This eminently readable collection of high-quality essays on Third World politics provides, through a variety of well-integrated themes and approaches, an examination of "state theory" as it has been practiced in the past, and how it must be refined for the future.

The contributors go beyond the previously articulated "bringing the state back in" model to offer their own "state-in-society" approach. They argue that states, which should be disaggregated for meaningful comparative study, are best analyzed as *parts* of societies. States may help mold, but are also continually molded by, the societies within which they are embedded. States' capacities, further, will vary depending on their ties to other social forces. And other social forces will be mobilizable into political contention only under certain conditions. Political contention pitting states against other social forces may sometimes be mutually enfeebling, but at other times, mutually empowering.

Whether the political struggles analyzed ultimately prove empowering or not, this volume shows why and how our understanding will be improved by greater sensitivity to the mutually transforming quality of state–society relations.

State power and social forces

CAMBRIDGE STUDIES IN COMPARATIVE POLITICS

General editor
PETER LANGE   Duke University

Associate editors
ELLEN COMISSO   University of California, San Diego
PETER HALL   Harvard University
JOEL MIGDAL   University of Washington
HELEN MILNER   Columbia University
SIDNEY TARROW   Cornell University
RONALD ROGOWSKI   University of California, Los Angeles

OTHER BOOKS IN THE SERIES

State power and social forces

Domination and transformation in the Third World

Edited by

JOEL S. MIGDAL
University of Washington

ATUL KOHLI
Princeton University

VIVIENNE SHUE
Cornell University

CAMBRIDGE
UNIVERSITY PRESS

PUBLISHED BY THE PRESS SYNDICATE OF THE UNIVERSITY OF CAMBRIDGE
The Pitt Building, Trumpington Street, Cambridge CB2 1RP, United Kingdom

CAMBRIDGE UNIVERSITY PRESS
The Edinburgh Building, Cambridge CB2 2RU, United Kingdom
40 West 20th Street, New York, NY 10011-4211, USA
10 Stamford Road, Oakleigh, Melbourne 3166, Australia

First published 1994
Reprinted 1996, 1997

Printed in the United States of America

Typeset in Times

A catalogue record for this book is available from the British Library

Library of Congess Cataloguing-in-Publication Data is available

ISBN 0-521-46166-9 hardback
ISBN 0-521-46734-9 paperback

Contents

Preface

The genesis of this volume lay in the individual writings of the authors. All ten participants had written about states in various corners of the world, noting how susceptible to the influence of their societies these states were. Over a period of nearly three years, these authors worked together – first in a preparatory meeting (of the editors plus Catherine Boone) in Princeton and then in two full-fledged workshops in Seattle and Austin – to develop a common approach to the study of state and society. This book is the product of those deliberations.

Although we came together from diverse intellectual backgrounds and studied a remarkably heterogeneous set of societies, we came to share a state-in-society approach. Joel Migdal's essay in Part I served as the initial discussion piece and intellectual framework at the workshops, generating debate, highlighting differences among us, and clarifying our points of agreement. We concurred that the struggles for domination in society do not always begin – and certainly do not end – at the commanding heights of the state. Nor are such battles always among large-scale social forces (the entire state organization, well-organized interest groups, various social classes, civil society, and the like) operating on some grand level. Many of the most important encounters determining who dominates in societies and how those societies change take place far from what scholars and journalists have usually considered the center of action.

The test of the utility of our approach is its usefulness for scholars attempting to understand particular societies. In Part II, "States: Embedded in Society," Frances Hagopian, Vivienne Shue, Atul Kohli, and Catherine Boone use and enhance the volume's framework by looking at particular states and the limitations social forces and processes have put on them. These social forces, in their real-world settings, are the focus in the third part, "Social Forces: Engaged with State Power." Elizabeth Perry, Robert Vitalis, Reşat Kasaba, Michael Bratton, and Naomi Chazan concentrate on specific elements in the society to see how they have been changed by interaction with the state and how they, in turn, affect the nature of that state. In the Conclusion, Kohli and Shue discuss some general themes as well as the individual papers in light of the approach offered in the volume as a whole.

Our workshops took place as the result of several small grants by the Committee on States and Social Structures, then of the Social Science Research Council; the Government Department and the Graduate School of the University of Texas at Austin; the Henry M. Jackson School of International Studies and the Graduate School at the University of Washington; and the Woodrow Wilson School of Public and International Affairs at Princeton University. Migdal's work was partially financed through a grant of the World Society Foundation. We thank them all for their assistance. Akhil Gupta, an anthropologist from Stanford University, also participated in the workshops, offering his usual incisive comments. Every one of the essays benefited from the thoughtful criticisms of all the other participants. This was truly a joint effort.

The Editors

Contributors

CATHERINE BOONE is Assistant Professor of Government at the University of Texas at Austin. Her work explores the political economy of capitalism and rentierism in West Africa. She is author of *Merchant Capital and the Roots of State Power in Senegal, 1930–1985* (Cambridge University Press, 1992).

MICHAEL BRATTON is Professor, Department of Political Science and African Studies Center, Michigan State University. His publications include *Governance and Politics in Africa* (Lynne Rienner, 1992) and *The Local Politics of Rural Development* (University Press of New England, 1980). His current interests include the comparative analysis of political transitions in Africa and the role of political culture in the consolidation of democratic institutions in Zambia.

NAOMI CHAZAN is on leave from the Hebrew University of Jerusalem, where she recently headed the Harry S. Truman Research Institute for the Advancement of Peace. Currently, she serves as a member of the Knesset in Israel as a member of the Meretz party. She is the author of *An Anatomy of Ghanaian Politics* (Westview Press, 1982). Her most recent edited book is *Irredentism and International Politics* (Lynne Rienner, 1991).

FRANCES HAGOPIAN is Associate Professor of Political Science at Tufts University. She is the author of *Traditional Politics and Regime Change in Brazil* (Cambridge University Press, forthcoming) and several articles on Brazil and Latin American democratization. Her current research focuses on the retreat of the state from the economy and the postauthoritarian reformulation of political representation in Latin America, with emphasis on Chile and Brazil.

REŞAT KASABA is Associate Professor of International Studies and Adjunct Professor of Sociology at the University of Washington. He is the author of *The Ottoman Empire and the World Economy: The Nineteenth Century* (SUNY Press, 1988). His current research includes a study of the domestic roots of international migration in the Middle East, and an examination of the project of modernity in Turkey.

ATUL KOHLI is Professor of Politics and International Affairs at Princeton University. He is the author of *The State and Poverty in India* (1987) and *Democracy and Discontent* (1990), both published by Cambridge University Press. His current research focuses on the role of states in late industrialization.

JOEL S. MIGDAL is Professor and Chair of the International Studies Program at the University of Washington's Henry M. Jackson School of International Studies. His books include *Palestinian Society and Politics; Peasants, Politics, and Revolution;* and *Strong Societies and Weak States,* all published by Princeton University Press, and (with Baruch Kimmerling) *Palestinians: The Making of a People* (Free Press, 1993).

ELIZABETH J. PERRY is Professor of Political Science at the University of California, Berkeley. Her most recent books include *Shanghai on Strike: The Politics of Chinese Labor* (Stanford, 1993) and *Popular Protest and Political Culture in Modern China* (Westview, 1992).

VIVIENNE SHUE is Professor of Government at Cornell University. She is the author of *The Reach of the State: Sketches of the Chinese Body Politic* (Stanford University Press, 1988) and of a number of other essays on state and society in contemporary China. Her current research is focused on private philanthropy, community welfare, and the renegotiation of class relations and of state-society relations in China today.

ROBERT VITALIS is Assistant Professor of Government and International Relations at Clark University. His book *When Capitalists Collide: Business Conflict and the End of Empire in Egypt* is forthcoming from the University of California Press.

State power and social forces

Introduction: developing a state-in-society perspective

Comparative political study of developing countries is a scholarly subfield that for nearly four decades has been in search of a theoretical core. Both modernization and dependency schools, as well as their debates, have come and gone. Over the last ten to fifteen years, a more state-oriented approach has instead attracted considerable attention. The present volume continues the dialogue with these intellectual traditions by offering a state-in-society perspective. Proceeding both at a general and at country-specific levels, the contributors to this collection hope to persuade others to move in several related but new theoretical directions: to go beyond "bringing the state back in" by resituating the study of states in their social setting and thus adopting a more balanced state-in-society perspective; to disaggregate states as objects of study, both as an end in itself and as a means toward a better understanding of states and political change; to rethink the categories used to conceptualize the evolving and fluid nature of social forces in developing countries; and to be continually sensitive to the mutually transforming quality of state–society relations.

Following the usual pattern for intellectual changes, our theoretical perspectives have developed as reactions to some prevailing scholarly tendencies. Although this volume does not attempt a critical evaluation of other schools of thought, but rather to develop a state-in-society approach, it may help the reader see where we are headed if we briefly recall some of the scholarly antecedents. The debate between modernization and dependency schools is well known to political development scholars, so well known that it does not need to be reviewed in this brief introduction (for further discussion, see Chapter 11). The more Weberian state–society literature of the 1970s and the 1980s, in turn, developed as a reaction to both structural-functional and Marxist assumptions that undergirded these earlier approaches. More specifically, state–society scholars began with two distinctive "first assumptions." On methodological grounds, they dropped the goal of creating a general social or political theory, aiming instead for middle-level theories informed by empirical analysis. And second, on analytical grounds, they reacted negatively to the tendency of both structural-functional and Marxist scholars to reduce politics to society, to see the nature of governments and states mainly as the outgrowth of certain social patterns. Instead, they argued for an analytical separation of state and society (authority and association) before proceeding with actual case studies. (An early statement of this theoretical position is Reinhard Bendix's *Nation Building and Citizenship* [Berkeley: University of California Press, 1977], ch. 1.)

The present volume shares these "first assumptions." The more recent state-oriented literature, however, which constitutes a subset of the larger body of Weberian scholarship of the 1970s and 1980s, has pushed some statist claims too far. (A prominent example of this genre of scholarship is Peter Evans, Dietrich Reuschmeyer, and Theda Skocpol, eds., *Bringing the State Back In* [Cambridge: Cambridge University Press, 1985].) State theorists have rightly pointed out that states have always been critical and direct agents of socioeconomic change, and this has been especially true in the twentieth century. Moreover, how state power is organized influences the incentives of social and economic actors, again contributing indirectly to patterns of change. These important assertions have helped sustain the case for "bringing the state back in." Nonetheless, we are of the view that some of the claims are overreactions and have misleading implications for development studies. It is time to offer some correctives.

States are parts of societies. States may help mold, but they are also continually molded by, the societies within which they are embedded. Once the state's importance has been emphasized, therefore, the intellectual attention immediately shifts to issues of why states do what they do, under what circumstances states are effective, and why states differ in their respective roles and effectiveness. These issues, in turn, cannot be discussed satisfactorily without looking at society, at the socioeconomic determinants of politics. So, although the important point that "states matter" has now been made – and, to repeat, it needed to be made – there is no getting around the mutuality of state–society interactions: Societies affect states as much as, or possibly more than, states affect societies.

More specifically, this volume asserts several interrelated claims – four of which we discuss here – that we hope will nudge the state–society literature away from a statist emphasis and toward a state-in-society frame of reference.

1. States vary in their effectiveness based on their ties to society. It is important not to mistake analytic constructs, such as the central role of the state in processes of social change or the autonomy of the state from society, for what happens in actual cases. In the real world, states are seldom the only central actors in societies and are almost never autonomous from social forces. By making these analytical claims into empirical ones, state-oriented theorists have mistaken what issues are important, for instance, privileging the study of states and their role in society over the study of social influences on the state's role.

They also have blurred the development of specific explanations; for example, a state's autonomy from society has come to be mistakenly viewed by some as a source of that state's effectiveness.

By contrast, we demonstrate that even where states were presumed to have been pervasive, domineering, and efficacious in the developing world, such as Maoist China and Brazil under military rule, the reach of the state turns out on closer inspection to have been limited. These limits of state power, in turn, draw attention to the rich social drama that has influenced processes of social change in low-income countries. Our shift in perspective also helps alter specific explanations. For example, we show that the concept of a state's "autonomy" is often an illusion and helps explain very little; a state's apparent disconnect-edness from social groups turns out to be associated in some cases with "strength" (as in some rapidly industrializing countries) and in other cases with "weakness" (as in several African countries). We suggest instead that a state's relative effectiveness is a function of the varied forms in which state–society relations are interwoven.

2. States must be disaggregated. A second, related claim follows from the first. If states have to be viewed in their social contexts, it is important to study not only the peak organizations of states and key social groups, often located at the center of the polity in the capital city, but also state–society interactions at the periphery. Our suggestion is that in their engagements with and disengagements from the scattered elements of society, the various components of the state encounter the same pushes and pulls, the blurring of boundaries, and the possibility of domination by others that other social organizations face. The overall role of the state in society hinges on the numerous junctures between its diffuse parts and other social organizations. The essays in this book stress the need to disaggregate the state, paying special attention to its parts far from what is usually considered the pinnacle of power; to recognize the blurred and moving boundaries between states and societies; and to view states and societies as mutually transforming. Several empirical studies in this volume demonstrate how an adoption of such a disaggregated perspective leads to a better understanding of state power in developing societies.

3. Social forces, like states, are contingent on specific empirical conditions. If it is important to resituate states in their social setting, we also need to consider the adequacy of the categories in which we are accustomed to conceptualize politically salient social structures and social actions. This is our third claim. We adopt the view that the political behavior and the power capacities of social groups are contingent, at least in part; in other words, the political action and influence of a social group are not wholly predictable from the relative position of that group within the social structure. For example, several essays in this volume rework the concept and the empirical salience of social classes, and a

few others investigate the development of civil societies in a low-income setting. We suggest that classes, such as the proletariat or peasantry, do not have
historically predesignated social roles and are not simply more or less powerful
depending on their relative control over property. Although property clearly is a
potent political resource, and the propertied often do get their way in politics, a
range of political power balances involving the propertied and the propertyless
are possible, even workable. Similarly, levels of nonclass associational activity
do not covary in any simple or direct fashion with levels of economic development; the emergence of civil society is not automatic but requires close empirical study.

4. States and other social forces may be mutually empowering.   Finally, we
urge scholars to eschew a state-versus-society perspective that rests on a view
of power as a zero-sum conflict between the state and society. Real-world power
struggles seldom pitch large collectivities called states against large collectivities
called societies. We accept that for some social groups, this is indeed an
accurate rendering of the nature of their interactions with the state. But it is not
always – and not even normally – so. Some interactions between state segments
and social segments can create more power for both. Some, of course, favor
one side over the other. Some vitiate the powers of each side. And in still other
cases, state actors ally with select social groups against other groups. This real-
world complexity suggests that our initial analytical position best avoid a statist
perspective that is misleading insofar as it renders the state in an adversarial
position vis-à-vis the society, and instead favor viewing the state as part of society.

   In sum, we propose a state-in-society perspective for the comparative study
of the state and politics in developing countries.

PART I

THEORETICAL AND METHODOLOGICAL CONSIDERATIONS

1

The state in society: an approach to struggles for domination

JOEL S. MIGDAL

Ever since Thomas Hobbes wrote *Leviathan* in the seventeenth century, 150 years before the full blooming of capitalism, thinkers have grappled with the increasingly powerful state and its role in society. Following the Industrial Revolution, Karl Marx, Max Weber, Emile Durkheim, and many others devoted themselves to what Karl Polanyi would later call the great transformation.[1] Like Hobbes, they too focused on the state, now in its relationship to the momentous social and economic changes overtaking European societies.

Some, such as the Hegelians, put the state – and the idea of the state – at the center of the social currents rushing through Europe. Others, including Marx, looked elsewhere for the source of historical change, notably to the organization of production. But even those who, like Marx, saw the primary motor of change outside the formal political realm felt called upon to address the notion of the transformative state. The new state was unquestionably a major component of life in the modern era and was understood by many as the driving force behind the astonishing changes of the time.

This statement holds true as much at the close of the twentieth century as in the latter decades of the nineteenth. Not surprisingly, then, the underlying questions dealt with in this volume echo the classical debates about major societal transformations and their relationship to the state. When and how have states been able to establish comprehensive political authority? When have they succeeded in defining the prevailing moral order or in determining the parameters of daily social relations, whether in preserving existing patterns or forging new ones? When and how have states been able to establish the economic agenda for their societies – to appropriate resources and to shape patterns of investment, production, distribution, and consumption? And when have other social forces, whether entire social classes or tiny cliques, large ethnic groups

I thank James Caporaso, John Keeler, Michael Keren, and members of several seminars for helpful comments on this essay. All the participants in the workshops leading to this book helped in the development of the ideas here. Atul Kohli took special time and care with my chapter.

or resourceful clans, thwarted or co-opted the state and had their own way in devising effective symbolic systems, molding daily social behavior, and shaping the patterns of economic life?

As in the classical debates, scholarship since World War II has seesawed between society-centered and state-centered theories to answer these questions. In the last decade or so, theorists have leaned toward state-centered approaches, explicitly acknowledging the central institutional role of the state in molding patterns of domination.[2] Although many state-centered researchers have written nuanced accounts of association and authority in various parts of the globe, the more theoretically oriented treatments have all too often tended to regard states in fairly undifferentiated terms. In presenting them as holistic, some scholars have given the misleading impression that states, at key junctures in their histories, pull in single directions. Some researchers have gone so far so as to reify and anthropomorphize the state, treating it as a unitary actor that assesses its situation strategically and then acts accordingly to maximize its interests. Unfortunately, by treating the state as an organic entity and giving it an ontological status, such scholars have obscured state formation and the dynamics of the struggle for domination in societies.

The participants in this book, coming from a variety of theoretical perspectives and drawing from the experiences of diverse regions, argue the need to move away from extreme state-centered theories. But we can go beyond simply establishing a balance in scholarship between state and society. We need to break down the undifferentiated concepts of the state – and also of society – to understand how different elements in each pull in different directions, leading to unanticipated patterns of domination and transformation. Once we think in more disaggregated terms, we can begin to imagine the engagement of state and society in very different ways from those found in existing theories.

By presenting a means to disaggregate the state, we do lose some of the elegance of nomothetic theories of power, such as those from the realist or rational choice perspective. These theories see the process by which states or specific social groups come to dominate, even in widely different circumstances and time periods, as occurring through a coherent logic, such as the single-minded drive of the state to garner larger revenues.[3] As inviting as such a logic is, an all-encompassing theory of this sort oversimplifies struggles for domination to such a degree that it obscures the actual outcomes in different societies. It also trivializes the question of state formation by trivializing historical contingencies and the struggles inherent in that process.

This essay and the following chapters point to the need for a theoretically informed, but more historically specific, treatment of power. Indeed, the ensuing chapters affirm the need for what the anthropologist Manning Nash has called "closely viewed crucial instances" – case studies reflecting the rootedness of the scholar in the society – in order to make persuasive comparative generalizations.[4] A close, historically specific treatment of power still leaves us room to indicate how to discern the key building blocks of states and societies and the sorts of interactions among social forces leading to various patterns of domination, even if the varying combinations do lead to different results in different circumstances.[5] My central argument is that patterns of domination are determined by key struggles spread through what I call society's multiple arenas of domination and opposition. Officials at different levels of the state are key figures in these struggles, interacting – at times, conflicting – with an entire constellation of social forces in disparate arenas. Any individual part of the state may respond as much (or more) to the distinctive pressures it faces in particular arenas as it does to the rest of the state organization.

Different responses from within the state mean that we cannot simply assume that as a whole it acts in a rational and coherent fashion, or strategically follows a defined set of interests. Scholars and journalists alike have paid far too much attention to who controls the top state leadership positions, as if those at the summit speak and act for the entire complex state organization. Similarly, they have overemphasized the major battles among large-scale social forces (entire states, social classes, civil society, and the like) operating on some grand level. In many societies, attention to struggles in multiple arenas may explain far more than easy assumptions about unified bodies like states and social classes. For example, a state official implementing birth control policies in Orissa, India, may have to take local landlords, religious leaders, and businesspeople into account at least as much as distant supervisors and parliaments, and such consideration of these figures may lead to a distinctly different disposition of program resources from what was conceived in New Delhi. The point is that to glean the patterns of domination, one must focus on the cumulation of struggles and accommodations in society's multiple arenas.

Such a focus is possible only by first conceptually breaking down states and societies and the junctures between them. In some cases, the numerous struggles may move a society toward *integrated domination,* in which the state as a whole (or possibly even other social forces) establishes broad power and in which it acts in a coherent fashion. In other instances, the conflicts and complicities in the multiple arenas may lead to *dispersed domination,* in which neither the state (nor any other social force) manages to achieve countrywide domination and in which parts of the state may be pulled in very different directions.

Some arena struggles may be limited to a depressed urban slum or a far-off neglected village; others may be countrywide and extend to the seat of state power itself. In the various settings is born the recursive relationship between state and society, the mutually transforming interactions between components of the state and other social forces – a central theme of this volume. Conflicts flare up over specific thrusts and parries: attempts by the state to increase tax collection, efforts by local figures to gain control over particular state offices and resources, initiatives by state agencies to regulate certain behavior, attempts by local strongmen to extend the area of their own dominance, and more. The struggles in these multiple settings end up reshaping both the state and society.

Often, state- or society-driven initiatives have been provoked by the fundamental changes associated with the great transformation – the growth of cities, the increased use of fossil fuels and other technological innovations, the decline of agriculture in terms of total domestic production, and so on. These changes have swept beyond Europe to every nook and cranny of the globe. Capitalism and the model of the strong European state have sent reverberations through every continent, precipitating massive dislocation and mixtures of appropriation of new ideas and methods, reactions against them, and their adaptations to local circumstances. These processes have constituted an onslaught on existing distributions of critical resources – land and other sources of wealth, personal connections, representation of meaningful symbols, and more – setting off new and renewed battles and accommodations throughout societies. At times these struggles have resulted in integrated domination as the state has played a leading role, but in other instances such centralization has proved elusive, ending in dispersed domination.

Whether the impetus for renewed struggle lies in the spread of world capitalism or in other factors, our first concern is the clashes and accommodations that these new circumstances have precipitated. We seek to develop an approach that can shed light on the nature of patterns of domination in society, that is, in where one might fruitfully look to study persistence and change. We also propose a number of educated guesses as to when and where we might expect to find certain patterns of domination prevailing.

Third World settings have thrown into stark relief the struggles for domination in societies.[6] In Africa, Asia, and Latin America, established social relations and institutions came under severe pressure during the last century as most areas outside Europe became what Eric Wolf called "dependent zones of support" in a single capitalist world.[7] Particularly in the period since World War II, state structures have been at the center of intense discord over how societies should deal with their integration into the larger world economy. The struggles are not simply over foreign economic policy but are, more fundamentally, about the very essence of how these societies are and should be constituted – their norms and rules, regulations and laws, and symbols and values. The dominance of state organizations in such domestic struggles cannot simply be assumed. People do not automatically consider the state to be the proper authority to settle the crucial questions or even the appropriate forum within which various social groups will struggle over the future course of the society. The role of the state is itself an object of the struggle.

We can think of the analogy of England and France as the last embers of feudalism were fading in Western Europe. The Wars of the Roses and the Fronde, among other struggles, illuminated the intense, ground-level disputes between states attempting to impose their will upon their societies and the social groups resisting that force. Max Beloff put it well: "In the sixteenth and seventeenth centuries, the modern idea of political sovereignty, the notion that over every man and every foot of ground, there must exist some single supreme authority was still something to be argued and fought over rather than the underlying presumption of all political action."[8] In the contemporary Third World, significant state autonomy and state capacity – so glibly, perhaps even teleologically, assumed and expected by some theorists – have not been assured outcomes at all.

Social science requires an approach that leads researchers to the struggles for domination that lie at the heart of twentieth-century social and political change. It is the elaboration of such an approach to which the participants in this volume aspire. In the sections that follow, I discuss the state, society, and state–society interactions in the arenas of domination and opposition. In these arenas, all sorts of social organizations, including components of the state, engage one another, attempting to impose their own stamp on ordinary life, everyday social relations, and the ways people understand the world around them. In brief, my aim is to draw the attention of those concerned with state–society issues to the appropriate focuses of analysis. The discussion highlights both a method of disaggregating states and societies as well as the recursive and mutually transforming nature of state–society interactions. Because such struggles may indeed be more obvious in the Third World than in the highly industrialized countries – just as in England and France in the seventeenth century – we hope that this volume's essays will also aid in understanding state and society where similar struggles are frequently veiled – in Europe, including the former Communist states, and in North America as well.

THE STATE

Any number of scholars have offered formal definitions of the state, most of which draw heavily on the notions of Max Weber.[9] These definitions have not differed markedly from one another. They have tended to emphasize the state's institutional character (as an organization or set of organizations), its functions (especially regarding the making of rules), and its recourse to coercion ("monopoly of the legitimate use of physical force").[10] At the core of these definitions lies the question of domination or authority in the state's claimed territory and the degree to which the state's institutions can expect voluntary compliance with their rules (legitimacy) or need to resort to coercion.

One work, for example, considers "the state to be a set of organizations invested with the authority to make binding decisions for people and organizations juridically located in a particular territory and to implement these decisions using, if necessary, force."[11] Another looks at the state as a power organization that engages in "centralized, institutionalized, territorialized regulation of many aspects of social relations."[12] By the "power" of the modern state, authors usually mean what Michael Mann has called infrastructural power, "the capacity of the state actually to penetrate civil society, and to implement logistically political decisions throughout the realm."[13]

Scholars understand the state to be the culmination of a process transcending the old localized organizations in societies, which had previously made the rules. It is "a more impersonal and public system of rule over territorially circumscribed societies, exercised through a complex set of institutional arrangements and offices, which is distinguished from the largely localised and particularistic forms of power which preceded it."[14] Since the sixteenth century, the theories maintain, the emergence of this new sort of public power with its large standing armies, formidable bureaucracies, and codified law has made the old forms of rule antiquated. The state has forged close-knit nations out of peoples who had been but loose associations of local groups. It is simply assumed that there is no longer any dispute that the state is the framework for the authoritative making of rules. "In the modern world only one form of political unit is recognized and permitted. This is the form we call the 'nation-state.' "[15]

Although there is much to recommend these definitions, they also pose certain problems. For one, they tend to feature one dimension of the state, its bureaucratic (or rule-enforcing) character. The accent on this side of the state highlights its capabilities, its proficiency in achieving a fixed set of goals and in implementing formal policies. Another dimension of the state exists that many of these definitions do not capture well: the formulation and transformation of its goals. As the state organization comes into contact with various social groups, it clashes with and accommodates to different moral orders. These engagements, which occur at numerous junctures, change the social bases and the aims of the state. The state is not a fixed ideological entity. Rather, it embodies an ongoing dynamic, a changing set of goals, as it engages other social groups. This sort of engagement can come through direct contact with formal representatives, often legislators, or, more commonly, through political parties closely allied with the state.

Resistance offered by other social forces to the designs of the state, as well as the incorporation of groups into the organization of the state, change its social and ideological underpinnings. The formulation of state policy is as much a product of this dynamic as it is a simple outcome of the goals of top state leaders or a straightforward legislative process. The results of the engagement with (and disengagement from) other social forces may modify the state agenda substantially; indeed, they may alter the very nature of the state.[16] Even as self-consciously an ideological state as that in postrevolutionary China – a state, as Vivienne Shue puts it, that set out to do nothing less than reinvent society – found itself transformed by its engagement with other social forces. Mao's China, to be sure, framed state policies in the language of class struggle, defending socialism and raising revolutionary consciousness. But the state's goals and actions were colored by the social networks that, in Shue's terms, insinuated themselves into all aspects of economic, social, and political relations, affecting the character of the state at both local and national levels. In the specific instance of Shanghai, Elizabeth Perry notes how the Chinese Communist Party (and, later, state) changed in character as the result of incorporating the most skilled components of that city's working class. Similarly, as Reşat Kasaba demonstrates, the nineteenth-century Ottoman state's engagement with principally non-Muslim merchants fundamentally changed its goals and character, drawing it into many new roles and procedures.

Problems with existing conceptions of the state go beyond lack of interest in the changing foundation upon which state goals are built; problems exist even on the issue of capabilities, which is the heart and soul of such definitions. There is a troubling tendency of authors to take too seriously actual states' abilities to make binding their decisions for people. This penchant to exaggerate capabilities has stemmed from states' near ubiquity in the struggles and accommodations occurring in arenas of domination and opposition, as well as from the presumptions of state officials themselves.

In the twentieth century, there have been very few places on earth, whether in the most remote corners of a country or in the heart of a capital city, where the state organization has not been a key actor in struggles for domination. Sometimes the state's initiatives have triggered intensified social battles; in other instances, it has simply reacted to the forays of other social forces. At times, it has championed economic development and redistribution. In other cases, its agenda has been to preserve existing patterns of economic domination. But in only rare instances (a number of which have been in Africa)[17] during the last several generations has the state been largely absent during conflicts over who exercises power in any segment of society. Along with technological change and industrialization, the idea of the transformative state has been, to be sure, a defining characteristic of the modern world. Indeed, what has distinguished the modern state from most other large-scale political organizations in history, such as empires, has been its insinuation into the core identities of its subjects (thus the emphasis on the nation-state). In their ordinary lives, people have come to think of themselves, among other central social roles, such as father or farmer, as French or Pakistani or Brazilian. Indeed, transformative states go beyond trying to establish people's personal identities; they aim to shape people's entire moral orders – the content of the symbols and codes determining what matters most to them. This penetration into people's daily lives means that a transformative state simply cannot let any struggle over domination within its official boundaries go uncontested;[18] state leaders want the state to matter most, enough to die for.

With only isolated exceptions, political leaders have sought to head a transformative state. They have seen it as an organization that can (or, at least, should) dominate in every corner of society. It should dictate the rules of daily behavior or, minimally, authorize and defend other social organizations to undertake some of those tasks. Even in recent cases of privatization and liberalization of markets, for example, a frequent underlying assumption is that the state should not entirely abdicate economic questions to markets. It should seek to carve out the limits to the autonomy of those markets and, at the same time, to authorize, regulate, and defend their operation.[19]

In short, throughout the territory they claim to govern, most political leaders have maintained that the state should have primacy. In some instances, that has meant privileging powerful social groups with which state leaders are allied as well as the organizations those groups dominate, such as markets or churches. But commonly the quest is for the state to exercise control directly – to impose its own systems of meaning and boundaries for acceptable behavior centrally on its subjects, in everything from sexual unions to labor–management relations.

State leaders attempt to create an aura of invincibility about the state. The more the state seems all-powerful, the more likely are subjects to accept it in their ordinary lives and, in the process, reduce the burden of enforcing all its dictates. In fact, those social scientists who, wittingly or unwittingly, exaggerate the capabilities of the state become part of the state's project to present itself as invincible. State sovereignty, the actual imposition of supreme state authority over its claimed territory, has simply too often been taken for granted.[20]

Despite their best efforts and to their never-ending frustration, state leaders have not had a clear way in imposing their domination – their systems of meaning, their rules for social behavior, and their economic plans – upon society. Like any other organizations, states have real limits to their power: what they can do and what they cannot do, when they can collect taxes and when not, which rules they can make binding and which not. Ambitious goals for states – aims of actually penetrating throughout the society, regulating the nitty-gritty of social relations, extracting revenues, appropriating resources that determine the nature of economic life, and controlling the most dearly held symbols – have seldom been achieved, certainly not in most of the new or renewed state organizations in the Third World.

The manner in which recent literature presents states results in consistently overestimating state power and autonomy. All too frequently the focus has been on the very top leadership, as if it alone constitutes the state, as if its collective will is re-created faithfully throughout the labyrinth of state branches and bureaus. "My principal interest," writes Mann, "lies in those centralized institutions generally called 'states,' and in the powers of the personnel who staff them, at the higher levels generally termed the 'state elite.' "[21]

But states surely consist of far more than this. As in ideology and policy formulation, policy implementation also reflects the state's engagement with other social forces. To study this, one must look at the multiple levels of the state through a new "anthropology of the state." A number of writers have elaborated what a truly cross-disciplinary political anthropology might look like.[22] Although the state as an institution has rarely been the central concern of these works, their insights could profitably lead to works shedding new light on the state. An anthropology of the state would lead to at least three advantages.

First, emphasis would change from what anthropologist Laura Nader called "studying up"[23] (focusing attention at the tops of agencies and institutions) to investigation at different levels of the state, including the lowest rungs on the organizational hierarchy where direct engagement with society often occurs, and the interaction among the levels. In short, such an approach helps us disaggregate the state and study its engagement with society.

Second, an anthropology of the state would open the study of its institutions to new methods, particularly participant observation. Techniques now commonly used to study state officials and others "are highly useful in dealing with articulate introspective respondents when those individuals are not otherwise engaged in socio-political behavior."[24] Participant observation would focus on the process of engagement of state officials in the contests of power with others inside and outside the state organization.

Finally, such an approach could go beyond the common concern with the theoretical study of the relationships of power to the interplay of power and symbols in state–society relations. No state can monitor all its rules; each needs what Peter Berger and Thomas Luckman called "legitimating universes,"[25] a constellation of symbols justifying state domination. It is this need that lies behind the attempts by states to shape the moral or symbolic order of their populations. Political anthropology, notes Abner Cohen, "specializes in unfolding the political implications of symbolic formations and activities – the 'mumbo-jumbo' of modern society – which are manifestly non-political."[26] It is the transformation of people as they adopt the symbols of the state and the transformation of the state as it incorporates symbols from society – both seemingly "non-political" processes – that an anthropology of the state can illuminate.

As Atul Kohli shows in the case of India, various levels of the state organization operate in markedly different structural environments. An anthropology of the state directs us to these distinctive environments and to the interaction among the levels. An understanding of the Indian national government's paradoxical growing inability to govern, even as it centralizes functions, demands that students of India look beyond the difficulties in New Delhi, to politics at the district and state levels of the country. This sort of approach, then, would not anticipate a single strategic and rational response of the state to its crisis of growing impotence. Indeed, political outcomes may not at all be in line with what seem to be the overall state's "interests," but may stem instead from the complex interaction of the different levels of the state and the peculiar pressures faced at each level.

An anthropology of the state, then, allows us to dismantle it analytically and to discern the distinct structural environments of its different components and the interaction among them. One possible way to disaggregate the state is to break it down into four levels, which differ markedly in the kinds of pressures they face from other state components and from nonstate actors. From bottom to top, they are:

(1) *The trenches.* Here stand the officials who must execute state directives directly in the face of possibly strong societal resistance. They are the tax collectors, police officers, teachers, foot soldiers, and other bureaucrats with the mandate to apply state rules and regulations directly. Their contacts are with the intended clients, targets, and beneficiaries of official state policies. Supervisors tend to be somewhat distant in district or regional capitals.

(2) *The dispersed field offices.* A notch higher are the regional and local bodies that rework and organize state policies and directives for local consumption, or even formulate and implement wholly local policies. They include the bureaus, legislative bodies, courts, and military and police units that work exclusively in a circumscribed territory within the larger territory claimed by the state as a whole, making key decisions about local appropriation of resources funneled through national ministries or garnered locally. Where will state schools be built? How will local postal distribution be organized? Which villages will benefit from the digging of new tube-wells or irrigation canals? Who will be hired in the trenches? They are more likely to face large, well-organized regional social forces, as well as direct intervention from the capital city, than those in the trenches.

(3) *The agency's central offices.* In the capital city are the nerve centers where national policies are formulated and enacted and where resources for implementation are marshaled. These agencies are technically responsible to the top political leadership, but they are also often in intense negotiations with each other and are targets for influence by large, well-organized interest groups at the national level.

(4) *The commanding heights.* At the pinnacle of the state is the top executive leadership. While top leaders depend on those in lower levels for everything from tax collection to keeping order, they may not fully identify with any other component of the state. Those other components become yet other pressure points among an array of large-scale domestic and international forces seeking to influence the top leadership.

Leaving aside momentarily the issue of nonstate forces, both domestic and international, that impinge on the various parts of the state, three sets of pressure from within the state organization itself bear directly on each level of the state. Those pressures are, first, from supervisors (at least for those neither elected nor at the very top of the hierarchy); second, from underlings, those that one directly or indirectly supervises; and third, from peers, staff in other agencies or politicians at roughly similar levels. Given the different constellations of these forces at each level, let alone the differing nonstate forces officials face, it is not surprising that states seldom generate a single, homogeneous response to an issue or problem, or even necessarily a varied but coordinated set of responses. The different constellations of forces each part of the state faces mean that various units have diverse histories of their own, leading to differing degrees of esprit de corps, purposefulness, and insularity. Political outcomes – the formulation and implementation of the state's policies – reflect the aggregation of a series of different actions based on the particular calculus of pressures experienced by parts of the state at each level.

There is certainly little guarantee that such outcomes will represent some harmonious mesh. They can just as likely be a sum of ill-fitting responses that stem from the different components of the state as they respond to their various pressures from within the state and from the broader environment. Shue writes of Maoist China, for example, "Frontline officials, despite their status as agents of the state, frequently found it advisable, or easier, or more natural, or just in accord with their own convictions, to throw in their lot with local people and departmental associates, against the impersonal requirements of the state bureaucracy above them."

At different points in the state organization, the calculus of pressures on state officials differs markedly, depending on the particular array of forces in their arenas and their relative weight. To speak of the overall autonomy of states, as some recent theory does, might not at all be the best initial point of inquiry for those studying politics and society. Researchers must first ask about the autonomy of the various components of the state, for which the calculus of pressures differs so markedly. What sorts of social forces predominate at different points in the state hierarchy, and why? Does the calculus of pressures allow for discretionary room for state officials and representatives? Do supervisors influence decisions of state offices, or are they outweighed by other social forces?

To conclude this section, there has been an unfortunate tendency in social science to treat the state as an organic, undifferentiated actor. Scholars have assigned the state an ontological status that has lifted it apart from the rest of society. As a result, the dynamics of the struggles for domination in societies, in which components of the state have played differing roles in various arenas, have been obfuscated. Those struggles have not only been about who seizes the commanding political heights in society. They have involved alliances, coalitions, and conflicts in multiple arenas, including various components of the state and other social forces. The cacophony of sounds from the wildly different arenas in which components of the state and social forces interact often have resulted in state actions that bear little resemblance to the original schemes or policies conceived by leaders of the state or by particular state agencies.

The more diverse and heterogeneous the arrays of pressures that various components of the state encounter on their different levels, especially when strong pressures are applied by multifarious domestic and foreign social forces, the less likely the state is to end up with complementary behavior by its many parts and the less likely it is to convey successfully a coherent system of "legitimating universes." Despite its international stature and its sheer bulk in society, the state may be a crippled giant in the quest for domination. Its bulk guarantees it cannot be ignored in conflicts over domination in society, but more meaningful initiatives and more coherent actions may come, if they come at all, from other social forces.

THE SOCIETY

We can start our discussion with a depiction of society offered by Liah Greenfeld and Michel Martin: Society's "only definitive characteristic is that it is the outermost social structure for a certain group of individuals who, whatever might be their attitude toward it, view themselves as its members and experience their identity as being determined by it."[27] This is a fairly loose characterization, which avoids assuming that there necessarily exists a central force guiding the disparate parts of society. Indeed, many of the difficulties in analyzing state–society relations arise from the tendency by theorists to impose some general analytical framework that can help discern patterns for all (or most) of society's disparate parts. Social scientists drawing on Marxism have thus portrayed the ruling class or the hegemony generated by a combination of the ruling class and the state as dominating across society and giving it a distinctive shape. Where society is seen as pulling in different directions, the struggles are then understood to be between this class and other broadly constructed social classes.

Like the Marxists, liberal social scientists have often accepted axiomatically that the existence of society presupposes the exercising of some sort of hegemony, or society-wide domination. For them, the integrated framework is the consensus of norms, partially expressed within the authoritative structure of a somewhat constrained state, about how individual and group competition proceeds over the question of who gets what.[28] Social struggle comes through a set of plural interests competing for influence on public policies, all under the umbrella of well-established rules of the game. Recent state-centric theories have, implicitly or explicitly, tended to accept the notion of society-wide domination or hegemony, with the important qualification that they have been more prone than either Marxists or liberals to focus explicitly on the frameworks and authority created by the society's state organization.[29]

The approach to society offered here accepts some of what the state theorists have presumed; namely, in the modern world, societies as we know them – their contours and boundaries, their sense of shared experience – have been products of state formation. At the same time, we must raise questions about theorists' presumption of a unifying framework (whether a ruling class, a consensus of norms about competition, or the state) to explain overall patterns of domination and distribution in Third World societies. We must ask a prior question: Have the outcomes of struggles in multiple arenas aggregated to create, in fact, broad classes with cohesive projects that can shape a society or a widely agreed upon normative framework or a state organization capable of containing competition? And, if we indeed find such classes or frameworks or states, must we assume that they will hold together beyond the short- or medium term?

In the case of the Marxists, unified social classes and wide-ranging social struggles for dominance – class struggles – have often been easier to find in imaginative theorizing than in real societies. Class, notes E. P. Thompson, has become a broad heuristic device when, in fact, it is the particular result of historical conditions in only certain places and times. "Class, as it eventuated within nineteenth century industrial capitalist societies, and as it then left its imprint upon the heuristic category of class, has in fact no claim to universality."[30] Referring to the mix of capitalists and large-scale agriculturalists in nineteenth-century England, Thompson states, "It arose, like *every* real historical situation, from a particular equilibrium of forces; it was only one of the seemingly infinite number of social mutations (in which each, nevertheless, maintains a generic affinity to others arising from a comparable conjunction) which actual history provides in such profusion."[31] In other countries of Europe and in other parts of the world, cohesive classes, which can lead society or around which the primary struggles in society revolve, may or may not exist at all or, when they do, may or may not succeed in achieving some sort of broad class project. Whatever the general utility of a "theory of class," then, our cases seem to indicate caution against an overgeneralizing tendency.

For example, the Egyptian business elites of the 1930s, as Robert Vitalis demonstrates, could in limited instances engage in broad forms of collective action. But in some of the critical issues revolving around state-fostered markets, the business leaders, despite all their privileges, did not develop unified class domination. Instead, rival coalitions of businessmen aligned with different elements of the state, each coalition seeking to secure access to the state's investment resources. The results were not only deep conflicts among the business elites themselves but the undermining of the state and its policies as well. Isma'il Sidqi, the strong-armed leader who took over the government in 1930, needed the businessmen as much as they needed him. In the end, however, neither could achieve their goals: Sidqi was forced to resign by 1933 and businessmen continued to pursue their conflicting interests in multiple arenas, with no semblance of pulling society in a single direction. The idea of a unified social class working toward some large class-project that can reshape society may be an elegant metaphorical device, Vitalis points out, but these metaphors "can obscure as much as they reveal about the nature of the institutions, strategies and power of capitalists."

Similarly for liberal theorists, battles over the distribution of authority have not always produced dominance for specific rules of competition. The struggles in societies have often been over who establishes the procedures, rather than competition on the course of public policy within an overarching legitimate framework for all of society. The establishment of legitimate authority over a large territory in which plural competition can occur has, like unified class rule, been exceptional in twentieth-century history and the result of distinctive historical conditions.[32] Even in as established a democracy as India, as Kohli argues, integrating frameworks of authority are difficult to find today. In fact, the opportunities provided by democracy for mobilization have opened the way for new groups, especially the lower and lower-middle strata, to expand their participation in politics substantially. The result has been an unanticipated one; instead of providing a long-term "solution" to management of conflict, democracy has increasingly facilitated the creation of fragmented politics, with few institutional or normative frameworks that could contain growing and increasingly vitriolic competition.

State-centered theories encounter similar difficulties when they assume the state organization is powerful and cohesive enough to drive society. Again, not only is that claim open to empirical verification, the theoretical assumption has frequently led to the tendency to strip the other components of society of their volition or agency, portraying them as malleable putty in the hands of the most powerful element of society, the state.[33] Such a perspective leaves us at a loss to explain such instances as Senegal. Rather than finding an increasingly capable state in the postcolonial years, Catherine Boone observed that political practices seemed to undermine the administrative capacities and resource bases of the Senegalese state. The state itself came to be based on a system of patronage in which chiefs and other local-level authorities exercised a tremendous degree of discretion in local arenas. These local patterns of domination came to be rooted in the state organization, crippling it and rendering it unable to deal with the pressing problem of eroding national production that left the state with a drastically declining tax base. Authoritative and autonomous forces in society shaped the state as much or more than they were shaped by it.

Social forces in society represent powerful mechanisms for associative behavior. These forces encompass informal organizations (such as Senegal's patron–client networks, or friendship groups and old-boy networks in other societies) as well as formal organizations (such as businesses and churches). They can also be social movements, including those held together by common, strongly motivating sets of ideas (even where obvious organizational ties are absent).[34] Such movements may range from those dedicated to squatters' rights to ones focusing on questions of ecology. All these sorts of social forces' ability to exercise power starts with their internal organization. The efficiency of their hierarchies, their ability to use resources at hand, their adroitness in exploiting or generating symbols to which people develop strong attachments, all affect their ability to influence or control behavior and beliefs.

But there is another dimension as well. Social forces do not operate in a social vacuum. Their leaders attempt to mobilize followers and exercise power in environments in which other social forces are doing the same. And there is rarely a neat division of the population or of issues that keep various social forces from conflicting. The focus here is on precisely those environments – those arenas of domination and opposition – where various social forces engage one another over material and symbolic issues, vying for supremacy through struggles and accommodations, clashes and coalitions.[35] These are not simply "policy arenas" in which various groups attempt to shape public policy. In addition to contestation over governmental policy, struggles and accommodations take place over the basic moral order and the very structure within which the rights and wrongs of everyday social behavior should be determined: Who has the right to interpret the scriptures? Who is to be respected over others? What system of property rights will prevail? How will water and land be distributed within the context of the prevailing system of property rights?[36]

Various social forces endeavor to impose themselves in an arena, to prescribe to others their goals and their answers to these and related questions. Their aims may vary and may be asymmetrical. Some use social forces to extract as much surplus or revenue as possible; others look for deference and respect or doing God's will or simply power to rule other people's behavior as an end in itself. Whatever the motivation and aims, attempts at domination are invariably met with opposition by others also seeking to dominate or by those trying to avoid domination. Rarely can any social force achieve its goals without finding allies, creating coalitions, and accepting accommodations. Landlord and priest, entrepreneur and sheikh, have forged such social coalitions with power enough to dictate wide-ranging patterns of belief and practice. Frances Hagopian, for example, demonstrates how in Brazil, the authoritarian military regime found it had to reinstate accommodations with local traditional, oligarchic elites after it had instituted a political system of domination that it believed had rid Brazilian politics of these very forces. "The military was no more successful at cleansing the political system of patronage politics than it was at purging the state of the traditional political elite." The old patrons' ability to manipulate resources in order to achieve domination in local arenas forced the state's leaders to seek an implicit coalition with them.

Coalitions and accommodations may transform as well as enhance a social force's ability to attain its goals. As a social force's constituency changes, it may incorporate a new material basis as well as new ideas and values into its constitution. To state this point in slightly different terms, in addition to a social force's capabilities, its social and ideological basis (whom it serves and with what goals or agenda) also may change radically as a result of its interactions in an arena. It makes little sense, then, to try to understand outcomes by deriving actions from a fixed set of goals, as too much social science does today. Those ends themselves may very well be in flux. In China, both the Nationalist regime in the 1930s and the Communist one from the late 1940s on were themselves transformed as they recruited different segments of the Shanghai working class as pivotal constituencies. Perry's chapter notes how deeply affected the Kuomintang was as it used organized crime to help it incorporate semiskilled workers from North China and how the Communist state absorbed the goals of the labor elite as it attracted the more skilled artisans from the south.

Power or social control can expand along three dimensions in order to extend a social force's domination. First, within an arena, a social force can dominate in an increasing number of issue areas, from dictating what crops to grow, through providing credit, to defining the nature of salvation. Second, arenas themselves can grow to incorporate a larger share of the population and a larger territory. The alignment of forces over which language people should use, for example, may begin in a particular city and spread to incorporate large portions of a country and its population. Third, a social force can use the resources it garners in any one arena to dominate in other arenas, with different sets of social forces. Chiefs in some countries of postcolonial Africa, for instance, used their command in tribal territories to catapult themselves into national questions such as issues of family planning.

Social forces attempt to appropriate the resources and symbols at hand to further their goals, and they often have wildly different abilities to do that. The mix of key elements in an arena – its physical geography, material resources, human resources, forms of social organization, and trove of beliefs – are the raw materials with which the patterns of relationships among social groupings are determined. Patterns of domination come as social forces, with their already unequal abilities and access to resources, seek to utilize and manipulate these key elements of the arena's environment. The introduction of new factors into an arena, such as additional capital, compelling ideas, or innovative forms of social organization, or the depletion of old elements, also benefits and harms social forces in very different ways. These new factors set off new and renewed struggles in arenas, ranging from struggles that proceed slowly and quietly to ones fraught with violence and recurring upheaval.

The struggles and accommodations of social forces in any local or regional arena of domination and opposition have not been hermetically sealed affairs. Resources have been reallocated from one arena to another in order to influence the outcome of struggles. Social forces have enhanced their position by sporting resources garnered from outside, by reassigning trusted personnel, or by riding on the backs of pervasive and powerful symbols. Factors such as the overall structure of production in society, existing institutional arrangements, and the saliency of certain symbols all influence who is in a position to reallocate resources and symbols from arena to arena.

Creating the conditions for domination in society and maintaining dominance – the reproduction of power within society – are the products of the multiple ongoing arena struggles and accommodations. Our approach to society analyzes whether particular social forces can create an integrated domination. That is, can they prevail within given arenas to produce resources and support – a material base and a normative framework – that can be used to dominate locally and then be carried into other domains to create society-wide domination? Or do the struggles in the arenas result in a pattern of dispersed domination by limiting the creation of authoritative, legitimate forces that can dominate broadly across society?

THE JUNCTURES OF STATES AND SOCIETIES

In the modern world, it is impossible to understand the term "society" without the state. The formation of the state has created and activated society. If society is the outermost limits with which people identify, then it is the state that initially determines those limits or social boundaries. But that does not mean that the state simply molds the groups that make up society. Indeed, interactions of state and society are mutually transforming. The results of the engagement and disengagement of states and other social forces are tangible, even momentous, but outcomes rarely reflect the aims and wills imbedded in either. The clash of social forces, including the state, is mediated through the struggles and accommodations in society's numerous arenas. For the social scientist, the challenge is to understand how those diffused struggles alter society's disposition of resources, the nature of its stratification, the character of its gender relations,[37] and the content of its collective identities. In the end, those local interactions cumulatively reshape the state or the other social organizations, or, most commonly, both; these interactions are the foundation of the recursive relationship between the state and other social forces.

The cumulative result of engagements and disengagements in arenas has been that societies have assumed "all manner of shapes," as Anthony Smith puts it.[38] Smith's observation seems, at first glance, rather unremarkable; of course societies have ended up with all manner of shapes. But Smith's comment, as he notes, flies in the face of much prevailing social theory. In contemporary social science writing, where states and societies have been portrayed with broad brushstrokes, different states and societies have had an uncannily uniform look. So much contemporary scholarship blurs the rich diversity produced in various societies' multiple arenas. The meeting grounds between states and other social forces have been ones in which conflict and complicity, opposition and coalition, corruption and co-optation have resolved the shape of countrywide social and political changes. They have determined whether domination is integrated or dispersed, as well as the varying contours of integrated or dispersed domination.

Arenas of domination and opposition have achieved periods of stable relations among their social forces in different times and places, but these may have been more the exception than the rule. A Nicaraguan earthquake, a Bengali tidal wave, the absorption of fundamentalist Islam in southern Lebanon, changing birth rates in Mexico, the penetration of the world economy throughout the Third World, all have created winners and losers and thus changed the balance of forces in arenas. Through its distinctive ideology and organization, the modern state has been at the core of destabilization of existing arenas in the nineteenth and twentieth centuries. The common core of ideology among the leaders of transformative states has been to create a hegemonic presence – a single authoritative rule – in multiple arenas, even in the far corners of society. The goal has been to penetrate society deeply enough to shape how individuals throughout the society identify themselves, and the organization of the state has been to effect such far-reaching domination. It has included vertically connected agencies, designed to reach to all pockets within the territory, and specialized components to promote the state's system of meaning and legitimacy (e.g., schools), to make universal rules (legislative bodies), to execute those rules (bureaucracies), to adjudicate (courts), and to coerce (armies and police). Major policy initiatives by the state have led to a massive inundation of new elements (from fresh ideas to personnel and hard cash) as well as to the depletion of others through taxation, conscription, relocation, mass murder, or other means. Even the most benign states have made extraordinary demands on those they have claimed as their subjects: to sequester their children in state institutions for thirty hours a week, to dispose of their bodily wastes in only prescribed ways, to treat their sick exclusively with state-licensed healers, to prove a proprietary relationship to land solely through state-issued deeds, and so on. Whatever their specific programs, states have shaken up existing social relationships, renewing active struggles for domination.

In the multiple meeting grounds between states and other social components, some social forces have tied their own fortunes to that of the state or accepted it as the appropriate organization to establish the proper practices for all of society. In such cases, we can speak of the relationship between state and social forces as mutually empowering. But, in other instances, the engagement between the state and social forces is a struggle for agency, for the ultimate autonomy to take initiatives and to make decisions in given realms. Here, the struggle is one marked not by mutual empowerment but by mutually exclusive goals. Some forces, for example, have sought to appropriate resources, positions, personnel, even whole bureaus of the state for their own purposes. Still others in society, such as peasants or slum dwellers, who were already dominated by other social forces, have also, at times, actively or quietly resisted the attempts of officials to impose new state domination.

These struggles and accommodations in the junctures between components of the state and other social forces have produced a range of outcomes. We can capture these in four ideal types of results. First is total transformation. Here, the state's penetration leads to the destruction, co-optation, or subjugation of local social forces and to the state's domination. In such cases, the components of the state successfully transform how the people of an arena identify themselves. Forced migration, replacement of the locals by a settler population, widespread use of violence, and other draconian means may nullify or destroy local dominating social forces and transform personal identity. Where there is no severe social dislocation, it is unlikely that total transformation will occur within a single generation. China, discussed in the two chapters by Perry and Shue, comes closest to this ideal type. The dislocation of the prolonged civil war, overlaid by the war against the Japanese, in addition to the later turmoil of the Great Leap Forward and the Cultural Revolution, gave the Chinese Communist state unprecedented opportunity to harness local forces. But even this case instructs us to proceed with caution in looking at transformative states; as both Perry and Shue demonstrate, China has fallen short of the ideal type. As the state incorporated new groups and engaged with old ones, it found itself transformed as well as transforming.

Second is state incorporation of existing social forces. In this type, the state's injection of new social organization, resources, symbols, and force into an arena enables it to appropriate existing social forces and symbols in order to establish a new pattern of domination. But it also forces changes and accommodations on the part of the state's components as they adapt to the specific patterns and forces in the arena. These changes in local components of the state may then affect the state's overall coherence – its ability to reallocate resources, establish legitimacy, and achieve integrated domination. Hagopian's chapter on Brazil illustrates this second type. The military coup there in 1964 brought a regime bent on transformation of society. But, for all the resources at its disposal, the state found itself reincorporating the old oligarchy at the provincial level and thereby relinquishing allocative discretion in key areas.

Third is existing social forces' incorporation of the state. In this type, the presence of the state's components spurs adaptation by dominating social forces, but does not produce radical changes in the pattern of domination. Or, in some cases, the new state presence does generate new patterns of domination, but ones in which new nonstate social forces rise to the top. In either case, the personal identity and moral order that result among the population are not the ones envisioned by state leaders. The organization and symbols of the state's components are appropriated by the local dominating social forces. In this scenario, the transformation of the local components of the state is so extensive as to harm significantly the state's overall chances of achieving integrated domination in society. Michael Bratton's chapter, for example, points to how the establishment of marketing boards and cooperatives for peasants in African states has precipitated arrangements not at all intended, or even imagined, by political leaders. Peasants reacted to the state initiatives by setting up their own informal trading networks. Bratton dismisses the notion that the interpenetration of parts of the state apparatus with this second economy implies some sort of state domination.

When public officials accept bribes to turn a blind eye to an illegal activity, they are not extending the state's authority but reducing it. And when officials engage in private accumulation and trade – even if only through relatives, intermediaries, and employees – they are acknowledging that their behavior is not governed by legal commands. The participation of state officials in the second economy amounts to a deconstruction of formal architecture of the state in the face of a more compelling set of social imperatives.

Again, with this ideal type, we must express some caution. Although African cases, such as that of Senegal discussed in Boone's essay, often demonstrate the co-optation of the state by particular social forces, even here the engagement between state and society may have mutually empowering aspects, a point brought out nicely in the chapter by Naomi Chazan.

Finally, the state may fail altogether in its attempt at penetration. Disengagement or lack of engagement of the state in the local arena will result in little transformative effect on the society – and limited effects of the society on the state. Failures to engage in arena struggles in even the most remote parts of the country can affect the state in the capital city by denying state components there resources and support from the larger society.

Only rarely have real cases in arenas approached the two extreme ideal-types, total transformation or disengagement. Most have offered some variant of the middle two types, where state components and other social forces have been involved in a recursive relationship, that is, mutually transforming struggles. In fact, states and other social forces not only may alter one another, they may also affect the very integrity of the other through encroachment. In the midst of arena struggles and accommodations, the boundary between the state and other parts of society may continually shift, as powerful social forces in particular arenas appropriate parts of the state or the components of the state co-opt influential social figures. Although state leaders may seek to represent themselves as distinct from society and standing above it, the state is, in fact, yet another organization in society. And, as one organization among many, it is subject to the pushes and pulls in society's arenas that can change the line between it and other social forces.

In parts of colonial Africa, for example, the British attempted to extend the scope of the colonial state by incorporating tribal chiefs as paid officials. Many chiefs, for their part, gladly accepted the salary and any other perquisites that they could garner but often ignored the directives from their superiors in the state hierarchy. The demarcation between the state and other parts of society in such instances was difficult to locate and was in constant flux. Chiefs were state officials but sometimes – indeed, many times – simply used their state office and its resources to strengthen their roles as chiefs.

To talk of the relations between state and society as if both always have had firm boundaries, as much recent social theory does, is to miss some of the most important dynamics of transforming struggles.[39] Chiefs, like other state employees and officials, play multiple roles. State organizations may succeed in having them suppress roles with different norms (as members, for example, of kinship or tribal groups) while performing their state duty. The desire to mold special state norms and suppress the norms of other roles is one reason that states attempt to create their own space for officials, such as separate state office buildings or new capital cities. In state-designated space, the assumption goes, officials would be less likely to succumb to the logic of the struggle being played out in specific arenas. But states may fail to "capture" chiefs or other state workers, resulting in the domination of the norms of other social forces.

In arena after arena, then, social forces have reorganized to deal with the new reality of ambitious states. Where those forces have created or found the spaces and methods to sustain, sometimes even augment, their own social and economic power outside the framework of the state's moral order and its rules, the society comes to be characterized by dispersed domination. Here, neither the state nor any other social force has established an overarching hegemony; domination by any one social force takes place within an arena or even across a limited number of arenas but does not encompass the society as a whole. Social life is then marked by struggles or standoffs among social forces over questions ranging from personal and collective identity and the saliency of symbols to property rights and the right to use force. People's identities and moral codes remain remarkably diverse in such a society.

Even in cases of dispersed domination, the state has rarely been a negligible actor. The junctures of the state with other social forces have taken place in the multiple arenas of society, and in most instances the state's agencies have created a formidable presence, precipitating realignments of local forces. But the components of the state have not achieved total transformation or even successful state incorporation of local powerful social forces in all or most of these settings. This pattern contrasts with integrated domination, which is inclusive, or society-wide. In cases of integrated domination, the state, whether as an authoritative legal system or a coercive mechanism of the ruling class, is at the center of the process of creating and maintaining social control. Its various components are integrated and coordinated enough to play the central role at all levels in the existing hegemonic domination. That domination includes those areas of life regulated directly by the state, as well as the organizations and activities of society that are authorized by the state within given limits.

In analyzing the junctures of state and society, many theorists have simply assumed the existence of integrated domination. The concept of civil society has been widely used by a number of liberals, Marxists, and statists to capture the relation between state and other parts of society, reinforcing the presumption of integrated domination in society.[40] The notion of civil society, to be sure, has had different shades of meaning in various theoretical contexts – in the works, for example, of Hegel and Gramsci.[41] But despite their differences, for many theorists, civil society has been a convenient term with some surprising commonalties. Various writers have used the concept to acknowledge the existence of sundry interests in society while still being able to treat them as if, on some level, the entire society (even the state, in many writings) pulls together in a single direction.[42] Note how Stepan, in his book on military politics, speaks of civil society in an anthropomorphic way: "Civil society must consider how it can make a contribution to the democratic control of military and intelligence systems."[43]

Civil society assumes the existence of a normative consensus or hegemony of fundamental ideas among social forces, even among contending groups; this consensus represents a prevailing moral or social order. For many writers, civil society expresses the ties that bind all, or nearly all, of society together, whether those are property rights or mutually felt needs or any other factors. Until the last decade or so, most theories posited a hand-in-glove relationship between state and civil society.[44] This interpretation does not mean there are never tensions between the state and civil society or questions about the boundary between the two. The concept of *pouvoirs intermédiares,* intermediary institutions, has been used to signify a civil society in which organizations guard a degree of autonomy from the state. Such autonomy leaves open the possibility of some differences between the state and nonstate associations.

But the critical point is that in most social science writing, state and civil society are mutually reinforcing, even when differences prevail between them. It is the existence of widely held norms, property relations, or modes of social behavior in myriad organizations across the totality of society – that is, the existence of civil society – which reinforces the dominance of the state and allows it to rule without constant recourse to coercion or without an outlay of resources that would cripple it. Conflicts may persist on particular issues, but implicit agreement prevails over the rules for interaction and competition. For the most part, it is the legal framework of the state that establishes the limits of autonomy for the associations and activities that make up civil society. If that framework is widely accepted, then the activities of the state and other social groups may be mutually empowering.

Only recently in Latin America, Eastern Europe, and even Western Europe has there developed a discourse that takes more seriously the possibility of civil society versus the state.[45] Even among those holding this position, the strain between civil society and the state is seen in overarching terms between these two integrative entities. Civil society is still an aggregate of diverse interests, which on one level pull in a single direction. Together, they attempt to oppose the state's moral order and impose one of their own.

There are several problems with analyzing the junctures of state and society through such a view of civil society. For one, as I have discussed elsewhere, even within civil society, various social forces are not always aggregative and inclusive, leading to a hegemony of fundamental ideas.[46] We need to develop a much more careful understanding of the constitutive elements in civil society and not assume it is made up only of interest groups and private voluntary organizations, which tend to create a harmonious consensus in society. Also, an integrative view of civil society misses entirely cases of dispersed domination. *Society* and *civil society* are not synonymous; the heterogeneous struggles in society's multiple arenas of domination and opposition in which social forces pull in different directions also affect the state profoundly. The way the concept of civil society is most commonly used leaves no room for these dispersed struggles over society's moral order. As Chazan points out in her chapter, "Civil society encompasses only one portion of what has become a complex and diverse associational scene. What distinguishes those groups incorporated in civil society from other associations is their partial nature: They are separate from but address the state." Society as a whole may include other organized components (not just marginal individuals), which strive to make their own rules and institute their own moral orders, without addressing the state directly. Here, goals of these groups and goals of the state are mutually exclusive.

Many contemporary societies have included significant elements that have struggled against all or many of the claims of the state to be the organization in society with supreme authority. Some social forces have not lent their support to the state's universal pretensions or, for that matter, the pretensions even of a civil society pitted against the state. Their relation to the state has been one of resistance (overt or covert) or one in which they have sought to transform or appropriate part of the state for their own purposes. Similarly, their orientation to the other forces that make up civil society has often ranged from disinterest to outright hostility.

The multiple arenas of society and the interactions among them have been the cauldrons within which the contingent, particular historical outcomes have been brewed for each society and its state. The form of the state (democracy or some other type of government), its goals, its capabilities, its scope, its domination by particular social forces or its autonomy, as well as the form, systems of meaning, capabilities, and autonomy of other social forces – all these have been determined through these critical struggles and accommodations in the multiple arenas of society and the relationships among arenas. States do not succeed in establishing their own domination by default. In fact, they may end up as much the transformed as the transformative states.

In brief, scholars need to ask if and how the struggles in arenas carry over to other arenas and, possibly, to domination in the society as a whole. Have resources and support generated in struggles and accommodations in one arena then been carried into other domains in society, possibly to create an integrated domination? Integrated domination, whether by states, social classes, civil society, or any other groupings, results from successful reallocation of resources and support garnered from activities in one arena into other arenas.[47] What Sidney Tarrow has called the "vast issues, roiling conflicts, and deep-seated social and economic cleavages" in societies cannot be understood divorced from the more limited arena conflicts. It is in the latter that people "organize their relations with the state, reconcile or fight out conflicts of interest, and attempt to adapt politically to wider social pressures."[48] The ability of any social force, including the state, to develop the cohesion and garner the material and symbolic resources to project a meaningful presence at the society-wide level depends on its performance in more circumscribed arenas. In those arenas, it must dominate successfully enough (close to total transformation or, at least, incorporation of existing social forces) so as to be able to generate resources for application in other arena struggles and, ultimately, the society as a whole. Whether any social force, from social classes to the state, will succeed as the basis for integrated domination is far from a foregone conclusion.

NOTES

1 Karl Polanyi, *The Great Transformation: The Political and Economic Origins of Our Time* (Boston: Beacon Press, 1944).
2 My use of "domination" refers to the ability to gain obedience through the power of command. Weber used such a designation for domination in *Wirtschaft und Gesellschaft*. See Max Rheinstein, ed., *Max Weber on Law in Economy and Society* (Cambridge, Mass.: Harvard University Press, 1954), pp. 322–337. The motivation to obedience can be the coercion or voluntary compliance that comes when one sees the rule maker as the legitimate authority. (Weber speaks of the sources of domination in slightly different terms, seeing domination as a virtue of one's interests, the monopoly position of the dominator, or, by virtue of authority, the power to command and the duty to obey [p. 324].) "Domination," as used here, is thus more inclusive a term than just coercion or just legitimate authority. Domination can be localized or it can be exercised broadly over society. The term "hegemony," on the other hand, while also having elements of coercion and legitimate authority, includes only domination exercised broadly over society. For a discussion of the literature that focuses mainly on the state, see the "Conclusion" of Weber's volume, especially the references cited there in note 1.
3 For a good recent example, see Margaret Levi, *Of Rule and Revenue* (Berkeley: University of California Press, 1988).
4 Manning Nash, *The Cauldron of Ethnicity in the Modern World* (Chicago: University of Chicago Press, 1989), p. viii.
5 Ibid., p. 5, states, "Which building blocks . . . are invoked to construct a category and what boundary forged to set the category off from others is historically specific."
6 The term "Third World" is not used with any special precision or analytical rigor here. A good case for the limitations in the term and its utility, nonetheless, is found in Christopher Clapham, *Third World Politics: An Introduction* (Madison: University of Wisconsin Press, 1985), ch. 1.
7 Eric R. Wolf, *Europe and the People Without History* (Berkeley: University of California Press, 1982), p. 296.
8 Max Beloff, *The Age of Absolutism, 1660–1815* (New York: Harper Torchbooks, Harper & Row, 1962), p. 20.
9 Max Weber, *Economy and Society* (New York: Bedminster Press, 1968), vol. 1, p. 64; and Rheinstein, ed., *Max Weber on Law in Economy and Society*, p. 342.
10 Max Weber, "Politics as a Vocation," in H. H. Gerth and C. Wright Mills, *From Max Weber: Essays in Sociology* (New York: Oxford University Press, 1946), p. 78.
11 Dietrich Reuschmeyer and Peter B. Evans, "The State and Economic Transformation:

Toward an Analysis of the Conditions Underlying Effective Intervention," in Peter B. Evans, Dietrich Reuschmeyer, and Theda Skocpol, *Bringing the State Back In* (Cambridge: Cambridge University Press, 1985), pp. 46–47.

12 Michael Mann, *The Sources of Social Power,* vol. 1, *A History of Power from the Beginning to A.D. 1760* (Cambridge: Cambridge University Press, 1986), p. 26.

13 Michael Mann, "The Autonomous Power of the State: Its Origins, Mechanisms and Results," in John A. Hall, ed., *States in History* (Oxford: Basil Blackwell, 1986), p. 113. Also see John A. Hall and G. John Ikenberry, *The State* (Minneapolis: University of Minnesota Press, 1989), pp. 1–14.

14 Roger King, *The State in Modern Society: New Directions in Political Sociology* (Chatham, N.J.: Chatham House, 1986), p. 30.

15 Anthony D. Smith, "State-Making and Nation-Building," in Hall, ed., *States in History,* p. 228.

16 Alfred Stepan's use of the term "political society," which he adapted from Gramsci, opens the way to consideration of the changing basis of the state's symbolic system and its behavior. Political contestation, Stepan argues, is within the framework of "political society" and is about "control over public power and the state apparatus." Alfred Stepan, *Rethinking Military Politics: Brazil and the Southern Cone* (Princeton: Princeton University Press, 1988), p. 4.

17 Victor Azarya and Naomi Chazan, "Disengagement from the State in Africa: Reflections on the Experience of Ghana and Guinea," *Comparative Studies in Society and History,* 29 (January 1987).

18 By transformative, we do not necessarily mean progressive. Even a state seeking to preserve an existing order must be transformative if it is to have its way in the context of international changes sweeping over its boundaries.

19 Evans and Stephens have noted, "The state is as central to the economics of development as to its politics." Peter Evans and John D. Stephens, "Studying Development Since the Sixties: The Emergence of a New Comparative Political Economy," *Theory and Society,* 17 (1988), p. 723.

20 King writes (*The State in Modern Society,* p. 51), that "the constitutional state is characterised by a unitary sovereignty which becomes manifest in a single currency, a unified legal system, and an expanding state educational system employing a single 'national' language. A literary tradition in this 'national' language erodes cultural particularism, and a system of national military conscription, which replaced the local recruitment of ancient military units, also tends to overcome 'peripheral' or localist identities."

21 Mann, "The Autonomous Power of the State," p. 112. The identification of the state with its top elites or leadership, with its own distinct interests and perspectives that are independent of specific other socioeconomic interests, does not mean that authors do not recognize what King (*The State in Modern Society,* p. 53) calls the "plurality of foci" of the state. But these focuses are seen largely as differentiated institutional expressions of a fairly singular will.

22 See, for example, Abner Cohen, "Political Anthropology: The Analysis of the Symbolism of Power Relations," *Man,* 4 (1969): 215–235; Clifford Geertz, "Ideology as a Cultural System," in David Apter, ed., *Ideology and Discontent* (New York: Free Press, 1964), pp. 55–72; Max Gluckman, *Politics, Law and Ritual in Tribal Society* (Oxford: Basil Blackwell, 1965); and Marc Swarz, Victor Turner, and Arthur Tuden, eds., *Political Anthropology* (Chicago: Aldine, 1966).

23 Laura Nader, "Up the Anthropologist: Perspectives Gained from Studying Up," in Dell Hymes, ed., *Reinventing Anthropology* (New York: Vintage Books, 1974), pp. 284–311.

24 David C. Schwartz, "Toward a More Relevant and Rigorous Political Science," *Journal of Politics,* 36 (1974): 130 (emphasis in original).

25 *The Social Construction of Reality* (Garden City, N.Y.: Doubleday, 1966), p. 171

26 *Two-Dimensional Man* (London: Routledge & Kegan Paul, 1974), p. 17.

27 *Center: Ideas and Institutions* (Chicago: University of Chicago Press, 1988), p. viii.

28 Vincent notes that the consensus that is assumed by liberal theorists is a collective good. But, he complains, "the pluralists seem at times to conjure this collective good out of thin air." Not all groups may accept the basic framework. "Groups can be as oppressive, mean-minded and destructive of liberty as any state." Andrew Vincent, *Theories of the State* (Oxford: Basil Blackwell, 1987), p. 216.

29 See Evans et al., eds., *Bringing the State Back In.* Vincent notes of the liberal pluralists that "they were trying to theorize an idea of the state incorporating maximal diversity of group life and some kind of central authority." He also notes that some have argued "that the State was smuggled in through the backdoor." Vincent, *Theories of the State,* p. 210.

30 "Eighteenth-Century English Society: Class Struggle without Class?" *Social History,* 3 (May, 1978): 150. Stedman Jones ends up taking a position different from Thompson's but is even more adamant about the tenuous relationship between heuristic devices and what was found in history. "One should not proceed upon the assumption that 'class' as an elementary counter of official social description, 'class' as an effect of theoretical discourse about distribution or production relations, 'class' as the summary of a cluster of culturally signifying practices or 'class' as a species of political or ideological self-definition, all share a single reference point in an anterior social reality." Gareth Stedman Jones, *Languages of Class: Studies in English Working Class History, 1832–1982* (New York: Cambridge University Press, 1983), pp. 7–8.

31 E. P. Thompson, *The Poverty of Theory and Other Essays* (New York: Monthly Review Press, 1978), p. 255 (emphasis in original).

32 In Gramsci's language, these historical contingencies are "conjunctural." *Selections from the Prison Notebooks.* Liberal theorists have tended to deny the existence of a real society in cases where an integrative framework, with clear rules of the game, does not exist. Shils, for example, has spoken of such cases as "proto-societies." But that simply accepts the reality of the bounded nature of society and the linking associative behavior and common memories while denying the status of society where conflict still exists over the framework for action. See Edward Shils, *The Constitution of Society* (Chicago: University of Chicago Press, 1972), p. 68.

33 "The inhabitants of countries also possess social attributes like language, a cultural heritage, and a common history. . . . Unlike the country's political structure, the common attributes of *society* do not possess any representative agency that speaks for the whole." Reinhard Bendix, John Bendix, and Norman Furniss, "Reflections on Modern Western States and Civil Societies," *Research in Political Sociology* 3 (1987): 2 (emphasis in original).

34 The existence of a social organization, formal or informal, necessarily implies domination. Note Weber: "A circle of people who are accustomed to obedience to the orders of leaders and who also have a personal interest in the continuance of the domination by virtue of their own participation in, and the benefits derived for them from, the domination, have divided among themselves the exercise of those functions which will serve the continuation of the domination and are holding themselves continuously ready for their exercise. This entire structure will be called organization." Rheinstein, ed., *Max Weber on Law in Economy and Society,* p. 335. I use the broader term "social forces" to signify such relations of domination in organizations

but also where there is obedience in movements where no clear organization is present.

35 An arena is not necessarily spatially limited but, rather, is a conceptual locus where significant struggles and accommodations occur among social forces.

36 Arenas of domination and opposition thus differ in some fundamental respects from Lowi's arenas of power. Such arenas of power, he writes, include "events, issues, and leadership [which should] be studied within defined areas of governmental activity. These areas are, in effect, the functions of government defined more broadly than a single agency, more narrowly than government with a single political process." Theodore J. Lowi, *At the Pleasure of the Mayor: Patronage and Power in New York City, 1898–1958* (New York: Free Press, 1964), p. 139. In contrast, arenas of domination and opposition are not functions of government (although they may include government actors), nor are they limited to governmental activity.

37 Of all elements concerning identity and the state, probably the least remarked upon has been gender. One good exception is a recent book by Parpart and Staudt. They write, "For us, gender is at the heart of state origins, access to the state, and state resource allocation. States are shaped by gender struggle; they carry distinctive gender ideologies through time which guide resource-allocation decisions in ways that mold material realities. Through their ideological, legal, and material efforts, states foster the mobilization of certain groups and issues. This mobilization usually benefits men rather than women. While over the long haul, state action may submerge and obscure gender conflict, over the short term, the obviousness with which male privileges are fostered may actually aggravate that conflict." Jane L. Parpart and Kathleen A. Staudt, "Women and the State in Africa," in Parpart and Staudt, eds., *Women and the State in Africa* (Boulder, Colo.: Lynne Rienner, 1989), p. 6. Also, see chs. 2, 3, and 10.

38 Smith, "State-Making and Nation-Building," pp. 229–230.

39 I am indebted to Timothy Mitchell for illuminating the point about the shifting boundary between states and societies. See Timothy Mitchell, "The Effect of the State," paper presented at the "State Creation and Transformation" workshop of the Social Science Research Council's Committee on the Near and Middle East, Istanbul, September 1–3, 1989.

40 Hegel put forth the notion of civil society as one that emerges from the interdependence of individuals, their conflicts and their needs for cooperation. Those needs give rise to the state; and it is the law, the principle of rightness, that links civil society to the state. *Hegel's Philosophy of Right* (Oxford: Clarendon Press, 1942), pp. 122–123, 134–135. Marx reacted to Hegel's conception, arguing that the state is merely the mechanism to defend privileged propertied interests in civil society. He understood civil society in a material sense, the expression of particular property rights: " 'Bureaucracy' is the 'state formalism' of civil society." David McLellan, ed., *Karl Marx: Early Texts* (Oxford: Basil Blackwell, 1979), p. 68. Gramsci noted that besides the educational agencies of the state helping maintain hegemony, there are, "in reality, a multitude of other so-called private initiatives and activities [that] tend to the same end – initiatives and activities which form the apparatus of the political and cultural hegemony of the ruling classes." This, for Gramsci, is civil society. Gramsci, *Selections from the Prison Notebooks,* p. 258.

41 One difference among them has been the direction of causality: Does the state create civil society or does civil society bring about the state? Whereas Hegel believed that society created the demand for the state, others, including Stepan, have argued that the state can create civil society. Otto Hintze alluded to this mutuality of the state and civil society and the role of the state in creating its own civil society, using the

term "nationalities" instead of civil society: "The European peoples have only gradually developed their nationalities; they are not a simple product of nature but are themselves a product of the creation of states." Hintze, "The Formation of States and Constitutional Development: A Study in History and Politics," in Felix Gilbert, ed., *The Historical Essays of Otto Hintze* (New York: Oxford University Press, 1975), p. 161.

42 Bendix et al. do note that "civil society comprises only a segment of the population." Those not in civil society tend to be marginal sorts – those abandoned by their parents, homeless people who do not participate in the market, illegal immigrants, and the like. "Reflections on Modern Western States and Civil Societies," p. 23. John Keane sees even larger elements of European societies, which have been excluded from civil society (most of those who are not white, heterosexual male citizens). *Democracy and Civil Society: On the Predicaments of European Socialism, the Prospects for Democracy, and the Problem of Controlling Social and Political Power* (New York: Verso, 1988), p. 14.

43 Stepan, *Rethinking Military Politics*, p. 128.

44 Bendix et al. note that "the independence of private associations is a synonym for civil society," and that for civil society to exist a "consensus" is required between state and society. "Reflections on Modern Western States and Civil Societies," pp. 14–15.

45 In the 1980s, the term "civil society" came to be used by analysts of Eastern Europe. They were looking for a way to break the theoretical umbilical cord between state and civil society. For them, civil society implied a spunky society, which develops autonomy through organizations in opposition to the state. See, for example, Andrew Arato, "Empire vs. Civil Society: Poland 1981–82," *Telos,* 14 (1981–1982): 19–48. For a critique, see Zbigniew Rau, "Some Thoughts on Civil Society in Eastern Europe and the Lockean Contractarian Approach," *Political Studies,* 35 (1987): 573–592. On Western Europe, see Keane, *Democracy and Civil Society* (see, for example, pp. 31–32). On Latin America, see Alfred Stepan, *Rethinking Military Politics*.

46 Joel S. Migdal, "Civil Society in Israel," in Ellis Goldberg, Reşat Kasaba, and Migdal, eds., *Rules and Rights in the Middle East: Democracy, Law and Society* (Seattle: University of Washington Press, 1993).

47 In the United States, social theorists have been particularly reticent about admitting that the state is, in fact, exercising supreme authority. More often the emphasis has been on social organizations that regulate themselves, with little attention as to how the state creates the authoritative legal framework within which markets and other social organizations function. See Gary C. Hamilton and John R. Sutton, "The Problem of Control in the Weak State," *Theory and Society,* 18 (January 1989): 15–16.

48 Sidney Tarrow, "Introduction," in *Territorial Politics in Industrial Nations* (New York: Praeger, 1978), p. 1.

PART II

STATES: EMBEDDED IN SOCIETY

2

Traditional politics against state transformation in Brazil

FRANCES HAGOPIAN

Recent military regimes in the Southern Cone of Latin America promised profound change, brought significant force to bear to support the cause of change, but delivered surprisingly little. Beginning in Brazil in 1964 and subsequently in Argentina in 1966, Uruguay and Chile in 1973, and again in Argentina in 1976, militaries staged coups not to transfer power to rival civilian factions – their traditional pattern – but to rule directly. Although their intentions were eventually to return their countries to civilian rule (albeit with no timetables for doing so), they defined theirs as regimes not merely of transition but of transformation.[1] By reorganizing economic and political life, by depoliticizing the state and weakening the capacity of society to make demands of it, they expected to create modified, more "workable" democracies, ones less vulnerable to future recurrences of economic and political chaos. Their steps were extraordinary and novel: They concentrated power in the ministries and agencies of the executive branch of government and handed major policy decisions over to technocrats. They achieved immediately high levels of state autonomy, most remarkably even from civilians who had supported military takeovers – traditional economic and political elites.[2]

With the salutary trend toward democratization in Latin America in the 1980s, which ended military rule on most of the continent, the failure of the region's military governors to translate quick sociopolitical reform into deeper change of a lasting nature became manifest.[3] In each country, the populist, Peronist, and socialist parties and party leaders whom the militaries obsessively attempted to drive forever from the political scene survived military rule to return with significant constituencies, as did former patterns of political and

I am grateful to my former colleagues who commented on an earlier version of this work, Jorge Domínguez, Ashutosh Varshney, and Jennifer Widner; to each of my fellow contributors to this volume for their penetrating criticisms of and useful suggestions for improving the draft version of this chapter; and above all to the volume's editors. I am indebted to Joel Migdal for encouraging me to think more deeply about state–society relations, and to Atul Kohli for insisting that I clarify the "military project."

social organization about which these militaries displayed more ambiguity. The inability of strategic state elites who enjoyed a monopoly of force and who were willing to resort to repression on a massive scale, and who did not lack, at least not initially, significant middle and upper class support,[4] to transform their states and reorganize their societies, and ultimately to sustain their regimes, underscores in a dramatic fashion the resilience of state–society relations.

This chapter explores the failure of the military to transform the state and to repattern political interaction between the state and society in Brazil, the first of the regimes that have come to be known as "bureaucratic-authoritarian."[5] The failure of the Brazilian military to impose successfully its transformative project is especially puzzling given that society was perceived to be so weak.[6] Indeed, after the brief administration of the "soft-line" president Humberto Castelo Branco (1964–1967), the military appeared able to shun its former political allies and govern exclusively with technocrats. The Brazilian military also had a longer period – twenty-one years – than the other South American dictatorships in which to rewrite the political map. Yet the political results of military rule were no more lasting than in neighboring countries.[7] Although legal socialist and Communist parties today attract only bare fractions of the electorate, other leftist and populist alternatives remain quite viable; indeed, they may be stronger than on the eve of the coup, despite being the object of intense repression during the dictatorship. Second and more intriguing, *traditional* politicians and forms of political practice that the military also initially favored expelling from the state outlasted military rule. Indeed, not only was politics not ultimately transformed in the direction that the military wanted, but after more than two decades of authoritarian rule and rapid economic development, it was changed hardly at all.

The failure of the military to realize its transformative project has been explained in two ways. The first is as a result of a crack in the Leviathan – that is to say, a split within the state and specifically within the military institution. According to this view, soft-liners in the government sought to curb the excesses of the hard-liners in the security community through a political liberalization and "courtship of civil society."[8] Second, the expectation that the military would succeed in reorganizing politics in the long term has also been treated as an analytical error, one that underestimated the capacity of Brazilian civil society to resist a state dictatorship. Perhaps for the first time in Brazilian history, voluntary, associational life flourished and became politicized, and civil society became empowered.[9] Without denying the military divisions that made the initial "relaxation" of authoritarian rule possible, and the extraordinary significance for the end of the dictatorship of the awakening (and heroism) of Brazilian civil society, neither the "liberalization from above" nor the "resurrection of civil society" thesis satisfactorily addresses the related, and more challenging, question of how to explain the *direction* in which the military project came to be reformulated and revised. While no bureaucratic-authoritarian regime ultimately could be institutionalized, in Brazil an ambitious project to transform the state gave way to an unlikely successor: traditional politics.[10] Indeed, when the project to transform the state became derailed, the military rerouted it back on the track of state clientelism administered by a traditional political elite. Even today, one-quarter century after military-sponsored rapid industrialization began, traditional politics and traditional political elites arguably predominate over unions, labor parties, and the autonomous associations of civil society.[11]

This chapter explores the problem of how the transformative project of a strategic state elite, the Brazilian military, came to be modified. It examines the nature of mediations between the state and society before and during the period of authoritarian rule, a research strategy in which "state" and "society" must be conceptually disaggregated and their arenas of intersection carefully identified. My overarching argument is that the degree and direction of political change possible under Latin American military dictatorships were constrained by the legacy of the way in which society was organized politically and attached to the state, and of how authoritarianism was formatted onto preexisting links between society and the state – that is, whether the political and economic programs of the authoritarian regimes nourished or undermined these inherited networks of state–society mediation.

In Brazil, the particular cast of the state–society relations the military inherited at the start set limits on its political project. Its initial decision to hold elections and temper repression can be traced to the fact that clientelism – the classic mediation for securing societal support for oligarchical and semicompetitive regimes through the selective channeling of state resources to state-dependent populations – worked reasonably well up to the coup in containing social and political conflict and buttressing a semicompetitive regime. Because preexisting networks of mediation between state and society could be repaired, the military was constrained from rebuilding them on a different foundation.

Subsequently, the military's political priorities and economic policies strengthened those preexisting networks. Even as it permitted electoral politics to function, the military, bent on dismantling populism, repressed and effectively closed corporatist networks of representation that had mediated the interests of labor in the postwar, competitive regime. At the same time, it broadened the scope for interaction between the state and society by expanding the state's productive and distributive roles in the economy, thereby creating a large class of state clients. The military's lack of mediation became particularly problematic in the second decade of its rule when it suffered electoral punishment. Forced to reinvent ways to mobilize societal support for its regime, it revitalized the clientelistic networks that were part of its political inheritance. Its own economic programs, moreover, nourished and made more pervasive, potent, and hardy those clientelistic networks that had traditionally been an especially effective mode of mediation between state and society. Because the Brazilian military could not effectively manage state patronage networks, resuscitating them required restoring the group that could distribute state resources in a politically expedient fashion – those veteran, traditional *political* elites who had been partially shunned but nonetheless survived the first decade of bureaucratic-authoritarian rule in the lower levels of the state. Ultimately, the traditional political elite skilled at mediation who commanded that part of the state that reached society outlasted in the state the military elite, which, although more strategically placed in the higher echelons of the state, lacked such connections to society.

Given the high degree of salience of regional-level politics for state–society relations in a federal political system, this paper draws empirical support for its arguments from the political and administrative life of the state of Minas Gerais, traditionally one of Brazil's most important states, and one in which scholars observed that state events have mirrored those at the national level.[12] But much of its evidence cannot be provided within the limited space of this chapter;[13] empirical detail has been sacrificed in order to place theoretical arguments in a comparative context. I proceed by sketching out the military project, its limits, and its revisions.

THE MILITARY PROJECT

When the Brazilian military seized power, it inherited a functioning populist system that was, with the notable exception of the peasantry, based on inclusion. The regime's initial goal, which always took precedence over all others, was to dismantle this populist system, and in this it was successful. Practically immediately and without significant resistance, the military tamed unions by sacking and jailing "militant" union leaders; transferred the administration and distribution of social security, the base of power of the union bosses known as *pelegos,* to technocratic branches of the state; and decapitated the leadership of the populist parties, the Brazilian Labor Party (PTB) and the Progressive Social Party (PSP), by stripping them of their political rights, above all, the right to stand for office.[14] In 1968, it viciously repressed what was to become the last major strike for a decade at Osasco. The entire array of corporatist labor legislation was used by the authoritarian regime as a club with which to enforce state control over labor.

In contrast to the single-mindedness with which the military ruthlessly implemented its "defensive" project of stabilizing an economy in crisis and restoring political order by demobilizing labor, its pursuit of its "offensive" designs for new patterns of state–society interaction – in Garretón's terminology, its "foundational" project – appeared to waver. The military aimed to depoliticize the state, believing that in order to increase the state's administrative capacity and efficiency, the state had to be liberated from the grip of politicians who put personal ambition ahead of the national interest, and insulated from their whims.

Yet, how it planned to reorganize state–society relations in order to achieve that was never clearly enunciated or acted upon without ambiguity, partly because the military spoke with more than one voice. "Soft-liners," the group surrounding military President Castelo Branco (1964–1967) who were allied with politicians of the National Democratic Union (UDN), one of three major and two-elite dominated parties of the 1945–1964 period, adopted the anticlientelistic, antipopulist, discourse of that party; their primary intention was not to evict all politicians from the state, but to govern with their allies in the UDN who had been unable to win power for themselves at the polls. Hard-liners who prevailed from 1967 to 1973, on the other hand, distrusted deeply professional politicians of all stripes, including those who had supported the coup of 1964, for their alleged mismanagement of the economy, failure to prevent political fragmentation and conflict, and widespread engagement in clientelism and corrupt practices that they believed compromised national security and economic development. Eventually, the differences between the two were submerged, and all military factions agreed to a reform project of purging the state and the political system of all vestiges of traditional, patronage politics. By forcing regionally based political elites to surrender their dominance over the political system, military governors hoped to fulfill a century-old military dream: to create a national politics out of the mosaic of states' politics, to discard regional identities and loyalties, and to make Brazil a "great power" (*grande potência*).

A two-prong strategy for revamping state–society relations pursued both political and fiscal centralization. Within a few years of assuming power, the military appropriated the executive branch of government, expanded its powers vis-à-vis the legislature, effectively insulated it from popular, electoral pressure, and made it immune from constitutional checks on its authority. Through a series of constitutional changes, Congress was barred from formulating budgets and the range of its responses to executive-initiated ordinary legislation and constitutional amendments severely curtailed.[15] The executive was also given and used on thousands of occasions the prerogative to enact legislation by decree, which bypassed the legislature altogether.[16] Any acts of defiance from a demoralized Congress were, moreover, swiftly punished; senators and deputies who dared openly to challenge the regime were expelled from the Congress and stripped of their political rights.

Within the executive branch of government, control of the economy was concentrated in a select group of ministries of the federal cabinet, banks, and interministerial councils – the ministries of planning and finance, the National Monetary Council, the Price Council, the Industrial Development Council, the Bank of Brasil, and the Central Bank. Named to head these ministries and state agencies responsible for economic policy-making were civilian and military technocrats.[17] Only 29 percent of federal cabinet ministers in the administration of Emílio Garrastazú Médici (1969–1974) had served in the legislature (as opposed to 60 percent in the 1946–1964 period), whereas more than half had had technical careers and 11 percent were military officers.[18] The key positions advising the president, the "inner group," were occupied almost exclusively by military and techno-bureaucratic elites. This sea change in patterns of elite recruitment led Cardoso to characterize the top echelons of the state apparatus as the *chasse gardée* of the military and bureaucrats.[19]

The second principal means by which the military planned to strengthen the national state was to purge state administration of clientelism through fiscal centralization. Traditionally, the dependence of local communities for their economic livelihood on state support in the form of development projects, public sector employment, and social services engendered a form of political clientelism that benefited the traditional elites who controlled branches of the central and subnational governments that distributed state patronage resources, such as the state departments of education and public works. The military's intention in centralizing state finances was to starve patronage networks of resources and to depoliticize federal–state–local relations. To this end, in 1965, it passed a sweeping tax reform package that concentrated fiscal revenues in the federal government and funded state and municipal governments through a revenue-sharing program with strict priority guidelines for how such transfers were to be spent; in other words, it set out to transfer municipal dependence from the states to central authorities. Together, the presence of technocrats in the economic ministries coupled with fiscal reform was intended to bring about the demise of traditional politics and to evict traditional political elites from the state.

At the same time that the military project to transform the state was attempted, however, the military permitted politics as usual to take place. Alone among South American military rulers, the Brazilian military, anxious to cloak its rule in a veil of legality, allowed Congress and the state legislatures, albeit emasculated as legislative bodies, to convene for most of the life of the dictatorship,[20] and it did not fail to hold direct elections for most national and state legislative positions, and all local-level offices (exceptions were the presidency, state governorships, and mayors of state capitals and areas of national security), even though repeated manipulations of electoral law left only the facade of political contestation and representation.[21] After it "lost" gubernatorial races in two important states in 1965, the military abolished existing parties and created two new ones, a progovernment party, the National Renovating Alliance (ARENA), and an official opposition, the Brazilian Democratic Movement (MDB). So limited were the electoral prospects of the MDB that it did not take itself seriously as a political party for nearly a decade. Despite this perverse political theater, the fact that regularly scheduled, direct elections were held for most legislative and some executive positions nonetheless was to have enormous implications for the need to mediate state–society relations.

THE LIMITS TO STATE TRANSFORMATION

As military rule drew to a close, it was apparent that, changes in national level politics notwithstanding, state and local politics changed little in bureaucratic-authoritarian Brazil. The composition of state cabinets by and large conformed to precoup patterns; precoup traditional elites fared quite well in circumstances of military governance; the practice of clientelism persisted – indeed was more pervasive than ever – and state resources were distributed in a highly politicized fashion.

The state elite

Outside Brasília, technocratic usurpation of the state apparatus was limited. Most state governors, even when appointed by the military, were politicians. Fourteen of twenty-two governors appointed in both 1970 and 1974 had held elected office; the 1974 governors enjoyed even better political connections than their 1970 counterparts, though both sets were chosen from within established regional political circles, and whereas three governors named in 1970 were military men, not one of the later cohort was drawn from the ranks of the armed forces.[22] Similarly, the composition of state cabinets was only temporarily and not significantly altered from the precoup period, when most cabinet secretaries rose because of family connections or through political channels. In the state of Minas Gerais, after the regime change, the participation in the state cabinet of "technocrats" – economists, engineers, and other persons technically qualified for their posts by their education or job experience – increased, peaked in the years from 1971 to 1975 at 55 percent, and then declined.[23] Politicians per se were once again rewarded for party service and their vote-drawing ability in the late 1970s and early 1980s, when 64 percent of state cabinet appointees were drawn from the ranks of elected officeholders. A sustained and definitive displacement of politicians by a technocratic elite did not occur during the military regime, and no new patterns of elite recruitment were established that outlasted military rule.

Far from having been neutralized politically and dislodged from the state in the postcoup authoritarian system, many prominent figures of *traditional* Minas politics before the 1964 coup fared quite well in circumstances of military governance. Two-fifths of the precoup political elite served in the executive branch of state government after the regime change, another 15 percent in state and federal legislatures and in the top echelons of the progovernment ARENA party, and when the field of potential "political survivors" is narrowed to reflect demographic change (ten members of the elite died before 1974), the political survival rate of the precoup elite rises to two-thirds. The political elite, moreover, was and remains largely a traditional elite. Virtually three-fourths of the postcoup state cabinet members, lieutenant governors, and mayors of the state capital can be classified as traditional: they had an "oligarchical heritage" (were descended from one of twenty-seven "governing families" of the state), or older relatives in politics, or had organized an "oligarchical" political party.[24] The traditional political elite even fared better after the coup than the "nontraditional" political elite. The survival rate of the traditional subset of the precoup elite (61 percent) is markedly higher than that of the nontraditional contingent of the precoup state elite (47 percent). Most remarkable, perhaps, all but two members of the postcoup elite had either a well-established precoup political career or older relatives in politics who enjoyed such careers. If Minas Gerais is not atypical, the military failed abjectly to promote a *renovação,* or renewal, of the Brazilian political elite; this elite was more closed than in the reasonably competitive period from 1956 to 1964.

Fiscal reform, clientelism restored

The military was no more successful at cleansing the political system of patronage politics than it was at purging the state of the traditional political elite. The regime's ambitious program of fiscal centralization neither deprived state governments of resources nor induced compliance with federal spending priorities; substantial evidence from the local level suggests that centralizing tax collection and pegging transfers to federal guidelines had little impact on local spending patterns, and subnational governments exhibited widely divergent patterns of spending in 1971.[25] In Minas Gerais in particular, the state oligarchy retained its capacity to marshal sufficient resources to sustain its patronage operations through state, transferred, and borrowed resources.[26] The centralization of finance and policy making introduced during the authoritarian regime did not transfer control over patronage from regional traditional political elites to the federal government and technocratic policy makers. At best, it produced a standoff between state and federal elites, and municipal dependence remained a political resource for both to dispute.

During the military regime the administration of these programs was not depoliticized. National policy-making by technical experts and their control of state departments of finance and planning notwithstanding, politicians retained or regained their positions at the head of most patronage ministries, and politician-governors continued to manage, and federal and state deputies to operate, the channels by which state resources reached municipalities and citizens. Deputies appealed to electors on the basis of their ability to deliver state patronage, and once in office both they and their constituents perceived the exercise of clientelism as their prime function; in one survey of Minas Gerais state deputies conducted in 1968–1969 (the height of the dictatorship), 83 percent reported that requests for jobs were the most frequent demands made of them.[27] Similarly, the institution of "majority deputy" functioned throughout the dictatorship: The majority deputy – a deputy who receives the most votes on the ticket of the winning party in a particular municipality – wins the "political command," or the prerogative to fill public posts and make other public sector decisions, in that municipality.

Two examples illustrate the politicization of the distribution of state program resources. In one especially dynamic city of approximately 100,000 inhabitants in the center of the prosperous south of Minas Gerais, Varginha, where the incumbent mayor had warded off a fierce challenge from the opposition MDB in the 1976 election, the vice-mayor bragged in 1981 of his city's inclusion in the Intermediate, or "Dike Cities," Program, which had brought a bonanza of public works to the city.[28] He revealed that Varginha had not appeared on the preliminary list of municipalities, but that the city's mayor, Eduardo Otoni, had fought for and won Varginha's inclusion in the program.[29] In Curvelo, a once powerful agrarian center in decline, a popular opposition mayor serving a third (nonconsecutive) term was unable to resist the governor's overtures, and bribes, to cross over to the progovernment party, then called the Democratic Social Party (PDS). Because his city and its environs were suffering from economic stagnation, when he was invited to the governor's weekend palace and promised an array of new public works projects – including a new bus station and a low-income housing program – on the condition he change his partisan affiliation, the poor mayor acceded. Immediately after he signed his affiliation with the PDS, agreements for low-income housing, electrification, telecommunications, roads, bridges, and urban development were delivered by the state government to the municipality. Olavo de Matos attributed what he saw as a radical and immediate difference in the level of benefits to Curvelo from the state and federal governments, to his switch to the PDS. "If I had continued in the opposition," he matter-of-factly explained, "I would have received nothing."[30]

THE MILITARY PROJECT CONSTRAINED: THE SEARCH FOR MEDIATIONS BETWEEN STATE AND SOCIETY

Why did the military fail in its quest to purge traditional politicians and patronage politics from the state? As most scholars writing at the height of the dictatorship were persuaded that the military could accomplish its project because it commanded the repressive arm of the state as well as those branches which controlled economic resources and decision making, the "failure" of the military project, to the extent it is explained at all, is attributed to either military choice or error.[31] Such a view, if fully developed, would contend that beyond its initial steps at fiscal centralization the military did not seriously attempt to eradicate clientelism and traditional politicians from the state, or that by not exploiting intra-elite rivalries, it failed to take full advantage of existing political opportunities. Upon reflection, this perspective neglects the question of how an elite who seized "the state" could build societal support or overcome societal resistance, and it fails to appreciate the boundaries within which the military had to make its strategic decisions.

Why the Brazilian military was unable to transform the state and remake society as it wished is better explained by focusing on the constraints placed on the military project by the regime's need to resort to state–society mediation, and by examining the structure of incentives and opportunities presented by historical patterns of state–society interaction. Guillermo O'Donnell more than a decade ago insightfully argued that because the bureaucratic-authoritarian regimes restricted citizenship and excluded popular classes from participation in the political system and the fruits of economic development, their pretensions to govern for the entire nation were transparently hollow and their rule exposed as naked domination.[32] This, he warned, was an uneasy and ultimately inadequate formula upon which to institutionalize their rule. In Brazil, this tension was more urgent and finding a solution more imperative because the regime multiplied the opportunities for the state to meet society. It expanded the state's productive, regulatory, extractive, and distributive capacities, and allowed politics to take place, even during the height of military repression.[33] The way in which the military defined its political regime and economic strategies at the outset was shaped, and constrained, by its political legacy; those initial constraints, in turn, forced the revision of the military project.

Historical legacies

The Brazilian political system is elite-dominated. Through the course of the twentieth century, most Brazilian citizens were incorporated into political life, if at all, through corporatist and clientelistic networks strictly controlled by the state. Formal corporatist structures were erected in the 1930s and 1940s to regulate functional networks of representation for all classes but especially for labor. By prohibiting plural representation and competition among organizations for membership, corporatist labor laws kept the interests of civil society segmented, weak, and subject to state control.[34] Clientelism dominated and deformed the political parties and most other forms of territorial mediation between the state and society. The hegemonic parties – the Republican Party during the Old Republic, the Social Democratic Party (PSD) in the postwar period, and finally, ARENA during the dictatorship, poorly performed their representative and interest-aggregating functions; they were little more than the patronage machines of regional oligarchies, and the principal division of party systems in Brazil was historically between the "ins" (*situação*), who had access to state patronage, and the "outs" (*oposição*), who did not.

Clientelism was historically practiced in Brazil above all by the traditional political elite, a group that includes members of the regional oligarchies who enjoy national prominence as well as their local allies, the political bosses of the cities and towns of the interior.[35] Unlike other so-called professional politicians and nontraditional or modern political elites, *traditional* political elites are related to each other and to previous political generations, and they exercise domination through highly personalized patronage networks that are themselves most often family-based. "Typical" traditional politicians may be the grandsons or -daughters of a senator or governor, have attended a prestigious preparatory school and subsequently earned a law degree from the Federal University, entered politics as university students, won their first election in local politics, and then demonstrated the strength of their local power base in a race for state deputy. Their family lands have usually either been sold or subdivided, and family assets transferred into finance and other modern sector economic activities. The traditional political elite encompasses and represents agrarian elites, exporters, industrialists, and bankers, but, from top oligarch to remote local boss, its political power is predicated on its access to state resources.

Even early in the state's development, when public authority could not penetrate the entire nation, private elites in most regions did not command autonomous sources of political power, but maintained their political positions only as they exercised power through the public sphere, and as long as they were useful to the state oligarchies. In the best-known form of political clientelism known as *coronelismo,* local political bosses, the *coroneis,* who were most often landowners, served as mediators between the state and citizens in rural areas.[36] By providing an economic livelihood, justice, and protection from police and local enemies, the *coronel* commanded the political loyalty of his dependents, whose support, in turn, he delivered to his overlords, either the incumbent state oligarchies or their challengers, in exchange for state resources or their future promise. Local political bosses and their rivals had to support the state oligarchy or its competitors because their municipalities were financially dependent on the state and subject to intervention by state militias. Thus, even the largest landlord needed state support to stay in power locally, lest he be replaced by a rival abetted by direct or indirect state intervention.

Economic development did not undermine traditional, clientelistic relations between state elites and private citizens. To the contrary, political clientelism, which had been used by traditional elites to deliver votes in the Old Republic and to survive the explosion in political participation accompanying the transition to democracy after World War II, became more ubiquitous as Brazil changed from a largely agrarian society to one industrializing under state auspices. But it was also modernized, transformed from a fundamentally private affair between lords and peasants into a state-based system.[37] The revolutionary modernization of agriculture of the past thirty years, which expelled the peasantry from the rural areas, produced an army of urban migrants who did not for the most part enter the industrial and modern service sectors but commuted to the fields as seasonal agricultural laborers and drifted into temporary construction employment, personal services, and other poorly remunerated economic activities of the "marginal" tertiary sector.[38] For these classes interposed between agriculture and industry, the state sector provided part or all of their material support through permanent and temporary employment, the provision of basic social services (sanitation, transportation, shelter), transfer payments, credit, and so forth. With the shift of the dependence of the client population from land to the state, the power of political bosses at the local level was increasingly based on their role as political mediator, and their dominance was sustained by the productivity of their alliance with state-level elites. At the regional level, the most important material resource in establishing class dominance became the prerogative to distribute public resources, which in turn emanated from controlling the state apparatus.

The effectiveness of these historical and modern forms of state–society mediation in Brazil helps explain the decision of the Brazilian military regime to hold elections, perhaps the most significant manifestation of its being by far the least repressive of the bureaucratic-authoritarian regimes.[39] The Brazilian military restrained its attack on Brazilian society in general and the political elite in particular not merely because the military was ambivalent about authoritarianism, lacking in political acumen, and internally divided, or even because of a tradition of political pluralism that set limits on civilian elite support for dictatorship and forced the military to seek ways to retain the legitimacy of its rule, the most commonly offered reasons for the military's decision to hold elections,[40] but because traditional elite–dominated networks had malfunctioned only slightly by the standards of the Southern Cone. Unlike in Chile, where frenetic competition among strong, ideological parties ultimately drove the political system headlong into class warfare,[41] and in Argentina, where Peronist economic policies and political strategies had given rise to "mass praetorianism," a condition marked by unyielding conflict within civil society,[42] in Brazil on the eve of the coup d'état, social mobilization and conflict took place on a modest scale, and existing channels of mediation between state and society forestalled political polarization and class warfare. Brazilian labor was less well organized and the union movement less of a threat to the established order than the more militant workers' associations in the neighboring bureaucratic-authoritarian regimes. And unlike in Uruguay, where broad segments of society were incorporated into the state distribution network by the "premature welfare state" erected by Battle y Ordóñez in the early part of the century, and second- and third-generation "clients" came to see state benefits as entitlements rather than as favors from their political representatives that required reciprocity – which explains why an overstretched state could not prevent the erosion of consent when economic stagnation set in and the "assistentialist" state became exhausted[43] – in Brazil, new clients welcomed whatever state patronage benefits were directed their way, and these were abundant. Economic growth was robust in the 1950s, and the coup-instigating economic crisis of 1964 did not stem from structural stagnation – in fact, the "deepening process" had advanced considerably in the late 1950s and early 1960s – but from an eminently curable inflation.[44] In Brazil, not only was the breakdown of the "democratic experiment" not inevitable, but it has been attributed to two highly avoidable phenomena: the foolish actions of an inept president, and the excessive fragmentation of the party system.[45]

Unmediated authoritarianism

The strategic decisions which the Brazilian military made under the heavy weight of its political inheritance in turn constrained its future political options. Because the Brazilian military held elections, it could not dispense with politicians as did the militaries of Chile, Argentina, and, at least until soldiers began to think of charting a transition to democracy, Uruguay. In Uruguay, one year after the coup, parties of the leftist Frente Amplio (Broad Front) were systematically dismantled, their presses confiscated, and their leaders arrested, and the traditional parties – the Blancos and the Colorados – were "suspended."[46] In 1976, fifteen thousand politicians lost their political rights for a period of fifteen years. In Chile, the regime closed Congress, banned elected local governments, and disallowed party activity. Even elections within private organizations and associations were circumscribed or monitored by the authorities.[47] In Argentina, where at least nine thousand middle-rank union officials, party cadres, teachers, and student activists died in a "dirty war,"[48] military repression was directed especially against Peronists.[49] Even the "moderate" repression of the Brazilian military was blunted against politicians and was directed hardly at all against the traditional political elite.

At first, the Brazilian regime's gamble to hold elections seemed well worth the risk. With the opposition MDB demoralized and disorganized, and riding the wave of extraordinary economic growth (however poorly distributed its fruits), ARENA won resounding victories in the congressional elections of 1970 and the municipal elections of 1972. In many rural areas, ARENA candidacies went unchallenged by the MDB. Confident of victory in 1974, the regime decided to hold relatively free elections to shore up collapsing legitimacy manifested in declining voting turnout, and to challenge the traditional elite.[50] In the 1974 congressional elections, however, the regime suffered an unanticipated defeat. The MDB won 16 of the 22 contested seats in the senatorial elections, and it increased its share of the seats in the Chamber of Deputies from 28 percent to 44 percent (it elected 172 deputies as compared with 192 for ARENA). It also took control of five additional state legislatures (before the election, it held the majority of seats only in Guanabara).[51] An effective media campaign waged by the MDB, and its new tack of protesting bread-and-butter economic issues captured for the party the allegiance of voters who previously had stayed home on polling day, cast blank votes, or spoiled their ballots. In other words, the party capitalized on a strong undercurrent of protest.

The military was stunned by the 1974 elections, which it interpreted as evidence of its own political isolation. To parry the electoral setback, the regime undertook nothing less than the revision of its political project. Although not threatened with outright defeat or brought to the point of surrendering power, it acted swiftly and decisively to safeguard its electoral advantage. It first strengthened ARENA through electoral manipulation; it appointed one-third of the Senate (without which the government party would have lost its Senate majority), and restricted access to the mass media by the political parties.[52] But it also recognized its longer-term need for, and developed a strategy to build, enhanced political support. This need became all the more imperative after important segments of Brazilian elite society, especially the Catholic Church and the bourgeoisie, defected from the authoritarian coalition, and stepped up their attacks on the regime.[53] Confronting internal splits, an increasingly militant trade union movement, a hostile, reawakening civil society, and declining polls in the nation's urban centers, it could only hope to prolong its "influence in retreat."[54] In accepting this course, it forsook its political project to transform the state and politics.

THE MILITARY PROJECT REVISED

The military's political options for revising its project were as restricted by its political inheritance as were its initial political decisions. It first sought to counter its declining popularity by priming the economy to avoid recession, even when that meant borrowing abroad heavily to compensate for the effects of the first and second oil shocks.[55] After years of squeezing wages to attract foreign investment, promote growth, and combat inflation, the governments of Ernesto Geisel and João Figueiredo attempted to increase real wages for the working class. The Geisel initiative fell short, but Figueiredo in 1979 enacted a wage readjustment law that in fact redistributed income from the higher income brackets to the lower.[56]

Soon, however, it become apparent that this strategy was unworkable and propping up the fortunes of ARENA would require reviving clientelism. It was much less expensive to the economy and less damaging to the government's anti-inflationary policies to buy votes through patronage than to attempt a direct appeal to broad segments of the population through wage hikes for the low-income population.[57] What made the resort to patronage on a massive scale feasible as a political strategy was the regime's economic programs, which had nourished clientelistic networks. The economic model pursued by the Brazilian military, above all the expansion of the state's roles in production and distribution, expanded both the resource base for state patronage operations and the number of program beneficiaries dependent on state clientelism. In Minas Gerais state expenditure per capita nearly tripled in real terms between 1960 and 1977,[58] the number of state agencies and parastatals tripled,[59] and state direct employment alone nearly doubled. Indirect employment rose substantially as well, especially in housing-related construction.

In line with this new strategy, in the mid- to late 1970s the Geisel and Figueiredo administrations reversed spending priorities on social programs, and abandoned all pretensions to excise patronage from the state. Agricultural credit was redirected toward small farmers, and there was a significant expansion of public housing for the poor and the near poor: almost 200,000 units were constructed in 1980, up from 7,831 in 1974.[60] Through state governments, these patronage programs reached a broad segment of society. In Minas Gerais, where urban and rural development programs were accelerated, the state's housing program was targeted to provide shelter to roughly 15 percent of the state's population. Its most ambitious urban development program, the "Dike Cities" Program, delivered basic sanitation, infrastructure, health and education, labor training, credit, and income-improving opportunities to 2 million low-income inhabitants of sixteen midsized cities (one in seven of the state's population). Agrarian credit for small landowners reached roughly 70,000 beneficiaries, or one in five of all small agrarian producers in the state.[61] Ninety percent of all agrarian credit in 1980 in Minas Gerais was disbursed by public entities.[62]

These urban and rural program resources were distributed for maximum electoral advantage, not according to any predictable electoral formula but through the intermediation of particular politicians. One popular regime tactic to build electoral support for ARENA was to win popular opposition figures over to the government party. As many as from one-half to two-thirds of MDB mayors elected in 1972 joined ARENA, a phenomenon in Brazil called *adesismo*.[63] Offering inducements to opposition mayors to join the government was the centerpiece of a regime strategy to broaden the government coalition by co-opting essentially nonpartisan mayors whose apolitical followings were based on the services they provided. Barry Ames, who has studied the pattern of allocation of state resources for housing and the complementary infrastructural investments (sewerage, water, etc.) of the National Housing Bank (BNH), has concluded that "the regime never fine-tuned these programs to its political needs" in that "politically marginal states did not gain at the expense of solidly progovernment and hopelessly antigovernment states." Rather, the pattern of federal allocations reflected the political strength of individual politicians.[64] In other words, to implement its electoral strategy based on state patronage, the military resurrected the traditional political elite, restoring its members to top-level positions in the state. In contrast to the technocrats and political newcomers and outsiders whom Médici had named to top cabinet positions and some governorships, the governors nominated by Geisel in 1974 were all civilians and highly placed in state and local party machines. The traditional elite were also invited to return to head various state departments and national cabinet positions from which they had been temporarily evicted.

Was it necessary that patronage be conducted by, and benefit, the traditional political elite? Why did the military not use state resources to exploit intra-elite divisions as a means of ridding the state of the relatively autonomous *traditional* politicians who carved up the state at its lower levels into personal fiefdoms? It initially tried to do just this, when it favored for state governorships politicians from the defunct National Democratic Union (UDN) at the expense of their traditional rivals in the PSD. But the political elite united during the harshest years of the dictatorship behind the most unlikely of rallying points: the 1968 speech in the Congress by the deputy Márcio Moreira Alves insulting military dignity (see note 20). However ambivalent this elite was about mild authoritarianism and open political competition, and however salient PSD–UDN rivalries remained *within the elite* for the entire period of the dictatorship, the traditional political elite defined its interests vis-à-vis the military as common interests.[65]

It was not by default that the military turned to the regional oligarchies for help, nor was it a random choice. Despite the fact that the military ultimately controlled state resources and should have been able to direct patronage funds through any officeholder, it was not able to replace traditional political elites with a new, perhaps more loyal, elite in the state. The traditional political elite controlled the national electoral network of the progovernment party, which was itself an inpenetrable amalgam of private support networks of local bosses and state oligarchs. Ward bosses who sustain such networks at the lower levels of these systems may remain loyal to a particular family for a lifetime. Seizing the state did not ensure being able to gain control over these separate, clientelistic networks, which, as private networks, belonged to the persons who organized them. Military-created "artificial" parties, moreover, reinforced and reinvigorated the clientelistic basis of Brazilian politics; because voter loyalties based on partisan attachments were unlikely to develop, deputies were able to retain personal clienteles and followings.[66]

Just as military rule resurrected traditional politics, so too did it abet the persistent dominance of the traditional political elite, in two principal ways. First, the enrichment of the public sector enhanced the political value of occupying federal and state cabinet and other top administrative posts. Second, controlling patronage networks became an even more valuable asset to the traditional political elite in an authoritarian political system. As incumbent state elites, they benefited from measures taken by the authoritarian regime – the redrawing of the party system and the appointment, or "indirect election," of governors – which sharply reduced political competition. The certain outcome of the partisan affiliation of every postcoup governor hardened once fluid lines dividing state and local political coalitions. The only practical recourse for most local challengers who hoped to come to power was to join the official party, ARENA, but only with great difficulty could a challenge be mounted within the party organized in 1965 and managed throughout authoritarian rule by the oligarchy. In the command of the party at all levels of the political system, the oligarchy regulated handily the subsequent entry of new contestants into the political arena.[67] Traditional local bosses easily dominated local politics and resisted any incipient challenges to their rule, helped elect and reelect federal and state deputies, and contributed to the durability of state elite factions. Even during an authoritarian regime that excluded the vast majority of the population from participation in political life and economic gain, administering state patronage allowed the regional oligarchies to win electoral victories not only in small cities and rural areas where they might be expected to poll well, but also in many mid-sized cities where they might not.[68] More than 90 percent of federal deputies elected from the state of Minas Gerais in each electoral contest during the authoritarian regime on the progovernment party ticket (or their fathers or elder brothers) had served in either the federal or state legislature before. Thus political centralization simply transformed the patronage system into an oligarchical monopoly.

Although the traditional political elite may in the long run be the ultimate beneficiary of the military's project to sustain itself in power, the revised strategy worked as it was expected to. The effective allocation of state patronage secured not only local victories but also majorities in the state houses and the Chamber of Deputies, races in which voters applied clientelistic criteria.[69] To the extent that the military successfully stoked clientelism and for as long as it could secure the support of the political elite (a total of eleven years), it sustained itself in power and it found a graceful exit that still permits it some say in government.[70]

PROSPECTS FOR CHANGE: A NOTE ON THE PERMANENCE OF STATE–SOCIETY RELATIONS

State–society relations are resilient, but not immutable. I have already suggested that the degree and direction of change that is possible, is constrained by the manner in which authoritarianism is formatted on state–society relations. In Chile, the principal accomplishment of the economic model of the military regime – the withdrawal of the state from a wide array of productive and distributive functions, undermined rather than nourished existing patterns of state–society interaction. But in Chile, too little time has passed to determine what the nature of enduring change may be.

A comparison with Uruguay is potentially more fruitful and instructive. In Uruguay, a more repressive form of bureaucratic-authoritarian rule that eliminated the possibility of alternation of national-level power was imposed, as in Brazil, upon a political system dominated by clientelism. Despite losing control of the government and public resources in 1973,[71] the traditional Uruguayan political parties reemerged after the thaw, but many members of the old political elite were not rehabilitated. Elite turnover rates in the 1984 elections, the first since 1971, were much higher in Uruguay than in Brazil: one-third of the senate (10 of 30), and 70 percent of (99) deputies elected in 1984 had no prior parliamentary experience. These rates do not vary by party or within party by ideological faction: overall, 60 percent of the Blancos, 69 percent of the Colorados, and 70 percent of the Frente Amplio's legislators had not before served in the legislature.[72] Rial has gone so far as to claim that the old caudillos and clientelistic leaders have passed from the scene and have been replaced by new political actors, especially in the provinces; however much "these new politicos might want to use the old methods, they will encounter severe limitations on the practice of traditional politics."[73] In subsequent elections held in 1989, the traditional parties declined to the clear advantage of the nonclientelistic parties of the Left – those in the Broad Front and the Nuevo Espacio coalitions – which captured 30 percent of the national vote.

Why a similar configuration of clientelism and authoritarianism in Uruguay and Brazil should have yielded differential rates of elite turnover, and perhaps even different prospects for the survival of clientelism, can be attributed to three factors. First, unlike in Brazil where the military unleashed a torrent of state patronage programs to shore up its sagging support among a state client class whose ranks were swelled by peasants who willingly left, and were unwillingly evicted from, the land, the military regime in Uruguay was unable to trade welfare state programs for votes because "sophisticated Uruguayans had already come to see these as their birthright."[74] Second, the Uruguayan political elite of the traditional parties was cut off from its sources of patronage during the military dictatorship; the full closure of the political and electoral arenas by the authoritarian regime left dormant clientelistic networks of mediation. Rial has observed that when the Uruguayan parties reemerged in 1980, they did so as coteries of notables; they had no party organization.[75] Third, these networks were also starved of economic resources: Although state expenditure grew by 3 percent per year, some limited privatization did take place and the public budget deficit was cut.[76] When inoperative, state–society relations can become "rusty." If and when they reemerge, this "rusty" quality may impede their normal functioning.

Unlike the Uruguayan political elite, the Brazilian traditional elite was able to sustain its patronage operations during the early years of fiscal and political centralization, and even to expand upon them during the latter years of bureaucratic-authoritarian rule, when the military injected private clientelistic networks with massive patronage resources. In Brazil, the networks which bridged state and society remained open for business as usual, especially but not exclusively at election time. "Modified competition" forced the traditional political elite to practice its craft, and especially to expand its influence at lower levels of the political system, which in turn made clientelism stronger even while unions and other civil organizations were also growing stronger. When traditional politicians could no longer deliver victory to the military under the umbrella of the party of government, the power-sharing arrangement between traditional elites and technocrats that had been in force during the early years of the bureaucratic-authoritarian regime finally collapsed, and the distribution of power within the ruling alliance was tipped toward the traditional political elite, who now re-emerged as dominant.

Because the traditional political elite was strong in Brazil, and most of its members sufficiently prescient to jump on the democratization bandwagon soon enough to avoid being tarred with the authoritarian tag, it was even able to play a leading role in a regime transition demanded by the masses of Brazil in the most significant public demonstrations in the country's history. Even after the military exited, the traditional elite remained to preside over the birth of the new regime.[77] The transition that took place with the participation of these traditional mediators in founding elections and the constitutional convention produced a civilian regime which, despite real constitutional change,[78] bears considerable resemblance in its political practices to both its authoritarian and its semicompet-itive precursors. The traditional political elite played a decisive role in shaping the political arrangements of the postauthoritarian order, leaving its particular imprint upon the Brazilian political system. This elite, more than any other force, shaped politics and state–society relations during the transition to democracy.

CONCLUSIONS

The view of the state and state–society relations embedded in most political analyses of Brazilian authoritarianism and the long regime transition that clings to a national focus, equates the state with the military – and views the state and society as separate entities that under authoritarianism did not intersect – inadequately explains how and why the political project of the military came to be revised. A more disaggregated view of the state, as suggested by Joel Migdal in the introduction to this volume, and an examination of the mediations between the state and society, help illuminate the failure of the Brazilian bureaucratic-authoritarian regime to transform a state it ostensibly controlled and to explain the direction in which politics evolved under the dictatorship. Such a focus reveals that the Brazilian state, a federal state with significant strength in the state governments, was not a state that if seized merely at the top could be molded to transform social and political organization as readily as its resources could be marshaled to produce growth. Its historic strength was based in large measure on the way it preemptively organized societal interests and attached these to itself in a dependent fashion. The use of torture by military rulers could not substitute for these historical mediations to society.

How a military regime organizes consent, or fails to, depends in great part on the configuration of state–society relations it inherits. In Brazil, traditional politics cast the project of the Brazilian military adrift, threw a life raft to the military regime struggling to stay afloat, and finally brought the military back to shore on its own terms. The Brazilian military could not operate existing channels of mediation, exercise state domination single-handedly, or structure new ones. When forced to revert to the best anticlass formula it had available to contain social conflict – patronage – it discovered that neither it nor its technocratic handmaidens had any political-organizational structures of their own through which to channel pork to substitute for oligarchical parties; the military could not draw electoral gain from dispensing state patronage; and it had no other basis upon which to organize consent. It needed to champion a political elite. As virtually the only group that could operate state clientelism on a grand scale in Brazil and secure the electoral victories needed to legitimize military rule, the traditional political elite was the military's best option to prevent the radicalization of the polity and the development of class- and interest-based politics. The military was unable even to sponsor a new political elite more to its liking because in such a clientelistic system in which representation and state outputs were organized and distributed according to the logic of clientelism, *traditional* political elites benefited from incumbency in an authoritarian regime that restricted political competition. They contested elections during authoritarian rule with the advantage of already established networks in place in an electoral game in which alliances and coalitions were precluded from shifting, and elite turnover was hence diminished. When important segments of the political class cooperated with military dictators to preserve their own positions in the state, as transpired in Brazil, it was possible for this alliance to collaborate during the transition as well. The survival of traditional politics and traditional political elites, abetted by the authoritarian regime that had initially hoped to be their executioner, had profound consequences for the Brazilian transition to democracy.

The Brazilian experience suggests that state–society relations, although brought into being and shaped by economic and political relations, are capable of outlasting economic development and regime change. These conduits between public and private arenas may ultimately even influence the "state" and "society" more often and more profoundly than the "state" and "society" can reshape these channels of mediation.

NOTES

1 Cf. Manuel Antonio Garretón, *The Chilean Political Process,* trans. Sharon Kellum in collaboration with Gilbert W. Merkx (Boston: Unwin Hyman, 1989); Arturo Valenzuela and J. Samuel Valenzuela, "Party Oppositions Under the Chilean Authoritarian Regime," in J. Samuel Valenzuela and Arturo Valenzuela, eds., *Military Rule in Chile: Dictatorship and Oppositions* (Baltimore: Johns Hopkins University Press, 1986), pp. 184–185.

2 Fernando Henrique Cardoso, "Associated-Dependent Development: Theoretical and Practical Implications," in Alfred Stepan, ed., *Authoritarian Brazil: Origins, Policies, and Future* (New Haven: Yale University Press, 1973), pp. 146–147, best articulated a common view that "the older ruling sectors [traditional agrarian elites,

industrial and merchant interests who could not adapt, and career politicians identified with the dominant classes in the previous political regime] have lost their relative power position in the total structure."

3 Garretón, *The Chilean Political Process,* p. 108, argues that these military dictatorships could not solve the national problems they swept to power to attack (stagnation, unemployment, dependence, inequality), nor were they able to transform politics. His claim that these regimes produced only economic failure is somewhat questionable. The Brazilian regime achieved spectacular growth rates, and the Chilean has been widely credited with effecting painful structural adjustment. Although most did not restructure politics and society, the Peruvian military regime, which effected significant political change, stands as an exception. Abraham F. Lowenthal, "The Peruvian Experiment Reconsidered," in Cynthia McClintock and Abraham F. Lowenthal, eds., *The Peruvian Experiment Reconsidered* (Princeton: Princeton University Press, 1983), pp. 415–430, argues that its failures to spur economic growth, reduce external dependence, and redistribute economic wealth notwithstanding, the Velasco regime did, through land reform, break the back of the oligarchy, and it strengthened an "anemic" state.

4 In Argentina, 66 percent of those questioned in one poll taken in greater Buenos Aires in 1966 approved the coup, while only 6 percent opposed it. In another survey, 77 percent of the respondents in Buenos Aires believed the coup was necessary. Guillermo O'Donnell, *Bureaucratic Authoritarianism: Argentina, 1966–1973, in Comparative Perspective* (Berkeley: University of California Press, 1988), p. 39.

5 "Bureaucratic-authoritarianism" was coined by Guillermo O'Donnell, *Modernization and Bureaucratic-Authoritarianism: Studies in South American Politics* (Berkeley: Institute of International Studies, 1973). Bureaucratic-authoritarian regimes were a response to the problems engendered by the "exhaustion" of the "easy phase" of import substitution, principally the inflationary pressures caused by the strains on the nation's balance of payments that this development model bred and the wage increases that the working class was able to extract as partners in the populist coalitions. The bureaucratic-authoritarian regimes swept to power to "deactivate" the popular sectors in order to contain inflation and attract foreign investment, and at the core of the coup coalition were technocrats.

If Argentina inspired O'Donnell's model – indeed, it was the case O'Donnell knew best, and mass praetorianism and the manifestations of the exhaustion of import-substituting industrialization the model describes were most visible there (see Albert O. Hirschman, "The Turn to Authoritarianism in Latin America and the Search for its Economic Determinants," pp. 70–71, and Robert R. Kaufman, "Industrial Change and Authoritarian Rule in Latin America: A Concrete Review of the Bureaucratic-Authoritarian Model," p. 252, in David Collier, ed., *The New Authoritarianism in Latin America* [Princeton: Princeton University Press, 1979]) – Brazil was the practical model for other militaries in the region and for those civilians who favored harsh authoritarianism over the loss of class privilege.

6 Although there is disagreement as to where the locus of power lay *within* the Brazilian state, whether the power of its regional and local branches superseded or was subordinated to that of the central state, few would doubt that the state apparatus inherited from the Portuguese monarchy was stronger than society. The Portuguese crown penetrated and dominated the sparsely settled colony, and when Brazil achieved independence in 1822, the center did not fragment as it did in Spanish America. Some scholars who view the Brazilian state as a bureaucratic apparatus superimposed upon a weakly organized society, following Weber, have called it "patrimonial." See Raymundo Faoro, *Os Donos do Poder: Formação do Patronato*

Político Brasileiro (Porto Alegre: Globo, 1958); Simon Schwartzman, *São Paulo e o Estado Nacional* (São Paulo: DIFEL, 1975), and *Bases do Autoritarismo Brasileiro* (Rio de Janeiro: Campus, 1982); Fernando Uricoechea, *The Patrimonial Foundations of the Brazilian Bureaucratic State* (Berkeley: University of California Press, 1980); and Riordan Roett, *Brazil: Politics in a Patrimonial Society,* 3rd ed. (New York: Praeger, 1984).

7 True, the military scored some quick and lasting political strokes. It increased the military presence in the state and usurped control of state police forces away from politician-governors. Economic policy is still formulated and carried out by high levels of the cabinet ministries and state banks with formal responsibility for the economy, with little input from elected representatives and virtually no public debate. Through the 1988 constitution, Congress has acquired the power to review the executive's budget, but it has yet to transcend the boundaries of its junior partner status. And even after its exit, the military was able to bully the constitutional convention to adopt the political system of its choice: presidentialism.

8 Alfred Stepan, *Rethinking Military Politics: Brazil and the Southern Cone* (Princeton: Princeton University Press, 1988), pp. 32–40; Guillermo O'Donnell and Philippe C. Schmitter, *Transitions from Authoritarian Rule,* Part 4: *Tentative Conclusions about Uncertain Democracies* (Baltimore: Johns Hopkins University Press, 1986). See Karen Remmer, *Military Rule in Latin America* (Boston: Unwin Hyman, 1989), pp. 34–43, for an interesting institutional analysis of why these rifts were more apt to form in some cases than in others.

9 A huge literature has emerged on the flourishing of Brazilian civil society during the authoritarian regime. The most important movements and new forms of voluntary association were the "new unionism," the local church groups known as Ecclesiastical Base Communities (CEBs), ecology and women's movements, and neighborhood associations. For a representative sampling of works taking up the theme of civil society confronting the state, see especially Ralph Della Cava, "The 'People's Church,' the Vatican, and *Abertura,*" pp. 143–167; Scott Mainwaring, "Grassroots Popular Movements and the Struggle for Democracy: Nova Iguaçu," pp. 168–204; Sonia Alvarez, "Politicizing Gender and Engendering Democracy," pp. 205–251; and Margaret Keck, "The 'New Unionism' in the Brazilian Transition," pp. 252–296, in Alfred Stepan, ed., *Democratizing Brazil: Problems of Transition and Consolidation* (New York: Oxford University Press, 1989). In his editor's introduction, Stepan has combined these two perspectives – the state-led liberalization and the strength of civil society – into a single concept: the dialectic of regime concession and societal conquest.

10 By "traditional politics" I mean a system of political organization that is authoritarian in the sense that political power is narrowly concentrated, access to decision making is restricted, channels of political representation are arranged hierarchically, and political competition is strictly regulated. I use "traditional politics" broadly to imply domination by oligarchies, clientelism, and local bossism, but within this rubric in Brazilian politics a variety of forms is evident, ranging from an extremely personalistic politics in the northeast backlands (*sertão*) to the more modern form of clientelism practiced during the dictatorship in the state of Rio de Janeiro by the official opposition party, the Brazilian Democratic Movement (MDB). In all forms of traditional politics, salient political divisions are based on particularlistic concerns rather than issues, and factions are defined by and identified with personal cliques.

11 I have based this claim in part on the results of the 1990 elections. One year after the candidate of the Workers' Party, Luis Inácio "Lula" da Silva, polled credibly in the 1989 presidential elections, traditional politicians returned in force to capture a series

of important gubernatorial races, and candidates of the Workers' Party suffered a disproportionate electoral decline. Bolivar Lamounier, "Brazil: Inequality Against Democracy," in Larry Diamond, Juan J. Linz, and Seymour Martin Lipset, eds., *Democracy in Developing Countries*, vol. 4: *Latin America* (Boulder, Colo.: Lynne Rienner), p. 153, has characterized the "wild clientelism" that gripped the federal government after 1987 as Brazil's "Jacksonian age." Current research confirms, moreover, that the systematic practice of clientelism in Brazil is as pervasive as ever. Barry Ames, "Electoral Strategy and Legislative Politics in Brazil, 1978–1990," progress report, 3 April 1991; Scott Mainwaring, "Clientelism, Patrimonialism, and Economic Crisis: Brazil Since 1979," paper presented at the Congress of the Latin American Studies Association, Washington, D.C., 4–7 April 1991.

12 Maria das Graças Grossi, "Minas Gerais: del Estancamiento al Boom: una Réplica Local del Modelo Brasileño," *Revista Mexicana de Sociología*, 39, no. 1 (January–March 1977): 251–267; Luis Aureliano Gama de Andrade, "Technocracy and Development: The Case of Minas Gerais," Ph.D. dissertation, University of Michigan, 1980.

13 The reader interested in this detail should consult my book *Traditional Politics and Regime Change in Brazil* (New York: Cambridge University Press, forthcoming).

14 On the repression of unions, see Kenneth S. Mericle, "Corporatist Control of the Working Class: Authoritarian Brazil Since 1964," in James M. Malloy, ed., *Authoritarianism and Corporatism in Latin America* (Pittsburgh: University of Pittsburgh Press, 1977), pp. 303–338; on the transfer of social security administration to *técnicos*, see James M. Malloy, *The Politics of Social Security in Brazil* (Pittsburgh: University of Pittsburgh Press, 1979), pp. 122–128.

15 Brazil, *A Nova Constituição do Brasil* (Rio de Janeiro: Gráfica Auriverde, 1981), pp. 40–45, and Roett, *Brazil*, p. 128. According to Robert Wesson and David V. Fleischer, *Brazil in Transition* (New York and Stanford: Praeger and Hoover Institution Press, 1983), p. 82, during the Médici presidency, 100 percent of executive-initiated bills were passed. Olavo Brasil de Lima Júnior, "Mudança política e processo decisório: análise da política orçamentaria brasileira," *Dados*, 14 (1977): 141–163, demonstrates the effective transfer of control over the budget to the executive.

16 During the administration of Castelo Branco (1964–1967), six thousand decree laws were passed, and during that of Costa e Silva (1967–1969), four thousand. Philippe C. Schmitter, "The 'Portugalization' of Brazil?" in Stepan, ed., *Authoritarian Brazil*, p. 190; and Ronald M. Schneider, *The Political System of Brazil: Emergence of a "Modernizing" Authoritarian Regime, 1964–1970* (New York: Columbia University Press, 1971), p. 200.

17 Thomas E. Skidmore, "Politics and Economic Policy Making in Authoritarian Brazil, 1937–71," in Stepan, ed., *Authoritarian Brazil*, pp. 3–46; Peter J. McDonough, *Power and Ideology in Brazil* (Princeton: Princeton University Press, 1981); Schneider, *The Political System of Brazil;* Barry Ames, *Rhetoric and Reality in a Militarized Regime: Brazil Since 1964* (Beverly Hills, Calif.: Sage, 1973); Luciano Martins, *Estado Capitalista e Burocracia no Brasil pós 64* (Rio de Janeiro: Paz e Terra, 1985); Cândido Mendes, "The Post-1964 Brazilian Regime: Outward Redemocratization and Inner Institutionalization," *Government and Opposition*, 15 (Winter 1980): 48–74; Luiz Bresser Pereira, *Development and Crisis in Brazil, 1930–1983*, trans. Marcia Van Dyke (Boulder, Colo.: Westview Press, 1984); and Malloy, *The Politics of Social Security in Brazil*.

18 Edson de Oliveira Nunes, "Legislativo, Política e Recrutamento de Elites no Brasil," *Dados*, 17 (1978): 61.

19 Fernando Henrique Cardoso, *Autoritarismo e Democratização* (Rio de Janeiro: Paz e Terra, 1975), pp. 178–179.

20 The national Congress was closed briefly on two occasions: in December 1968, after it refused to lift congressional immunity for one of its members, Márcio Moreira Alves, whose speech "insulting military dignity" provoked the notorious Institutional Act No. 5; and in April 1977, when the regime enacted the "April package" of electoral measures designed to preserve government party majorities.

21 Cf. Bolivar Lamounier, "O Voto em São Paulo," in Bolivar Lamounier, ed., *Voto de Desconfiança: Eleições e Mudança Política no Brasil, 1970–1979* (São Paulo: Vozes/CEBRAP, 1980), p. 18. After the 1974 elections, one-third of the Senate seats were removed from direct election and became appointed positions.

22 Margaret Sarles Jenks, "Political Parties in Authoritarian Brazil," Ph.D. dissertation, Duke University, 1979, pp. 335, 361–362, 380, 385; and Nunes, "Legislativo, Política e Recrutamento," p. 60.

23 Hagopian, *Traditional Politics.*

24 The "twenty-seven governing families" of Minas Gerais were boldly identified in Cid Rebelo Horta, "Famílias Governamentais de Minas Gerais," in Universidade de Minas Gerais, *Segundo Seminário de Estudos Mineiros* (Belo Horizonte, 1956), pp. 45–91. Working from Rebelo Horta's published information on these families, and an update of this story in the regional newspaper (*Estado de Minas,* 18 January 1981), I was able to trace the family lineage of officeholders to these families.

25 Instituto Brasileiro de Administração Municipal (IBAM), *O FPM e a Política de Receitas Vinculadas* (Rio de Janeiro: IBAM, 1976), pp. 41–57, and *Municípios do Brasil: Quinze Anos Depois* (Rio de Janeiro: IBAM, 1975), p. 53.

26 In the 1970s, the state came to borrow regularly more than 10 percent of its total revenue and, in some years, as much as one-fourth of state revenue. Secretaria de Estado de Planejamento e Coordenação Geral (SEPLAN), *Comportamento da Economia Mineira Período 1960–1977,* vol. 6: *Setor Público* (1978), pt. 2, pp. 355, 356. According to data from the state finance department, 24 percent of state income in 1980 and 19 percent in 1981 derived from borrowed monies, some from foreign development banks.

27 Tocary A. Bastos and Thomas W. Walker, "Partidos e Forças Políticas em Minas Gerais," *Revista Brasileira de Estudos Políticos,* 31 (May 1971): 147.

28 Dike cities were so called for their anticipated role in stemming the tide of migration from the northeast and the rural areas of the center-south to state capitals and the metropolitan region of São Paulo. By investing in housing, urban infrastructure, and job creation, it was hoped, these cities could attract transient migrants to settle permanently.

29 Interview with Ronaldo Venga, Varginha, 13–14 October 1981.

30 Interview with Olavo de Matos, Curvelo, 9 October 1981.

31 There are at least three important exceptions. Juan J. Linz, "The Future of an Authoritarian Situation or the Institutionalization of an Authoritarian Regime: The Case of Brazil," in Stepan, ed., *Authoritarian Brazil,* pp. 233–254, anticipated that the Brazilian military would lack a formula upon which to legitimate its rule. In writing about the difficulties of institutionalizing the Onganía regime in Argentina, William C. Smith, *Authoritarianism and the Crisis of the Argentine Political Economy* (Stanford: Stanford University Press, 1989), p. 160, noted the paradox that the "elimination of mediating institutions and popular exclusion constituted the source of the Argentine authoritarian project's apparently unchallengeable power as well as its extreme fragility and exceptional rigidity." And Garretón, *The Chilean Political*

Process, provides a sophisticated argument about the evolution of these "new" military regimes.

32 Guillermo O'Donnell, "Tensions in the Bureaucratic-Authoritarian State and the Question of Democracy," in Collier, ed., *The New Authoritarianism,* pp. 294–298.

33 One hundred and eight federal state enterprises were added to the state sector from 1967 to 1973. Braz José de Araújo, "Intervenção Econômica do Estado e Democracia," in Carlos Estevam Martins, ed., *Estado e Capitalismo no Brasil* (São Paulo: Hucitec-Cebrap, 1977), p. 238. By 1983, there were 683 public sector companies (195 federal, 372 state, and 116 municipal), many of which dominated the petroleum, transportation, mining, metallurgical, and public utilities sectors of the economy. More than half of Brazil's financial institutions, moreover, were state-owned. *Visão,* "Quem é Quem na Economia Brasileira," 32 (31 August 1983), 35A: 431. For an overview of the expansion of the fiscal, regulatory, and productive roles of the state, see Werner Baer, Richard Newfarmer, and Thomas Trebat, "On State Capitalism in Brazil: Some New Issues and Questions," *Inter-American Economic Affairs,* 30 (Winter 1976):69–96.

34 Philippe C. Schmitter, *Interest Conflict and Political Change in Brazil* (Stanford: Stanford University Press, 1971); and Kenneth P. Erickson, *The Brazilian Corporative State and Working Class Politics* (Berkeley: University of California Press, 1977).

35 These regional oligarchies are political and should not be confused with the "export oligarchies" who were dominant at the turn of the century, although their members may be descended from that elite group. Their numbers are relatively small, their ranks relatively closed, and their power concentrated in few hands.

36 See Antônio Octávio Cintra, "Traditional Brazilian Politics: An Interpretation of Relations Between Center and Periphery," in Neuma Aguiar, ed., *The Structure of Brazilian Development* (New Brunswick, N.J.: Transaction Books, 1979), pp. 127–166; Eul-Soo Pang, "Coronelismo in Northeast Brazil," in Robert Kern, ed., with the assistance of Ronald Dolkart, *The Caciques: Oligarchical Politics and the System of Caciquismo in the Luso-Hispanic World* (Albuquerque: University of New Mexico Press, 1973), pp. 65–88; and the classic, Victor Nunes Leal, *Coronelismo: The Municipality and Representative Government in Brazil,* trans. June Henfrey (New York: Cambridge University Press, 1977); originally published in Portuguese as *Coronelismo: Enxada e Voto. O Município e o Regime Representativo no Brasil* by Revista Forense (Rio de Janeiro, 1949).

37 Similar arguments have been advanced by Ronald H. Chilcote, *Power and the Ruling Classes in Northeast Brazil: Juazeiro and Petrolina in Transition* (Cambridge: Cambridge University Press, 1990); and more generally by René Lemarchand, "Comparative Political Clientelism: Structure, Process, and Optic," in S. N. Eisenstadt and René Lemarchand, eds., *Political Clientelism, Patronage, and Development* (Beverly Hills, Calif.: Sage, 1981), pp. 7–32.

38 Brazil's urban population rose from 36 percent in 1950 to two-thirds by 1980. Vilmar Faria, "Desenvolvimento, Urbanização, e Mudanças na Estrutura do Emprego: A Experiência Brasileira dos Ultimos Trinta Anos," in Bernardo Sorj and Maria Hermínia Tavares de Almeida, eds., *Sociedade e Politica no Brasil Pós-64* (São Paulo: Brasiliense, 1983), p. 131.

39 Far fewer persons lost their political rights and their lives than in Chile, Argentina, and Uruguay. According to the account of military repression compiled by the Archdiocese of São Paulo from the records of the military tribunals, *Brasil: Nunca Mais,* the Brazilian government was responsible for "only" 333 deaths from 1964 to

1981, a per capita death toll one hundred times lower than that of neighboring Argentina. The regime also displayed leniency: At the height of the repression (1969–1973), the Supreme Military Tribunal acquitted 45 percent of the cases brought before it, and for the entire period from 1965 to 1977, 68 percent. Thomas Skidmore, *The Politics of Military Rule in Brazil, 1964–85* (New York: Oxford University Press, 1988), p. 132. Only about five hundred persons lost their political rights.

40 Bolivar Lamounier, *"Authoritarian Brazil* Revisited: The Impact of Elections on the *Abertura,"* in Stepan, ed., *Democratizing Brazil,* pp. 45–51.

41 Arturo Valenzuela, *The Breakdown of Democratic Regimes: Chile* (Baltimore: Johns Hopkins University Press, 1978).

42 "Mass praetorianism" is the highly politicized climate described by Samuel P. Huntington, *Political Order in Changing Societies* (New Haven: Yale University Press, 1968), pp. 80, 88, 196. See O'Donnell, *Modernization and Bureaucratic-Authoritarianism,* and Carlos Waisman, *Reversal of Development in Argentina: Postwar Counterrevolutionary Policies and Their Structural Consequences* (Princeton: Princeton University Press, 1987), for applications of this idea to Argentina.

43 The term is from Juan Rial, "Continuidad y Cambio en Las Organizaciones Partidarias en el Uruguay: 1973–1984," in Marcelo Cavarozzi and Manuel Antonio Garretón, eds., *Muerte y Resurrección: Los Partidos Políticos en el Autoritarismo y las Transiciones del Cono Sur* (Santiago: FLACSO, 1989).

44 José Serra, "Three Mistaken Theses Regarding the Connection Between Industrialization and Authoritarian Regimes," in Collier, ed., *The New Authoritarianism,* p. 117, and Michael Wallerstein, "The Collapse of Democracy in Brazil: Its Economic Determinants," *Latin American Research Review,* 15, no. 3 (1980): 3–40.

45 Alfred Stepan, "Political Leadership and Regime Breakdown: Brazil," in Juan J. Linz and Alfred Stepan, eds., *The Breakdown of Democratic Regimes: Latin America* (Baltimore: Johns Hopkins University Press, 1978), pp. 120–133; Wanderley Guilherme dos Santos, "The Calculus of Conflict: Impasse in Brazilian Politics and the Crisis of 1964," Ph.D. dissertation, Stanford University, 1979, *Sessenta e Quatro: Anatomia da Crise* (São Paulo: Vértice, 1986).

46 Charles Guy Gillespie and Luis Eduardo González, "Uruguay: The Survival of Old and Autonomous Institutions," in Diamond, Linz, and Lipset, eds., *Democracy in Developing Countries: Latin America,* p. 220.

47 Arturo Valenzuela, "Chile: Origins, Consolidation, and Breakdown of a Democratic Regime," in Diamond, Linz, and Lipset, eds., *Democracy in Developing Countries, Latin America,* p. 159.

48 Some unofficial estimates range as high as twenty thousand.

49 Marcelo Cavarozzi, "Peronism and Radicalism: Argentina's Transitions in Perspective," in Paul W. Drake and Eduardo Silva, eds., *Elections and Democratization in Latin America, 1980–85* (San Diego: Center for Iberian and Latin American Studies, University of California, San Diego, 1986), p. 155.

50 Linz, "The Future of an Authoritarian Situation"; O'Donnell, "Tensions in the Bureaucratic-Authoritarian State"; Barry Ames, *Political Survival: Politicians and Public Policy in Latin America* (Berkeley: University of California Press, 1987); Lamounier, *"Authoritarian Brazil* Revisited"; Scott Mainwaring, "The Transition to Democracy in Brazil" (Kellogg Institute Working Paper No. 66, 1985); Bolivar Lamounier and Alkimar R. Moura, "Economic Policy and Political Opening in Brazil," in Jonathan Hartlyn and Samuel A. Morley, eds., *Latin American Political Economy: Financial Crisis and Political Change* (Boulder, Colo.: Westview Press, 1986), pp. 165–196.

According to Margaret Sarles, "Maintaining Political Control Through Parties: The Brazilian Strategy," *Comparative Politics*, 15, no. 1 (October 1982), 45, 70, "the technocratic-oriented military, disgusted with traditional corrupt electoral practices, systematically purged the electoral lists of phantom voters, disproportionately depriving ARENA of many voters," in some northeast states, by as much as from 25 percent to 50 percent.

51 Roett, *Brazil*, pp. 146–147; Maria Helena Moreira Alves, *State and Opposition in Military Brazil* (Austin: University of Texas Press, 1985), pp. 144–145. Guanabara was, until 1975, the state that encompassed the city of Rio de Janeiro.

52 Alves, *State and Opposition*, pp. 144, 147.

53 On the defection of the bourgeoisie from the ruling coalition, see Luciano Martins, "The 'Liberalization' of Authoritarian Rule in Brazil," in Guillermo O'Donnell, Philippe C. Schmitter, and Laurence Whitehead, eds., *Transitions from Authoritarian Rule*, Part 2: *Latin America* (Baltimore: Johns Hopkins University Press, 1986), pp. 72–94; Luiz Carlos Bresser Pereira, *O Colapso de uma Aliança de Classes* (São Paulo: Brasiliense, 1978); and Philippe Faucher, "The Paradise That Never Was: The Breakdown of the Brazilian Authoritarian Order," in Thomas C. Bruneau and Philippe Faucher, eds., *Authoritarian Capitalism: Brazil's Contemporary Economic and Political Development* (Boulder, Colo.: Westview Press, 1981). McDonough, *Power and Ideology in Brazil*, was one of the first works to focus on "the tensions within the Brazilian establishment that have contributed to the undoing of authoritarianism" (p. xix).

54 Ames, *Political Survival*.

55 Lamounier and Moura, "Economic Policy and Political Opening," pp. 167–185.

56 Ames, *Political Survival*, p. 198.

57 Ibid., p. 206.

58 Fundação João Pinheiro, *Análise da Evolução da Despesa Pública do Estado de Minas Gerais – Administração Direta, Autarquias, e Fundações*, vol. 3 (Belo Horizonte: Fundação João Pinheiro, n.d.), pp. 141, 145.

59 SEPLAN, *Comportamento da Economia Mineira*, pp. 252, 254.

60 Ames, *Political Survival*, pp. 157, 168.

61 *Estado de Minas*, 24 May 1981, p. 14.

62 Instituto Brasileiro de Geografia e Estatística (Fundação IBGE), *Censo Agropecuário, 1980, Minas Gerais* la parte (Rio de Janeiro: IBGE, 1984), p. 52.

63 Paul Cammack, "Clientelism and Military Government in Brazil," in Christopher Clapham, ed., *Private Patronage and Public Power: Political Clientelism in the Modern State* (New York: St. Martin's Press, 1982), p. 68.

64 Ames, *Political Survival*, p. 205.

65 Commenting on the durability of the PSD–UDN schism, the regional newspaper commented in 1981, sixteen years after they had been abolished: "The PSD and UDN evoke a deep longing in our politicians. What's more, after two party reforms [1965, 1979] they defy every law and threaten eternity." *Estado de Minas*, 18 January 1981.

66 In four local elections (1966, 1970, 1972, 1976) in a sample of twenty-five municipalities in Minas Gerais, how individual politicians aligned in the postcoup parties was more strongly correlated with the local MDB victories even *after* the "realigning" election of 1974 than such more frequently cited factors as municipal size and the percentage of the population residing in urban areas. Hagopian, *Traditional Politics*.

67 Eli Diniz, *Voto e Máquina Política: Patronagem e Clientelismo no Rio de Janeiro* (Rio de Janeiro: Paz e Terra, 1982), pp. 90–91, demonstrated that through the Organic Party Law the "Chaguista" group (which was headed by and loyal to

Governor Chagas Freitas) controlled the admission of new members to the state branch of the MDB.

68 Research I conducted in 1981 showed that in such boomtowns as Varginha and Montes Claros, electors returned to office the political representatives of the local traditional elite despite rapid urban and industrial growth.

69 Lamounier, "O Voto em São Paulo," p. 78; Eli Diniz, "Máquinas Políticas e Oposição: O MDB no Rio de Janeiro," *Dados,* 23, no. 3 (1980): 335–357. When the resources of the state could be employed to support ARENA candidates, and voters could visibly recognize the advantages of state assistance, they voted ARENA; when they wished to protest government performance in such areas as the high cost of living (a salient issue for the poor, whose adjustments to indexed wages lagged up to six months behind double- and later triple-digit inflation), they voted for the MDB.

70 See Stepan, *Rethinking Military Politics,* on the prerogatives retained by the military under civilian rule; and Frances Hagopian and Scott Mainwaring, "Democracy in Brazil: Prospects and Problems," *World Policy Journal* (Summer 1987): 491–493.

71 Why these parties survived has been attributed to: (1) their long duration and "solid roots" in society; (2) the fact that the military regime did not create rival parties, but expressly named the traditional parties as its only successors; and (3) the inability of the military to demobilize society and sever the links between the parties and civil society. See Rial, "Continuidad y Cambio," pp. 259–263.

72 Rial, "Continuidad y Cambio," p. 257.

73 Ibid., pp. 257–258.

74 Gillespie and González, "Uruguay," p. 223.

75 Rial, "Continuidad y Cambio," p. 269.

76 Remmer, *Military Rule,* pp. 175–176.

77 In "The Compromised Consolidation: The Political Class in the Brazilian Transition," in Scott Mainwaring, Guillermo O'Donnell, and J. Samuel Valenzuela, eds., *Issues in Democratic Consolidation: The New South American Democracies in Comparative Perspective* (Notre Dame, Ind.: University of Notre Dame Press, 1992), I discuss at length the role of the traditional political elite in the Brazilian transition.

78 The democratic constitution ratified in 1988 is exceptionally strong on civil, social, and political rights.

3

State power and social organization in China

VIVIENNE SHUE

PROLOGUE

There is an odor of righteous vindication in the air. Communism is in disarray around the world. Little wonder then if some influential voices emanating from the capitalist camp have been heard now claiming not just the missile victory and the moral victory, but the economic and the philosophic victories as well. The unmistakable turning point, both in Europe and in China, came in 1989, amid a staggering series of unlooked-for events at once thrilling and terrifying in their intensity. And by the time 1989, that year of living dangerously, had given way to the new decade, American observers of various persuasions, but especially those on the political right, were already to be found confidently casting those events in the categories of free market economic growth and liberal democratic values versus centrally planned economic stagnation and communist political repression. These categories are not by any means entirely without force and relevance, of course. Yet if we insist on viewing recent events primarily in terms so tinged with partisan self-congratulation, we will miss much that can be known and learned.

For, after all, the evidence is exceedingly plain that there is only very mixed enthusiasm, in all parts of the socialist world now undergoing systemic reform, for the social realities of laissez-faire market competition and for the societal norms and consequences of untrammeled individualism. The evidence has also been pretty plain, as we have heard the demands of demonstrators from Beijing to Bucharest, that at least for many groups in these societies, elemental desires for an end to bureaucratic corruption, nepotistic incompetence, and other fla-grant abuses of power – longings for the ideals of simple, honest, popularly responsive government – have been at least as salient and potent discursive themes as the more explicitly westward-leaning appeals for multiparty electoral competition or other liberal democratic institutions and procedures. Communist

The author wishes to thank Guo Junsheng, Wang Shaoguang, and Yue Ming for able assistance with some of the research for this essay.

parties may indisputably be held in disdain all over the East and Far East now; but the humanistic and communitarian ideals associated with socialism have by no means been so utterly rejected. In 1989 citizens and victims of one Commu- nist dictatorship after another did cast their ballots of blood and honor in favor of more just, accountable, and humane government. But were they voting also for *less* government, for a weakening of state power and authority? And is a weaker state what all of them are likely to get?

STATE POWER AND CIVIL ASSOCIATION

Students of state building sometimes speak as if the consolidation of strong and centralized state power necessarily entails the displacement or at least the weakening of alternative loci of authority and control already existing in society. State power and social power are presented as confronting each other in a generally very protracted yet ultimately zero-sum competition for both the right and the capacity to command obedience. Yet, there does appear to be an intriguing relationship – one deserving better social scientific exploration – between the emergence of a robust sphere of civil associational life, on the one hand, and the consolidation of social power in a relatively strong or resilient state organization, on the other. Putting it in simple terms, we might propose that a prima facie case could as well be made for thinking that, under certain conditions at least, strong and robust civil associations can "go together" with powerful and resilient states.

Or, to state the hypothesis more precisely, where the institutions of associa- tional life are relatively potent and well developed, state power may be rela- tively more difficult to organize in the first instance; but once consolidated, the state in question is more apt to endure and to evolve in ways that permit it to retain and expand its capacities to govern. Such states, at first glance, may all too easily be misclassified as "weak" because they appear much fettered by social compromise and vulnerable even to more aggressive challenges from interests and institutions in society. The United States, in the nineteenth and twentieth centuries, may serve as a familiar example of such a robust associa- tional life–resilient and expansive state combination.

When the institutions of associational life are relatively undeveloped, by contrast, pretenders to state power may more readily arise and may even prove able to consolidate their regimes if not quite effortlessly, at least with little opposition. But regimes thus made may also tend to be brittle. With their roots not buried very deep in the social soil of normative and historical construction and negotiation, such governing structures may grow up fast and stand very tall yet be prone to snap and blow away in the high winds of social upheaval. Such regimes may appear very "strong" however, and may even deserve to be classified as dictatorial, while they *do* manage to exert their power "over against" society. But the very scope of their declared dictatorial ambitions may yet mask many crippling incapacities.

It might prove useful to think of many of the Communist governments established in the postwar period as belonging to this type. In such a light, the dilemmas of governance in these states would not be conceived primarily in terms of the failures of socialist ideology, or the failures of the command economy, or even the dangers of excessive state control. The difficulties of these regimes would be posed instead as problems of engagement between state and society, problems in the intimate articulation of the relationship between state power and social organization. This chapter explores the applicability of an analytical approach such as this to an evaluation of the capacities and the frustrations of the Chinese state over the last forty years.

SOCIAL ORGANIZATION AND THE REVOLUTIONARY PARTY-STATE IN CHINA

The traditional institutions of Chinese associational life were subjected to extraordinary strains and erosions in the first half of this century. The customary forms of civil association in both rural and urban China were, in fact, distorted very nearly beyond recognition during those fifty years of rapid but uneven economic modernization and industrialization, of dynastic ineptitude and collapse, of imperialist military and financial meddling, of warlordism, missionaries and Christian converts, opium trafficking, banditry, famine, refugee migrations, occupation by the Japanese, and finally civil war. Old forms of social organization were subjected to the challenges of obsolescence and adaptation while fresh forms – and not always salutary ones – were improvised.[1] The extent of the collapse need not be overstated; the overall picture was not by any means one of full and uniform exhaustion of traditional social institutions. There were some surprisingly vigorous adaptations and revivals. The general condition, from the last serious Qing Dynasty attempt at self-renewal in 1898 until the ultimate victory of the Communists in 1949, should probably be conceived, rather, as one of tragic disarticulation; a failure of constructive engagement among the still viable customary forms of social organization, the newly evolving, avowedly more "modern" social institutions, and the other key elements of social power (such as the military) that were prominent in the several regimes of that era.

When the Chinese Communist Party (CCP) finally achieved national state power in 1949, then, it confronted a society made up of mostly frayed, discredited, and poorly integrated institutions. The most vigorous associations, in fact, tended to be those that the party itself had mobilized into being – peasant associations, mutual aid associations, women's associations, and labor unions, for example. These institutions were, of course, *very* well articulated with the rising state organization. They were plainly dominated by and quite readily bent to the purposes of party-state authority.

The new-minted party-state then took as its first and most important task nothing less than reinventing Chinese society. It imposed its own class categories on literally every citizen and social institution. Rich peasants, poor peasants, middle peasants, and landlords, petty capitalists, national capitalists, workers, intellectuals, religious practitioners, criminal elements – and so on. The personal history of every Chinese was investigated and a classification assigned; then reinvestigated and reclassified finally into one of the officially recognized categories.[2] This monumental social classification process was completed within a couple of years after 1949. In the immediate postwar atmosphere, when spies, saboteurs, and Guomindang agents were still expected to be found in any and every social unit, the classification process not only had the effect of reconfiguring social structure and social status; it also served to identify those citizens who could be supposed to be friends, and those who would be enemies, of the state.

Not only were individual and family classifications assigned, but the very boundaries of communities and other basic social units were redrawn during those very early years of CCP rule. In the countryside mutual aid teams and then cooperatives, collectives, and communes were fashioned out of the lineage organizations, temple associations, hamlets, villages, and market towns that had previously constituted the rural social space.[3] And in the cities, individuals were assigned permanently to certain workplaces and were given residence rights in specific blocks and neighborhoods officially designated as basic units of social life.

The old elites were simply swept away, and old social units were redefined. Agrarian reform, collectivization, and the nationalization of business and commerce deprived members of the former socioeconomic elites of their wealth, privileges, political influence, and social status. The social hierarchy of the ancien régime was, in fact, stood on its head. The previously poor and lowly were raised up and dignified as the noble bearers of revolutionary proletarian consciousness. The previously grand and powerful were reconceived as reactionary exploiters and class enemies. In certain respects, to be sure, only the names were changed as underlying social realities and relations persisted. Still, there can be no gainsaying that the social revolution in China brought with it a social transformation that was both wholesale and profound.

SOCIAL CELLULARIZATION

As postrevolutionary society was reconfigured in accord with Marxist class categories, it was also segmented into numerous small and uncommonly discrete cells or parcels. Collectivization of agricultural production, for example – which by shared land, shared labor, and shared harvests tied the welfare of each household very tightly to the fortunes and performance of only the other households in its collective – effectively divided the Chinese peasantry into very small, comprehensive, and discrete units of life and labor. Rural free commerce, through which individual families might supplement their incomes and thus alleviate their dependency on the collective, was tightly regulated and suppressed. Peasants rarely had opportunities for social intercourse of any kind with individuals outside their collective unit. Their opportunities for physical and social mobility were strictly circumscribed, especially after 1958 when, by means of the household registration system, they were effectively forbidden to travel without permission, whether in search of supplementary work, or for any other reason. The restrictions on mobility locked virtually the entire farming population into diminutive communities of work and welfare that were peculiarly cut off from easy social interchange with other communities. Old networks of trade and exchange, of religious worship, and even of marriage and family – networks that had traditionally functioned to bridge the isolation of small peasant communities – were very effectively weakened, even dissolved, by some thirty years of state policies promoting local self-reliance, economic self-sufficiency, and social cellularization.[4]

In urban areas, job assignments made for life, plus the socialist system's magnification of the role of the work unit (*danwei*) in the distribution of valued goods, services, and opportunities, likewise served to intensify the individual's dependency on and isolation in a small but comprehensive cell of social activity.[5] Even when living in the heart of a vast and seemingly modern metropolis, the range of contacts and experiences available to an ordinary Chinese worker was astonishingly limited by the extreme parcelization of social life.

To be sure, the highly centralized apparatus of state, arching over and doing its best to penetrate these social cells, was intended to coordinate and connect their activity – even to give voice and potency to the "demands" emanating from society. But social interests and issues, as processed through the apparatus of state, had to be conceived and articulated in the categories of the state's own ideology – categories of class struggle and revolutionary purity, anti-imperialism and antirevisionism. The party-state relied on its organs of mass mobilization – the peasant associations, labor unions, the women's federation, the youth league, and so on – to press these categories of social analysis and concern into the popular mind. Where indigenous institutions of social organization are not well elaborated, or where they have been artificially cramped in their development, state dominated organizations and techniques of mass mobilization can sometimes serve as substitutes for more genuine or spontaneous state–society engagement.

In a way, we might say, institutions of civil association in China were not so much made weak as miniaturized under Mao. A whole lifetime's social experience, for the vast majority of the Chinese people, was exceedingly confined or, more precisely, contained. For most people, social experience was almost entirely *local* experience. Thus, issues and interests emerging out of society itself tended necessarily to be conceived in terms that also were local and highly contained. The authentic, non-state-dominated institutions of civil association that were available were likewise highly confined; they did not *span* or *join* communities and units. Interests and needs originating in society could not very readily, therefore, be aggregated and articulated at supra-local levels of the polity. Genuine regionwide civil associations, engaging the state at intermediate levels of the political system, were virtually nonexistent.

The very form and functioning of the state's own apparatus, not oddly perhaps, came to resemble this fragmented distribution of force in society. It was a highly centralized bureaucracy, of course. So, much real power was lodged at the very top. And there it was that social issues were conceived and broadcast in the macrosocial categories of Marxist revolutionary struggle. Much real power was also lodged in the hands of the most local of local officials, however, who had responsibility for actual policy implementation and for reporting local conditions accurately to superiors. And it was among them, in their millions, that social issues and interests were conceived and interpreted in localized categories and personifications of value. The collective capacity of these small-unit and local officials to evade, neglect, embellish, or distort central directives – their capacity to dissemble and to cheat their superiors where local interests were at stake – did much to determine the central state's actual capacity to govern. *Between* these two spheres of real power – at the intermediate levels of the system – there was much administration but little authority. The macrosocial conceptual categories of Maoist Marxism were not adapted to the politics of sectionalism or regionalism. And genuine interests emanating from the cellularized society of the time were not adapted, nor were they aggregated, for regional expression and political action.

None of this is to imply, however, that Chinese society under Maoism was either passively manipulated or wholly remade by state policy and practice. The state's designs were met only in part by categorical social compliance. In part they were met by social adaptation and invention as well. Individual and group adaptations to social cellularization and to the absence of authoritative intermediate-level institutions of civil association took many forms, both cunning and tough. Just two of the more important adaptations can be noted here: patronage networking and localist protectionism.

PARTICULARISTIC ADAPTATIONS

The cultivation of personal influence networks (*guanxi wang*) – more or less typical patron–client systems energized by the exchange of favors – was one very crucial means by which people with individual or small group interests at issue could propel those issues, along with their own preferences as to the outcome, *into* the realms where decisions about them were made. Where no institutions of associational life exist to sift and give expression to specific needs and demands, networks of personal relations and reciprocal obligations can serve as substitute vehicles.[6]

The blatant favoritism of these elaborate patron–client networks, although it had always been a feature of Chinese social life, became much more pronounced after the revolution, insinuating itself into all aspects of economic, social, and political relations. Personal influence networks became the foundations and the perpetuators of political factions, as well, both in small communities and on the national scene. State policy was always publicly crafted in terms of class struggle, defending socialism, or raising revolutionary consciousness: But real politics in China too often boiled down to cabals and conspiracies, to factional duels and ploys. Thus patron–client networks and factions became critical arenas in and through which state and society interacted and accommodated each other's purposes.

Localist protectionism – sometimes called "departmentalism" – on the part of low-level officials and functionaries in small units, also emerged in Maoist China as a hardy adaptation to social cellularization and to the dearth of unit-spanning experiences, institutions, and loyalties. Subordinate-level officials found numerous ways to protect their own units of workers, peasants, or technicians against what they viewed as unwarranted or unfair restrictions and demands made by superior organs of the party-state. These, after all, were units of co-workers and co-residents in which those very officials could confidently (if mournfully) expect to spend the remainder of their careers, indeed their entire lives. Loyalties within these social cells, though subject to cleavage along clique and factional lines, tended to be fierce.

Frontline officials, despite their status as agents of the state, frequently found it advisable, or easier, or more natural, or just more in accord with their own convictions, to throw in their lot with local people and departmental associates, against the impersonal requirements of the state bureaucracy above them. They dragged their feet in implementing unpopular policies; sent up false figures and other misleading data; hoarded resources; cooked the books; bent the rules; and dissembled under questioning by special investigators sent in from above. They often found in these activities, of course, ample opportunities for personal corruption as well. But whether ultimately inspired by evil and avarice or only by empathy and affection, the activities of these localist officials constituted new arenas of power struggle; and the vibrancy of these arenas gradually reformatted state–society interactions, setting limits on political possibility that could not be acknowledged in party-state rhetoric.

Patron–client factionalism and localist deception, then, were main ingredients in the *real* politics of postrevolutionary China. They are ingredients present in almost all political systems, to one extent or another. But they became ever more prominent in China during the two or three decades following 1949, precisely *as responses to* state policies of social cellularization. Still, patronage and localist particularism, however practical in the circumstances, could be accorded no ethical standing in the normative order of Maoism. Although absolutely functional, these social adaptations had to be treated (publicly and officially) as tainted. However widely practiced, they had to be concealed. The really operative dynamics of Chinese social organization and politics may have been largely localistic and factional; but the official dynamics were still those of class struggle or class capitulation, of ideological purity or ideological decay. The disjuncture between the state's social philosophy and the people's lived social reality widened. But this gap could not be acknowledged.

Two important political consequences of this gap are worth noting specifically. First, in day-to-day affairs, the actual capacity of the party-state to govern on the ground was much eroded over time by the workings of patronage systems and of localist administrators. The capacity of the state to gather accurate information for policy planning, to mobilize support for its policies, and to implement its policies as they were intended to be implemented *declined* during the late Mao era, however dictatorial might have been regime appearances to the contrary.[7] In one sense it is possible to say, therefore, that gradual adaptations by society to state policies very vigorously pursued and implemented in the early postrevolutionary period were in due course to undermine that same state's vigor and capacity for regularized administration and policy implementation.

Second, in more extraordinary affairs of heightened political significance – mass mobilization campaigns, for example, or the Great Proletarian Cultural Revolution itself – the gap that could not be acknowledged tended to make the engagement of state philosophy with genuine social reality more and more attenuated, even illusory. Repeated mass mobilization drives had been carried out over the years, targeting people in accord with their classifications and personal dossiers into official social categories of less and less real salience to their own lived experience. State–society engagement by these means had thus tended to become a ritualized matter. And in the Cultural Revolution what we finally witnessed was the nearly complete disjuncture of state rhetoric and social action.

Call after call for class-based, unified, and militant proletarian action went forth from the center all through the Cultural Revolution. Yet the actual struggles that ensued were fought school by school, factory by factory, and faction by faction. The real arenas of political battle were revealed then in all their cellular and personalistic miniaturization, while the state center incongruously continued to demand a struggle waged in terms both epic and universal.

By the time of Mao Zedong's death in 1976, it was already apparent that party-state and society in China were failing to engage each other in ways that produced empowering outcomes. Where state and society did most effectively intersect, it was precisely in those arenas structured by localistic or factional interests; arenas that were morally or ideologically tainted and could not be regarded as holding a valid place in the state's own normative constructs. The real power of the party-state apparatus to mobilize society was by then seriously eroded. And the real power dispersed throughout society was deeply parcelized and nearly exhausted in phony political struggles.

REFORM-FROM-ABOVE

Clearly, a reform project of major proportions would be required to realign and reengage state power and social organization in China. And the reform project that did in fact emerge, under the nervous tutelage of the Deng Xiaoping leadership coalition, aimed precisely at such a reorganization of society *and* reinvigoration of the state. There was never any secret or any mystery about a reinvigorated state authority being a key goal of Dengist reform. On the contrary, this central premise of the reform effort has been trotted out again and again over recent years, to calm the nerves of jumpy powerholders and to justify and explain the need for transitions that many in China found unpleasant or painful. Decentralization of power to lower levels of state bureaucracy, for example, or more of a role for the market, even the relaxation of many oppressive social restrictions – these were the means, but not the ends of the reform initiative Deng captained. The object of the Chinese party-state's post-Mao reform-from-above was never to replace socialism with capitalism or single-party dictatorship with liberal democracy. The object was to clean, repair, and restore the corroded connections linking the dispersed power in society with the concentrated power in the state.

The reform program began to take effect in earnest only in 1979. And it has proceeded since then unevenly, in fits and starts. The extent to which fundamental reforms have actually been implemented varies considerably from place to place and from segment to segment of the Chinese economy and polity. Over a decade and a half of such ad hoc and improvised systemic reform, nonetheless, has produced some very marked modifications of the arenas in which state agents and social forces commonly meet to contend for authority or to achieve accommodation. No comprehensive or even summary overview of the reform project can be attempted here. But certain aspects of the systemic changes under way, those which have had especially important implications for the nature and the loci of state–society interaction, can be highlighted in brief.

Decentralization of bureaucratic controls

Several of the more critical reforms of the bureaucratic-administrative system undertaken since 1979 have had the effect of pushing both decision-making discretion and financial responsibility downward, away from central ministries and offices in Beijing and out to intermediate and lower levels of the state hierarchy. A gradual trend toward bureaucratic reconstruction – in the aftermath of the wholesale purges of the Cultural Revolution – and toward simultaneous decentralization of authority within the system, had actually already been under way all through the decade of the 1970s. But the state finance, planning, credit, and investment reforms of the 1980s accelerated the decentralizing trend so precipitously that by the end of the decade, the question most observers were asking was no longer *when* or *if* central authorities might order restraint, but *whether* they still had it in their power at all to regain control of their badly overheated, underregulated, and superinflated national economy.[8]

By far the greatest beneficiaries of this massive move toward bureaucratic decentralization have been party-state authorities placed at the middle and lower-middle reaches of the system. Cadres working in town and county governments, and those in small, medium, and large city offices, have gained even more in discretionary authority and independent freedom to maneuver than have bureaucrats higher up in district and provincial departments. Whereas before the reforms county, city, and regional officials did administrative work primarily of the "transmission belt" variety, they have recently been acquiring new roles as key gate-keepers and rulemakers, and as underwriters and power brokers in command of considerable resources.

Expanded market relations

Meanwhile, the very widespread introduction of more marketlike systems and relations throughout the economy has had a very jarring effect on the cellularized socioeconomic substructures of everyday life. Expanded markets in commodities, labor, services, money, and knowledge have presented people in almost all walks of life with new opportunities to provide for their own welfare by working or investing in ventures *outside* the scope of their home units. Nationwide decollectivization of agricultural production, and official determination to release surplus labor, so long tied to the land, for free participation in what would become much bigger and better integrated commercial and service sectors of the economy – these were necessary preconditions for the very substantial reallocations of peasant labor and rural investment that have characterized the Chinese pattern of economic growth and development over the past few years. The greatly enhanced freedoms to travel, to mix employments and to change jobs, to participate in far-flung networks of exchange on the basis of individually negotiated contracts and agreements, to start up businesses and invest in independent or collective enterprises – these new freedoms have truly revolutionized peasant opportunities and have done much to break down the cell walls of community and collective that previously so tightly contained them.

Market reforms in state-sector enterprises and many other urban occupations have proceeded less far. But in the cities, too, trends away from social cellularization have been strong. Many urban dwellers work two jobs now; some taking valuable skills acquired in state-sector industries out to suburban enterprises with them on the weekends, where they not only earn extra income for themselves but shop in local markets, listen to different strands of gossip, and absorb information about local politics, all while keeping an eye out for additional jobs, connections, and opportunities for their family members or friends. The reverse employment flow – that of peasants *into* urban areas – has become a major flood in recent years. And the so-called floating population, people who move from place to place in search of opportunity, is now estimated in the tens and tens of millions. All this recent physical and job mobility has greatly expanded, if it has not always enriched, the social experience of ordinary Chinese citizens.

Thanks to all the splendid opportunities – and to all the terrible risks – that come with marketization of social relations, a great many people in China today are less dependent on the very contained local communities that characterized Chinese social life in the recent past. And, it must be added, with all the unsettling changes in welfare, employment, and investment systems and priorities, those local communities and little units are often much *less to be depended on.* Individuals are now able and indeed must begin to conceive of themselves as members of social groupings with common interests (and quite possibly demands) that span the old cellular social divisions, extending past locality to metropolis or region, and beyond.

New intermediate-level arenas of state–society interaction

The possibility that a convergence of forces will take place in the middle and lower-middle reaches of the Chinese political system is, thus, apparent. Just as more extensive state power has come to be lodged in these midregions of the polity, new social groups and forces have been generated with the potential, at least, to aggregate and express their needs, demands, and preferences at those very political midlevels. Whereas in the prereform past state–society struggles and accommodations most powerfully occurred at the very bottom of the system – in tiny units and localities or in private patronage and other highly particularistic settings – now the *possibility* at least exists for salient state–society struggles and accommodations to occur in new arenas of engagement at more elevated levels of the polity. Whereas in the prereform past there were few social elites not defined by and incorporated within the state power system as such, now the *possibility* at least exists for influential social forces to take shape more independently, outside the state apparatus.[9] But if such a trend toward convergence of state power and social organization at the intermediate levels of the polity is now actually under way in China, it still remains to be seen whether (and how precisely) this trend proves empowering for newly organized social interests. Might it rather prove empowering for the party-state itself in the effort to channelize and control newly rising social forces? Or finally, might such a convergence perhaps prove empowering for *both* sides as they go about learning to deal with each other within these newly demarcated arenas of state–society engagement?

ASSOCIATIONAL LIFE AND STATE-SOCIALIST CORPORATISM

One pattern of ongoing change deserving to be closely watched at present is the widespread emergence of civil associations of much greater variety, and on a much more elaborate scale, than we have seen in China since 1949.[10] These cover a broad range: from essentially apolitical common interest associations, such as sports clubs and specialized technical associations;[11] through professional associations, such as those for lawyers[12] and journalists; to mass constituency associations with an implied social or economic agenda, such as religious associations,[13] senior citizens' associations,[14] and consumers' groups;[15] to very broad-based economic interest groups, such as municipal chambers of commerce,[16] or more specialized interest groups, such as trade associations[17] or associations of the self-employed;[18] and even to politically uncertain and open-ended entities, such as discussion groups and "salons" of young educated technical and professional people who gather together regularly because they have an interest in questions of social philosophy, political economy, and culture.[19]

Some of these organizations are national in scope; others are regional or very local. The greatest density of activity appears, as we would expect, to be in large urban centers.[20] But it is clear that smaller cities and towns, and even many grassroots rural communities, are involved as well. Furthermore, it is evident that at least some of these organizations, set up in the first instance without any direct political-economic functions to perform, can and do readily become enmeshed in matters of policy and governance. In Shaanxi Province in 1986, for example, faced with persistent rumors about a predicted decline in demand for fruit exports, an independent farmers' association, originally organized to provide technical information and assistance to fruit growers in just one county, took it upon itself to intervene with local and regional foreign-trade officials insisting that purchase contracts be negotiated with growers immediately, to avoid unnecessary crop loss.[21] The contracts were offered promptly and production went up, instead of down, that year. The magazine report on this incident stressed just how beneficial such specialized organizations could be in "serving as a bridge between farmers and the state."

Most reports from China do not distinguish among the varieties of such social organizations, treating it as obvious nonetheless that they all can and should serve as valuable "bridging" agents between state and society. As one *People's Daily* headline pointedly repeated in January 1990, "Social Groups Are Actively to Develop Their Role in Safeguarding Stability."[22] The story under this headline makes it clear that the proper task of social groups in the Chinese polity is "to support social peace and unity consciously, to handle properly the relationship between the particular interests the social group represents and the fundamental interests of the Chinese people at large, and to put particularistic interests at the service of the general interest." Social groups are also charged with "actively reflecting the masses' wishes, opinions, and needs to the party and government while propagandizing and implementing party lines and policies, and making the relations between party and people even closer." They are also expected "to solve social problems, alleviate social contradictions, effectively promote the stable development of society, and to create the best possible social climate for economic construction."

This, the official line, is a patently state-corporatist vision of the proper nature of associational life in China, stressing as it does intimate and continuous consultation, along with the values of social harmony and overall party-state leadership and control. One very pressing topic for research on contemporary political and social change in China, therefore, is to investigate the degree to which this official and idealized state-corporatist vision now adequately characterizes the *actual* operations of the host of new groups we now note emerging at the shifting frontiers of state and society. To what extent might these new social organizations be regarded as independent actors expressing interests and attitudes formed outside the realm of the state? To what extent, on the other hand, are they constrained to act as buffers defusing potentially unwieldy social conflict? To what extent is it accurate to regard these new organizations as mere handmaidens of the party-state's authority and facilitators for its corporatist purposes?[23]

CASES AND VARIATION: A CONTINUUM?

During the second half of 1990, I interviewed a number of association representatives to collect additional information on the organization and operations of some dozen different civil associations in two largely rural Chinese localities – Xinji (an average-income small town that has grown up around a railroad junction on the North China plain in Hebei), and Anxi (a heavily populated tea-producing county in the Fujian mountains, officially classified as "poverty-stricken"). To my knowledge, this effort was the first by a Western field researcher at a systematic gathering of data on *rural* grassroots civil associations,[24] and although the sample is admittedly tiny and far from scientifically selected, the material collected is diverse enough to suggest a good deal of variation among China's present-day local-level civil associations on the question of greatest concern to this discussion: associational autonomy versus state-corporatist interpenetration.

Most of the associations studied were neither entirely self-organized nor entirely independent of state leadership and guidance in their activities. Structurally as well as philosophically, there is a state-corporatist cast to both the organization and the raison d'être of all the associations surveyed. Yet the dissimilarities among them are also striking enough to suggest a possible continuum of associational structures and experiences stretching from those relatively incorporated and state-dominated at one extreme, to those relatively self-constituted, self-governing and autonomous organizations, at the other.

The Xinji Association of the Self-Employed (*Geti laodong zhe xiehui*) can serve as an example at the state-dominated end of the spectrum. This is the local branch of a nationwide organization of peddlers and small traders, the first of whose two basic tasks is described as "providing education for the socialist motherland, for science and for service to the people."[25] Because development of the civil and criminal legal systems and of the requisite local judicial apparatus has obviously not been keeping pace with expansion of more freewheeling marketized economic relations all across China lately, it is no surprise that public fear of being cheated by "private" traders has reached new peaks in recent times. This is a much discussed and highly sensitive issue around the country, and there can be little doubt that the national Association of the Self-Employed and all its branches exist primarily as means by which the party-state may instruct peddlers and traders about proper and permissible business practice, and regulate their conduct in the market. The very formation of the association in the mid-1980s must, in fact, be understood as a regulatory response by the state to the perceived dangers and disorderliness of a freer market. The second basic task of the association is "representing and protecting the legal rights of members,"[26] presumably when they are suspected or accused of illegal activity.

The association operates under the watchful eye of the Commerce Control Bureau of the town government. (In fact, the association shares office quarters with the government bureau and, in response to an invitation to the association for a representative to come for an interview, a Commerce Control Bureau official arrived at the briefing room instead, in uniform, with the explanation that he was fully informed and could answer any and all questions there might be about the association.) The Commerce Control Bureau of the town government is responsible for licensing all private traders who conduct business in Xinji. According to the bureau spokesman, although membership in the association was not "compulsory" for licensees, there had been *no* instances of licensed self-employed workers *not* joining. The individual membership fee was forty cents (*fen*) per month. At monthly branch meetings members reportedly "studied party documents relevant to their activity in the market, and discussed matters of common interest."[27]

The Xinji Association of the Self-Employed, in its propaganda–education and regulatory functions, so resembles the paradigmatic "mass organizations" of the Maoist past that one may wonder whether it belongs at all on the spectrum of "new" civil associations. Perhaps it does not; but it is included here since it seems worth noting that association members do elect their own governing committee (members of which need not all be party members or government officials), and worth noting also that not all association activities are obviously politicized. The Xinji association, for example, came to the aid of some of its members running a knitting shop that had operated in the red for two years in a row. Through the association's (not the Commerce Control Bureau's) own contacts (with the Second Light Industry Bureau, another government body), workers and technicians were invited in to demonstrate a different and better knitting technique to the floundering entrepreneurs – apparently with some encouraging results.

In the same locality, but at the other end of the state-corporatist continuum, we might consider the Chive Farmers' Association headquartered in Xinji's Junqi village.[28] This association began from the bottom up, and although it works on and off in tandem with government entities, it also seems to try to keep an arm's length distance from officialdom. During the late Mao era, Junqi village farmers were obliged by the dictates of the state plan to plant almost all of their land to grain and cotton. But with the advent of the household responsibility system,[29] many again found themselves free to return to cultivating chives, a traditional local specialty vegetable crop for which the soil around Junqi is especially suitable. Chive farming got off to a profitable revival in the early eighties, and by 1984 farmers in the village who were specializing in this particular cash crop started meeting together with village committee members and agricultural technicians, on an informal basis, to pool their experiences and to study relevant technical pamphlets and other information. (A number of the new civil associations have interesting links to the agricultural technical or scientific technical communities and bureaucracies in China, as noted in succeeding paragraphs.)

By 1984 the Junqi chive farmers and agricultural technicians decided to form their own organization, and they went to the Agricultural Technical Center (of the Xinji party committee) for guidance on how to go about constituting themselves as a formal association (*xiehui*). They began with a mixed membership of fifty-one farmers, agricultural technicians, and village committee members. Among their earliest activities as an association were some launched entirely independently and others for which they accepted a helping hand from the local party-state. On its own responsibility, for example, the association sent some representatives outside Xinji (to a few northeastern provinces as well as to the Xi'an area, where popular consumption of chives is high) to bring back samples of chive varieties grown there. Shortly thereafter, however, they approached the Xinji Agricultural Technical Center again, this time with a plea for special assistance, because their crops had come under a serious pest attack. The association members also accepted financial help from the village government when they first began trucking their crops to northeastern cities in an attempt to break into the market there. (This has since become a highly lucrative business but, at the very beginning, the Junqi chive farmers lacked access to insurance on their vegetables in transit and could not afford the risks of long-distance marketing without some subsidy from the village.)

The association established and maintained its own independent "lateral" relations with chive farmers' associations in other localities where there was reason to believe production techniques were relatively advanced. They exchanged materials of various sorts and even attempted some swaps of seed varieties – which unfortunately have not proven hardy under local growing conditions. The association's main task is conceived as finding solutions for problems of all kinds that its members may face in production. And this mission can extend to applying a little pressure on local officials and semiofficial institutions when necessary. For example, the association intervened with the local credit co-op to help negotiate a loan deal for members who wanted to purchase additional plastic coverings for fields planted with early-sprouting chives. And the association has also used its outside contacts at times, in what amounts to doing an end run around the local state-supply system, to get hold of extra fertilizer for its members when local supplies have been short.

The Chive Farmers' Association, thus, is a self-constituted and mostly independent organization that represents and promotes the interests of a certain (relatively affluent) subsection of the Xinji farming population. It works with the local government at times, and accepts small amounts of financial aid and other support from state institutions on an ad hoc basis. But none of its functions are politicized, and many of its activities involve voluntary linkage with similar associations of cash crop farmers and agricultural technicians operating outside Xinji, and thus outside the jurisdiction of the Xinji government.

On the state-corporatist continuum, lying somewhere between the two Xinji extremes just described, is the Anxi Chamber of Commerce. This new association, which represents the interests of Anxi County business and industry, was formed in mid-1987 at the state's initiative. It has some 540 members who represent the leading manufacturing, commercial, and financial institutions of the county. The special characteristic of the Chamber of Commerce format, and this is an important departure from the vertical segmentation of industry in the pre-reform period, is that its member enterprises cut right across all the various ownership systems now prevailing in China to embrace state-run, collective, *and* private businesses within a single organization.[30] The chamber has several professed purposes. First, it seeks to find markets, attract investment, and generally expand business opportunities for local enterprises *outside* the province and *outside* the country. (Specifically, it works to interest overseas Chinese businesspeople in the possibilities for investment in and trade with Anxi enterprises.) Second, the chamber seeks out relevant domestic and international market and business information, which is provided to its members. (Some of this is done through standard printed source materials, but much is also accomplished through informal contacts with overseas Chinese.) Third, the chamber is "the voice and advocate" for member enterprises, interceding with government offices and departments on their behalf to secure raw materials in short supply, to help find markets for their products, and so on. Fourth, the chamber speaks for member enterprises and may act for them in disputes over contractual obligations that may arise with foreign or other corporations. Likewise, it may act for member banks and credit organizations to put pressure on loan defaulters or to help work out revised repayment schedules. And fifth, the chamber is authorized to run its own enterprises, both for profit and for the "convenience" of members. As of 1990 it was already running its own credit organization, deputized by the Quanzhou municipal government to issue loans to businesses in Anxi.

Representatives of the Chamber of Commerce would not discuss the level of capitalization of their credit office, nor were they willing to be very specific about their annual budget. But they did explain that their organization's expenses, including salaries, travel and entertainment allowances, the purchase of cars and trucks, newspaper and magazine subscriptions, and so on, were all paid for by the county government. No dues were yet being collected from members. The chamber is publicly funded, therefore, but while it clearly works hand in glove with local officials, it does not take direct orders from any unit of the county government, and it may at times approach local state officials with requests and demands of its own – requests and demands that can be said to articulate the long-term or short-term interests of Anxi businesspeople.

More different points along the continuum could be identified. The National Internal Combustion Engine Cylinder Cover Trade Association, whose president happens to work as an engineer in the Xinji Cylinder Head Factory,[31] seems in some ways to resemble the Association of the Self-Employed. It, and other nationwide trade associations like it, are certainly intended to be harmonizing responses to the potential conflict and "chaos of the market." This type of association is designed to coordinate planning and moderate competition among enterprises in the same trade that are now exhorted to treat profit, not the plan, as their bottom line.[32] But the Cylinder Cover Association showed signs of having been more genuinely "self-constituted" than the Association of the Self-Employed. And, like the Chive Farmers' Association, it had some interesting links to institutions in the national science and technology complex.[33]

The Anxi County Tea Study Association, on the other hand, seems very close to the Chive Farmers' Association in its main goals of raising production technique and solving local production problems encountered in the cultivation of a local cash crop.[34] But the tea study group was set up on the initiative of one of the offices of the county government, rather than on the initiative of planters and field agronomists themselves. It interacted more with offices of the county government as well, in something resembling a professional consulting relationship. And although the Tea Study Association had some of the same types of links into the national agricultural technical institutional hierarchy as the Chive

Farmers' group,[35] it lacked the voluntary lateral contacts with similar small associations that the Chive Farmers' Association had gone to some lengths to develop.

This small set of examples by no means exhausts the range of associational patterns now observable; not even the range noted in just these two particular localities.[36] The set should be sufficient, nevertheless, to suggest some very considerable variation where the constitution, activity, and autonomy of the new civil associations in the Chinese countryside are now concerned.

"CIVIL SOCIETY" AND "POSTSOCIALISM"

The bureaucratic and market reforms of the post-Mao era have touched off many complex and intertwined social processes. A renegotiation of both state–state and state–society relations is now well under way in China but is likely to be protracted. The very arenas in which state and society have been accustomed to interact are being redrawn. And most of the rules of competition and accommodation are being rewritten. The ongoing decentralization of state power and the simultaneous deminiaturization of social organization have created some of the conditions required for *both* the empowerment of newly rising social forces *and* the enhancement of the state's capacity to govern. Whether both state and society will ultimately emerge in some sense strengthened by the wrenching processes of renegotiation now so precariously under way cannot, however, be predicted. The material this chapter has presented on civil associations, gathered in the Chinese countryside during late 1990, is obviously too sparse to do more than point us in the direction of a few modest and tentative hypotheses. But even that can be of some value if it keeps us from the temptation to jump to conclusions.

We may consider, for example, the concept of "civil society," deployed very fruitfully in some of the other chapters in this volume to analyze apparently fairly similar processes of social change,[37] but not made use of here to characterize current trends in China. Some specialists, it should be pointed out, have already concluded that an emergent "civil society" may in fact be just what we are witnessing now taking shape in China following more than a decade of reform.[38] Yet some rather crucial conceptual problems are involved here, on which the material summarized above may shed some light. The idea of civil society has a long and none too pure pedigree in the social science literature.[39] It has been and continues to be defined in many ways, some arguably fairly consistent with current Chinese realities, but others very much less so. Even the most permissive and adaptable of these many definitions,[40] however, tend to emphasize that organizations of civil society must be self-constituted and for the purpose of expressing and pursuing their own interests, in a relationship of relative autonomy from the state and its interests. And definitional conditions such as these, when held up against the interview and other data gathered on real rural associations in contemporary China, make it seem premature at best to assume that what the ongoing reform of the Chinese socialist order is generating are the undoubted conditions for the flowering of civil society.

What the data will support is more limited. We can be certain that the scope and intensity of associational life have recently greatly expanded in China. And we may surmise that this tendency has been especially marked in localities that are economically relatively better developed. We can note also that many of these new and vibrant civil associations are constituted at supra-local levels of the polity and do have direct interactions with government offices at the midlevels of the political system as well as with semiofficial bodies, such as scientific and research institutions, that are in turn directly linked into even higher-level state offices. The exaggerated cellularity characteristic of past patterns of social organization does appear to be waning, in part as a result of the activity of all these new, more broadly conceived and constituted associations. The arenas in which state and society confront each other are being significantly redrawn, in part by the entry of all these associations onto the political scene.

But most of these associations are by no means entirely self-constituted, nor do most of them apparently seek or enjoy much relative autonomy from the state. Some are more autonomous, and others are less so. All, however, are enveloped in a rhetoric of corporatist interpenetration and encapsulated in a self-conception that stresses corporatist consultation, cooperation, and harmony in action with the party-state and its aims. There can be little doubt that in the very act of overcoming the enforced cellularization of the past, these associations are playing a role in strengthening and empowering the social groups they represent (or speak for) in the Chinese system. But it seems just as clear that the party-state itself, in its information gathering, policy planning, and even in its policy implementation modes, may also be strengthened (i.e., empowered) by these new arrangements. There is little doubt, further, that the reinvigoration or reempowerment of the state and its authority are the chief goals to be served by these arrangements, in the view of state officials and bureaucratic reformers. If these goals were not being served, then tolerance for some of the activities of the new associations could well be foreshortened. The party-state, which is still in hot pursuit of a reinvigorated, modernized, rationalized, and more credible image and administrative structure for itself, may in fact be the main beneficiary of the activities of a good many of these new associations. A species of state strengthening could well be, after all, a plausible outcome of the processes of reform-from-above that have been responsible for bringing the associations into being.

Still, at various points on the continuum just sketched, it may also be possible to glimpse some "sprouts" of civil society, as it were – some organizations that are relatively self-constituted and relatively autonomous of state penetration and regulation in their activities. Although they are not now very weighty in the overall system, perhaps they are the nucleus of a future trend. They bear watching. And the party-state's fluctuating degree of tolerance for them bears watching as well. From the vantage point of the early 1990s, however, we should perhaps remind ourselves again that there is little inevitability and much contingency to consider in the further development of associations such as these. The evolution of a vibrant civil society may not be anymore the "necessary" result of "postsocialism" in China than was social cellularization the "necessary" result of the socialists' coming to power there.

In Chapter 2 of this volume, Frances Hagopian makes the point that no matter how ambitious and determined they may be, how seemingly in control, how apparently unopposed, authoritarian-transformative regimes mostly *do not* manage, even after several decades in power, to remake entirely the stuff of politics in their societies. The transformative capacities of even highly authoritarian regimes are, simply, limited; and when we look at them probingly, we may be surprised by how limited also are the real, on-the-ground capacities of the state machines created (some used to say "perfected") by such regimes. What I have suggested briefly in this chapter, concerning *both* the fallibilities of Chinese party-state control in the sixties and seventies *and* the cunning responses and adaptations of Chinese society to the awesome transformative initiatives of Maoist political economy and ideology, all certainly resonates well with Hagopian's important insight. Her point may work as well for left-wing as for right-wing authoritarian regimes.

In seeking to understand the forces that may lead to the demise of authoritarianism and to understand also the real postauthoritarian range of political possibility, we must look again at individual country histories and at the fundamentals of the sociopolitical systems those would-be transformative regimes were trying to displace. But as we apply this important caution about comparison to the small host of left-wing authoritarian (state socialist) states now embarked on simultaneous (but not always so similar) projects of systemic reform, it seems worth remembering also that thirty or forty or fifty years of searing historical experience are not nothing, either.

The presocialist states and societies of the peoples of, say, Hungary, Romania, and China were certainly deeply disparate. But so also were the experiences of these peoples under socialism. In none of the Eastern European countries did socialism come to power on the back of a peasant revolution. And in no other socialist state was there a historic episode quite like the Great Proletarian Cultural Revolution in China. The particularities of the state socialist project from place to place must also be made to enter our comparisons. Several decades of state socialism have surely not entirely remade the state or the society where it was imposed. But several decades of differing experiences of state socialism have just as surely made some important alterations in the political landscape from place to place. And, at the very least, the patterns of exit from socialist authoritarianism should, therefore, be expected to be different also.

In China as in Europe it seems, men and women do have the power to remake state socialism, but not exactly as they wish. The possibilities for future reform cannot help but be structured by very particular past histories of accomplishment and compromise. And these distinctive histories – national, regional, ethnic, and so on – although they may share some important similarities, differ enormously from socialist state to state and society to society. Whatever we may be thinking, then, about the prospects for "civil society" in Europe, we should be sure to think again about China. As there was no single state socialism, there will be no single "postsocialism."

Exactly how specific state structures crystallized and their capacities evolved, exactly how the repertoire of organizational forms available within societies shifted over time, and exactly how the scope and nature of contemporary state–society interactions emerged – all these particularities condition future political possibilities, both structural and ideational. If we are interested in probing, comparatively, the underlying processes animating and directing the rapid changes we are now witnessing in so many postsocialist systems, then analyses framed in the vocabularies deployed in this essay (and in the other essays in this volume) should prove most applicable. An analytical approach featuring questions about state structure and capacity, and about social organization and civil society, as well as questions about shifting arenas of state–society struggle and accommodation – such an approach holds considerable promise of improving our understanding of the forces at work in state socialist systems now undergoing rapid transformations. Such an approach should take us a good deal farther down the road to adequate explanation than we have so far traveled, anyway, with the aid of analyses featuring premature announcements about the death of statism and the worldwide victory of democratic capitalism.

NOTES

1 Elizabeth Perry in Chapter 6 of this volume, on gangsters and unionism in Shanghai, provides a host of good urban commercial and industrial examples. Rural improvisations from tradition, somewhat akin to metropolitan gangsterism, included secret societies, sworn brotherhoods, (female) marriage resistance sects, and bandit gangs and associations.

2 For a classic account of this classification process as it was carried out in one north China village, see William Hinton, *Fanshen* (New York: Vintage Books, 1966). Also, Vivienne Shue, *Peasant China in Transition* (Berkeley: University of California Press, 1980), esp. chs. 1 and 2.

3 For more detail on these institutional changes and creations, see Shue, *Peasant China in Transition,* chs. 4–7.

4 These policies and their effects are discussed at greater length in Vivienne Shue, *The Reach of the State* (Stanford: Stanford University Press, 1988).

5 See, for example, Andrew G. Walder, *Communist Neo-Traditionalism: Work and Authority in Chinese Industry* (Berkeley: University of California Press, 1986).

6 For an account of recent Chinese social life and politics that emphasizes patron–client networks and strategies, see Jean C. Oi, *State and Peasant in Contemporary China: The Political Economy of Village Government* (Berkeley: University of California Press, 1989).

7 The pattern of decline in state capacity between 1949 and 1979 is explored, along several different dimensions, in my "Powers of State, Paradoxes of Dominion: China 1949–1979," in K. Lieberthal, J. Kallgren, R. MacFarquhar, and F. Wakeman, eds., *Perspectives on Modern China: Four Anniversaries* (Armonk, N.Y.: M. E. Sharpe, 1991), pp. 205–225.

8 See, for just one example, the front-page story by Nicholas D. Kristof, "Beijing Authority Being Challenged by Local Powers," *New York Times,* 11 December 1988.

9 The reforms have thus created a host of new possibilities for struggle and accommodation between elements of state and elements of society. If state power and social forces do tend to converge at the midlevels of the system, the convergence process might, as entertained further along in this chapter, produce gains in *both* state capacity *and* social influence. But on such a scenario, elements of state and elements of society would not necessarily "gain" evenly. Both central state officials and the little local strongmen of the old parcelized system would suffer losses of discretionary power, in fact. Thus some party–state bureaucrats would experience reform as a net loss of state authority while others, inhabiting the midregions of the system, would experience it as opening new realms for their own action and influence. Likewise, participants in informal patronage networks and old-style local-protectionist community leaders would find the amplitude of their influence in society challenged by the emergence of broader-gauged groupings, groupings intent on pressing their interests vis à vis the state through alternative political channels. Some social groups, inevitably, would be better placed than others to exert such leverage. And those less favored, far from experiencing the reform environment as empowering, would be prone to regard it as dangerous and disenfranchising. In fact, from the early 1980s on, there was evidence that each of these cross-trends may be at work inside China's changing polity.

10 The emergence of these associations, and the underlying linkage of this expanding realm of associational life with changing patterns of socioeconomic stratification and of social interests in post-Mao China, are trends already noted by a number of Chinese scholars and academics. Preliminary analyses of these trends by Chinese social scientists, published in learned journals, are frequently insightful and quite broad-ranging. See, for example, Zhang Wanli, "Exploratory Analysis of China's Social Interest Groups" (*"Woguo shehui liyi . . ."*), *Society (Shehui)* (November 1988): 1–3ff; Wang Guangming and Liu Wenkai, "The Current Condition and Reform of Enterprise Labor Unions" (*"Qiye gonghui de . . ."*), *Society (Shehui)* (August 1988): 16–18; Zhu Qinglao, "On Changes in China's Social Class Structure and Stratification" (*"Woguo shehui jieji, . . ."*), *Research on Industry and Transportation (Gongyun Yanjiu)* (April 1988): 42–45, reprinted in *Zhongguo Renmin Daxue Fuyin Baokan Ziliao* (April 1988): 97–100; Wang Jie, "Social Structural Changes in the Midst of Reform and My View on Countermeasures" (*"Gaigezhong de jieji jiegou . . ."*), *Sociological Studies (Shehuixue Yanjiu)* (March 1987): 1–13; He Jianzhang, "Actively Unfolding Studies of Classes and Strata in Socialist Society" (*"Jiji kaizhan shehuizhuyi shehui . . ."*), *Sociological Studies (Shehuixue Yanjiu)* (May 1987): 1–9; Yu Zhen and Tan Mingfang, "The Theory of Social Interest Groups and the Development of the Marxist Perspective on Social Class Structure" (*"Shehui liyi qunti . . ."*), *Shanghai Social Science Academy Quarterly (Shanghai*

Shehui Kexue Xueshu Jikan) (April 1988): 112–123, reprinted in *Zhongguo Renmin Daxue Fuyin Baokan Ziliao* (January 1989): 29–39; and Yu Xianyang, "The Present Social Structure of China and Prevailing Problems" (*"Woguo shehui zuzhi . . ."*), *Journal of Chinese People's University* (*Zhongguo Renmin Daxue Xuebao*) (June 1988): 101–104, reprinted in *Zhongguo Renmin Daxue Fuyin Baokan Ziliao* (January 1989): 41–44.

11 See, for example, "Rural Specialized Technical Associations Get off to Good Start on Mainland" (*"Dalu nongcun zhuanye . . ."*), *Liaowang Weekly* (Overseas Ed.), 25 January 1988, pp. 15–16.

12 "The Evolution of the Organization of Chinese Lawyers" (*"Zhongguo lushi . . ."*), *Liaowang Weekly* (Overseas Ed.), 10 October 1988, p. 12.

13 See *China Yearbook, 1988* (*Zhongguo Nianjian, 1988*) (Beijing: Xinhua Publishing Co., 1988), p. 641, for a breakdown of types and numbers of religious organizations.

14 "The Current Situation with Regard to Elderly Affairs in China" (*"Zhongguo laonian . . ."*), *Liaowang Weekly* (Overseas Ed.), 17 October 1988, pp. 11–12.

15 "Mainland Consumers' Associations Exceed Seven Hundred" (*"Dalu xiaofeizhe . . ."*), *Liaowang Weekly* (Overseas Ed.), 15 February 1988, p. 40.

16 "Xiamen Chamber of Commerce – Good Friend to Taiwan Investors" (*"Xiamen shanghui . . ."*), *Liaowang Weekly* (Overseas Ed.), 21 November 1988, p. 19.

17 For example, "Conscientiously Support and Protect the Interests of Unions" (*"Qieshi weihu . . ."*), *Liaowang Weekly* (Overseas Ed.), 10 August 1987, pp. 3–4. Also, "New Changes in the All China Federation of Industry and Commerce" (*"Quanguo gongshanglian . . ."*), *Liaowang Weekly* (Overseas Ed.), 19 December 1988, p. 15. And also, "Promoting Trade Associations: Urban Reform in Nanjing" (*"Hangye xiehui . . ."*), *Liaowang Weekly* (Overseas Ed.), 7 December 1987, pp. 15–16.

18 "Xiamen Establishes Association of Privately Run Industrial and Commercial Enterprises" (*"Xiamen chengli . . ."*), *Liaowang Weekly* (Overseas Ed.), 31 October 1988, pp. 15–16.

19 See, for example, "Liaoning Province 'Theory Salon' " (*"Liaoning sheng de . . ."*), *Liaowang Weekly* (Overseas Ed.), 19 October 1987, pp. 11–12. Also "Dynamic 'Salon' of Beijing Entrepreneurs" (*"Huoyue de Beijing . . ."*), *Liaowang Weekly* (Overseas Ed.), 19 September 1988, pp. 17–18.

20 See "Social Organizations Are an Important Force for Establishing a Democratic Socialist System" (*"Shehui tuanti shi . . ."*), *People's Daily,* 29 April 1988, where it is reported that in Shanghai between 1980 and 1984, the total number of social organizations "of all types" rose from 628 to 2,627.

21 *Liaowang* (Overseas Ed.), 25 January 1988, p. 15.

22 *"Shetuan yao wei weihu wending fahui jiji zuoyung,"* *Renmin Ribao* (Overseas Ed.), 11 January 1990.

23 A few scholars publishing in China are already trying to make some distinctions in their studies with respect to the relative independence or nonindependence of new "intermediate organizations." One such study, appearing in the journal of the Ningxia Provincial Academy of Social Science, divides these organizations into three types: those instigated and run by the state; those that are partly state and partly civil organizations; and those that are fully independent civil organizations. See Chen Tongming, "On the Origins, Potential Contributions, and Special Characteristics of Intermediate Organizations in China," *Ningxia shehui kexue* (May 1988): 52–58, reprinted in *Zhongguo Renmin Daxue Fuyin Baokan Ziliao* (June 1988): 35–40.

24 Gordon White had earlier conducted some research on urban associations. See White, "Chinese Economic Reform and the Rise of Civil Society," manuscript, n.d.

25 Interview, 9 July 1990, pp. 173–174.

26 Ibid., p. 174.

27 Ibid., pp. 175–176.

28 Interview, 21 July 1990.

29 Which did not come to Xinji until 1982.

30 For those interested in the details, the Anxi Chamber of Commerce represented 37 state-run, 21 county-run collective, 49 township-run (*xiang zhen qiye*), 10 village-run, 11 private (*siying qiye*), and 5 individual (*geti*) enterprises. Interview, November 25, 1990, p. 126.

31 Interview, 28 July 1990, pp. 344–349.

32 For an explanation of the principles and procedures guiding this and other similar trade associations, see "Some Points of Information on Industrial Trade Associations" (*"Guanyu gongyexing hangye xiehui . . ."*), *Zhongguo Jidian Bao,* March 4, 1989.

33 See Interview, 28 July 1990.

34 Interview, 26 November 1990, p. 148. And Interview, 30 November 1990, pp. 175–176.

35 The technological rationale for coming together, and the real linkages with Chinese scientific and technical networks and organizations that so many of the new civil associations display are probably worth some sustained study. Among other things, this fact of organizational life seems at present to give something of a "white collar" or "specialist" cast to the quality of associational life in both rural and urban environments.

36 Xinji, with a considerably smaller population than Anxi, is, on any measure of economic development, the more advanced of the two localities. It is interesting to note, therefore, that Xinji appears to have many more functioning civil associations already in place than Anxi. Some twenty-eight different associations, for example – including a consumers' group, a youth and teenage education association, an orchards and forestry association, a rabbit raisers' study group, and even a Ping-Pong club – are grouped loosely under the Political Consultative Committee (PCC) of the town government. And PCC representatives complain that new associations are sprouting up so fast that it is hard to keep track of the total (Interview, 27 July 1990). The Xinji PCC is chaired by the former mayor of the town. And the apparent fact that, through the PCC, this group of civil organizations should have a ready-made conduit for expression of their needs and interests to inner party and government circles, may prove relevant and important to the issues under discussion here. But further exploration of this topic must be deferred.

37 And employed also by some scholars trying to develop a rigorous analysis of apparently like processes taking place in Russia; for example, see M. Steven Fish, "The Emergence of Independent Associations and the Transformation of Russian Political Society since 1985," paper presented at the 1990 meeting of the American Political Science Association.

38 See White, "Chinese Economic Reform"; and Clemens Stubbe Ostergaard, "Citizens, Groups and a Nascent Civil Society: Towards an Understanding of the 1989 Student Demonstrations," *China Information,* 4 (1989): 28–41.

39 For a useful review of this pedigree, see Michael Bratton, "Beyond the State: Civil Society and Associational Life in Africa," *World Politics,* 41, no. 3 (April 1989): 407–430. In this very helpful essay, Bratton also raises for discussion the conditions under which a mutual empowerment of state forces and social forces may take place.

40 One such would be Stepan's, employed by Naomi Chazan in Chapter 10 of this volume. She quotes Stepan defining civil society as "an arena where manifold social movements . . . and civic organizations from all classes . . . attempt to constitute themselves in an ensemble of arrangements so that they can express themselves and advance their interests."

4

Centralization and powerlessness: India's democracy in a comparative perspective

ATUL KOHLI

During the 1970s and 1980s, a recurring pattern characterized political change in India: Control over governmental decisions tended to centralize in leaders who ruled by virtue of personal popularity, but who found it difficult to transform their personal power into a problem-solving political resource. A number of political consequences typically followed. Governmental legitimacy became hard to sustain; there was a high leadership turnover below the highest ranks; the state continued to perform at a low level of efficacy – in terms both of accommodating conflicting interests and of solving developmental problems; and political violence as well as poverty continued to dominate the political landscape. This chapter attempts to explain the roots of the simultaneous tendencies toward centralization and powerlessness in India's low-income democracy.

It is argued that such tendencies toward centralization and powerlessness are generated by the near absence of systematic authority links between the state's apex and the vast social periphery. In years past, especially during the 1950s, India's nationalist party, the Congress, forged patronage links with regional and local influentials, thus creating a chain of authority that stretched from the capital city to villages. Over the last two decades or so, these links in the authority structure eroded, owing to a number of forces: The spread of democratic politics undermined the influence of regional and local traditional elites; and the nationalist party-qua-organization was destroyed by intra-elite conflict and by the recalcitrance of power-hungry national leaders.

Given India's plural diversity, the erosion of both traditional authority in the social structure and of the nationalist party created a highly fragmented political society. Leaders with populist and personal appeal offer one ready mechanism for forging a modicum of political coherence in such a fragmented political situation. Once in power, however, populist leaders do not readily perceive the need to build political institutions; rules and procedures of such institutions as parties only put limits on the discretionary power of personalistic leaders. Without parties or other political institutions, however, the links between leaders and their supporters remain weak. Elections are won on general, nonprogrammatic promises, and it becomes very difficult to translate such general mandates into specific policies. Major policy decisions repeatedly evoke considerable opposition, even from former supporters, and, just as repeatedly, governmental initiatives falter. Policy failure in turn paves the way for other populist challengers, thus perpetuating the cycle of centralization and powerlessness.

The argument developed here with reference to India may also be of some general relevance. First, India is one of the few developing countries that has sustained democracy for nearly forty years. Political patterns within it may thus help analyze what is likely to happen in other low-income democracies over time. One insight of possible general relevance is that the spread of democratic politics in preindustrial societies undermines domination between traditional "superiors" and "inferiors." As this happens, struggles of domination and opposition emerge from localized, social arenas and enter the national political sphere. One should then expect difficulties in forging new and coherent patterns of national authority. Such a political context, in turn, encourages the emergence of leaders who rule by personal and populist appeal. More often than not, however, personalistic rule of this nature is likely to lead to disappointing results. Without parties and programs, populist leaders promise too much and are capable of delivering little, especially to the bottom half of the population. The problem of forging coherent authority thus continues. Besides Indira and Rajiv Gandhi in India, this analysis may also apply to such other recent cases as Cory Aquino in the Philippines or Garcia in Peru.

The second general point worth noting at the outset concerns how this chapter's approach relates to other prevailing ones. The issues raised here are similar to some of the earlier concerns of Samuel Huntington insofar as the problem of centralization and powerlessness is an integral aspect of the imbalance between institutional development and mobilized demands.[1] The causal analysis, however, is different. Instead of conceptualizing mobilization primarily as a function of socioeconomic change, this chapter conceives of growing political activism as additionally resulting from the spread of democratic politics.[2] This modification enables one to understand considerable political activism, even in fairly low-income, preindustrial settings. Moreover, because power-hungry national leaders in India have destroyed or inhibited institutional rebuilding, those who control the state are not viewed here as necessarily the agents of political order and the public good.

Finally, this chapter emphasizes the mutual interaction of the state and society – the "recursive relationship" – which neatly complements that proposed by Joel Migdal in the volume's introductory essay. On the one hand, the centralizing and populist antics of India's national leaders are not comprehensible without situating them in the larger sociopolitical context, especially at the regional and local levels. On the other hand, the changing societal context of growing authority fragmentation cannot be understood without reference to how India's democratic and interventionist state molds the incentives of local and regional actors.

In the first of three parts, I analyze the recurring tendency in contemporary India toward the emergence of centralized and personalistic rule. The second part discusses the reasons why personal, concentrated power, while enabling leaders to bloc the access of others to the state, does not readily translate into developmental efficacy. The conclusion investigates the consequences of this recurring tendency towards centralization and powerlessness, as well as some of the broader implications of the Indian materials. (I should note at the outset that the empirical materials for this essay build on some of my other research; details of the Indian materials may be found in this larger body of work.)[3]

THE RECURRING TENDENCY TOWARD CENTRALIZATION

By "centralization" I mean control over key national decisions in the hands of a very few (or even a single) political elite. Understood as such, India has always been a fairly centralized democracy. Even during the 1950s and the 1960s, control over important decisions was highly concentrated in Jawaharlal Nehru and those close to him. Nevertheless, important contrasts between India of the 1950s and 1960s, and India of the 1970s and 1980s, help define the analytical problem I seek to explain.

To simplify drastically a rather complex picture, levels of political mobilization in India during the 1950s and the early 1960s were relatively low, and elite politics tended to accommodate intra-elite struggles. While Nehru was definitely "first among equals," the fact is that cabinet government during this early period was a reality, the parliament functioned as an important deliberating and debating forum, opposition was treated with respect, the Congress Party had internal democracy and an identity independent of the government, chief ministers of states often possessed independent political base, and such other state institutions as the constitution, the civil service, and the judiciary enjoyed a degree of nonpartisan integrity. There were thus important institutional checks on the personal power of Nehru. It is also important to recognize, however, that political struggles in this early stage involved primarily a relatively small group of elites, especially nationalist and other wealthy urban and rural elites. The large majority of the Indian population, especially those in villages, were not as yet actively mobilized political actors. Members of dominant castes and other influential "big men" in villages were thus often able to sway the political behavior of those below them, namely, the middle and lower rural strata. As these rural elite were incorporated into the fold of the Congress Party via patronage links, India's democracy took on the appearance of a relatively well constructed, elitist democracy in which competing elites managed to work with each other, and into which the elites professed a hope of actively incorporating India's masses.

Political changes over the next two decades present an intriguing paradox: The more the power relations in the social structure, especially in the villages, were democratized, the more personalized and centralized became decision making at the top of India's political pyramid. Can these two processes of change be conceived to have been systematically linked? Before such a case is made, the fact of growing centralization needs to be documented briefly.

Specialists on Indian politics should agree with the broad observation that from the late 1960s onward, decision making in India became more and more centralized in the person of Indira Gandhi. The old Congress Party was marginalized and the new Congress Party of Indira never became a real party. Indira Gandhi instead won considerable popularity by adopting a populist posture and by establishing direct links with the masses. In turn, she used this popular electoral base as a power resource to make key political appointments. More and more individuals, both in the party and in the government, were appointed rather than elected to power. Issues of personal loyalty and favoritism thus became crucial in this top-down political system. Over the 1970s and the 1980s, nearly all members of the cabinet, the parliament as well as the Congress Party officers and chief ministers of states lost their political autonomy; these positions came to be filled by those deemed loyal and useful by Indira Gandhi. As challenges to such personalistic use of power grew, the civil service and the police were also politicized. Eventually, even the armed forces and the constitution were not spared from partisan political struggles.

How does one interpret this trend toward growing centralization in the person of Indira Gandhi? One line of analysis views it as a product of an intra-elite conflict that Indira Gandhi won, partly because of her manipulation skills, and partly because of her populist appeal to India's numerical majority, the rural poor. This victory, the argument would continue, was then used to create a top-down political system to preserve and enhance Indira Gandhi's personal power.[4] Such an argument is not wrong but is incomplete. It is not wrong in the sense that a leader with greater vision, and a greater sense of the public good, would have realized that such a ruling strategy would not only weaken democracy but would also, over the long run, prove self-defeating: As discussed later in this section, when Indira Gandhi needed institutional support to implement her programs, having destroyed the institutional base of the state, she found the state's arms rather limp. Programmatic failures, in turn, contributed to her political decline, and to her tragic assassination.

The emphasis on power-hungry Indira Gandhi is incomplete, however, because other Indian leaders have also ended up creating a very similar personalistic, centralized, and top-down political system. For example, Rajiv Gandhi sought to reverse these trends after coming to power in 1985, but by 1989, gave up any such effort as quixotic and reestablished a personalistic, highly centralized regime.[5] As important are other examples from several Indian states. Non-

Congress leaders, such as the actors-turned-politicians, M. G. Ramachandran in Tamilnadu and N. T. Rama Rao in Andhra Pradesh, also failed to institutionalize their power. They concentrated power in their persons, appointed loyal minions to positions of power, and continued to rule as long as their personal popularity could be maintained.

The wider prevalence within India of a tendency toward centralization and personalization of power suggests the following: Certain broader political forces in contemporary India encourage the rise of leaders who rule by virtue of personal popularity and who, in turn, following the logic of personal rule, tend to concentrate power and create top-down systems staffed by dependent appointees. These forces came into play sometime in the 1960s, and over time their significance has grown. Stated baldly, the lower-middle and the lower strata of rural India emerged during the 1960s as independent and significant political forces. The less these groups were swayed by leaders of the so-called dominant castes, the less electoral utility was served by the old Congress system of a chain of influential "big men." As a clever politician, Indira Gandhi sensed this political change rather early and, facing power competition from rival elites, quickly shifted her energies into reaggregating the newly released political forces. The populist slogan of "alleviate poverty" was aimed precisely at winning electoral majorities in an increasingly fragmented political society, where traditional influentials were losing their influence. Indira Gandhi's repeated electoral successes further confirmed this hypothesis. The large majorities she won in turn freed Indira Gandhi from coalitional responsibilities and enabled her to create a top-down state system.

Numerous local examples from India's political hinterland buttress the claim that, from the 1960s onward, India's political society became more and more fragmented. I will cite only three empirical cases, and those only very briefly, from three different parts of India.[6] The first example is from Kheda district in the western state of Gujarat. Well into the 1960s, the politics and society of this area were controlled by the landowning dominant castes of the Patidars (the Patels). Even though the Patidars were a numerical minority (some 20 percent of the local population), their power rested both on control over land and on a relatively high position in the caste hierarchy. Over time, a heterogenous middle group, the Kshatriyas – who constituted nearly 40 percent of the local population – slowly awoke to the possibility that their numbers could be translated into political power. The more these "backward castes" were mobilized as an electoral bloc, the more their leaders wanted to control the local state – for both symbolic and direct material rewards (patronage) that control of a local state provides in rural India. Unfortunately for the Kshatriya elite, the old, undivided, district-level Congress, as well as local government offices, were dominated by the Patidars – well into the 1960s. The resulting political conflict thus posed a fairly classic question of democratic politics: How were Congress's national leaders, like Indira Gandhi, going to incorporate the support of numerically significant groups, like the Kshatriyas, while local party and governmental structures were controlled by hitherto dominant groups like the Patidars?

A second example is from Guntur district in the South Indian state of Andhra Pradesh. The dominant community in the 1950s and the 1960s in this area were the Reddys, who often competed for power and influence with another landowning, relatively high caste community, the Kammas. As long as power conflict was limited to these two elite castes, the old Congress often succeeded in incorporating rival elites. Over time, however, here as elsewhere in India, the capacity of Reddy and Kamma leaders to sway the political behavior of the backward and scheduled castes declined. This became clear in the 1960s as many of the old Congress leaders (like a significant national politician, Sanjiva Reddy, who had opposed Indira Gandhi within the Congress) started losing their electoral support. The challenge to the power of the dominant castes was not as dramatic in Guntur as it was in Kheda. Nevertheless, it was becoming clear throughout the 1960s that "backward castes" would need to be incorporated on a new basis by any leadership seeking their support. Segments of the rural poor in this area had, in any case, been successfully mobilized by the Communist Party of India. How was the new Congress going to respond to these growing power challenges?

The third and most dramatic example of growing power challenges is provided by India's eastern state, West Bengal. Always more susceptible than other parts of India to radical appeals, parts of the state in the 1960s experienced quite a few radical movements. The well-known Naxalbari movement in the north of the state successfully organized tribal peasants for confiscation of land, till it was brutally repressed. Less dramatic, but probably more threatening, was the fact that the political significance of the old *bhadralok* elite (the Bengali intelligentsia, with a base in land wealth) declined both in cities and in the countryside. Simultaneously, Congress's capacity to win elections declined. As various communist parties gained in significance, the same political question emerged at the forefront: How was a new national leadership of the Congress going to reaggregate electoral majorities in a political context of growing power challenges?

Similar examples could be multiplied. The general point, however, is fairly simple: Introduction of democratic politics and competitive mobilization was slowly chipping away at the corporate cohesiveness of India's traditional social structure. As this happened, the old Congress system of patronage-chains-of-big-men was losing its ability to mobilize an increasingly fragmented political society. The sharp downturn in Congress's electoral fortunes in the 1967 national elections must have confirmed this hypothesis for the more astute Indian political leaders, including Indira Gandhi. A new ruling strategy was clearly needed. Many political changes in contemporary India, in turn, are comprehensible if one thinks of them as by-products of the new ruling strategy: namely, populism aimed at building and sustaining majority coalitions in the context of a highly fragmented political society.

We know in retrospect that Indira Gandhi in the early 1970s adopted a political posture that emphasized the alleviation of poverty as a key theme. This populist strategy paid handsome political dividends, generating large electoral majorities for her. Before investigating the implications of this strategy further, however, we should note that pro-poor populism was by no means an inevitable by-product of a changed political context. It was, rather, a choice from among a handful of other available strategic options. For example, as it became clear during the 1970s that poverty was not going to be readily alleviated, and that empty promises to that effect could not continue to bring electoral rewards, the Congress in the 1980s sought to create winning majorities by flirting with ethnic themes – for instance, Hindus against other Indian minorities. This electoral strategy has, of course, been pursued with a vengeance by other Indian political parties in the 1990s; that, however, is another story.

One question remains a puzzle: Given a number of available ruling strategies, why didn't Indira Gandhi attempt systematically to rebuild institutions – such as a reformist party – that could enable her to deliver on her reformist promises, and that at the same time could help solidify her electoral base? A definite answer will never be known, but three possible contributing factors can be proposed. First, it would have required a more visionary leader with a greater sense of the public good than Indira Gandhi possessed. Second, building of parties and institutions takes both time and sustained political attention; Indira Gandhi instead devoted most of her energies to blocking real or imagined power threats. Third, and most important, parties can not be readily decreed from above. More often then not, parties develop as vehicles for capturing power. Those who are already in power, and especially if their power rests on personal popularity, tend to find rules, procedures, and a robust second tier of leaders, unnecessarily constraining; they often view institutions more as obstacles and less as facilitators of effective rule.

To return to the main theme, growing political fragmentation in the 1960s encouraged the rise of personalistic populism. The forces that have propelled political fragmentation, as well as the consequences of personalistic, populist rule now need to be discussed, if only briefly.

Both socioeconomic and political forces have propelled growing mobiliza-tion, although, on balance, peculiarities of India's democracy have played a very significant role. Students of development often anticipate growing social mobilization in the context of "modernization." The spread of commerce, new modes of economic activity, literacy and urbanization, are generally associated with what Karl Deutsch had labeled "social mobilization."[7] Social mobilization, in turn, is supposed to erode traditional domination, release social actors for new political commitments, and lead to greater levels of political activism, owing either to anomie or to formation of new interest groups. Marxist analysis of the transition from "feudalism to capitalism" is also consistent with this "modernization" analysis; it, too, emphasizes the corroding role of economic change, especially of capitalism, that supposedly renders class inequalities naked, and thus contributes to class conflict and to new levels of activism.[8] There is enough evidence in contemporary India to sustain an analysis that would emphasize socioeconomic changes as the basic motor of growing political mobilization. For example, the roots of radical activism of poor peasants in parts of West Bengal, Andhra Pradesh, and Bihar, and of growing political efficacy of the newly wealthy green revolution farmers of northwestern India are located primarily in socioeconomic changes.

What is less well understood in the general literature, and to which the Indian experience can contribute, is how peculiarities of democracy in a low-income setting themselves propel higher levels of political mobilization. For example, the state in India seeks to promote development and is thus highly interventionist. This means that a fair amount of a poor society's free-floating economic resources is accessible primarily through the state, which thus becomes an object of intense political attention. Moreover, since this state is accessible via democratic means, the stakes of winning or losing the electoral game become very high. Rival elites thus use all available means, fair or foul, peaceful or violent, to mobilize support from their respective communities so as to secure access to the society's main milking cow, the state. The diversity of India's plural social structure easily lends itself to competitive mobilization. Because political parties are weak in any case, and also do not organize and thus systematize participation, intra-elite political competition is readily transformed into what the Rudolphs have rightly identified as India's growing number of "demand groups."[9] The dynamics underlying this process of overpoliticization is both political and economic. Spread of egalitarian values, and of competitive politics within the context of India's low-income democracy and an interventionist state, have politicized social conflict in a manner that has greatly contributed to fragmentation of India's political society.

Some of the evidence for these claims is embedded in the local examples already cited. To recall, the mobilization of Kshatriyas in parts of Gujarat was both political and economic; it was aimed at winning elections and capturing state power, it was led by partisan political elite, and its main demands were economic rewards from the state (e.g., more "reserved" employment for the "backward castes" or state subsidies). The backward caste movements for "reservations" across India have followed a more or less similar pattern. Mobilization of various ethnic groups also has not been all that different. Whether at issue are smaller movements, like those of the Gurkhas in West Bengal or Marathi speakers in Belgaun, Karnataka, or movements of much greater significance, like those of the Sikhs of Punjab, or even the Hindu–Moslem conflict in various parts of India, the political dynamics are identifiable: Leaders mobilize communities so as to strengthen their own political demands. If demands are met, movements often die down. Just as often, however, demands are not met and movements are intensified, or worse, in spite of concessions – as in the case of the Sikhs – leaders of movements loose control over mobilized followers and fragmented movements develop in volatile and often unpredictable ways.

The most compelling evidence to support the claim that the dynamics of growing political activism are not "social mobilization" à la Deutsch, but are politicoeconomic, emerges from regional patterns within India. For example, states as diverse as prosperous Gujarat and poor Bihar have experienced considerable political activism over the last decade. If economic development was the primary driving force, how would one explain the very high levels of activism and political violence in an economically stagnant state like Bihar? A better explanation is, rather, this: Changing political consciousness and competitive democratic mobilization in a stagnant economy have bequeathed to political demands a zero-sum quality, thus intensifying the sense of threat that political demands pose and periodically lead to political violence. Similarly, the fact that the highly mobilized state of West Bengal has been relatively free of violence and agitations since 1977 must be attributed to a rule by a relatively well organized reformist party. Political and organizational variables are thus crucial for understanding patterns of political activism in India.

To connect the argument back to the main point, introduction of democracy into a highly rigid and inegalitarian social structure has slowly but surely unleashed diverse patterns of mobilization. These activities started intensifying sometime in the 1960s and have continued over the last two decades. A major consequence has been the difficulty in forging moderately consensual authority; the more fragmented the political society, the more difficult it has become to form a democratically constituted, coherent center of power. This political context, in turn, has encouraged personalistic populism. Leaders who promise a little something to everyone, even if vaguely, and those who possess personal appeal – or, as it were, charisma – often emerge powerful in settings of political fragmentation.

Personalistic and populist rule, in turn, tends to be inherently centralizing and deinstitutionalizing and does not offer a long-term solution to the problem of building democratic authority. Because power lines link diffuse masses to a single leader, the person at the top is not as constrained by coalitional pressures as are other democratically elected leaders. Of course, such leaders must respect the socially powerful, but they also possess a considerable degree of freedom, not in social restructuring, but in creating a top-down political system. The more the second- and third-tier officers of the polity come to be appointed from above, the less independent power exists within the polity and the more centralized becomes the top of the political pyramid. Thus emerges the first important paradox of contemporary India: Democratization of traditional authority, especially in the rural social structure, has paved the way for centralization of power at the top. The paradox, however, does not stop there. The related, and second, paradox to which I now turn my attention is, why this centralization and control at the top is difficult to transform into real power to solve problems.

THE RECURRING TENDENCY TOWARD POWERLESSNESS

The use of "powerlessness" refers to the repeated incapacity of rulers to fulfill their stated objectives. Leaders who manage to centralize control over decision making often appear to be very powerful. This, however, can be and often is misleading, especially in low-income democracies. Therefore, one needs to make an analytical distinction between centralizing power and developmental power. Centralizing power, as already noted, involves growing control over decisions in the hands of a few leaders and, by the same token, exclusion of the second and lower level of political elite from decision making. Developmental power, by contrast, refers to a capacity not only to make decisions but also to carry them through. Developmental power thus is the ability of political leaders to alter successfully the behavior of social actors and groups.

Some authoritarian regimes within the Third World are able to transform centralized control into developmental efficacy, mainly by utilizing coercion to alter the behavior of social groups. But, as both Frances Hagopian and Vivienne Shue demonstrate in this volume, this is rare, even under authoritarian conditions. When the polity is organized as a democracy, coercion definitely cannot be the main currency that leaders utilize to influence socioeconomic change. Instead, positive and negative incentives, persuasion, and selective use of laws backed by the threat of coercion – legitimate domination – take on an increased significance. Within a democracy, therefore, the capacity to initiate major developmental changes from above comes to rest on a prior capacity of leaders to institutionalize "blocs of consensus," or to build majority coalitions to support a specific path of change. For majority coalitions not only to elect specific leaders, but also to provide sustained support for the implementation of leaders' programs, in turn requires that the link between rulers and supporters, or between the political center and social periphery, be durable. This durability is likely to exist if the relationship of leaders and supporters is institutionalized through such mechanisms as political parties. Democratic leaders, whose power rests on well-organized parties, are thus in a better position to implement developmental programs than are leaders with a diffuse and populist support base.

These generalizations can be supported with some empirical materials from India. However, one general caveat needs to be made. Leaders in democracies often need the support of multiple constituencies and thus often pursue multiple goals. This simple observation has two important implications for the discussion that follows. First, under the best of circumstances, democratic governments seldom act decisively but, rather, tend to muddle through. This should raise one's tolerance for what is a "normal" level of developmental performance in a democracy; the "decisive and flexible" South Korean state under Park Chung Hee, for example, and the "flabby and muddling through" Indian state reflect, in part, the differences in regime type. The weakness of parties and other institutions that could systematically link the state and society in India is an additional variable that further contributes to the powerlessness of that country's centralizing and personalistic leaders. Second, the capacity to fulfill goals often varies from goal to goal. Whether parties are weak or strong, varying with the nature of the coalitional support, some goals are easier to pursue than others, and the pursuit of some goals makes it difficult to achieve other goals.

Given these caveats, a few examples from contemporary India can now be provided to explain how and why growing centralization did not lead to increased power to achieve developmental goals. Two different types of examples are discussed: the incapacity of Indira Gandhi to follow through on her major commitment to alleviate poverty; and the political difficulties that Rajiv Gandhi ran into when he attempted to redirect India's import-substitution development model in a more "liberal" direction.

Indira Gandhi and poverty alleviation

Garibi hatao or "alleviate poverty" was Indira Gandhi's main political slogan throughout the 1970s. Yet we know in retrospect that Indira Gandhi did not have much success in alleviating India's rural poverty, certainly not through the mechanism of redistributive state intervention. Because such gaps between rhetoric and outcome are fairly common in the Third World, the gap itself is not very surprising. Why it nevertheless poses an interesting analytical puzzle is because of the following: Indira Gandhi won sizable electoral majorities on the basis of her populist slogan; she came to have tremendous personal control over India's crucial political decisions; and for a short while (1975–1977), she even possessed near authoritarian powers. Why did it prove so difficult to transform these power resources into a capacity to implement some redistributive programs, such as land reforms?

The reason is in part that it is very difficult for any state to reach out into the nooks and crannies of a society and hope to restructure social relations in a manner that would benefit the weak at the expense of the socially powerful. Next to making war, redistributive reform is probably the most difficult task a state can undertake. If leaders use standard operating procedures, such as pass laws, and hope the bureaucracy implements them, land reforms do not get implemented. Given that those who own land are often powerful, the lower reaches of the state's bureaucratic arm are seldom efficacious enough to fight the powerful on the behalf of the weak, especially in a society's periphery, where bureaucratic supervision tends to be slack. What is more likely is that lower-level state officials and the socially powerful rural elites establish cozy working relationships and redistributive laws are not implemented. If such reforms are to be implemented, what is needed instead is much more of a political intervention, one that can simultaneously strengthen the weak by organizing them, and utilize politicized implementing agents, usually party cadres, that more readily respond to the decisions of rulers than bureaucrats.

I have argued elsewhere in a book-length study that redistributive intervention in India's low-income democracy has been best facilitated by well organized, left-of-center ruling parties.[10] The absence of such an instrument made it almost impossible for Indira Gandhi to follow through on her political platform of *garibi hatao*. The argument in this other study was developed by a comparative analysis of regional Indian materials. It was documented that redistributive reforms were much more successfully implemented in a state like West Bengal than in several other Indian states, including those run by Indira Gandhi's party. I traced this success to the role of the ruling party in West Bengal, a party that calls itself communist – the Communist Party of India, Marxist (CPM) – but is essentially social democratic in ideology, though sharing a tight organization with other Leninist parties. The party rests its power on a coalition of middle and lower rural classes. This social base, combined with a good party organization, enabled CPM successfully to implement mildly redistributive tenancy reforms in one part of India.

More recent regional evidence from India further supports the significance of well-organized parties as agents of redistribution, although it is also important to reaffirm the issue of the regime's social base. West Bengal continues to be one of the few states in which tenancy reforms have been successfully implemented over the last ten to fifteen years. Nevertheless, having implemented these reforms, the CPM regime has stopped short of implementing any further land redistribution that could benefit the really poor, the landless agricultural laborers. The CPM also has not made any real effort to organize these laborers so as to improve their wages. The main reason for this is the difficulty the CPM faces in holding together a coalition of middle peasants and landless laborers. Because the middle peasants often employ these laborers and some of their lands may be affected by radical land reform, the CPM has decided to go slow. The analytical point is clear: Party organization is only one significant variable in successful redistribution. The social base of the ruling party is another important factor that conditions a regime's policy proclivities.

Lest the correspondence between social base of power and a state's policy behavior be overdrawn, the case of Gujarat in the 1980s provides a ready check. The winning coalition that the Congress Party under Madhev Singh Solanki put together in Gujarat was nearly identical to CPM's power base in West Bengal. As in Bengal, Solanki succeeded in excluding the elite, landholding groups – the Patidars – and rested his power instead on Kshatriyas and Adivasis, the middle and the lower strata. Once in power, however, in contrast to West Bengal, Solanki did not even attempt land reforms. When he tried to implement something as mild as the "reservation" policy – a policy that would have done little more than ensure a few thousand future jobs in the public sector to the middle and lower strata – Gujarat became embroiled in major riots. These riots were initiated by the Patidars and they severely checked Solanki's power to attempt even token redistribution. Solanki, in turn, could neither hold together the coalition of his own supporters nor fight the opposition with any success. The root of this weakness was the absence of a well-organized party. Without a party, the government's supporters were not deeply attached to a program, the ruling elite remained factionalized, and a coherent force could not be generated to confront the socially powerful. Clearly, identical social coalitions do not provide a ready explanation of regime's redistributive performance. The ideology and the organization of the ruling party remain crucial variables for understanding success or failure at redistribution in contemporary India.

The absence of a well-organized, left-of-center party was what made it difficult for Indira Gandhi to translate her left-of-center political goals into reformist outcomes. In other words, without an instrument to systematically link the state and society, personalistic power enabled centralization but did not generate power to achieve goals. It is important only to add – although the point is relatively obvious – that the presence of a specific type of instrument does not mean that the capacity of leaders to accomplish all types of goals will be enhanced. A well-organized left-of-center party, for example, may enhance the leadership's redistributive capacity but may have no bearing on the capacity to deal with ethnic conflicts, or may well have negative impact on economic growth. The issue of when states have capacities to achieve their goals thus remains a highly complex one, varying not only across countries but also across issues within a country.

Rajiv Gandhi and economic liberalization

Having recognized that India's industrial growth was relatively sluggish, especially in comparison with such other developing countries as South Korea, Rajiv Gandhi attempted to alter India's development strategy. This was in the aftermath of Indira Gandhi's assassination, and after Rajiv Gandhi had ridden a "sympathy wave" to power with a massive electoral majority in early 1985. We know in retrospect that Rajiv had some success in implementing "liberalization," but also that he faced numerous obstacles. Eventually, he had to backtrack in a more populist direction. Moreover, whatever success he may have had probably cost him electoral support in the 1989 elections.[11] A brief discussion of this example, therefore, highlights a somewhat different analytical point than the one already discussed with reference to the issue of redistribution. The general point continues to be the same, namely, the inability to translate personalistic power into developmental results, but the more specific point here is that the attempt to translate nonspecific electoral mandates into specific policy goals quickly runs into obstacles.

The first issue that needs to be understood is why recent elections in India have all been won on fairly nonspecific mandates. For those who do not follow Indian politics, it is important to know that ever since 1967, most national elections in India have been conducted in the shadow of some extraordinary event. The 1971 election, for example, took place when the nationalist euphoria over the dismemberment of Pakistan (and the birth of Bangladesh) was high, and when Indira Gandhi's sharp shift toward populism had also raised the hopes of many. National emergency was imposed in 1975 as a result of growing and violent political opposition. Indira Gandhi lost the 1977 elections, mainly owing to the Emergency, but the dramatic failure of the opposition to hold the coalition together catapulted her back to power in 1980. There was a widespread feeling in India in the early-1980s that, had Indira Gandhi not been assassinated in 1984, she would have done poorly in the national elections of 1985. Her assassination, which created a widespread fear of impending turmoil, as well as sympathy for her son, brought Rajiv to power with a large electoral majority in early 1985. The 1989 elections were one of the few "normal" elections in India since 1967, and it is not surprising that, as in 1967, the Congress Party again lost its dominant position. The elections in 1991 that brought Congress back to power again reflected the inability of Congress's opposition to work together, as well as the dramatic assassination of Rajiv Gandhi.

The general point is that the Congress Party lost its nationalist hegemony over India sometimes in the 1960s, and ever since then it has been difficult for Congress leaders to put together a winning coalition. This task has become especially difficult because the memory of unfulfilled populist promises is fresh, and populism has probably lost its electoral efficacy. Without parties, programs, and stable coalitions, therefore, electoral victories have had to be "manufactured" by creating, or taking advantage of, extraordinary events that generate electorally consequential national moods like euphoria or crises. Electoral majorities based on nonspecific and nearly sensational mandates are thus not only fortuitous, they have become an integral part of how to create a coherent center of power in contemporary India. The analytical issue for us now is, how leaders who win power through such means fare while in power.

Rajiv Gandhi was elected on a very general, nonspecific mandate and did rather poorly while in power. His attempts to "liberalize" India's economy afford important glimpses into the underlying dynamics. Liberalization in India mainly has meant providing incentives – or at least removing disincentives – for the profitability of private production, with the hope that this will improve both the levels and the quality of investment, and lead to higher levels of economic growth. Although eminently "rational" from the standpoint of improving production output from private sources, attempts to implement such policy measures created major political problems for Rajiv Gandhi.

Rajiv Gandhi did not win by putting together a pro-growth coalition that sought to liberalize India's economy. As a matter of fact, his electoral victory had no or little economic component. As soon as he attempted to translate his broad mandate into a specific economic direction, the first major source of resistance was his own party. Even though the Congress is not much of a party anymore, many of those who had been in appointed positions from the time of Indira Gandhi balked at Rajiv's attempted redirection. The motives behind this resistance were mixed: Some feared that the abandonment of "socialist" economic policies in favor of a more "liberal" approach would cost the party electoral support among India's majority, the rural poor; others worried that "liberalization" would eventually lead to the opening of the economy to external economic influences, thus threatening sovereignty; and yet others saw the new policy regime as signaling that new officers would come to run the party and thus sought to bloc any major change as a way of preserving personal power. Whatever the motives, and they were mixed, the general point is this: Because a major policy initiative was not part of the party platform that had facilitated electoral victory, there was no cohesive support for the initiative, even within the ruling party.

Because Rajiv Gandhi stood at the apex of what was by now a top-down political system, the resistance of the party may have slowed his initiatives but was by no means decisive. Rajiv replaced those who really resisted with those who were more loyal, and, at least during 1985 and 1986, continued with his liberalization measures.

Very soon, however, opposition to his new policies grew. For example, Rajiv's attempts to reduce India's public expenditures on poverty programs evoked considerable opposition, including, once again, that from Congress's own senior political officers. Rajiv backtracked. When plans to remove subsidies on prices of essential goods, like kerosene, were announced, numerous opposition parties threatened a general strike across urban India. Once again, Rajiv Gandhi backtracked. And when plans to invite Japanese auto manufacturers to produce automobiles in India were leaked, India's import-substitution-coddled businesspeople brought pressure on the government and attempts to alter India's foreign investment policies were put aside. Clearly, different components of the "liberalization" package evoked opposition from all social groups likely to be affected.

Finally, the opposition that really hurt Rajiv Gandhi was that of rural groups, who started viewing the new policy measures as pro-city and pro-rich. While such an interpretation was not necessary, especially because measures like devaluation can shift the terms of trade in favor of the peasantry, the problem was one of political management. Without a party, Rajiv Gandhi simply did not have the political resources needed to persuade and incorporate sections of the rural population behind his program. What happened instead was that other political actors, at lower levels of the polity, succeeded in countermobilizing. Rajiv's new economic policies had led to an increase in industrial production, especially in durable consumer goods. Worried that these goods might not clear the market, the government had also provided numerous incentives for urban consumers to consume more. The resulting development strategy was, and could thus be easily characterized as, benefiting the urban rich. Peasant leaders took advantage of the new opportunity and successfully mobilized rural groups against the Congress Party. When Congress lost elections in 1987 in the crucial, Hindi-heartland state of Haryana, only then did Rajiv Gandhi realize how politically expensive the new economic rationality had become.

After 1987 one heard less and less about economic liberalization in India, at least until 1991, when another new government started pushing this agenda; that again, however, is a different story. There was no major policy reversal during 1987 and 1991, but there was also no major policy movement. Instead, Rajiv Gandhi readopted some of the more populist economic programs. It should be noted in passing that, the more torn he became by the conflicting pulls of economic and political rationality, the less he used economic policies as tools of electoral mobilization. It can be argued that Congress's renewed interest in mobilization around religious sentiments was rooted in this contradiction. Indira Gandhi's populism had won majorities, but poverty alleviation policies were never implemented. As Rajiv Gandhi attempted to reorder economic policies in a progrowth direction – which might eventually benefit India's poor – the short-term problem became one of securing electoral majorities. If the majority–minority pie is not to be cut along the poor–rich angle, the other obvious angle in India is Hindus versus minorities, especially Moslems. Congress's growing flirtation with a pro-Hindu orientation, and the electoral success of other political parties with similar commitments, is thus partly rooted in these contemporary political tensions.

Rajiv Gandhi did implement some liberalization measures but was also forced to curtail many of his other planned actions. Where he did succeed in implementation, the moves may have cost him important political support. It thus becomes clear that in spite of a massive electoral majority, Rajiv Gandhi could not translate this general support into a force to help him pursue his own policy priorities – mainly because the support he had enjoyed in early 1985 was very diffuse and without a strong mandate to do anything specific. If economic liberalization is what Rajiv Gandhi stood for, it should have been tested in the marketplace of electoral politics. If he could have thus put together a proliberalization, progrowth majority coalition, and given this coalition some durability by incorporating its representatives into a party organization, the problem of implementation would have been qualitatively different. As already argued, however, without parties, programs, and stable coalitions, nonspecific electoral mandates have become a near necessity in contemporary India. Attempts to translate these victories into specific new policies have, in turn, become very difficult. The greater the gap, therefore, between how power is won and how power is used, the more India's political system continues to muddle through at a relatively low level of efficacy.

CONCLUSION

This chapter has sought to identify and explain a recurring tendency in Indian politics toward centralization and powerlessness. Its purpose has been both to analyze an important political problem and to demonstrate the utility of the state–society approach that this volume seeks to advance. It is now important to conclude by drawing together some arguments concerning the substantial analytical puzzle and the approach embedded in the analysis.

The puzzle I have sought to analyze here plagues many developing countries: Control over national decisions comes to centralize in the person of a single leader or a few leaders, but the leadership finds it difficult to transform this control into developmental efficacy. The argument I have developed regarding India may or may not apply to other developing countries. My hunch is that it is likely to have some relevance to other low-income democracies but that the dynamics within authoritarian systems are different.

The main condition that helps explain the tendency toward centralization and powerlessness in India is the weakness of systematic authority links between the political center and the social periphery. The spread of democracy has eroded patterns of traditional domination in the social structure. Numerous groups have thus been mobilized into the political arena, but such mobilization has not been accompanied by a systematic reorganization of the newly mobilized forces. Political parties could have been one major institutional means of such reincorporation. Parties, however, take time to emerge. In India, moreover, power-hungry leaders contributed to the destruction of old, established parties. Weakness of parties and fragmentation of power in the social structure have made the task of forging effective government – a government able to resolve conflicts without violence and follow through on its policy promises – very difficult.

One of the few alternatives for creating a coherent political center in a fragmented polity is leaders with personal appeal. Following the logic that leaders like power, such leaders characteristically create top-down political systems of loyal minions. Since rules and procedures constrain personal discretion, personalistic leaders also do not always view – especially, if they are shortsighted – the need to create institutions as desirable. Fragmentation of power in India has thus provided the context that encourages personalistic and centralizing leaders to emerge.

We have also noted that personalistic control in India has proven hard to translate into power to achieve policy goals. This was true of both redistributive and growth goals. In both cases, our analysis has suggested, leaders needed a political instrument to translate their goals into outcomes, but such an instrument was missing. Instruments such as parties could have helped bring together leaders and supporters into a durable "power bloc." This institutionalized power, in turn, could have been used to pursue specific goals.

The question that remains is this: Supposing Rajiv Gandhi's power had rested on a well-organized growth coalition, what would have been the implication of such a power configuration for redistributive goals? The answer in the abstract is that the implication may well have been negative. The reverse is probably also true: A well-organized redistributive coalition in power can hurt economic growth. How,'then, can states simultaneously pursue goals that may be in tension? There is no easy answer. One possible way of thinking about the problem, however, is as follows.

Because interests of social actors vary, one needs in societies parties that emphasize alternative goals. It is no accident that many well-established democracies are served well by alternating rule between growth- and redistributive coalitions. Within developing country democracies, where political communities are not well established, and where the state must perform important economic functions, the need for well-organized parties of competing orientations becomes that much greater. Well-organized parties are one of the few available political instruments that can both represent interests and concentrate them at the top, enabling party leaders, if they win majority support, to pursue development democratically. Crafting well-organized parties thus remains an important long-term goal of political engineering in the Third World.

A last set of concluding comments concerns the state–society approach embedded in the analysis here. First, if the argument developed in this chapter is persuasive, it should strengthen the general claim of the volume, namely, that state and society condition each other continuously, and that patterns of political change must be analyzed by focusing on state–society interaction. Second, this chapter's analysis suggests that what the national leaders do, or do not do, cannot be discovered without traveling down the political and social hierarchies, where at the "periphery" the social and political forces provide the context that condition the nature of central rule. And last, this analysis also leads to the argument that our understanding of state and society ought to be deeply political. Instead of a bureaucratic vision of the state, and a tendency to view social structures as given, it is important to recognize that both political and social actors wish to shape the use of authority in social change, and in the process, both the state and society are formed and re-formed. The struggles for domination and opposition are struggles over life chances and thus tend to generate political struggles. How the resulting political struggles are co-opted, repressed, or utilized is essential to an understanding of how political change in developing countries proceeds.

NOTES

1 See his *Political Order in Changing Societies* (New Haven: Yale University Press, 1968), esp. ch. 1.
2 This idea has a long intellectual lineage, from Tocqueville, through T. H. Marshall, to Reinhard Bendix and Charles Tilly. See, for example, Reinhard Bendix, *Nation*

Building and Citizenship (Berkeley: University of California Press, 1977), esp. pp. 62–65, 419–434.

3 See mainly *Democracy and Discontent: India's Growing Crisis of Governability* (New York: Cambridge University Press, 1990). Also see *The State and Poverty in India: Politics of Reform* (New York: Cambridge University Press, 1987); and an edited volume, *India's Democracy: An Analysis of Changing State-Society Relations* (Princeton: Princeton University Press, rev. paperback ed., 1990).

4 See, for example, Paul R. Brass, *The Politics of India Since Independence* (New York: Cambridge University Press, 1990).

5 See Kohli, *Democracy and Discontent,* chs. 11 and 12.

6 For details, see ibid., chs. 3–7.

7 See his "Social Mobilization and Political Development," *American Political Science Review,* 55 (September 1961).

8 See, for example, Antonio Gramsci, *Selections from the Prison Notebooks* (New York: International Publishers, 1971), esp. p. 276.

9 See Lloyd and Sussane Rudolph, *In Pursuit of Lakshmi* (Chicago: University of Chicago Press, 1987), esp. Part 4.

10 See *The State and Poverty in India.*

11 The liberalization attempts begun in mid-1991 have been somewhat more successful. The analytical lessons of that experiment, however, will be materials for another essay.

5

States and ruling classes in postcolonial Africa: the enduring contradictions of power

CATHERINE BOONE

INTRODUCTION

Goran Hyden remarked that postcolonial African states appear to be "suspended balloon-like in mid-air."[1] Much of the literature on African states conveyed similar images. Both modernization theory and dependency–underdevelopment approaches emphasized the external sources or superimposed character of political power in contemporary Africa. Concepts like "Westernized elite," "auxiliary bourgeoisie," and "overdeveloped postcolonial state" underscored the extent to which contemporary states and forms of domination were grafted onto African societies. Assumptions about state autonomy went hand in hand with the notion that the most fundamental sources of state power were external, rather than rooted in African society. Implicit in modernization theory was a belief in near absolute autonomy of the political sphere, and in the capacity of the new political elite of tropical Africa to reshape societies in their own image. Political economists challenged modernization theorists' notion of state autonomy by pointing to neocolonialism and dependency. Underdevelopment theorists argued that African ruling classes enjoyed little autonomy vis-à-vis neocolonial interests and little autonomy to act in ways that systematically violated the logic of global capital. Yet dependency and underdevelopment theorists, like modernization theorists, tended to view postcolonial states and ruling classes as remarkably unconstrained by the societies over which they sought to preside.[2]

On the basis of such a view, many political economists argued that over time, Africa's ruling elite would entrench and guarantee their own power by transforming themselves into capitalist classes.[3] Some form of peripheral capitalism or dependent development would serve Africa's ruling classes (and international capital) better than chronic economic stagnation. The "logic of capital" and the driving interests of rulers both seemed to point in the direction of capitalist development, propelled by the relatively autonomous postcolonial state.

The problem with this scenario is that after some thirty years of political independence, it does not seem to have materialized in most African states. Rulers have often used state power in ways that compromise, rather than promote, economic growth. Paradoxically, patterns of political practice have worked to erode the administrative capacities and resources bases of states. Such practices are manifest dramatically in the domain of rural development, where regimes appear to have pursued policies that limited the growth of agricultural surpluses and constrained, or even degraded, the productive potential of this sector. Both trends compromise the long-term interests of ruling classes and of international capital.

What many analysts describe as the growing "dysfunctionality" of the African state raises new questions about forces that have shaped, constrained, and compromised state power in the postcolonial context. What accounts for the "weakening" of the African state and for forms of economic stagnation that belie expectations for dependent development?

An important part of the answer lies in an analysis of how state power in Africa *is* grounded in societally based forms of power. Despite the images and the partial reality of externally imposed rule and rulers, the forms of domination and economic exploitation that have emerged in contemporary Africa have been shaped in decisive ways by the societies that rulers seek to govern. This chapter directs attention to the agrarian bases of postcolonial society and to the political structures built upon them. The analysis sketches out ways in which both colonial and postcolonial states sought to base their authority – and their powers to appropriate wealth from agriculture – in social institutions that transcended the domain of state power and control. Institutional linkages, political fusions, and social antagonisms born of this process promoted regime consolidation in early postcolonial Africa. Simultaneously, they constrained rulers' willingness and capacity to accelerate processes of rural transformation that promised to enhance productivity, maximize marketed output, increase investment in agriculture, and concentrate rural surpluses in the hands of capitalist producers. The chapter argues that how state power was rooted in rural societies helps to account for regimes' ambivalence in the face of changes associated with the rise of rural capitalism, for the paradoxically counterproductive strategies they have employed to extract wealth from agriculture, and for the persistent fragility and weaknesses of ruling coalitions.

My argument draws in part on studies of colonial rule. Anne Phillips and Bruce Berman are among those who argue that in colonial Africa, the state's interest in promoting the exploitation of African land and labor could not be fully reconciled with its interest in political domination.[4] The imperatives of rule gave rise to forms of domination that obstructed the full development of capitalist social relations. This basic insight is relevant to understanding *post*colonial regime consolidation. Regime consolidation involved efforts by those who assumed state power at the time of independence to consolidate ruling coalitions, reproduce their own power, and establish some basis for rule. This process was shaped by social forces that compromised the hegemony and cohesion of emergent political classes. Most importantly, small-scale farmers across most of the continent retained direct control over the land, and thus preserved a measure of autonomy from both the state and capital. This feature of agrarian social and economic structures led colonial as well as postcolonial regimes to govern the countryside "indirectly," through a "politics of collaboration" with strongmen and political authorities who were rooted in the social relations and exchange networks of peasant society. Strategies of governance and exploitation that emerged under these conditions reproduced forms of political domination that constrained the willingness and capacity of postcolonial regimes, like their colonial predecessors, to promote capitalist transformation.

The first section of this chapter deals with the colonial period, concentrating on economic and political contradictions that shaped the colonial state. It relies on a few, basic generalizations about colonial rule in sub-Saharan Africa and about small-scale, African producers of export commodities. These generalizations lay a groundwork for discussing similarities that characterized regime consolidation across much of the continent. The chapter's second part turns to the peaceful transfers of power of the 1960s. This section discusses the role of clientelism and state patronage in welding fragmented and fissiparous ruling coalitions into regimes capable of maintaining a hold on state power. I argue that these patterns of political practice were rooted in, and worked to reproduce, material conditions and social relations that created and shored up peasantries during the colonial period. The emphasis, then, is on continuities that span the historical divide of decolonization, and on regularities that have emerged across African settings and over time.

This approach to uncovering connections between state and societally based forms of power emphasizes institutional and economic structures, and the kinds of political and social relationships that underpin them. The relationships that are privileged in this analysis are patronage ties that develop around authority-based controls (rather than market-based controls) over access to material resources. Patronage ties crisscross the analytic boundaries of class categories. They also blur the state–society distinction. Clientelistic hierarchies, factions, and clans form both within the state apparatus and on the local level, revealing divisions, competition, and power struggles that exist *within* the categories of "rulers" and "ruled" as well as patterns of alliance and conflict between them. I argue that hierarchies of power found in rural social institutions were harnessed to the task of extending state power in modern Africa, and that this process constrained the willingness and capacity of regimes to promote the capitalist transformation of agricultural production.

The general argument comes at the expense of systematic attention to variation of setting, circumstance, and manner *within* the African context, and at the cost of analyzing the infinite variety of ways in which these social and political realities were actually constructed and contested on the ground. Accepting such analytic limitations makes it possible to highlight features of setting and circumstance that combine to produce specificities that stand out when colonial and early postcolonial Africa is placed in a broader historical and comparative context.

From the perspective of a broader historical context, it is overwhelmingly clear that the arrangements of the early postcolonial period have proved difficult to sustain. In the chapter's conclusion, I argue that contradictions inherent in the exercise of state power that emerged under colonialism, and that were reproduced in the early postcolonial period, have culminated in the political and economic crises of the present. Naomi Chazan's and Michael Bratton's contributions to this volume trace the related emergence of new patterns of political practice in the late 1970s and 1980s.

FARMING COMMUNITIES, MERCHANT CAPITAL, AND "INDIRECT RULE"

Africa's newly independent states and emergent ruling classes were shaped by social forces that bore the heavy imprint of colonial rule. Postcolonial regime consolidation involved efforts to create new structures and relations of power. At the same time, regime consolidation involved efforts to (re)subordinate *existing* structures of societally based power to the state. These existing power structures were rooted in material conditions that were not transformed by the granting of independence in the 1960s.

The colonial project itself was political as well as economic, for governance was the necessary precondition for economic exploitation. The critical question is how tensions between these dual imperatives shaped the character of the colonial state, colonial modes of domination, and the success of the colonial project. Analysts who have framed this question argue that the dual imperatives were ultimately contradictory, for ever-intensifying levels of economic exploitation threatened to undermine the political arrangements through which colonizers sought to govern. Colonial domination and exploitation remained unstable and incomplete processes. Political independence did not resolve these contradictions.

In most of sub-Saharan Africa, colonial states undertook the project that private capital had achieved only on a limited basis: harnessing African land and labor to the production of low-cost agricultural commodities for European markets. The project involved efforts to promote the rapid expansion of export crop production and to undercut African political authorities and traders who stood in the way of European profit and ambition. The resort to coercion and political domination – that is, colonial rule – was a cumbersome means to these ends. The blatant and latent role of coercion in underpinning the colonial project made the task of colonial administrators complex. They were charged with using state power in strikingly *instrumental* and exploitative ways to promote European economic interests, while simultaneously constructing a stable political order that would make this possible.[5] Outside the settler colonies and plantation enclaves, the strategies that emerged by the time of World War I involved efforts to *modify,* rather than to sweep aside, the political infrastructure of conquered societies and precolonial systems of agricultural production.[6]

Across much of the continent, colonial states pressed African cultivators to allocate an increasing share of their productive resources to growing crops destined for Europe. Colonial states often relied on force to erode the self-sufficiency of households and communities, and thus to subject cultivators to the demands and pressures of colonial markets. Compulsory cultivation of export crops and taxation were the instruments of choice. Robert Shenton describes how this worked in one part of Nigeria:

In 1934, one study indicated that agricultural producers in . . . Zaria Province [of Northern Nigeria] were paying 41 percent of their total income in taxes while others were paying as high as 70 percent of their cash income. Since export crops were the single largest source of cash, it is clear that they were being produced almost entirely to meet the demands of the state. In some areas even food crops had to be sold to meet the growing burden of taxes.[7]

The particular ways in which communities responded to these demands were as varied as the ways in which African societies organized relationships between people, and between people and the land. In export crop–producing regions, agriculturalists found ways to bring new land under cultivation, redeploy fallow or food crop–producing land to export crop production, reorganize labor use within households, or to draw labor from outside their communities into household production units. These processes modified the structures of existing rural societies. In export crop–producing regions, African *peasantries* emerged.[8] Significantly, this process was most successful where export crop production developed without major transformations of existing methods and techniques of production – where tree crops such as coffee and cocoa requiring low labor input could be grown alongside or among existing food crops.[9]

As export crop producers, African farmers were drawn into the world economy through markets for commodities, imported consumer goods, and agricultural inputs. As peasantries, they remained independent household producers. Anne Phillips writes that through "most of the continent, pre-colonial property relations survived – at least to the extent of providing the majority of Africans with access to land."[10] Access to land was the key, for it allowed African producers to retain control over the primary means of production, family labor, and the production process itself. Households remained the primary unit of agricultural production, and families were able to provide part of their own subsistence needs. Peasant farmers' control over the land constituted one of the most fundamental constraints on European power in Africa.

In promoting the peasantization of African agriculturalists, the colonial state was instrumental in the expansion of the European trading companies that dominated the colonial import–export trade. Outside the limited regions of European settlement and plantation enclaves, European capital was not invested in agricultural production. European merchant houses extracted rural surpluses through the commercial circuits of the colonial economy, buying cheap and selling dear.[11] Colonial states underwrote the profitability of these operations by imposing controls over exchange circuits (through price-fixing, crop-purchasing monopolies, and other forms of administrative fiat). European firms interested in African commodities, however, had no direct control over the volume or quality of the coffee, cocoa, groundnuts, cotton, or palm nuts produced by independent African cultivators.[12] Without direct control over African land and labor, European industries and merchants could not reorganize the production process itself, change production techniques to suit their needs, invest capital to enhance productivity, divert land and labor away from food crop production, or force laborers to work faster, more productively, or more intensively. Once again, coercion and administrative fiat provided a partial solution. Through physical force, law, taxation, and persuasion, colonial administrators intensified pressure on Africans to produce more for export markets and to adjust methods of cultivation in ways deemed to enhance the quality of output (use of fertilizers, new seed varieties, monocropping, etc.).

For the colonial state, the problem was to create a stable political order that would facilitate and underpin the spread of export crop production. This was no simple task. Conquest of precolonial African societies, the heavy hand of the colonial state, and the economic exploitation of rural communities tended to provoke forms of direct and indirect resistance. Revolts, rebellions, sabotage, and population migrations are constants in the history of European colonialism in Africa. Just as important, according to Phillips, were Europeans' *fears* of revolt and the specter of disorder. "The fragility of colonial control was such that proposals were abandoned on the faintest suspicion of [political] disaster."[13] Resistance and the threat of resistance often grew out of Africans' efforts to protect the coherence of established communities. In places like the cocoa-producing regions of the Gold Coast and Côte d'Ivoire, by contrast, the success of the colonial economic project threw up challenges to colonial rule. Expanding commodity production in the most prosperous regions of colonial Africa gave rise to indigenous farmers and traders who were prepared to challenge the colonial state, "native authorities," or European monopolies in order to expand their own spheres of accumulation. As Phillips and Berman argue, colonialism itself produced social forces that were difficult to contain within the framework of the colonial political economy. Yet if Africa became ungovernable, it would be impossible to exploit.

What was the political order through which the Europeans sought to govern? Throughout most of the continent, colonial domination was rooted in a "politics of collaboration."[14] Where small-scale African farmers produced export crops, colonizers sought to work through and modify, rather than to destroy, preexisting political and social structures. When conquest destroyed established states, kingdoms, or chieftancies, colonial rulers usually tried to constitute "native authority" in some image of traditional forms. Lord Lugard coined the term "indirect rule" in spelling out principles to guide this process. The aim of indirect rule was to weaken existing African political structures and subordinate them to the colonial state without completely undermining the capacity of local authorities to control their subjects.

Colonial rule fully compromised precolonial forms of political authority through conquest and the appropriation of many of the established rule-making and economic powers of African kings, courts, chiefs, and councils. Changes in rural production and in the locus of control over economic surpluses also destabilized precolonial political structures. Under the aegis of the colonial state, the power of local-level authorities over communities tended to increase at the expense of aggregated and centralized political institutions such as kingship. In part, this reflected deliberate strategies of colonizers. Elliot Skinner quotes a pre–World War I French commander in what became Upper Volta:

"We have no interest in strengthening the power that is regarded as central, nor in increasing the power of the various Nabas; on the contrary, we must look for points of stress which will permit us to divide the country. . . . [T]he authority of the Mogho Naba itself will be weakened, because we can easily acknowledge the independence of these great [princes] and free them from his influence. . . . This is the course which has been followed. . . . It has produced excellent results, and the requested taxes have come in regularly."[15]

The suppression of slavery and pawnage, the demise of craft guilds, the imposition of European trading monopolies, and the expansion of export crop production weakened old political structures. African authorities tended to become increasingly dependent on resources mobilized and distributed by the colonial state.

At the same time, indirect rule confirmed or bolstered many of the powers of local-level authorities (such as chiefs) over the land and labor of their rural subjects. In this sense, indirect rule was rooted in, and shored up by, the material conditions of peasant society as it emerged in colonial Africa. As Beverly Grier argues, this connection was explicit in British administrators' preoccupation with "native land tenure." The West African Lands Committee, set up in 1912 to review land tenure policy in the Gold Coast, Nigeria, Sierra Leone, and Gambia, wrote: "Native rule depends on the native land system. If it is the policy of the Government to govern the natives through themselves, subject to European supervision, retaining what is useful in their institutions, the native system of land tenure must be preserved at all costs."[16]

In rural Africa under colonial rule, capitalist social relations developed on a limited scale. This meant that much of the rural economy was organized around *nonmarket* mechanisms for allocating productive resources. Households usually were the basic unit of agricultural production, and within households the allocation of resources was influenced by efforts to reproduce authority relations within the family and to maintain the family's "subsistence floor." Land distribution among households in a given community was organized through ongoing modifications of precolonial law and practice rather than through open and competitive land markets. Usufruct rights (land-use rights) for all members of a community were usually guaranteed. Chiefs, elders, and lineage heads exercised continuing powers (sanctioned by the colonial state) over the regulation of communal lands.[17] These conditions tended to shore up the power of local-level notables like chiefs, for they slowed the rate at which market forces chipped away at existing social structures. "Native land tenure" ensured that authority-based controls over productive resources would continue to play a role in organizing rural production. Although these arrangements reproduced some old forms of rural inequality and created new ones, they also tended to militate against the creation of ever larger production units and the consequent rise of a landless class of laborers. In prosperous export crop–producing regions of West Africa such as the Gold Coast, British colonial administrations attempted to *counter* tendencies toward the commoditization of land, working instead to confirm the powers of chiefs and lineages over land allocation and the transfer of land-use rights.

Because most people retained some access to land, labor markets developed in partial and uneven ways. Colonial Africa "lacked what had been the *differentia specifica* of capitalist development elsewhere: free wage labor."[18] In the pre–World War II era, the demands of the colonial state for labor (used in the building of roads and railroads, for example) were met through forced-labor regimes. This blatantly instrumental exercise of state power was carried out through "native authorities." Chiefs in French West Africa rounded up each village's quota of workers and received salaries from the colonial state for services rendered. Elsewhere, chiefs collected house and head taxes, keeping a cut for themselves. They exercised powers to fine, conscript, imprison, and banish. Coercive powers that were exceedingly arbitrary were thus vested in village-level authorities. In effect, chiefs were charged with manipulating personalistic relations of dependency, authority, and even fear to maintain order on the local level under the most oppressive of conditions.

If indirect rule provided a machinery for extracting taxes and labor from rural communities, then it also provided conduits for state efforts to intensify smallholder production of export crops. Colonial administrations often took a leading role in distributing agricultural inputs (better plant varieties, fertilizers, tools) required to intensify export crop production. Here again, colonial states were forced to deal with the contradictions of their own policies, for low producer prices (often set by the government itself) and the lack of competition in crop purchasing (often enforced by official purchasing monopolies) reduced the capacity and the willingness of most African farmers to undertake risky or costly investments in export crop production. Land tenure law also made it difficult to use land as loan collateral. Under these conditions, many colonial administrations resorted to nonmarket means to enhance the volume and quality of output. Working through village-level authorities and village agricultural cooperatives became the means of choice.[19] In the most dynamic export crop–producing zones, the opposite forces produced the same response. Where debt was forcing peasants to surrender control over their land and labor to would-be estate farmers or capitalist farmers, cooperatives were viewed as a way to drive a wedge between household producers and moneylenders, thus slowing the much feared process of rural class formation.[20]

Colonial states created agricultural cooperatives on a widespread basis in the post–World War II period. These institutions served to link peasant producers to the large-scale purchasers of export crops (i.e., the European import–export companies or the state marketing boards). Cooperatives circumscribed the activities of African moneylenders and middlemen, reduced competition in crop purchasing, and thus worked to concentrate the profits of the export trade in the hands of European trading conglomerates and the state.[21] After World War II, colonial regimes sought to increase the productivity (and output) of peasant producers by distributing credit and agricultural inputs through village cooperatives. To finance this, cooperatives acquired debt in the name of the collectivity. Pressuring families to repay debts, allocating state-financed credit, distributing inputs, and weighing and purchasing the crop were tasks placed in the hands of village-level cooperative officials. The system enhanced the power of these authorities and the vulnerability of farming families to decisions made by local-level agents of the state. The financial cycle was completed when debt payments were deducted from the proceeds from sales to the marketing boards. Cooperatives gave local-level authorities another means of controlling the distribution of productive resources within the community. Simultaneously, they gave the state and European merchant houses another mechanism for extracting surpluses from peasant farmers.

While indirect rule constituted a political infrastructure that promoted the process of peasantization, it also helped to contain the process of rural economic transformation by ensuring the continuing salience of preexisting systems of authority, law, and custom. This created an indispensable role for authority-based systems of allocating productive resources within communities. The material bases of peasant society forced the colonial state to work through, and to depend on, the cooperation of local authorities, or "strongmen." Chiefs and other local-level authorities were charged with maintaining order and advancing the colonial economic agenda. They exercised discretionary powers in using force on behalf of the colonial state or in the name of tradition. While they played key roles in mobilizing, distributing, or withholding resources belonging to communities, they also mediated flows of resources claimed or allocated by the state. Strongmen embodied a decentralized and particularistic form of local administration that was, as Berman writes, one version of colonial divide-and-rule.

African political and social forces were fragmented, isolated and contained within the framework of local administrative units, which both protected the institutions of the colonial state from constant involvement in local issues and conflicts, and inhibited the coalescence of African opposition and resistance into a colony-wide challenge to the colonial order.[22]

Like caciques and patrons elsewhere, the strongmen of rural Africa were links in hierarchical chains made up of various forms of "personal rule."[23] Material conditions and the threat of revolt gave colonial administrators little choice but to project their power in this way. Above the chiefs in the colonial chain of command were European field administrators, the district officers and *commandants de circle*. Like chiefs, these administrators found themselves wielding starkly instrumental forms of power. As isolated figures with little military force at their immediate disposal, how were field officers able to maintain and exercise control within their jurisdictions? Berman argues that their success depended on their skill in manipulating the dependency of rural authorities and communities on the exercise of their personal discretion and prerogative. Out of necessity, central authorities were obliged to grant district officers considerable autonomy and room for maneuver. Field officers, in turn, used their prerogatives to cultivate patronistic relationships with those under their command, accommodating social forces that they feared they could not control. Through this process, coercion "faded into, although never disappeared from the background of day-to-day governance."[24] For the colonizers, the ideology of paternalism turned this necessity into a virtue.[25]

Governance through hierarchies of personal power was a pervasive mode of domination under colonialism. Personal discretion gave local-level authorities room and opportunity to modify policies from the center in response to local circumstances, or in order to promote or protect their own interests.[26] Berman writes that for "the central authorities, the issue was the degree to which [European] field agents' accommodation of local social forces could be tolerated before they became in fact agents of those interests against the center."[27] Colonial administrations faced a similar dilemma in dealing with their African allies.

When Lugard presented "indirect rule" as workable strategy of governance, he acknowledged limits to European domination in the African colonies. The colonial state's dependence on local intermediaries and allies created new privileged groups within African societies or allowed established powerholders to sustain their status and wealth. Collaborators were able to use their positions in the colonial system to their own advantage, often in ways that were not fully consistent with colonial ambitions. Berman writes that the chiefs

> showed constant tendencies to extort money from the populace, especially where they were responsible for collecting tax and received a cut of the proceeds as part of their rewards; to accumulate land and other property by means fair or foul, and to become the focus of intense local political struggles. Increasingly seen by the populace as creatures of the state, the chiefs compromised its authority.[28]

Colonial chiefs and the old oligarchies were often able to establish control over prime lands, call subjects to work their fields, and accumulate wealth through export crop production. They diversified their assets by investing in commerce and urban real estate, and by financing Western educations for their children. Grier writes that these processes placed the chiefs of the Gold Coast "at the center of the simultaneous destruction and preservation of the precapitalist modes of production" – and thus at the center of contradictions that marked the rural economy at large.[29] Colonialism's "collaborators" accumulated political and economic assets that enabled many of them to reproduce their power across generations, often in ways that were not wholly dependent on access to the state.

Colonial administrations displayed marked ambivalence toward economic transformations that worked to erode systems of social control associated with indirect rule.[30] The expansion of export crop production – a development so desired by colonial administrations – tended to produce social and political changes that were incompatible with the colonizers' ideal vision of an acquiescent peasantry securely under the thumb of "native authorities." Uneven economic development produced regions marked by relative rural prosperity, the rapid expansion of export crop production, and the emergence of increasingly distinct class divisions in rural society. Other regions were marked by rural decay, declining agricultural production, and increasing dependence on the "export" of migrant labor to cities and farms in more dynamic regions.[31] From the Great Depression onward, colonial administrations confronted the growth of permanently urbanized strata of the working poor. The social forces arising from these transformations worked to dissolve the political and economic structures of peasant society and, thus, the underpinnings of "native authority" and indirect rule. "Political unrest, in the form of local class conflict and anticolonial sentiments, was the usual consequence."[32]

Yet the continuous expansion of production and productivity in the rural economy necessarily implied the dissolution of peasant forms of production. Generalized access to land and the resilience of peasantries limited possibilities for investment, land consolidation, and reorganizing labor use to maximize output and lower real costs of production. Colonial administrators faced a dilemma, for they feared the political consequences of the economic changes required to extract ever-growing surpluses from the agricultural sector. The Europeans feared that attacks on the most fundamental interests of African farming households would produce political backlashes that they could not contain. They also feared the political implications of landlessness and proletarianization. Anne Phillips quotes Lord Lugard's summary, that

> the problem of today is to ensure that service with Europeans shall not result in the premature disintegration of native society. For the illiterate worker who has lost faith in the approval or the anger of the spirits of his forebears, who has renounced his tribal loyalties and his claim to a share in the family or clan land and the ready help of his fellows in time of need, has now no motive for self-control and becomes a danger to the State.[33]

Colonial administrations responded with efforts to find ways of "blocking or retarding the disintegration of the peasantry."[34] The basic contradiction in the dual project of accumulation and political control was manifest on this level. Inherent in the political vision that guided European colonialism was a recipe for economic stagnation.

For the colonial state and African producers, however, there was no stable equilibrium. Colonial economies and societies inevitably produced social forces that could not be contained within peasant society and the structures of indirect rule. African professional strata, merchants, big commercial farmers, proletarianized populations (including increasingly assertive working classes), and "the unemployed" had no place within the Europeans' vision of the ideal colonial order. In the post–World War II years, African colonies were rocked by political and economic crises that could not be contained or resolved within the framework of colonial modes of governance.

The crises and transitions of the early postwar years marked the beginning of the decolonization era. More broadly, the war can be seen as inaugurating the long transition from the "heyday" of European colonialism in Africa – the interwar years – to the present, when the political innovations of the decolonization era seem to have run their course. Some analysts have argued that decolonization gave capital a second chance in sub-Saharan Africa, for the new political order brought with it possibilities for transcending the political dilemmas and constraints that had paralyzed the colonial state. I argue, however, that decolonization did not prove to be this watershed. Instead, decolonization created opportunities for reconstructing colonial modes of governance and exploitation on a new footing. The first generation of African independence succeeded in neutralizing the immediate crises of the 1940s and 1950s by expanding, elaborating, and infusing new blood into old structures of political control and surplus appropriation. Ultimately, postcolonial regime consolidation and ruling-class formation were constrained by the same contradictions that had compromised the colonial project. Within two decades, it became clear that the untransformed bases of African agriculture could not bear the weight of the new political arrangements built upon them.

PEASANT FARMERS, THE MERCHANT STATE, AND THE CONSOLIDATION OF POSTCOLONIAL REGIMES

The crises of capital accumulation and political control that confronted colonial states after World War II intensified pressures on all sides for decolonization. In the span of about a decade, the British and French scrambled to devolve and delegate power in orderly and acceptable ways. They devised new institutions to channel social forces that threatened to swamp the colonial state: legal labor unions, legislative assemblies, and political parties. These institutions drew hitherto "uncaptured" elements into the embrace of the state and created new conduits for the distribution of state resources.[35] Worthy successors were groomed as colonial administrations tried with considerable success to exclude radical social forces from the political playing field. The mobilization of votes – a process manipulated by the colonial powers as well as by their aspiring successors – brought presidents, prime ministers, and parliaments to power.

For most political economists, institutions and actors were not the critical issue. At the time, what was seen as important was the political character of ruling strata and the inherent functions of the postcolonial state, and these were often seen as overdetermined by the circumstances attending transfers of power to neocolonial regimes. Analysts sought to theorize the issues at stake by defining Africa's new ruling strata as comprador classes, state bourgeoisies, bureaucratic bourgeoisies. These concepts underscored the intimate connections between access to state power and the emergence of new politically and economically dominant social strata. In seeing these new social strata as fully formed social classes, however, analysts overlooked the political uncertainties and economic contradictions of the times.

Roger Murray was one of the first within this analytic tradition to stress the fluidity of the historical moment, arguing that decolonization brought "unformed" social classes to power.[36] By definition, those who came to power were elites. But as Murray argued in analyzing the leadership and cadres of Ghana's ruling party in the late 1950s and early 1960s, this political elite was a "mixed stratum, concentrating many of the . . . tensions of colonial society. It is precisely the socially ambiguous and unstable character of this stratum which helps us to understand its *relative autonomy and volatility* in the political arena. The CPP 'political class' did not express or reflect a determinate economic class."[37] If this was true of the Convention People's Party and the "petty bourgeois salariat" at the core of its leadership and rank and file (clerks, primary schoolteachers, storekeepers, etc.), then it was also true of the other political parties born of the nationalist era. "Nationalist movements . . . in African colonies were inevitably *composite formations* embracing in an externally imposed unity elements which were extremely heterogeneous, both socially and ideologically."[38]

Conflicts of the nationalist era revealed tensions rooted in the disparate power bases and political needs of the aspiring postindependence elite. In their most obvious form, such tensions appeared in struggles over federal versus unitary constitutions and in competition between African authorities anchored in the politics of "indirect rule" and the new politicians of the cities. Closer inspection, however, reveals that territorially based parties and movements were built on multiple, overlapping, and potentially contradictory sources of political power and influence. Politicians at the helm of nationalist parties often built their personal treasuries and influence on power and wealth accumulated by chiefly or aristocratic families, and thus represented in part an extension and diversification of established social hierarchies.[39] By the same token, chiefly and aristocratic elements often pressed their "rightful claims to power" not only by appealing to tradition, but also by finding common cause with other wealthy farmers and merchant interests.[40] Within regions and at the national level, political infrastructure was erected for leaders of the late 1950s and the early 1960s largely through the *aggregation* of existing power structures. "Mass" nationalist parties pulled together leaders of urban communes and labor unions, holy men, prosperous farmers, poor farmers, merchants, professionals, colonial chiefs, and old oligarchies into regional-level coalitions capable of advancing bids for state power. Themes of ethnic chauvinism that ran through the discourse of the times gave expression to the material and political realities of localism, regionalism, and uneven development. Political notables who stood on the scaffolding of local and regional power bases had a stake in reproducing power *already achieved*. They correctly perceived access to the postcolonial state as a means of doing so.

For leaders newly installed at the national level, the challenge was to "balance rival power brokers who based their influence on ethnicity, religion or region and prevent their mutual antagonisms from getting out of control."[41] Decolonization opened new struggles between and within loosely integrated, heterogeneous, and often multiple coalitions for control over the state apparatus itself. The dynamics of this process shaped the subsequent course of change, including the trajectory of ruling-class formation. Seeing these elites as emergent, weak, or state "bourgeoisies" presupposed an answer to what, as Lonsdale points out, was a logically prior question: How were these classes formed?

It was not enough to point to one specific asset, property, or state office. No bourgeoisie can reproduce itself in its fragmentations. . . . One has to look at the formation of coalitions through conflict in order to understand how classes gather. If . . . coalition building is accepted as a problem, then the state ceases to be a thing and becomes rather a channel of action, or a resource. [This] . . . model can apply to not only postcolonial but to colonial and indeed to precolonial states in Africa. Precolonial kingdoms [can be seen] . . . as political arenas for the conflict of separate power holders, rather than as autonomous third parties above such competition.[42]

Lonsdale argues that from this perspective, the national ruling strata of contemporary Africa can be seen as not necessarily homogeneous in their origins and interests but, rather, derived from "a fusion of elites. They may not have had any joint interest other than the maintenance of a social order, but quite what social order . . . was itself a question. *Its answer depended very much upon the way in which the fused elites had themselves been formed and the type of power they now exercised.*"[43] To the extent that the type of power they now exercised was institutionalized, it was institutionalized in modes of surplus appropriation and domination established under colonialism.

These modes of appropriation and domination were intensified and extended as postcolonial regimes sought to consolidate power and forge some basis for rule. Grier provides an overview of this process in a succinct analysis of Ghana in the immediate postcolonial period:

A petite bourgeoisie which was predominantly state employed was being consolidated and many other lower-class elements found unskilled employment in the state sector. The material base for incorporating the petite bourgeoisie and for absorbing lower-class tension in general lay in appropriating surpluses from peasant producers. However, only if rural social and political relations remained untransformed could this appropriation take place. It was essential that land not take a commodity form, that labor relations remain dependent, that peasant producers grow most of their own food, and that all independent forms of political expression and social reorganization be blocked.[44]

In Ghana and elsewhere, state trading monopolies took over positions held by European merchant houses in the earlier period. This extended the "merchant functions" of the state and concentrated control over rural surpluses in the hands of bureaucrats, politicians, and others linked to new regimes.[45]

Like European merchant capital of the colonial period, state marketing boards were able to "buy cheap" from peasant farmers who cultivated nonmortgaged land by relying primarily on non-wage, family labor. Rates of accumulation in smallholder agriculture remained low, reproducing forms of rural poverty that had emerged during the colonial period. Low rates of productivity, technological innovation, and private capital formation in the rural sector were the socioeconomic consequences. Like colonial administrations, newly independent states sought to intensify production within the framework of the peasant farming economy by distributing productivity-enhancing (or -sustaining) inputs in the rural areas – on state-financed credit, through state-controlled cooperatives.[46] Indebtedness to cooperatives worked to protect farmers from the loss of their land, but at the same time tied them to the state and to production for state-controlled markets.[47] Through marketing boards, rural cooperatives, and the intensification of rural development schemes (including settlement schemes), postcolonial states pursued what had been central to the colonial project: the quest to "capture the peasants."[48]

Commercial mechanisms for "buying cheap and selling dear" in rural Africa,

along with localized and personalized modes of political control, were reproduced after independence. The struggle to draw cultivators into state-controlled
commodity markets proceeded alongside efforts aimed at ensuring that this
process would not culminate in the rise of landless and dispossessed rural
classes and, thus, the swelling of the urban lumpen proletariat. Tanzanian-style
rural socialism created a peasantry by resettling part of the rural population in
government-created villages organized around the production of crops for the
market.[49] Kenyan-style rural capitalism was tempered by the government's fear
of throwing independent freeholders off their land when they defaulted on the
mortgages and loans that had been sold so deliberately by both the colonial
and postcolonial regimes.[50] The Senegalese government undertook a holding
operation: "Inspired by the principles of 'African socialism,' this [land] reform
[of June 1964] aimed to restore the communal aspect of customary tenure, took
all land into national domain except that which was held under individual title,
and provided for the creation of local councils to allocate land to farmers and to
oversee the use of the land."[51] Back-to-the-land programs in places like Nigeria
and Côte d'Ivoire repatriated unemployed urban youths to the rural areas so that
they could cultivate in state-sponsored settlement schemes or in their home
areas. In characteristic fashion, the South African state carried this logic to its
extreme, attempting to "retribalize" and discipline its unruly proletariat by
consigning workers' families to below-subsistence agriculture and indirect rule
in "bantustans" and "homelands."

In postcolonial sub-Saharan Africa, state marketing boards, the extension of
rural cooperatives, and the intensification of rural development schemes targeted
at peasant farming communities expanded the presence of the state in the
countryside and increased state spending in the rural areas. To varying degrees,
access to opportunities for private accumulation through rural trading circuits
was also mediated by state agencies, giving the state an even broader role in
organizing the rural economy in general and rural commerce in particular.[52] The
political forces structuring the postcolonial rural economy worked to channel
the energies and capital of rural power brokers and accumulating classes toward
the most lucrative, least risky avenues for private gain: opportunities in the
political arena and in state-mediated business activities.

Bureaucratization of control over rural markets – markets for export commodities, agricultural inputs, and credit – created new, expanded roles for rural
strongmen who could use their discretionary control over the flow and distribution of state resources to reinforce or re-create networks of political control in
the countryside. As Bates writes, these forms of control over resource flows
help to explain the "intense politicization of farm input programs."

In Zambia [for example], access to subsidized inputs could best be obtained by most
rural dwellers by membership in agricultural cooperative societies. The societies were
formed by local units of the governing party and are now dominated by them; access to
inputs is therefore contingent upon political loyalty. The rural loans program . . . was

run at the local level by former party "militants" who helped to insure that [loans] were given to those who contributed to the cause of the party in power.[53]

As farming families' usufruct rights were "privatized" and as population pressure on the land increased, control over terms of access to markets, inputs, and credit eclipsed control over allocating land as the linchpin of rural authority.[54] Rural authorities remained anchored in the economic structures of peasant commodity production.

Even where incumbents changed, the role of "rural strongman" was thus preserved and often extended on terms quite favorable to local-level notables and agents of the state. They gained access to and control over new resources and opportunities for private gain. State structures in the countryside absorbed rural traders, the most dynamic farmers, and professionals in the small towns into state employment, the ruling party apparatus, or state-mediated commercial opportunities. "Collaborators" and "progressive farmers" of the colonial period were often incorporated into the patronage networks and governing structures of new regimes. Where the institution of chieftaincy was abolished in response to popular discontent, the rural strongmen of the colonial period were replaced by rural administrators, party men, and local notables linked securely to those now in power. Building and strengthening political machines in the countryside was part of the process that modernization theorists called "national integration." Bayart calls this same process *la recherche hégémonique* – the quest for state hegemony.

Agrarian societies structured around peasant farming underwrote the consolidation of political power in the hands of those controlling the state apparatus. The chief productive asset under private African control – land – remained in the hands of small-scale, household producers who continued to grow export crops alongside food crops that were consumed, for the most part, in-house. Peasant farmers' control over land reflected and worked to perpetuate the absence of a class of large-scale, capitalist or estate farmers in most of sub-Saharan Africa. Farming regions settled by European colonialists (like parts of Rhodesia, Zambia, and Kenya) were the exception that proved the rule. It was in these places that African cultivators had been forcibly alienated from the land to clear the way (and provide labor) for politically powerful commercial farming interests.[55] Throughout most of postcolonial Africa, the structure of agrarian society did not provide the basis for the development of vigorous, accumulating classes independent of the state. State control over rural surpluses – and the related weakness of local capital – provided the material and political base for incorporating heterogeneous elements of the independence era elite into new "political classes" linked to the state.

Control over commercial circuits placed the state at the "commanding heights" of economies organized around the cultivation of export crops by peasant farmers. Trade remained the primary locus of capital accumulation and the most important mechanism for concentrating resources in the measure and forms necessary for investment. Most regimes moved quickly to institutionalize state control over postcolonial commerce, preempting and circumscribing possibilities for the spontaneous movement of private African traders into commercial niches left open by the partial restructuring of colonial forms of trade. Building on the regulatory apparatus of the colonial state, postcolonial governments licensed wholesalers and importers, controlled imports through tax and tariff regimes, and fixed the prices of agricultural commodities, agricultural inputs, and staple consumer goods. Controls over trade, especially government monopolies over the purchase and sale of export crops, generated the bulk of state revenue derived from internal sources. Administrative controls over trade and traders also allowed governments to regulate private access to commercial opportunities in the city as well as in the countryside. By suppressing competition among merchants, regulating the supply of imported commodities, and allocating subsidized credit, state intervention in markets generated rents that could be appropriated by the state itself or allocated to private traders who were singled out for preferential treatment.[56]

The sedimenting of bureaucratic control over the postcolonial economy was not confined to the commercial sector. Regimes expanded parastatal banking sectors and invested in industry, usually in partnership with foreign capital. In the 1960s, urban infrastructure and social services (including state-built housing) expanded rapidly, guaranteeing the government's position as the leading spender and employer in the urban areas. Under these conditions, the appropriation and distribution of wealth by the state constituted the primary internal force shaping patterns of social stratification. The political monopoly of ruling parties and the continued *étatisation* of the economy narrowed avenues for aggregating power in society – especially economic power – outside of the aegis of the state, working to block the emergence of rival political estates.[57] As Naomi Chazan writes in her contribution to this volume, "middle-level social organizations were enfeebled."

These structural conditions underwrote the efficacy of state patronage as a mechanism of political integration and control. Repression narrowed the scope of the political arena, and regimes undertook to "colonize" social groups that colonial "indirect rule" failed to control or contain: nascent capitalist strata, African traders, the urban middle classes of professionals and civil servants, and the skilled urban proletariat. Corporatist forms of control worked to domesticate labor unions and to integrate women's, youth, student, teacher, and merchant associations into vertically structured patron–client networks loosely centralized at the level of the ruling party and the state. Economic ascent and privilege (through access to jobs, housing, higher education, business opportunities) became ever more dependent on the discretionary allocation of state-controlled resources, and thus ever more contingent on political loyalty or acquiescence to those already, or more firmly, in power. Co-optation – largely through the distribution of state jobs and state patronage – became an attractive option under these conditions. "Access [became] the key resource."[58] Through this process, organized political forces were "embraced and suffocated in the bosom of the party."[59] Repression, co-optation, and state patronage revamped and expanded the system of parochial political control that had worked to fragment and isolate social forces during the colonial period.

The branching out of political machines within political machines drew new social strata into the orbit of state patronage and state control. State employment, or reliance on state contracts or licenses, placed some urban social groups in a position of structural dependency on state resources. For other urban professional groups, industrial workers in the private sector, and the poorest of the urban poor, however, patronage politics could elicit political acquiescence only on continuously renegotiated terms. Patronage politics thus provided a tenuous basis for regime consolidation and governance. To finance state spending in the urban areas, regimes systematically siphoned off the surpluses generated by peasant farmers. Institutional structures such as cooperatives and marketing boards, input-distribution programs, and hierarchies of political patronage rooted in communities all worked to organize and facilitate this process of surplus appropriation, but these arrangements were themselves increasingly dependent on the flow of state resources and patronage to the countryside. Regimes' capacities to mobilize the needed resources were strained severely. They "squeezed the peasantry" and turned to foreign borrowing.

These processes promoted "the coalescing of elites within the matrices of the state."[60] Co-optation widened access to the state and state resources, expanding ruling coalitions while reducing the autonomy of power brokers incorporated into them. Infusing state resources into existing social networks worked to tie local-level structures of political and social control to the center. Zolberg provides an illustration of this process when describing the "Ivorian political formula" circa 1970.

This formula appeared around 1950 . . . [The strategy consisted of] the building up of a heterogeneous coalition in which components would retain their distinctive identity. This coalition would be maintained only by enhancing the legitimacy of its leader, Houphouët-Boigny, and by distributing tangible benefits to key components, including the emerging bourgeoisie and the ethnic groups. . . . From this vantage point, there [was] no need for a direct confrontation between modernity and traditionalism.[61]

Notables in the rural areas, religious leaders, union leaders, politicians, and business magnates remained or became more dependent on resources distributed by the state. At the same time, these power brokers amassed private wealth through salaries, perquisites, government contracts, state-allocated business opportunities, rent collecting, and the privatization of state resources. Members of emergent political classes built personal fortunes at impressive rates and, as Donal Cruise O'Brien states with reference to Senegal, in measures "roughly proportional to each individual's standing within the official hierarchy."[62]

"Politicized accumulation" promoted the embourgeoisement of ruling strata and provided a material basis of consensus, otherwise lacking, for the cohesion of the ruling coalition.[63] To see the process as unstructured, unconstrained, or guided solely by individual and corporate interests in material gain is to miss the key fact, however. Clientelism and patronage were necessary corollaries of politicized accumulation, organizing the process into a system of political control. State resources flowed through vertically structured patron–client networks held together by the gravitational pull of self-interest and personalistic relationships of political loyalty, dependency, and vulnerability to sanctions from above. Within the corridors of power as well as outside them, the system created formidable incentives "to go along for fear of losing out entirely."[64] The particularistic and politically contingent allocation of state resources interlaced and broadened ruling coalitions. Patronage politics provided a material basis of consensus *and control* within ruling coalitions, oiling and structuring the processes by which regimes coalesced into economically dominant social strata.

As the expression "fusion of elites" implies, regime consolidation involved qualitative transformations in the nature of ruling coalitions and in the kind of power they exercised. There is a clear sense in which control over state power and politicized accumulation transformed ruling elites into economically dominant "classes-in-themselves." Members of the political elite shared a common position in what could be called the social relations of surplus *appropriation*. Rural surpluses flowed systematically "from peasants to bureaucrats."[65] Yet as Roger Murray emphasized, this new, dominant social stratum did not occupy a shared and determinate position in the *production* process. Their coherence as a social group and their position vis-à-vis subordinate social strata were defined by their ability to siphon off rural surpluses through the merchant functions of the state. New ruling coalitions quickly emerged as social classes in this sense, and were often perceived by their subjects as such. Factional and coalitional conflict centered around the allocation of this wealth, taking on the character of intraclass conflicts that, at the end of the day, betrayed an underlying and common commitment to enhancing means by which the state could distribute wealth to its agents and clients. The peasant base of these agrarian societies, the enduring weakness of local capital, and the disparate nature of the ruling elite turned out to be critical in this regard, for in spite of their heterogeneity, ruling alliances found common cause in aggrandizement through the state itself.[66] For emergent ruling strata, patronage politics and politicized accumulation provided a composite solution to the problem of governance and exploitation.

Yet patronage-based access to the state was not sufficient to reconcile, much less homogenize, the more fundamental interests represented by disparate elements contained within postcolonial regimes. The distribution of resources per se could not organize the programmatic exercise of state power or unite ruling coalitions in support of a broad, "transformative" social project. Class formation, urbanization, uneven development, and pressure on the land had created social strata with disparate and even conflicting needs and interests. These differences produced fault lines within regimes and inherent strains in territory-, ethnicity-, and religion-based forms of political power. Those managing regimes from the top sought to mediate and contain these tensions by incorporating power brokers with potentially contradictory political needs into ruling coalitions. Limits to state power were manifest in regimes' dependence on the acquiescence and political survival of their allies, and in the irreducible measure of autonomy that these elements retained. Power brokers rarely became wholly dependent on state resources, for the forms of authority, legitimacy, and power they enjoyed could not be fully reproduced, reconciled, or superseded through the exercise of state power. The ability of urban bosses, rival politicians, *marabouts,* ethnic leaders, and old oligarchies to secure and sustain access to state resources – in effect, to demand co-optation – was a function of their ability to influence constituencies, followers, and communities. Although the "fusion of elites" expanded ruling coalitions and their social bases of support (or acquiescence), the power of states hinged on the strength of particularistic, localized, and potentially contradictory forms of authority and modes of social control.

At a fundamental level, tensions inherent in the composite character of ruling coalitions were manifest over questions of land. Land remained the most political of issues, for patterns of control over the land undergirded the political and social organization of rural society, and defined the channels and mechanisms through which agricultural surpluses could be appropriated. Mandating land reform from above remained a live or latent option, pressed by those committed to increasing the productive capacity of the rural sector as well as by those interested in breaking the backs of reactionary "feudal," chiefly, or "petty bourgeois" power brokers in the countryside. In the early 1960s, populist proposals to reorganize patterns of land tenure in Senegal were advanced as a way of freeing small producers from the grip of the "aristocratic" Islamic *marabouts* – clearing the underbrush of local-level networks of dependency, control, and exploitation. This process would open new avenues for influencing production itself. As things turned out in Senegal, it was the reformers, rather than the *marabouts,* who fell from power. In Tanzania, *ujamma* in the countryside consolidated a peasantry and weakened the most prosperous commercial farmers and rural merchants, two groups that compromised the hegemony of the emergent "bureaucratic bourgeoisie." The structures and processes of *ujamma,* however, created a rural party-bureaucratic elite ensconced in new villages and state-controlled production and marketing schemes. The position of this new stratum was staked on defending the status quo, rather than on pushing forward "transformative" and productivity-enhancing projects mandated from above. The Tanzanian government created a new group of rural power brokers that it could undercut only at the risk of destabilizing its own networks of influence and control in the countryside.[67]

The political issues at stake in struggles over land reforms involved much more than center-versus-periphery competition, or struggles between old and new elites. State-mandated changes in land tenure and land-use systems imposed political costs and risks not only on rural authorities, but also on those managing ruling coalitions from the top. Where state-led restructurings of rural society would subvert the authority of rural strongmen linked to regimes, the costs and risks were high. Reforms could threaten the cohesion of established hierarchies of power by undercutting existing channels of resource appropriation and allocation, intensifying centrifugal pressures within ruling coalitions, and inviting local- and regional-level notables to defect along with their subjects, followers, and constituents. Proposals for state-initiated changes in systems of land tenure and land use often produced stalemates, for the power of those on the top rested on the cohesion of ruling alliances and on the power structures that produced political order and acquiescence on the local level.[68]

Postcolonial regimes, then, constructed forms of "indirect rule" that in many ways were similar to those of the colonial period. The capacity of smallholding farmers to retain the measure of autonomy that came from control over land goes far in explaining the parallel. Postcolonial regimes remained dependent on wealth extracted from peasant farmers, and thus on the commercial and patronage hierarchies that linked peasant farming communities to state-controlled networks of trade and political power. The state's role as a dominant force structuring wealth appropriation and accumulation, in turn helped perpetuate the weakness of local capital. Local capital tended to remain weak not only because governments monopolized potentially lucrative economic activities such as export crop purchasing, but also because individuals able to use their status and authority to promote their business interests were often absorbed into regimes' rent-generating and rent-collecting patronage networks. Yet, as in the colonial period, "indirect rule" and co-optation were inherently contradictory processes, for rulers depended on, and were compromised by, the power brokers through which they sought to govern.

As Bayart points out, political independence did represent a decisive rupture with the earlier period: Powerful elements within African society began to "reappropriate" the institutions of the state.[69] The fusion of elites found its institutional corollary in transformations in the structure and workings of the inherited state apparatus. New administrative structures and sprawling bureaucracies were the concrete manifestations of "inclusionary," co-optive, and patronage-based strategies of regime consolidation.[70] Existing hierarchies of political power and access were extended upward, into the institutional structures of the state itself. Patron–client networks reconfigured the distribution of power with state institutions, fracturing, dividing, and redividing administrative prerogative along the horizontal and vertical lines of patron–client networks that formed within the party, bureaucracies, and agencies of the government. Control at the top extended downward through these networks, rooting the state in social processes that lay outside the scope of direct state control. This was a process of state formation that allowed most postcolonial regimes to establish a loose and unstable form of hegemony. The failures of politics emerged out of the same process. In settings such as Ghana, Nigeria, and Sudan, the ruling party and the civil service "came to reflect all the cleavages in the country . . . [and] political system[s] collapsed under the strain of . . . particularly fierce struggle[s] over the spoils of power."[71] Hegemony and its antithesis, disintegration, arose out of the social processes that embedded postcolonial states and regimes ever more securely in underlying structures of power in society. Donal Cruise O'Brien's image of states entangled at the grass roots is apposite.[72]

By expanding and intensifying colonial modes of governance and exploitation, postcolonial regime consolidation worked to reproduce contradictions that had paralyzed the colonial state. Monopoly control over trading circuits allowed postcolonial states to extract peasant surpluses via "unequal exchange," just as European merchant houses had in the earlier period. Like European capital, most regimes refrained from investing directly in production, finding it more profitable, less risky, and more expedient to intensify peasant production. Frustrated attempts to "bypass the peasantry" through the creation of state farms reinforced the lesson that European capitalists and the treasurers of the colonial state had learned during the colonial period.[73] Without large-scale alienation of the land from smallholders, labor was hard to mobilize and control. Hired labor tended to raise the financial costs of estate production above those prevailing in the peasant farming sector, and competition from smallholders tended to undercut large-scale producers. Given the existing structure of control over land, extracting peasant surpluses through commercial circuits remained as "necessary" for the postcolonial state as it was for the colonial state.

Transcending the limits of peasant forms of production through deliberate state action threatened to accelerate the erosion of prevailing social structures and the old and new political arrangements built upon them. Using state power to accelerate movement toward forms of rural production based on wage labor and open land-markets (through reforms that would register, title, and mortgage land, for example) would intensify the formation and polarization of social classes in the countryside, driving more landless and indigent people to the cities and fueling the rise of independent, rural accumulating classes. Postcolonial regimes, like colonial administrations, had much to fear in the social and political consequences of such processes. Private appropriation and reinvestment of rural surpluses would come at the expense of the state's capacity to control these resources directly. The positions of postcolonial ruling classes would become increasingly vulnerable, for the shrinking of the resource base of the state would erode the material basis of consensus, accommodation, and control that promoted and sustained a "fusion of elites."

Could ruling coalitions find common cause in promoting changes that would erode social relations of production and power that underpinned their dominance? When this question is confronted, it becomes much more difficult to sustain the expectation that postcolonial regimes would use state power programatically to promote capitalist development and rural transformation.[74] The trade-off helps explain regimes' ambivalent stance in the face of reform proposals aimed at promoting rural capitalism at the expense of peasant farmers. More generally, the material bases of established forms of political domination help account for the ambivalence and caution of postcolonial rulers with regard to "market logic." Survival strategies of both rulers and peasants have militated against the emergence of fully capitalist forms of control over land and labor.

The postcolonial state, like the colonial state, remains caught between what Berman called "the contradictory demands of accumulation and political control." These tensions have been compounded over the course of the postcolonial period, contributing to what social scientists have come to understand as the persistent economic and political crises of the African state.

CONCLUSION

Debates between those who stress the "strength" of African states and those who stress their "weaknesses" underscore the contradictions of the postcolonial state. The process of regime consolidation sharpened both faces of power, bringing some of the most acute tensions in the political economy at large to full expression within the core structures and processes of the postcolonial state. "Inclusionary" and co-optive regimes were built by inflating the inherited state apparatus, strengthening armies, neutralizing legal structures for popular political participation and representation, and enhancing the state's capacity to appropriate and allocate resources. These changes in the structure of the state were integral to regime consolidation as it unfolded in postcolonial Africa, and analysts were not off the mark when they pointed to the "strength" of the African state as an institution of authoritarian rule, repression, and the extraction of rural surpluses via state-monopolized commercial circuits.

State patronage and clientelism emerged as loosely centralized modes of political control and governance, operating both at the level of the regime and within the political economy at large. This system of control helped to consolidate regimes by offering access to state resources in exchange for political acquiescence. Disparate elements could be welded into ruling coalitions on the basis of their stake in this all-or-nothing game, which not only enriched its principle players but also provided them with resources needed to build or sustain power bases of their own. As disparate patron–client networks were extended and pulled together at the level of the regime, bureaucratic power was fragmented along the same lines. Factionalism at the top, which appeared in the form of "palace politics" or personal power struggles, often grew out of fissures that extended far beyond the boundaries of the state itself. The private appropriation of state resources and the use of state funds to strengthen personalistic power networks were not aberrations or by-products of postcolonial political practice – they lay at the very heart of the process by which postcolonial regimes were consolidated and by which they sought to govern.

Over time, however, it has become increasingly clear that the same processes weakened the state as an instrument for organizing, exercising, and ultimately reproducing state power. Through the process of regime consolidation, state power was fragmented and privatized. The power of the state became increasingly contingent on the capacity of individual power brokers to use instrumental and material rewards and sanctions to enforce quiescence to the political status quo. As this system took shape, the postcolonial state – so much "softer," less coherent, and more "permeated by local social forces" than the colonial state – displayed a trait that it inherited from its predecessor: immobilism.[75] The colonial state had proved to be incapable of containing social forces that emerged out of the economic transformations that colonialism itself had set in motion. If the Europeans had opted for governance over economic development in the rural areas when faced with a choice between the two, then postcolonial regimes also opted, implicitly but in strict accordance with "rulers' imperative," for political control at the cost of social and economic transformation. The strains and limits of this process were cumulative and mutually reinforcing.

These strains and limits are manifest in the economic and political crises of the current period. On one hand, the postcolonial strategy of regime consolidation drove the expansion of the merchant functions of the state. This provided the state with material resources that could be used to build networks of power linked to the regime, increased state control over the process of private accumulation (and therefore over the distribution of power in society), and preempted deliberate strategies aimed at accelerating the process of capitalist transformation in the rural areas. On the other hand, this process could not be sustained over time. As colonial merchant houses and colonial regimes had discovered, the capacity of the rural economy to produce a growing surplus within the framework of peasant farming structures could not be expanded infinitely. The postcolonial state, like the colonial state, was forced to turn to borrowing abroad to sustain and enlarge its resource base. The scale and intensity of foreign borrowing were magnified in the postcolonial period, largely because the political imperatives that fueled the demand for resources became so much more acute.

Struggles over rural surpluses may have weakened postcolonial states long before "structural" limits to peasant-based export crop production were reached. In a peasant farming economy, a monopsonistic commercial system is vulnerable to producers' strikes, the corrosive rise of competition, and the process of rural decay. In sub-Saharan Africa, producers' strikes can take the form of gradual divestment of land and labor from export crop production in order to favor self-provisioning and the localized exchange of food surpluses. Competition can take the form of parallel markets. Both processes deprive the state of resources, making it difficult to sustain (much less expand) existing state-centered patron–client networks, and difficult to ensure that multiple and disparate power hierarchies remain linked to and dependent upon the center.[76] Meanwhile, the parallel economy gives rise to sources of wealth and power that lie beyond the reach of direct political control, eroding the capacity of the state to suffocate potentially competing loci of power.[77] The political threat of rural decay presents itself in the form of the urban poor, who create and sustain economic and social networks (the so-called informal sector) that lie outside established structures of political and economic control. Forces that have conspired to produce the current crisis – external debt, dependency on imported foodstuffs, and rural decay – coalesce, producing explosions like "IMF riots" when the urban poor take to the streets to protest increases in the price of (imported) food staples imposed by the International Monetary Fund.

What about the capacity of Africa's ruling classes to transcend what appear to be "inherent limits" to the political and economic systems consolidated in the 1960s? Dependency theorists looked to the international system and international capital to find structural constraints on the continuous development of Africa's productive capacities. Analysts such as Bill Warren responded with a logical and plausible counterargument, saying that the interests of capital were best served by the full development of capitalist social relations in Africa.[78] This was the reasoning that provided grounds for the argument that the process of primitive accumulation (mostly through the private appropriation of state resources), and pressures to enhance the productive bases of African economies, would gradually transform Africa's political classes into capitalist classes.

Analysis of postcolonial regime consolidation makes it possible to qualify this argument in several critical ways, and to see why stagnationist tendencies might prevail in the face of "capital logic." The capital logic school tends to abstract postcolonial ruling classes from historical and political context, and thus to posit the existence of coherent "state classes" or "political classes" that are unconstrained by interests and social relations reproduced outside the processes of the state. This model seems "to allow for an almost infinite variety of political practices" guided only by the corporate, long-term interests of members of this social stratum.[79] If, however, regime consolidation, coalition building, and the structural underpinnings of these processes are taken as serious analytic issues, a rather different picture emerges.

Regime consolidation was a political process that involved not only creating new structures and relations of power, but also tying existing structures of societally based power to the state. Modes of governance and exploitation were shaped by social forces that could subvert or strengthen these underpinnings of state authority, as well as by societally based competition for advantage within and through the institutions of government. Subsequent courses of change were mediated by the specific ways in which rulers sought, through political action and by using "the state as a resource," to manage and contain these conflicts, govern, and thus retain their hold on power. This process qualified and constrained state power – and the possibilities for development of any kind.

Ruling classes in postcolonial Africa were constituted through the use of state resources to satisfy the multiple and sometimes conflicting interests and political needs of the heterogeneous elements embraced within ruling coalitions. Patronage politics provided an instrumental, material basis of consensus – a lowest common denominator – for building ruling classes, working to divert political conflicts away from broader issues concerning the purposes of state power and toward short-run competition for access to state resources. If it was possible to bring about a "fusion of elites" in this sense, it was also quite possible that this fusion would remain partial, tenuous, and based on instrumental political alliances. It would not necessarily "fuse" elites on the basis of a common commitment and political need to promote a certain kind of structural transformation of economy and society. Absent this common interest, regime consolidation was likely to be aimed at sustaining and expanding the ruling alliance rather than transforming the disparate elements within it. The way in which ruling coalitions were constituted, and the political actions undertaken in the effort to sustain them, limited the likelihood that as a "ruling class" they could act upon what can be construed a shared, long-term interest in using political power to ensure the reproduction of state power, the material base of the state, and their own existence as a dominant class via capitalist transformation.

Most regimes in sub-Saharan Africa turned to efforts to intensify the extraction of wealth produced by peasant farmers. Forms of rural decay, impoverishment, and de facto resistance that often resulted made it increasingly difficult to reproduce the political and economic relationships that shored up postcolonial regimes. The material bases of ruling classes and states began to erode. The observation that African ruling classes constitute "classes in themselves" but not "classes for themselves" seems to take on its most explicit meaning in these circumstances. The patterns of political practice that led to the growing dysfunctionality of the state as an instrument for organizing and exercising power, counterproductive efforts to "squeeze the peasantry," and the unproductive buildup of wealth in the hands of ruling strata are symptoms of forces that have produced the current crisis. In many cases, there seems to be no social agent at the level of the state capable of transcending the crisis, and just as importantly, state power does not seem to exist in the measure or forms necessary for such an undertaking.

NOTES

1 Goran Hyden, *No Shortcuts to Progress* (London: Heinemann, 1983), p. 19.
2 Bruce Berman makes this point in "Structure and Process in the Bureaucratic States of Colonial Africa," *Development and Change,* 15 (1984): 166. See also J.-F. Bayart, "Le politique par le bas en Afrique noire: Questions de méthode," *Politique Africaine* (January 1981): 53–82.

3 See, for example, Nicola Swainson, *The Development of Corporate Capitalism in Kenya: 1918–1977* (Los Angeles: University of California Press, 1980); Bjorn Beckman, "Whose State? State and Capitalist Development in Nigeria," *Review of African Political Economy*, 23 (1982): 37–51; Richard Sklar, "The Nature of Class Domination in Africa," *Journal of Modern African Studies*, 17, no. 4 (1979): 531–52.

4 Berman, "Structure and Process"; Anne Phillips, *The Enigma of Colonialism: British Policy in West Africa* (London: James Currey, 1989). See also Michael J. Watts, "Class in Northern Nigeria, 1900–1945," in Paul Lubeck, ed., *The African Bourgeoisie* (Boulder, Colo.: Lynne Rienner, 1987), p. 69 inter alia.

5 Berman, "Structure and Process."

6 In settler colonies (Kenya, Rhodesia, and South Africa), this strategy was played out through the creation of "reserves" that were governed "indirectly" through African authorities. The economies of the reserves were organized around food crop production and the supply of labor to settler farming areas.

7 Robert Shenton, *The Development of Capitalism in Northern Nigeria* (London: James Currey, 1986), pp. 102–103.

8 "Peasant farming" is one variant of household-organized agricultural production. My definition of the term underscores two features of peasant farming that are important to the argument advanced here. First, peasant farmers are independent commodity producers who use simple tools and rely largely on family labor to produce both food for themselves and surpluses that are sold outside the community. Second, the commodity surpluses that these farmers produce are appropriated in large part by other (nonfarming) social groups. They are "independent" farmers in the sense that control over the land they work, control over their labor power, and ownership of most of the tools they use lie within communities or households, rather than in social groups able to accumulate most of the surplus generated by commodity production. I use the terms "peasant farmers," "peasantries," "peasantization," and "peasant economy" with reference to this definition. On this, see Jonathan Barker, *Rural Communities Under Stress: Peasant Farmers and the State in Africa* (Cambridge: Cambridge University Press, 1989), pp. 36–43, 54–69; Gavin Williams, "The World Bank and the Peasant Problem," in Judith Heyer, Pepe Roberts, and Gavin Williams, eds., *Rural Development in Tropical Africa* (New York: St. Martin's Press, 1981), pp. 16–51; and Goran Hyden, *Beyond Ujamaa in Tanzania: Underdevelopment and an Uncaptured Peasantry* (University of California Press, 1980), esp. pp. 9–16.

9 See, for example, Jannik Boesen, "Les paysans et l'exportation du café – Une région exportatrice de café en Tanzanie," in Samir Amin, ed., *L'agriculture Africaine et le capitalisme* (Paris: Editions Anthropos-IDEP, 1975), pp. 107–142.

10 Phillips, *The Enigma of Colonialism*, pp. 2–3.

11 For an analysis of merchant capital in colonial Africa, see G. B. Kay, *The Political Economy of Colonialism in Ghana* (London: Cambridge University Press, 1972), and *Development and Underdevelopment: A Marxist Analysis* (London: Macmillan, 1975).

12 As Shenton writes, merchant capital in Northern Nigeria "was essentially parasitical in nature, . . . it sought to batten on to pre-existing forms of surplus appropriation, and . . . it sought, in a profoundly conservative fashion, to preserve rather than to transform the pre-existing forces and social relations of production in Northern Nigeria" (Shenton, *The Development of Capitalism in Northern Nigeria*, p. xiii.). See also Michael Cowen, "Commodity Production in Kenya's Central Province," in Heyer et al., eds., *Rural Development in Tropical Africa*, p. 128.

13 Phillips, *The Enigma of Colonialism*, p. 158.

14 See Lonsdale, "States and Social Processes in Africa: A Historiographical Survey," *African Studies Review,* 24, nos. 2–3 (June–September 1981): 139–225.

15 Elliot P. Skinner, *The Mossi of Burkina Faso: Chiefs, Politicians and Soldiers* (Prospect Heights, Ill.: Waveland Press, 1989), p. 156.

16 Cited by Beverly Grier, "Contradiction, Crisis, and Class Conflict: The State and Capitalist Development in Ghana Prior to 1948," in I. L. Markovitz, ed., *Studies in Power and Class in Africa* (New York: Oxford University Press, 1987), p. 35.

17 Phillips (*The Enigma of Colonialism,* pp. 156–157) writes that through colonial law in British West Africa, the "chiefs were confirmed in their position as political authorities with continuing powers over the regulation of communal land."

18 Ibid., pp. 2–3.

19 See Shenton, *The Development of Capitalism in Northern Nigeria,* p. 126.

20 In regions such as the Gold Coast, peasant indebtedness did lead to land alienation and thus threatened the peasantry itself. Credit and marketing cooperatives were introduced in the 1930s to "shore up the peasantry" (Grier, "Contradiction, Crisis, and Class Conflict," p. 47). See also Phillips, *The Enigma of Colonialism,* p. 131.

21 See Shenton, *The Development of Capitalism in Northern Nigeria,* pp. 107, 127 inter alia.

22 Berman, "Structure and Process," p. 187. As Naomi Chazan states in Chapter 10 of this volume, the "social order in these frameworks was fragmented and dispersed. In most situations, European rules stringently demarcated local communities to facilitate administrative control. . . . The British, and in some instances the French, ruled through local potentates and were as dependent on their durability as these strongmen were dependent on the colonial state."

23 Jackson and Rosberg use the concept of "personal rule" to describe governance in postcolonial Africa. What is interesting are continuities along this dimension that span the colonial and postcolonial periods. The continuity raises questions about the extent to which "personal rule" is rooted, as Jackson and Rosberg argue, in a distinctly indigenous "political style." The continuity suggests that "personal rule" may be rooted in underlying, structural conditions. See Robert H. Jackson and Carl G. Rosberg, *Personal Rule in Black Africa* (Los Angeles: University of California Press, 1982).

24 Berman, "Structure and Process," p. 175.

25 Phillips, *The Enigma of Colonialism.*

26 Personal discretion gave field officers "substantial opportunity to modify or ignore policies from the centre they disliked." Berman, "Structure and Process," p. 181.

27 Ibid., p. 176.

28 Ibid., p. 189. For example, see Robert Bates, *Rural Responses to Industrialization: A Study of Village Zambia* (New Haven: Yale University Press, 1976), pp. 82–87.

29 Grier, "Contradiction, Crisis, and Class Conflict," p. 35.

30 This ambivalence marked British and French colonial projects in West Africa and even, according to Lonsdale and Berman, in the mixed settler–peasant economy of Kenya. See J. Lonsdale and B. Berman, "Coping with the Contradictions: The Development of the Colonial State in Kenya: 1895–1914," *Journal of African History,* 20 (1979): 487–505. Giovanni Arrighi makes a similar point about pre–World War II Rhodesia in "Labor Supplies in Historical Perspective: A Study of the Proletarianization of the African Peasantry in Rhodesia," in Giovanni Arrighi and John S. Saul, eds., *Essays on the Political Economy of Africa* (New York: Monthly Review Press, 1973), pp. 180–234.

31 Taxation was used to "draw forth" migrant labor rather than export commodities from the "labor reserve" economies of colonial Africa. In East and southern Africa,

deliberate state action held back commodity production in "reserves" in order to ensure a continuing supply of labor to mines and European-owned farms. With time, overcrowding and exhaustion of the land in the reserves had the same effect. In West Africa, parts of Sahel (Upper Volta, for example) evolved as "labor reserve regions" supplying migrant labor to export crop–producing zones closer to the coast.

32 Grier, "Contradiction, Crisis, and Class Conflict," p. 28.

33 Phillips, *The Enigma of Colonialism*, p. 139.

34 Grier, "Contradiction, Crisis, and Class Conflict," p. 28. Phillips, Grier, and Shenton all use the case of the West Africa Lands Commission to drive home the argument that colonial administrations displayed marked reluctance to endorse or promote open land markets, private markets for rural credit, and permanent settlement of workers in the cities.

35 "[Marketing board] price stabilization funds began to be channelled [in the mid-1950s] into 'development' under the auspices of those Nigerians who would soon inherit state power. Through this action the floodgates of politics were opened. In the north and in the south, the regional marketing board surpluses were raided for 'development' expenditure which became synonymous with the use of these funds as a major tool in the construction of the political parties of independence." Shenton, *The Development of Capitalism in Northern Nigeria*, p. 115.

36 Roger Murray, "Second Thoughts on Ghana," *New Left Review,* 42 (March–April 1967): 25–39. For context and commentary, see John S. Saul, "The Unsteady State: Uganda, Obote, and General Amin," in John S. Saul, *The State and Revolution in East Africa* (New York: Monthly Review Press, 1979), esp. pp. 350–366.

37 Murray, "Second Thoughts," p. 29.

38 Ibid., p. 27.

39 To take one example, the man who has dominated Ivoirian politics since the 1940s, Félix Houphouët-Boigny, was not only a medical doctor but also a landholder, a prosperous cocoa farmer, and the son of one of French colonialism's chiefly families. For general discussions, see Lonsdale, "States and Social Processes in Africa," p. 201, and Bayart, *L'Etat en Afrique* (Paris: Librarie Arthème Fayard, 1989).

40 David Apter quotes an Asanti chief: "We are the rightful rulers." D. Apter, *Ghana in Transition* (New York: Atheneum, 1968), p. 18.

41 Bill Freund, *The Making of Contemporary Africa* (Bloomington: Indiana University Press, 1984), p. 208.

42 Lonsdale, "States and Social Processes in Africa," p. 153.

43 Ibid., p. 153. Emphasis mine. Nelson Kasfir highlights the importance of the notion of the state as resource: "The emphasis that both Marx and Weber placed on the state as a critical organizational resource in the struggle of local interests [is critical]. . . . Neither would think of the state as merely the arena in which these struggles occur." See N. Kasfir, "Class, Political Domination and the African State," in Zaki Ergas, ed., *The African State in Transition* (New York: St. Martin's Press, 1987), pp. 46, 51.

44 Grier, "Contradiction, Crisis, and Class Conflict," pp. 48–49.

45 Gavin Kitching, "The State as Merchant Capital," ch. 13 in *Class and Economic Change in Kenya* (New Haven: Yale University Press, 1980). See also Susanne D. Mueller, "Retarded Capitalism in Tanzania," *Socialist Register* (1980): 208 inter alia.

46 See Hyden, *Beyond Ujamaa,* p. 82; Barker, *Rural Communities Under Stress,* pp. 110–120; Sheldon Gellar, "Circulaire 32 Revisited: Prospects for Revitalizing the Senegalese Cooperative Movement in the 1980s," in Mark Gersovitz and John Waterbury, eds., *The Political Economy of Risk and Choice in Senegal* (London: Frank Cass, 1987), pp. 123–159; and Roger King, "Cooperative Policy and Village

Development in Northern Nigeria," in Heyer et al., eds., *Rural Development in Tropical Africa,* pp. 259–280.

47 King, "Cooperative Policy and Village Development in Northern Nigeria." See also Gavin Williams, "The World Bank and the Peasant Problem," esp. pp. 33–36.

48 Hyden, *Beyond Ujamaa.*

49 Ibid.

50 See Colin Leys, *Underdevelopment in Kenya: The Political Economy of Neo-Colonialism* (Los Angeles and Berkeley: University of California Press, 1975), ch. 3, esp. p. 102.

51 R. Verdier, "Evolution et réformes foncières de l'Afrique noire francophone," *Journal of African Law,* 15, no. 1 (1971): 85–101.

52 The imposition of state monopolies to collect and export agricultural commodities accelerated a more general restructuring of control over rural commerce. European merchant houses that had dominated the import–export trade in the earlier period downscaled their presence in the rural areas and concentrated their activities at the most lucrative stage of the commercial circuit–wholesale importation. This process widened niches for private African accumulation in trade and transport. The role of the state in structuring access to these opportunities for private accumulation in rural commercial circuits grew as governments licensed private traders and transporters, created credit schemes to finance African-owned commercial enterprises, and, in cases like Senegal and Tanzania, created chains of government-owned stores to distribute consumer goods.

53 Robert Bates, *Essays on the Political Economy of Rural Africa* (Los Angeles: University of California Press, 1983), pp. 127–128. For the example of cooperatives in Senegal, see Edward J. Schumacher, *Politics, Bureaucracy and Rural Development in Senegal* (Los Angeles: University of California Press, 1975), ch. 7; and Donal Cruise O'Brien, *Saints and Politicians: Essays in the Organisation of a Senegalese Peasant Society* (Cambridge: Cambridge University Press, 1975), ch. 4.

54 John Waterbury makes the point that this system of controlling access to resources operates at the level of production (and consumption) units organized around extended families in Senegal. The *chef de carré,* the authority figure in extended households comprising two to five nuclear families, may be the sole member of the cooperative, and thus "he may control the distribution of seed and fertilizer [to male heads of nuclear families, bachelors, married women, and temporary members of the compound who provide seasonal labor while cultivating small plots for themselves]. In some ways, distribution of these inputs has supplanted the older role of the *chef de carré* as allocator of the *carré*'s land." John Waterbury, "The Senegalese Peasant: How Good Is Our Conventional Wisdom?" in John Waterbury and Mark Gersovitz, eds., *The Political Economy of Risk and Choice in Senegal* (London: Frank Cass, 1987), p. 54.

55 It is significant that Michael Bratton finds commercial farmers' associations that are able to promote their members' interests in these areas. (See Chapter 9 of this volume.)

56 On rents, see Robert Bates, *Markets and States in Tropical Africa* (Los Angeles: University of California Press, 1981).

57 Looking at the interwar period, Caglar Keyder describes "the propensity of [Turkish] government activity to colonise the society" – to block the emergence of what he calls "rival political estates." Caglar Keyder, *State and Class in Turkey* (London: Verso, 1987), p. 98.

58 " 'Access' is . . . a key resource in conditions of political departicipation" (René

Lemarchand, "The Dynamics of Factionalism in Contemporary Africa," in Zaki Ergas, ed., *The African State in Transition*, p. 159.

59 Ruth First described Houphouët-Boigny as "a master at embracing his radical opposition to suffocate it in the bosom of his party." Ruth First, *Power in Africa* (New York: Pantheon, 1970), p. 118.

60 Bayart, *L'Etat en Afrique*, pp. 230–240.

61 Aristide R. Zolberg, "Political Development in the Ivory Coast Since Independence," in Philip Foster and Aristide Zolberg, eds., *Ghana and the Ivory Coast: Perspectives on Modernization* (Chicago: University of Chicago Press, 1971), pp. 13–14. For a recent overview of "ethnic arithmetic" in regime building, see Donald Rothchild and Michael W. Foley, "African States and the Politics of Inclusive Coalitions," in Donald Rothchild and Naomi Chazan, eds., *The Precarious Balance: State and Society in Africa* (Boulder, Colo.: Westview, 1988), pp. 241–248.

62 D. Cruise O'Brien, *Saints and Politicians*, p. 194.

63 On "politicized accumulation," see Sara Berry, "Agrarian Crisis in Africa? A Review and an Interpretation," paper presented at the 1983 annual meeting of the African Studies Association, Boston, December 1983.

64 This paraphrases the words of Nelson Kasfir, "Class, Political Domination and the African State," p. 55.

65 Ibid., p. 46.

66 See Richard Joseph, *Democracy and Prebendal Politics in Nigeria: The Rise and Fall of the Second Republic* (Cambridge: Cambridge University Press, 1987); Thomas Callaghy, *The State–Society Struggle: Zaire in Comparative Perspective* (New York: Columbia University Press, 1984).

67 On Tanzania, see Goran Hyden, *Beyond Ujamaa*, ch. 5.

68 This dependence was reflected in clear ambivalence on the part of those at the top of the political hierarchy when it came to ensuring that state resources channeled through patron–client networks were deployed according to criteria formally specified at the center.

69 "The state, born of the colonial occupation, has been the object of multiple processes of reappropriation which move it steadily away from its original form." Bayart, *L'Etat en Afrique*, p. 258.

70 "The struggle for power is perhaps above all a struggle for wealth. . . . This explains in part the seemingly exaggerated value attached to the creation of new administrative structures. These institutions are themselves conduits and sources of wealth *[pourvoyeuses de richesses et d'accumulation]*." Ibid., p. 122.

71 Ruth First, *Power in Africa*, pp. 120, 126.

72 D. Cruise O'Brien, *Saints and Politicians*, p. 126.

73 On bypassing the peasantry, see Bjorn Beckman, "Ghana, 1951–78: The Agrarian Basis of the Post-Colonial State," in Heyer et al., eds., *Rural Development in Tropical Africa*, pp. 161–162.

74 This does not mean that elements within political classes could not, would not, and do not invest in productive enterprise. It merely suggests that ruling classes are unlikely to undertake, in the collective and deliberate way that the systematic exercise of state power implies, a broad-reaching project aimed at promoting the expansion of local private capital, and thus at redefining the process of accumulating power and wealth.

75 Jacques Marseille, *Empire colonial et capitalisme français: Histoire d'un divorce* (Paris: Albin Michel, 1984); Berman, "Structure and Process."

76 René Lemarchand, "The State, the Parallel Economy, and the Changing Structure of

Patronage Systems," in Rothchild and Chazan, eds., *The Precarious Balance,* pp. 149–70.

77 Janet MacGaffey, *Entrepreneurs and Parasites: The Struggles for Indigenous Capitalism in Zaire* (Cambridge: Cambridge University Press, 1987). See also Bratton, Chapter 9 of this volume.

78 Bill Warren, "Imperialism and Capitalist Industrialization," *New Left Review,* 81 (September–October 1973): 3–44; Bjorn Beckman, "Whose State?"

79 As Lonsdale says, "the plasticity of most African bourgeoisies . . . seems to allow for an almost infinite variety of political practices – at least until one adds to the analysis some of the sterner necessities of material reproduction" ("States and Social Processes in Africa," p. 153).

PART III

SOCIAL FORCES: ENGAGED WITH STATE POWER

6

Labor divided: sources of state formation in modern China

ELIZABETH J. PERRY

Recent generations of labor historians, disappointed by the failure of twentieth-century workers to live up to the exalted expectations of Karl Marx and Frederick Engels, have focused their explanatory energies on the limitations of proletarian politics. Central to this new wave of scholarship is attention to the fragmented character of labor. Divided along lines of gender, age, ethnicity, and skill, workers are shown rarely to have acted in the cohesive, class-conscious fashion predicted by communist visionaries. There is a pessimistic tone to much of this recent analysis, as students of labor reluctantly come to grips with the shortcomings of their object of study. There is also a note of irony, as scholars discover that what little indigenous support there was for a radical labor movement tended to be concentrated in the most privileged sectors of the working class, far removed from the heroic proletariat of the *Communist Manifesto*.[1]

In wrestling with the unfulfilled promises of Marxism, studies of labor have been obsessed with "why not" questions: Why did workers not develop a class identity? Why did workers, especially the most downtrodden of them, not flock to radical political parties? Why did working-class parties, especially in advanced capitalist societies, not engineer Marxist revolutions? When phrased in this manner, the questions prompt one to search for sources of weakness in the working class. And that search has led to sophisticated analyses of divisions within the labor force. A host of careful studies have convincingly demonstrated that contradictions between men and women, old and young, black and white, or skilled and unskilled have prevented workers from exhibiting the class-conscious party allegiances or revolutionary behaviors we might otherwise expect of them.

The disaggregation of labor that this line of analysis has entailed is indeed a salutary trend. We now have a much more realistic appreciation of the powerful centrifugal forces at play within the modern working class. But must such intraclass divisions be seen only in a negative light, as obstacles to the fulfillment of the "true" mission of the proletariat? I suggest instead that the fragmentation of labor can itself provide a basis for politically influential working-class action, not only in support of one or another political party but even in the emergence of new states. An approach linking class fractions to state formation is especially appropriate to studies of the Third World. It is commonplace to remark on the high level of social fragmentation in Third World countries. To acknowledge that a society is internally divided is not to concede that it is politically impotent, however. Different segments of society – and even different segments of one class within society – may link up with state allies in such a way as to affect decisively the fate of both parties. This is not to say that social groupings will always have their way; usually neither partner gets quite what it wanted or anticipated in these often uneasy relationships. Nonetheless, by beginning our analysis from the ground up – taking seriously the political potential of these subclasses, fragmented as they may be – we have a concrete means of exploring patterns of state–society interaction.

OUTLINE

This essay examines the relationship of two very different "modern" Chinese states – the Nationalist regime of 1927–1949 and the Communist regime of 1949–1989 – to the Shanghai labor arena. Although neither state was fundamentally based on the working class, both were in fact a good deal more dependent on worker support than is generally recognized. Each regime, however, drew its labor constituency from a different sector of the Shanghai working class. Whereas the Nationalists (with the assistance of organized crime) relied primarily on semiskilled operatives from North China, the Communists attracted skilled artisans from the south. This difference in labor base helps account for fundamental distinctions in the character of the two states. The Nationalists reflected a gangster mentality, extorting money from Shanghai capitalists yet cooperating with that same bourgeoisie if the price was right. The Communists, by contrast, operated on principles more in tune with the values of the skilled craftsman – severely curtailing capitalist prerogatives and constructing a new system of industrial relations in which the state assumed major responsibilities for worker welfare.

Despite its relatively small size in a country that remains to this day overwhelmingly rural, the Chinese working class (concentrated in the industrial metropolis of Shanghai) has shown itself to be a political factor of exceptional importance. This is partly for the universal economic reason that workers with access to expensive industrial equipment are capable of wreaking enormous damage – in terms of both property and production. But there is also an ideological explanation for the power of Chinese labor. Whether pledging allegiance to Sun Yat-sen's Three Principles of the People or to Marxism–Leninism, political leaders in twentieth-century China (as in many other developing nations) have accorded the working class a prominent place in their vision of a new society. Since modernization was seen as virtually synonymous with industrialization, workers were esteemed as the agents of development. A party claiming to represent the forces of progress thus needed a working-class constituency. This ideological consideration lent labor a far greater political voice than its small size might otherwise have suggested. Both the Nationalists and the Communists made active efforts to channel the labor movement in directions favorable to their own political agendas. In the process, parties and states – as well as labor itself – underwent fundamental change.

To be sure, the ideological formulations of these rival parties were substantially different. Whereas Communist labor organizers stressed the importance of class struggle spearheaded by a militant proletariat, the Nationalists emphasized the need for class harmony, with labor and capital cooperating for the economic development of the nation. The contrasting programs help account for the bifurcated reception that their overtures elicited among the workers. Skilled artisans, who boasted a long history of struggles to maintain high wages and job control, had little difficulty in relating to the radicalism of the Communist message. Semiskilled workers, who were typically factory-trained and who lacked the independence of guild-based artisans, were more inclined to support the conservative "yellow unions" founded by Nationalist organizers.

Ideology was not the only basis of division between these two sectors of the work force. Organizational differences were also of critical importance in shaping their relationships with parties and regimes. Skilled craftsmen in China, as elsewhere in the world, lay claim to a rich tradition of corporate organization. Guilds, native-place associations, and the like imbued their members with a communal spirit that encouraged collective action on behalf of shared interests. By contrast, semiskilled workers – who lacked the occupational training and security of skilled craftsmen – became dependent on underworld gangs to ensure their success in the competitive game of urban survival. As recent arrivals to the inhospitable world of the industrial city, these semiskilled workers were ready recruits to the powerful Green and Red gangs that dominated the economic landscape of early-twentieth-century Shanghai.

Nationalist cadres, relying on close connections with gang bosses – more than a few of whom were also factory foremen, developed a patron–client network of labor relations. In return for delivering the support of labor, gangsters were awarded key positions in the regime. The patronage system that emerged (in which opium czars mediated between semiskilled workers and top-level politicians) set limits on the ability of the Nationalist regime to effect either economic or political reform. By contrast, Communist cadres, building on the guild traditions of skilled workers, established radical unions advocating class struggle and worker welfare. Although such organizations were, of course, effectively tamed just as soon as the Communists assumed state power, the legacy of the guilds lived on in the *danwei* (unit) structure of urban China under the People's Republic (PRC) – a system now seen by many as an impediment to further industrial reform.

THE BATTLE FOR SHANGHAI LABOR

In retrospect, the fact that the Chinese Communist Party (CCP) was founded in China's industrial capital of Shanghai seems only natural. At the time, however, the location struck young Marxist organizers – accustomed to the more "cultured" atmosphere of the political capital, Beijing – as anything but ideal. Chen Duxiu, cofounder of the CCP, wrote contemptuously in a series of essays on Shanghai published less than a year before the first party congress convened in the city in the summer of 1921:

> In analyzing Shanghai society [we find] a large portion are totally ignorant laborers who suffer privation and hardship. Another portion are traitorous businessmen who make a living directly or indirectly under foreign capitalism. Another portion are swindlers who sell fake Western medicines or lottery tickets. Another portion are prostitutes. Another portion are evil gangsters and police. Another portion are "black curtain" writers and book sellers dealing in promiscuous romances, superstitious formulas, and profitable new magazines. Another portion are gangster politicians. Committed young students are only a small portion, and situated in this sort of environment they have barely enough strength for self-protection, let alone for overcoming the environment. . . . Because of this, I believe that *if a national congress can be convened, it should not be held in Shanghai.* . . .
>   What types of people are most powerful in Shanghai? A superficial look shows that major political and economic power is in the hands of the Westerners, but the internal social situation is quite different. The majority of factory laborers, all of the transport workers, and virtually all of the police . . . are under the control of the Green Gang . . . The commands of gang leaders are more effective than those of the Municipal Council. . . . The only way of eliminating them is to publicly establish legal unions in each industry.[2]

Unionization, it was quickly discovered, was most easily accomplished among the small subset of workers who shared many of the cultural prejudices of their would-be Communist organizers. The first unions to be founded under Communist sponsorship were in the trades of metalworking and printing, skilled occupations dominated by artisans from the same prosperous South China region from which many of the young CCP cadres themselves hailed. Not surprisingly, the new unions reflected long-standing concerns of skilled craftsmen. The Shanghai Mechanics' Union, whose seventy or so initial members were drawn from industries as diverse as shipbuilding and cotton, pledged in its founding manifesto to uphold customary practices of apprenticeship and mutual aid.[3]

For the Communists to move beyond the world of the literate artisan to make common cause with the less skilled rank and file of the Shanghai proletariat (many of whom were gang members from the poorer regions of the North China countryside) was a more challenging project. An early activist remembered,

Our work met with many difficulties. . . . Hardest to handle were the Green and Red gangs. Finally we decided that several comrades should infiltrate their ranks. But at that time our comrades were all students. If we wanted them to jump up on a stage and deliver a speech or jump down and write an essay, there were always volunteers. However, to enter the Green or Red Gang one had to knuckle down and learn their customs and regulations. Then, through various guises, one could begin work. Who had the patience for that?[4]

As it turned out, conservative members of the Nationalist Party (Guomindang or KMT) were a good deal more successful at using their connections with factory foremen to generate gangster support. Thanks to gangster assistance, by 1920 more than a dozen labor unions had already been founded in Shanghai under right-wing KMT auspices.[5]

The divergent results of Communist and Nationalist efforts to mobilize Shanghai labor soon became apparent in the emergence of distinctive working-class constituencies. The general trend can be illustrated by a close look at the British American Tobacco Company (BAT) in Shanghai, the most strike-prone of any factory in the history of the Chinese labor movement. The subject of intensive scrutiny by students of Chinese labor, BAT has usually been characterized as a bastion of united proletarian support for the Communist Party.[6] In fact, however, the picture was a good deal more complicated.

BAT, like most cigarette factories, was divided into three major production departments: leaf (where tobacco leaves were removed from the stem by hand), rolling (where machines rolled the dried tobacco silk into cigarettes), and packing (where cigarettes were placed in cartons). In addition, there was a machine shop where skilled metalworkers (known popularly as "coppersmiths") built and repaired the factory equipment.[7] Before outside political parties demonstrated any interest in the workers of BAT, the factory had developed a reputation for labor unrest. Significantly, virtually all of this early protest activity (which included twelve strikes during the fifteen years before Communist cadres first arrived on the scene) was initiated by unskilled women workers in the leaf and packing departments.[8] This pronounced militance on the part of women tobacco workers resonates with the findings of researchers focusing on very different societies.[9] However, once outside parties become embroiled in labor struggles at BAT, the situation changed markedly. Skilled male metalworkers from the machine shop (nearly all of whom were natives of South China) became active in Communist-inspired protests, while semiskilled rolling-machine operators (who were also male, but hailed predominantly from the north) enlisted on the side of the KMT.

The bifurcated pattern of labor politics at BAT began to emerge only a few weeks after the establishment of the Chinese Communist Party in the summer of 1921. At that time, metalworkers at the factory had gathered to grumble about a new British manager assigned to their division. Outraged by the new overseer's attempts to curtail their customary privileges, these mechanics – inspired, most probably, by the recent establishment of the Shanghai Mechanics' Union – declared a strike. Within two days, a young Marxist labor organizer had been dispatched to the temple where the strikers had congregated. Under his tutelage, a strike fund was collected and a set of specific demands was drafted. Thanks in part to this assistance, the strike ended more than twenty days later in complete victory with management's acquiescence to all demands. To solidify their gains, a BAT union was formed with Communist guidance at another mass meeting convened at the local temple.[10]

When a walkout again erupted at BAT the following year, however, management turned to a local Green Gang mobster in an attempt to prevent another lengthy work stoppage. Promising his followers a better settlement than any that could be negotiated by the CCP-sponsored union, the gangster managed to recruit hundreds of rolling-machine operators, all of whom were prepared to cross picket lines and resume work. Although the strike ended quickly without achieving any of its initial demands, management did grant concessions to the more than three hundred rollers who had returned to work early.[11]

Gangster involvement in the BAT labor movement intensified after the Nationalists took power in the spring of 1927. Having witnessed the influence of Communist-sponsored unions, the KMT was anxious to try its own hand at labor mobilization. The BAT union was reorganized "to improve workers' living conditions, develop the tobacco industry, and further the national revolution under the Three Principles of the People."[12] A Communist with Green Gang connections remained director of the union, but was joined on the standing committee by two Green Gang leaders in the factory. With generous financial backing from the new Nationalist regime, the BAT union quickly reduced Communist influences (the director was soon arrested) and pledged its support for government policies. When the BAT Company, whose foreign owners were accustomed to favorable tax breaks under previous warlord regimes, refused to pay a new tobacco impost levied by the Nationalists, the KMT-backed union declared a strike.

Thanks to a strike fund buoyed by secret subsidies from the ministry of finance, the walkout lasted for nearly four months, making it the longest industrial dispute of the KMT era.[13] But a strike sustained by government funds could also be squelched by government fiat. In early 1928, the KMT – through the negotiations of Finance Minister T. V. Soong, Chiang Kai-shek's brother-in-law – came to an understanding with BAT. The resulting agreement, signed during a dinner party at Soong's posh Shanghai residence and sealed by a payment of 3 million yuan, pledged the multinational tobacco giant to remit taxes (albeit at a much reduced rate) and to recognize the bargaining authority of the union.[14] Thanks to this settlement, BAT taxes became an important source of revenue to government and union alike. According to a confidential memo by BAT's general manager, the Shanghai KMT received some 1,750 yuan a month from the tobacco tax, of which it kept 550 yuan for its own purposes and divided the remainder among three Green Gang factions at the BAT union. This symbiotic relationship between local politicians and labor union leaders reminded the general manager of nothing more than Tammany Hall.[15]

Not until the Japanese invasion, when KMT forces retreated to the interior of China, did this state-sponsored form of yellow unionism weaken. By the late 1930s Communists had reestablished a foothold in the BAT machine room. After the Japanese took control of BAT following Pearl Harbor, the Communist Party branch at the factory (led by three metalworkers) instigated a number of slowdowns to interfere with production and promote worker welfare. With the Japanese surrender in the summer of 1945, CCP members were determined to reestablish a leftist union at BAT. Their first planning meeting was held at the home of a metalworker, indicating that Communist support was largely confined to the machine shop. The rolling department, by contrast, was controlled by Hong Meiquan, a Green Gang chieftain and KMT member who had been active in yellow union affairs a decade earlier. A longtime rolling-machine operator himself, Hong led a powerful sworn brotherhood society of workers from North China in the rolling department. In the spring of 1946, Hong Meiquan was appointed director of a new, government-approved BAT union.[16]

The pressing problem for the Communists was their confinement to a limited segment of the work force. As an intraparty report on the BAT situation confided, "All our foundation is in the coppersmiths' room [i.e., the machine shop] . . . Although a few of our people work in other departments, we have been unable to develop a mass following there."[17] To be sure, the metalworkers were an active group. But their very militance was attracting an increased level of surveillance. If the radical labor movement at BAT were to continue, it would have to shift its base of operations to a less closely monitored workshop. In the summer of 1947, as demand for a Sunday wage began to sweep the BAT work force, Communist organizers made a bold decision to relinquish leadership of the struggle to a few trusted allies in the rolling department. A leader of the strike recalled,

At that time the reactionary union was watching the coppersmiths closely. Since they were already very "red," we tobacco rollers were charged with this struggle. I was a sworn brother of Hong Meiquan, the head of the Yellow Union. The chief of the Rolling Department was also Hong's sworn brother. So Hong harbored no suspicions about our workshop and hadn't blacklisted any of our workers.[18]

The success of this strike led to an erosion of the gangster's power. But it was not until the KMT's flight from Shanghai in the spring of 1949 that the Communists attained unchallenged control of the BAT labor movement. A metalworker, imprisoned under the KMT, was released from jail to serve as chairman of a new union at the factory. His nemesis, Hong Meiquan, although shielded for some time by friends within the Public Security Bureau, was finally arrested in the spring of 1951 as part of the campaign to suppress counterrevolutionaries.

By the time that the British American Tobacco Company fell under Communist rule, its workers had compiled an impressive history of labor protest, spanning nearly half a century. It is hardly surprising, then, that historians of the Chinese labor movement have devoted a good deal of attention to the workers of BAT, praising them as exemplary proletarian fighters. But the BAT case, important as it is, is not primarily the story of a patriotic, revolutionary working class united in the struggle to seize power on behalf of its own interests. It is instead a story shaped in important ways by the competing agendas of outside partisans: gangsters and state authorities as well as young Communist intellectuals. And, most importantly, it is a story that reveals the complexity of the workers themselves. Although sometimes capable of united action, the workers of BAT were divided by differences in skill, wages, gender, and native-place origins. Such divisions contributed to a complicated labor movement, some of whose participants became enthusiastic advocates of Communist revolution, some of whom threw support to the KMT and their Green Gang henchmen, and some of whom remained outside the reach of would-be organizers.

The divisions at BAT were, moreover, far from unusual. Other enterprises and industries showed a similar segmentation among the work force. In cotton mills and silk filatures, where unskilled women workers from North China constituted the vast majority of employees, a small coterie of skilled male metalworkers from the south supplied the backbone of support for the Communist movement. In silk-weaving factories, where skilled and literate men and women (from South China) worked for high wages, a substantial percentage of workers of both sexes joined the revolution. In the tramway industry, skilled southern metalworkers formed a bastion of support for the CCP, whereas among semiskilled drivers and conductors (from the north) Green Gang and KMT influence was dominant.[19]

When viewed in comparative context, the political divisions of the Shanghai labor force are not surprising. As Eric Hobsbawm has noted, during World War I metalworkers "became in most countries of the world the characteristic leaders of militant labor movements."[20] By way of explanation, Michael Hanagan observes that "nowhere was artisanal survival inside the factory more clear that in metalworking. Although shut behind factory walls, metalworking artisans continued to behave as if they were in their own small shops."[21] A Russian journalist, trying to explain the militance of the skilled metalworkers of Petrograd at the time of the revolution, concluded:

Workers in machine production are always in the forefront of every movement . . . Turners, founders, blacksmiths, mechanics and machinists – all of these are developed people with a well formed sense of individuality and rather good wages. . . . The worker must think a great deal, reason in the very process of work. . . . In the form of their conversation and even their language, they are almost indistinguishable from our intellectuals. In my opinion, they are more interesting because their judgments are fresher and their convictions, once taken, are very firm.[22]

In fact, the radicalism of European metalworkers preceded World War I by more than half a century. In 1851, the Toulouse police, in an effort to explain why the factory metalworkers were "almost all socialist," pointed to the ease of spreading propaganda because of their concentration in *grands ateliers.*[23]

As a consequence of close on-the-job interaction – encouraged by the apprenticeship system – skilled workers took pride in their profession. Accustomed to steady employment and decent treatment, they held their employers to high standards. A privileged segment within the work force, factory artisans nevertheless saw themselves as spokesmen for the interests of labor as a whole. In their minds there was no necessary contradiction between what we may term "craft consciousness" – awareness of the collective interests of one's particular skill group – and "class consciousness" – awareness of one's common interests with other working class groups.[24]

Unlike unskilled laborers, whose attachment to the city was usually a temporary and insecure one, most skilled workers were committed to urban life. As permanent residents of urban society, they took an interest in public affairs that transcended the horizons of the workplace. The high levels of literacy that characterized most artisan professions further contributed to the process of politicization.[25]

Artisan trades in which these traits – of literacy, urbanization, and pride in one's product – were most pronounced, were also trades that generated a disproportionate share of working-class militants. Natalie Davis points to the printing industry as an example.[26] Robert Bezucha highlights the silk-weaving industry.[27] Eric Hobsbawm and Joan Scott identify the shoemaking trade.[28] It may be worth reflecting on the background of several of Shanghai's most active Communist labor leaders. Chen Yun – later to become architect of socialist China's industrial system – apprenticed at the Commercial Press, the city's largest printing house. (During the Great Leap Forward, when Chen Yun's economic policies were out of favor, he busied himself by writing essays on the *pingtan,* an operatic tradition of the South China region from which he hailed.)[29] Zhang Qi – later to become director of the Shanghai Federation of Labor Unions under the PRC – was a skilled craftsman at Mei-ya, Shanghai's premier silk-weaving enterprise. And Liu Changsheng – later to become deputy director of the All-China Federation of Labor Unions – had been a shoemaker.

Although the European labor movement is usually held up as the standard for international comparison, in the case of Shanghai the parallels with American labor are at least as instructive. Behind this similarity lies a recruitment process that in both countries relegated workers from certain regions and backgrounds to certain lines of work. As John Cumbler has described the American pattern,

Selective recruitment directed immigrants with various skills and experiences into particular occupations. Contacts with relatives and friends, often made before migration, steered newcomers into occupations and neighborhoods already identified with particular regions and origins. . . . Social and ethnic divisions channeled workers into worlds separated by traditions, customs and skills carried over from their past and reinforced by the experiences of their present life and work in ethnic groupings.[30]

Skill and native-place differences, in America as in China, were reflected in political orientations. In a study of the U.S. labor movement, Stanley Aronowitz has pointed out that initially the Socialists found their key base of support among skilled workers who were either native-born or of Northern European origins. By contrast, the unskilled laborers – most of whom hailed from Eastern and Southern Europe – remained largely outside the radical labor movement.[31]

But there was, in both America and Shanghai, an intermediate group of semiskilled laborers who also played an important role in labor politics. Lacking the job security or social status of the skilled worker, such individuals were often prompted to turn to gang networks in search of protection. Gangs helped rural immigrants make the difficult transition to urban life. They also served as brokers between workers and politicians. The case of Tammany Hall, the infamous Manhattan Democratic organization, illustrates the linkage clearly.

In the United States, as in China, the 1920s witnessed a transformation of gangster operations to more sophisticated political activities. The involvement of organized crime in the Teamsters Union was symptomatic of this development. The union had been open to corruption ever since it was first formed to represent drivers of horse-drawn wagons (hence the name "Teamsters"). As a student of the mob has explained its hold over American transport workers: "Every worker was a little guy out on a limb, and therefore easy to intimidate."[32] Racketeering and conservative politics were hallmarks of the union.[33]

For rank-and-file workers, patron–client gang ties were a means of getting ahead in an otherwise forbidding environment. As Teamsters leader Jimmy Hoffa recognized,

Personal contact is the key to service and giving the membership service is the only reason we are in the business. That political and social stuff – it's not important. I don't think the drivers expect me to be holding social gatherings for them or to go on the air and tell what's wrong in Germany or Italy. We're in the business of selling labor. We're going to get the best price we can.[34]

Much of the success of gangsters in mobilizing semiskilled workers lay in a public denial of political interests, while at the same time their unions forged close links to powerholders. As Anton Blok has analyzed the Mafia, its key distinction from common banditry lies in its symbiosis with those who hold formal political office. The mafiosi act as political middlemen or power brokers in patron–client networks that link politicians to the rank-and-file citizenry.[35] The insecure position of semiskilled workers – whose futures were tied to the city, but who enjoyed few advantages in the struggle to stake out a permanent urban niche for themselves – made them especially receptive to this variety of organized crime. As employer-trained operatives who lacked the autonomous guild traditions of the skilled workers, they were easy recruits for "yellow unions" advocating economic gain rather than political resistance.

If the political division separating skilled and semiskilled workers is a common enough feature of labor movements around the globe, the Chinese case holds a special significance in light of the fact that each of these "natural" political tendencies became associated with a major state: the Republic of China (1927–1949) and the People's Republic of China (1949 to the present). By exploring the relationship that these rival polities bore to Chinese labor, we have an opportunity to analyze the impact of social movements on state formation. We begin with an examination of the Nationalists during their ill-fated tenure on the mainland, after which we turn to the contemporary Communists.

SHANGHAI LABOR AND THE NATIONALIST STATE

Chiang Kai-shek's momentous coup of April 12, 1927, which shattered the Communist labor movement and forced the radicals out of the cities and into their twenty-year exile in the countryside, was, of course, executed by the Shanghai gangsters. In late March, three of Chiang's closest associates – all of whom had underworld ties – had been dispatched to Shanghai to establish contact with gangster leaders. There they met secretly with the powerful opium triumvirate of Huang Jinrong, Du Yuesheng, and Zhang Xiaolin to lay plans for the anti-Communist offensive that was soon to follow.

The KMT's reliance on gangsters was a recognition of their influence as local strongmen in early-twentieth-century Shanghai. Huang Jinrong, the "godfather" of the Shanghai Green Gang, had come to Shanghai originally in 1900. After leading the life of a petty gangster for several years, he was recruited into the French police force as a plainclothes criminal detective. Police work in Shanghai's French Concession certainly did not require severing ties with the underworld, and Huang kept a foot in each camp. His big break came a few years later, when he succeeded in obtaining the release of a French bishop who had been kidnapped while on a trip to North China. The bishop was a close friend of both the French consul and the French chief of police in Shanghai, so Huang was handsomely rewarded for his service with a newly created post as chief inspector for the Frenchtown police. Promotion to this powerful position greatly enhanced Huang Jinrong's standing as a gang master in the Shanghai underworld; as many as twenty thousand of the city's residents subsequently pledged their discipleship to him.[36]

Among those who took Huang as mentor was Du Yuesheng. Born into a poor family and orphaned at an early age, Du worked for several years at his uncle's fruit stand along the wharf by the old Chinese city of Shanghai. The boy's penchant for throwing rotten fruit at well-dressed rickshaw passengers did not endear Du to his uncle, however, and eventually he was fired for having stolen money for gambling. In this jobless state, Du made the acquaintance of the powerful Huang Jinrong. Huang's paramour, a former brothel madam, took an immediate liking to "Fruit Yuesheng," as he was then known, and saw that Du was given work in Huang's criminal empire. Like generations of secret society chieftains before him, Du Yuesheng rose to fame and fortune through Shanghai's lucrative opium trade. First assigned as an assistant in a Cantonese-owned opium den in Hongkou, Du was soon promoted to manage one of Huang's large dens in the French Concession. More entrepreneurial than his mentor, Du quickly saw the possibilities for turning Huang's Frenchtown connections to maximum advantage. With his master's sanction, Du established the "Black Stuff Company" to extract a monthly fee from every opium shop in the French Concession in return for a guarantee of freedom to sell openly without police interference. The system was maintained by substantial monthly payoffs to the French authorities.[37]

Soon Du's ambitions reached beyond the boundaries of Frenchtown. To expand the scale of opium operations, he made contact with another gangster-cum-opium magnate in the city: Zhang Xiaolin. Zhang's close relations with the Shanghai garrison command had allowed him to gain control of the opium trade at the critical juncture where the Yangzi and Huangpu rivers joined. In 1920, Zhang agreed to cooperate formally with Du Yuesheng and Huang Jinrong. The close relationship among Huang, Du, and Zhang – sealed by a sworn brotherhood ceremony – was further solidified in 1924 when Huang allocated some of his extensive land holdings in the French Concession to build adjoining residences for his two righthand men.[38]

Chiang Kai-shek's Northern Expedition, by challenging the political status quo in the Yangzi valley, also threatened to undermine the opium business. Thus it was more than revolutionary spirit or personal goodwill that inspired the opium triumvirate of Shanghai to offer their services to the generalissimo in 1927. Uppermost in their considerations was the maintenance of their profitable trade. Chiang's willingness to work out a mutually agreeable modus operandi ensured the support of these powerful gangsters.

On the night of April 11, only hours before the attack began, the opium triumvirate met with Chiang's trusted lieutenants to drink wine and swear mutual loyalty.[39] At two o'clock in the morning of April 12 the offensive commenced. Hundreds of mobsters wearing armbands marked with the character for "labor" (*gong*) fanned out from the concessions into the neighboring Chinese areas to wrest control from Communist-led workers' pickets. The battles were brief, as soldiers quickly took command of picket stations and union offices. Hundreds of workers and labor organizers lost their lives in the ensuing bloodbath.[40]

Having crushed the Communist labor movement, Chiang Kai-shek's men immediately undertook to impose their own organizational framework on Shanghai workers. The objective, in classic corporatist style, was to create a network of tamed labor unions under governmental direction.[41]

On April 13, only one day after Chiang's stunning coup, his lieutenants presided over the formation of the Unification Committee for Shanghai Union Organization – a gangster-staffed operation that quickly developed a reputation for extreme ruthlessness. Communists and others suspected of harboring leftist sympathies were summarily rounded up and put to death. The draconian methods of the Unification Committee proved unpalatable even to some members of the Guomindang, who soon formed their own umbrella associations to compete for allegiance of the city's labor unions.

Internecine warfare between rival KMT factions was brought to a halt only in the fall of 1928 when a newly established Bureau of Social Affairs of the Shanghai municipal government was charged with overall responsibility for the city's labor movement. In spite of the good intentions of many of the newly appointed staff members, however, the bureau was stymied in its efforts to revamp the city's industrial system. In 1930, the director of the Bureau of Social Affairs, Pan Gongzhan, reported that only 157 unions had registered with his bureau.[42] This was a far cry from the more than five hundred unions active in Shanghai on the eve of the Guomindang takeover, although it did indicate the government's interest in the matter of labor organization. Pan complained that his bureau faced two formidable obstacles in carrying out its responsibilities in the area of labor control. First was the continued existence of the foreign concessions, where foreign residents governed with their own councils, courts, and police. With the great majority of Shanghai's factories located in the International Settlement and French Concession, the cooperation of foreign authorities was required for Chinese officials to play their assigned role in union registration and dispute mediation. Such cooperation was seldom forthcoming. The second problem that Pan identified as an impediment to the proper functioning of his bureau was that of "people who instigate labor unrest for their own profit." No doubt Pan was here referring in part to remnant underground Communist organizers trying to resuscitate their radical labor movement. But he was surely also alluding to elements within his own Guomindang coalition. The most vexing source of intraparty dissension came from the very group to which Chiang Kai-shek had turned in mounting his April coup: the Green Gang. Although the dissolution of the highhanded Unification Committee had brought to an ignominious close the Nationalists' first experiment in gangster-dominated labor control, soon to follow was another – more subtle and successful – form of gangster intervention.

Aware of the Nationalist government's inability to control labor, Green Gang chief Du Yuesheng decided to try his own hand at organizing the labor movement. Du's first move was to reach out to reformist union leaders at the Shanghai Post Office. A Chinese government agency which was nonetheless directed by a foreigner, the Post Office was targeted by Du as an institution with sufficient social and political clout to serve as an ideal entrée to the unions. First among the postal unionists to ally with Du Yuesheng were Lu Jingshi and Zhu Xuefan.

Under the patronage of the opium czar, Lu Jingshi quickly rose to become a member of the executive committee of the Shanghai Guomindang and director of the martial law division of the Shanghai Garrison Command. Fellow postal unionist Zhu Xuefan soon assumed the chairmanship of a newly created Shanghai General Labor Union, established to provide overall direction to the city's labor movement.[43]

But it was, of course, Du Yuesheng whose star rose most spectacularly. In 1933 an English-language "Who's Who" of China described the opium magnate as "one of the leading financiers, bankers and industrial leaders of China," with "a long and honourable record of important achievements in public and civic service, having on many occasions rendered invaluable aid to his country." Among Du's many official positions were listed those of "advisor to the Military Commission of the Nationalist government, member of the Legislative Body of the Municipality of Greater Shanghai, member of the Supervisory Committee of the Chamber of Commerce of Shanghai, and chairman of the Executive Committee of the China Merchants Steam Navigation Company, which is government controlled."[44] As a foreign contemporary remarked, Du "was a combination of Al Capone and Rockefeller."[45]

The mutually advantageous partnership between gangster Du Yuesheng and his followers from the Post Office was built on the foundation of labor control. Through the introduction of Lu Jingshi and Zhu Xuefan, their patron was invited to intervene in virtually every major strike that broke out in the city. Du's services as labor negotiator par excellence were employed – often in a fashion quite beneficial to labor – in industries as diverse as cotton, printing, silk weaving, jewelry, journalism, and rickshaw transport. On more than one occasion Du drew on his personal bank account first to subsidize the strike committee and then to augment the financial settlement that management was willing to grant. Such displays of benevolence earned the gangster the gratitude of workers, employers, and public opinion (and often they netted him a significant share of the company stock, as well).[46]

Zhu Xuefan recalls in a recent memoir how Du's intervention in strikes helped the gangster shed his unsavory reputation and become a Shanghai celebrity. Each time that Du Yuesheng negotiated a settlement, Shanghai's four major Chinese-language newspapers (whose board of directors was chaired by Du) printed glowing reports of the occasion. Coverage of these events was facilitated by the Labor News Agency, which Zhu Xuefan established specifically for the purpose of publicizing his patron's exploits.[47] As Du Yuesheng's biographer on Taiwan has argued, these activities were directly responsible for the opium czar's rapid rise to fame:

> Regardless of whether it was Du Yuesheng or Lu Jingshi who sallied forth to settle labor disputes, their actions were perfectly coordinated into the smoothest of operations. Several years later, Du Yuesheng and the Shanghai municipal party branch joined forces in leading the labor movement. Shanghai industrialists and labor leaders in both the Chinese areas and the foreign concessions, regardless of trade or occupation, rushed to enter Du's gate. The confluence of these forces gave Du Yuesheng enormous power. The ease with which he subsequently launched his monumental undertakings can be traced back to the firm foundations laid during this period.[48]

Though Du Yuesheng's ascent was certainly attributable to the support of both government and big business, the primary loyalty of the gangster chieftain and his henchmen lay with no constituency but themselves. As a result, the gangsters were quite ready to champion the cause of labor – and even to promote labor strife – when such a strategy promised greater payoff. It was actually with some justification that Zhu Xuefan could boast to a foreign visitor to his Labor News Agency that "we are the only people who defend the Shanghai workers against exploitation."[49] Zhu and several other Green Gang labor organizers even founded a small printing house to surreptitiously print up strike handbills which regular presses, subject to tight government censorship, dared not handle.[50]

The targets of gang-directed strikes were various. We have already seen how Green Gang union leaders in the British American Tobacco Company launched a strike for higher wages that quickly became linked to a Guomindang effort to extract increased taxes from the multinational giant. But governments as well as corporations could fall victim to Du's labor strategems. In 1932, the Green Gang instigated a strike at the French Tramway Company to protest the unfriendly policies of a new French consul and police chief who threatened to curtail opium and gambling in the French Concession.[51] That same year, Du's followers in the Shanghai Post Office launched a politically motivated strike that spread rapidly to postal workers in Beiping, Tianjin, and Nanjing. Although the strikers complained that recent increases in the price of stamps had not been accompanied by commensurate wage hikes, the real target of the protest was the leadership of the ministry of communications. At the time, the ministry was controlled by Wang Jingwei's "Reorganization Faction" – a rival to the "CC Clique" with which Du Yuesheng was more closely connected.[52]

These examples suggest the range of concerns that motivated Du Yuesheng's promotion of labor unrest. Sometimes, as in the BAT strike of 1927, Du's objectives coincided with those of the Nationalist government. However, at other times, as in the 1932 postal strike, the protest could be directed against an agency of the government itself. By deputing the Green Gang as its chief labor organizer, the state had created a powerful challenge to its own hegemony. The outcome was identical to the situation found in so many Third World countries whose leaders feel compelled to reach an accommodation with local strongmen. Joel Migdal writes, "The paradox . . . is: while the strongmen have become evermore dependent on state resources to shore up their social control, state leaders have become evermore dependent on strongmen, who employ those resources in a manner inimical to state rules and laws."[53]

The power of gangster strongmen in Nationalist China ultimately foiled government efforts to carry out reformist labor policies. A telling example was the case of the dockworkers. Offended by the unreasonable profits that gangster labor contractors were extracting from workers' wages and hoping to win the gratitude of ordinary dockers, Nanjing in 1928 passed a "2–8 regulation" whereby the contractors' cut of wages would be limited to 20 percent, leaving 80 percent for the workers themselves. Such a regulation aroused the immediate ire of the contractors, who had grown accustomed to a much larger piece of the pie. Drawing on their gangster networks, contractors throughout the 1930s prevailed upon gang members within the Shanghai government to subvert implementation of the regulation. Rather than giving rise to a unified and loyal dockers' union, as lawmakers in Nanjing had imagined, the 2–8 regulation opened the door to a plethora of warring unions under the direction of rival contractors.[54]

The fascinating interplay among state, gangsters, capitalists, workers, and foreigners – all of whom suffered from internal divisions as well – defined Shanghai politics under the Nationalists. When the Shanghai branch of the Guomindang first authorized the formation of a General Labor Union headed by Zhu Xuefan, the Bureau of Social Affairs – which was a government, rather than a party, institution – refused to recognize its authority. Not until three years later, when Nanjing intervened in the dispute, did the bureau agree to accept the new umbrella union. By that time the General Labor Union's standing committee of five labor organizers was made up entirely of Green Gang members. Eventually the bureau itself was forced to open its doors to the gang. By 1936, three of the four departments at the bureau were headed by disciples of Du Yuesheng. Needless to say, the Labor Dispute Department and its subordinate Mediation Office were among the agencies that fell under Du's command.[55]

Du Yuesheng was not content merely to reap the economic rewards that his control over labor made possible. He was also determined to gain social respectability. In June 1931, all of Shanghai came to a standstill for several days to celebrate the founding of Du Yuesheng's ancestral temple. In honor of the special occasion, Lu Jingshi and Zhu Xuefan even arranged for the local post office to dispense a special postmark.[56] The lavish festivities (complete with colorful parade, three days of operatic performances, a worship ceremony presided over by the mayor of Shanghai, and banquets for fifty thousand guests per meal) reflected Du Yuesheng's desire to translate his substantial economic and political capital into a commensurate cultural and social standing.[57] To complete the genteel image, Du began to dress in long mandarin robes and to write his name with a studied calligraphic flair that belied his lack of formal education.[58] An institutional expression of Du Yuesheng's acquired respectability was the formation in 1932 of the Constant Club, an association of some fifteen hundred of Du's more prestigious followers.[59]

By the mid-1930s, Du Yuesheng was a cornerstone of Shanghai high society. A typical day would see him entertaining anywhere from one hundred to two hundred guests, many of them top officials and wealthy businessmen, at his posh Frenchtown residence.[60] No less a personage than Sun Fo, president of the Legislative Yuan, turned to "Mister Du Yuesheng" – as he was respectfully addressed – for a happy resolution of his complicated love affairs.[61]

The meteoric ascent of Du Yuesheng was telling testimony to the efficacy of gang connections in promoting upward mobility in republican Shanghai. Du's obsession with social acceptance underscored the distance the parvenu had traveled on his journey from orphaned fruit seller to powerbroker. The thousands of followers who flocked to Du's fold in the 1930s were motivated by a similar desire for promotion and prestige. Lacking the head start of a comfortable family background, these disadvantaged yet ambitious elements of Shanghai society were attracted to Du Yuesheng's gangster network as an alternative path to fame and fortune. As one of Du's former followers recalled, most of his fellow clients were "people with a certain ability and potential who faced formidable obstacles in fulfilling their aspirations." Affiliation with Du Yuesheng was a calculated strategy for getting ahead in an otherwise inhospitable environment.[62]

Within the working class, such recruits – although evident in virtually every industry – were especially numerous among semiskilled laborers. Lacking the remuneration and job security enjoyed by factory artisans, yet more committed to urban life than the transient unskilled worker, the semiskilled laborer was easily persuaded of the advantages of an accommodation with labor racketeers. Under the combined sponsorship of gangsters and government, the middle portion of the Shanghai labor force gained a political importance it had not previously known. This political trend reinforced developments in the structure of production that had substantially increased the size of the semiskilled sector. By the Nanjing decade (1927–1937), the "second industrial revolution" that had swept European and American industries around the time of World War I was in full swing in Shanghai. Less skilled, employer-trained male operatives could be found in increasing numbers in both Chinese and foreign-owned factories.

The Japanese invasion of 1937 brought to an end the Nanjing decade in which the Guomindang had enjoyed its heyday. Taking control first of the Chinese-ruled areas of Shanghai and then, after Pearl Harbor, of the foreign-ruled areas as well, the Japanese imposed their own order on the workers of China's largest city. Not until the Japanese defeat in the summer of 1945 did the KMT have an opportunity to reassert leadership over the Shanghai labor movement. Many of the same individuals who had promoted the system of yellow unions after Chiang's April coup were reassigned to positions of influence in the postwar period. Most notable among the returnees was Lu Jingshi, the former post office worker whose discipleship under Green Gang master Du Yuesheng had won him a series of prominent posts in the Nationalist regime. After the Japanese occupation of Shanghai, Lu had followed the Nationalist government westward to its wartime capital in Chongqing. There he formed a close friendship with Dai Li, head of the KMT's secret police. In 1945 when Lu was ordered back to Shanghai to wrest control of the labor movement from Communist competitors, his connection with the secret police proved immensely helpful. Thanks to a generous supply of weapons from Dai Li, Lu Jingshi was able to arm a group of faithful followers among the work force.

Influential as Lu Jingshi was in the postwar labor scene, his power did not go unchallenged. And the opposition came not only from underground Communists. Although Lu publicly named communism as his principal foe, he actually faced more insidious adversaries within his own Guomindang Party. Prominent labor leaders with whom Lu Jingshi had cooperated in the past now cultivated their own constituencies so as to diminish his control.[63]

As a result of the debilitating factionalism of the postwar period, many individuals who had served as bulwarks of government strength in the Nanjing decade now found themselves increasingly estranged from the Guomindang regime. Lu Jingshi's patron, Du Yuesheng, had returned to Shanghai after the war hoping to be named mayor of the city. Instead, perhaps to deflect attention from his own gang connections, Chiang Kai-shek named a rival of Du Yuesheng to head the municipal government. When the Shanghai Legislature was established some months later, Du again had ambitions of assuming the leading post. Again he was disappointed. But the biggest wound to Du Yuesheng's pride came in the fall of 1948 when his son was arrested by Chiang Chingkuo, son of Chiang Kai-shek, for illegal dealings on the Shanghai stock exchange. Seeing a picture of his handcuffed son on the front page of *Central Daily* was unbearable to Du Yuesheng. For more than a month the distraught father refused either to venture outdoors or to entertain guests. It was probably this incident more than any other that made Du decide to leave for Hong Kong, rather than Taiwan, at the time of Shanghai's Communist takeover.[64]

A number of other Shanghai notables chose not to leave at all, but instead to throw in their lot with the new socialist regime. Gu Zhuxuan, Shanghai rickshaw magnate and Green Gang chieftain, agreed to cooperate with his nephew, a Communist cadre responsible for liaison with the city's gangsters. A second-floor office in one of Uncle Gu's dance halls became the meeting place for Communist–gangster rendezvous in the early postwar period. Gu Zhuxuan was rewarded for his cooperation by being made special delegate to the first Shanghai people's congress convened after liberation.[65] By far the most significant defection to the Communist side by a Shanghai labor-leader-cum-gangster was that of Zhu Xuefan. Contacted by Communist agents as early as 1936, Zhu developed an increasingly close relationship with the CCP during the war years. In the postwar period, especially after Zhu was wounded in an assassination attempt by rival KMT agents, his allegiance shifted irrevocably to the Communist side.[66] With the founding of the People's Republic in 1949, the former gangster and postal unionist became first minister of post and telecommunications in the new socialist regime. Today, Zhu Xuefan serves as vice-chairman of the People's Political Consultative Conference and head of the "Revolutionary Committee of the Guomindang" in Beijing.

Built upon the foundation of gangster support, the Nationalist state was a highly personalistic and thus highly fragile regime. Gangster networks enabled the state to make contact with workers (especially the less skilled workers who were most tightly controlled by gangster-foremen), but these same networks could withdraw support whenever their gangster leaders found a more promising ally. If the Nationalists had looked like a good bet in 1927, the Communists seemed an even better bet two decades later.

SHANGHAI LABOR AND THE COMMUNIST STATE

Important as turncoat gangsters were in facilitating the Communist takeover of Shanghai, the heart of CCP support in the city remained with skilled workers. From the earliest days of Communist mobilization efforts through the 1940s, factory artisans were the most enthusiastic and committed labor recruits to the radical cause. Thus for the Communists, in contrast to their Nationalist predecessors, it was the guild rather than the gang that served as the prototype for state-sponsored labor organization.

The importance of artisan support had been dramatically demonstrated at the conclusion of World War II. The Japanese surrender precipitated, in Shanghai as elsewhere across occupied China, a scramble between Communists and Nationalists for control of abandoned territory. Initially the Communists harbored the hope that with proletarian support they might claim the country's largest industrial city. A year before the war's end, in anticipation of the internecine struggle that lay ahead, CCP Central had ordered the establishment of a Shanghai workers' underground army (Shanghai *gongren dixiajun*). Charged with the formidable task of recruitment for this army, labor cadres in Shanghai turned first to gangster elements. Several petty hoodlums did indeed cooperate in supplying the original manpower for the workers' army. It soon became apparent, however, that sustaining the allegiance of gangster mercenaries required substantial payoffs. Strapped for funds, the party returned to a more reliable source of recruits: South China metalworkers.[67] On August 23, 1945, more than seven thousand of these committed fighters – many of whom were party members – assembled at the Xinyi machine works in preparation for an armed uprising aimed at seizing weapons from nearby police stations and then marching to the city center to assist the New Fourth Army in the liberation of Shanghai. That same afternoon, however, the rebellion was canceled on orders from Party Central. After having initially approved the uprising three days earlier, Party Central had received a cable from the USSR calling for peaceful coexistence with the KMT in keeping with a new treaty of friendship between the Soviet Union and the Republic of China. The workers' army was dissolved a few days later and members whose identities had been revealed were transferred north to join the New Fourth Army.[68]

Ill-fated as the workers' army was, its development illustrated the degree to which party organizers in Shanghai were compelled in times of duress to fall back upon their staunchest ally among the Shanghai working class. Although gangster elements could be instrumental in launching militant engagements, ultimately it was the skilled workers who proved willing to sacrifice for higher political goals. Happily for the party, the size of this sector of the working class grew substantially in the postwar period. Thousands of skilled workers – copper fitters, ironsmiths, and mechanics in particular – returned to Shanghai from the interior after the Japanese surrender.[69] In addition, more than thirty thousand Chinese workers – largely educated, skilled workers from the south – were repatriated from Japan.[70]

The division of labor among members of the CCP's Shanghai Labor Committee during the civil war period reflected this heightened interest in factory artisans. Zhang Qi, secretary of the Labor Committee and a skilled silk weaver by training, was put in charge of railroads, shipping, and cotton (with special attention to mechanics). A worker at the Shanghai Power Company handled water and electricity plants as well as the machine industry. A staff worker at the French Tramway Company was in charge of that company, the silk-weaving industry, and some of the bus companies. A printer was assigned to the publishing industry – with responsibility for producing propaganda for the workers' movement as well as organizing among fellow printers. He also handled some hospitals, movie theaters, and other service enterprises.[71]

Skilled craftsmen who had long been active in the CCP labor movement became designers of the Communist industrial system after 1949. Chen Yun, widely acknowledged as China's "economic czar" in the decade following liberation,[72] had joined the CCP in the mid-1920s when he was still a worker at the Shanghai Commercial Press. The radical union at the press, of which Chen was an active member, was an outgrowth of a printers' guild that had predated the communist movement by years.[73] It was hardly surprising, then, that the system created by people like Chen Yun put such a premium on welfare and security, issues central to the guild milieu in which they had originated.

Ironically, the guild heritage was most visible in the sector of the industrial economy that most exemplified the "new" socialist system: state-owned enterprises. It was these organizations that guaranteed lifetime employment, high wages, and substantial welfare measures to their employees. As Andrew Walder points out,

The 27 million permanent workers in state sector industrial enterprises are the only segment of the industrial labor force to participate fully in the welfare state. . . . In 1981 their average annual wage . . . was almost 40 percent higher than that of the average in urban collective industry and well over twice the average of the other groups in the labor force. Just as important, however, are the many fringe benefits, wage supplements, government subsidies, on-site services and welfare and insurance provisions that the state provides. . . . These workers enjoy virtual lifetime tenure. . . . Large and medium-sized enterprises are usually able to provide them with subsidized meals, housing, medical care, and many other services and benefits that are unavailable elsewhere.[74]

Thanks to the perquisites it brought, a job in a state factory came to be known as an "iron rice bowl," in contrast to the less durable and less desirable "earthen rice bowl" of the collective sector.[75]

The exclusivity and paternalism of the socialist enterprise were reminiscent of the artisan guild. One needed the introduction of friends or relatives to join these selective organizations, which offered lifetime benefits to their privileged members. Like its guild forerunner, the socialist factory also stipulated certain behavioral norms for its membership.[76] But whereas the traditional guild had relied on the authority of its patron deity to enforce these values, the new state enterprise claimed legitimacy from the Communist Party.

In each province and city, the special prerogatives of workers at state factories were overseen by the local federation of labor unions, an arm of the state charged with responsibility for worker welfare.[77] In the case of Shanghai, the city's federation of unions has been dominated by former activists in the Communist labor movement, most of whom rose from the ranks of South China artisans.

If the new Communist order was a dream come true for skilled craftsmen, the same was not the case for excluded sectors of the labor force. Resentment against the benefits accruing to veteran workers at state enterprises was an important precipitant of the waves of labor unrest that have rolled across Chinese cities every decade since liberation.

In 1956–1957, under the inspiration of the Hundred Flowers Campaign, strikes erupted at hundreds of factories. As François Gipouloux has found, these labor protests were instigated for the most part by "marginal" workers: temporary and contract laborers, workers in the service sector, apprentices, and others who failed to share in the privileges bestowed upon veteran employees at state enterprises.[78] Despite the vociferous protests of that period, the gap between permanent state workers and temporary or contract laborers grew even greater in the years ahead.[79]

In 1966–1967, during the Great Proletarian Cultural Revolution, serious struggles again broke out in factories across the country. Divisions within the central leadership fanned the flames of local antagonism. The strife was most severe at older factories where generational animosities were especially pronounced. When Chairman Mao called upon the proletariat to undertake revolution, many of Shanghai's veteran workers joined the "conservative" Scarlet Guards to agitate for improvements in wages and working conditions. With some tacit support from members of the Shanghai Party Committee, they launched a general strike that paralyzed the city for days. Younger workers, including a substantial number of contract and temporary laborers excluded from the privileged state system, joined the rival Revolutionary Rebels. Charging the Scarlet Guards with "economism" and "guild mentality," the Revolutionary Rebels advocated a direct assault upon the Party Committee and its subordinate Federation of Labor Unions.[80] As Lynn White has explained the support of disprivileged workers for the radical cause,

Unemployed and contract workers may not, at first, have been passionately excited about the errors of historians, the ideologies of novelists, or the philosophies of musicians – even though these issues concerned editorialists from the radical group that launched the Cultural Revolution in late 1965 and early 1966. Unemployed workers seem to have had some idea what political leaders they disliked, however. When men like Mayor Ts'ao Ti-ch'iu [of Shanghai], who had espoused the "worker-peasant system," were criticized for cultural policies, some enthusiasm was stirred within the lower proletariat. The famous attack on "economism" is comprehensible only in terms of the fact that extra bonuses were commonly offered only to regular workers, not to temporary workers.[81]

Subjected to repeated lectures by their elders about the revolutionary exploits of bygone days, younger workers laboring under less favorable conditions longed for an opportunity to even the score. The Cultural Revolution offered them the chance. Interestingly enough, however, the methods that young Revolutionary Rebels employed in their own struggles bore an uncanny resemblance to the protest repertoires of the previous generation.[82] It was probably no coincidence that the Shanghai Number 17 cotton mill, where Revolutionary Rebel commander Wang Hongwen worked, had in the mid-1920s been the scene of labor violence strikingly similar in form to that of Cultural Revolution struggle sessions. In a 1925 incident at the factory, workers had tricked a hated foreman into attending a mass meeting at which he was publicly denounced. The hapless foreman was forced to kneel in front of the crowd with hands tied behind his back, dunce cap placed on his head, and a placard reading "Down with this traitor and running dog" hung across his chest. Photographs of the occasion were posted at the factory gate to serve as warning lest the unseated overseer should ever try to resume his post.[83]

When radical workers adopted similar tactics during the Cultural Revolution, their targets were the older generation and the institutions (e.g., the Federation of Labor Unions) that symbolized its privileged position in the new socialist order. In Shanghai, the year 1967 saw a string of attacks by Wang Hongwen's Revolutionary Rebels against the former party underground labor organizers who then controlled the Shanghai Federation of Labor. Zhang Qi, the former silk weaver who had served as secretary of the Shanghai party underground on the eve of liberation and was now director of the Shanghai federation, was subjected to repeated humiliation in public struggle sessions. His hands were forced behind his back in the painful "jet plane" position, a dunce cap adorned his head, and a placard across his chest announced him as a "running dog" who had committed "revisionist crimes." In December, Zhang was imprisoned in the basement of the building of the federation that he had helped to create.[84] Although Zhang Qi survived the Cultural Revolution in remarkably good health, many of his colleagues were less fortunate. A recent listing of fatalities in radical assaults on the Shanghai Federation of Labor illustrates the vulnerable position of former underground party organizers – most of whom were skilled craftsmen from South China.[85]

While the communitarian rhetoric of the Cultural Revolution may have seemed consonant with long-standing artisan values, the material sacrifice demanded by the movement was anything but popular with skilled workers whose privileged status had always been reflected in higher pay. In 1974–1975, a wave of strikes and slowdowns swept across China's factories to demand bonuses and wage hikes, anathema as these were to the Maoist orthodoxy of the day. The most serious work stoppage, a series of strikes in the city of Hangzhou, was resolved only when Deng Xiaoping went in person to assure the restive workers of an impending wage reform.[86]

Repeated labor protests bespeak fundamental dissatisfactions with the existing industrial pattern, but the state has found it extremely difficult to effect reform of a system around which so many embedded interests have coalesced. In many respects, the post-Mao reforms reflect a return to the status quo ante. Walder characterizes Deng Xiaoping's industrial policy as a "shift from asceticism to paternalism" in which "the state enterprise continues to play a central role in the delivery of free or highly subsidized goods and services."[87]

The prevailing arrangement, reintroduced by rehabilitated economic czar Chen Yun, offers certain advantages to central planners. Although Chen Yun, in contrast to Mao Zedong, has envisioned an important role for the market in China's socialist economy, it is nevertheless a subsidiary role. As Nicholas Lardy and Kenneth Lieberthal point out, for Chen the market is "solely a supplement to centralized planning." Bureaucratic allocation, especially of skilled labor, remains the cornerstone of his program.[88] Under such an arrangement, the basic components of which were fashioned in the first decade of the People's Republic, reforms of a more market-oriented variety are extremely difficult to implement. The demand of the central government for a steady source of revenue, based on reliable output from veteran workers at its state-owned enterprises, inhibits the prospects for industrial change in a more liberal direction. Moreover, the workers privileged by such a system are an important source of its perpetuation.

CONCLUSION

China's Nationalist and Communist states have shown the development of an increasingly intrusive pattern of government intervention in the labor arena. Both of these "modern" states acceded to power with substantial working-class support. Both endeavored to rechannel labor activism into government-controlled institutions: the "yellow unions" under the KMT, the Federation of Labor Unions under the PRC. Both evidenced ambivalence toward the labor strife which persisted after their consolidation of state power.[89] And both sought, successfully, to co-opt labor leaders as state officials. (The meteoric rise of Wang Hongwen and his Revolutionary Rebels after the January power seizure of 1967 was more than a little reminiscent of the prominence which Green Gang labor organizers enjoyed in the aftermath of the April coup of 1927.)

To be sure, the gang base of the Nationalists and the guild base of the Communists imply very different social constituencies. The competing ideologies of these rival parties had elicited divergent popular responses. As we have seen, it was not coincidental that skilled artisans were attracted to the radicalism of the Communist message, whereas semiskilled workers were drawn to the moderation of the KMT. The states established by both political parties were, moreover, substantially constrained by the nature of their working-class support, dissimilar as it was.

The common restraints faced by both Chinese states, despite their contrasting ideologies, points to a problem shared by many other fledgling regimes, regardless of their espoused political values. Trying to impose rule on highly fragmented societies, new states necessarily enter into pacts with receptive social elements. Yet such accommodations may imprison the state in preferential relationships that serve ultimately to inhibit a broader base of support. As a consequence of their confining partnerships with particular class fractions, regimes are likely to prove stubbornly resistant to fundamental economic and political reform.

In making an argument for societal constraints, I depart from a considerable body of scholarship that emphasizes the alleged immunity of the modern state from social forces. In the field of Chinese studies – thanks to China's ancient bureaucratic tradition as well as its contemporary Communist experience – the emphasis on state autonomy has been especially pronounced. This emphasis is seen even in studies of the Nationalist interregnum. Lloyd Eastman, perhaps this country's most prolific student of the Nationalist regime, has proposed an "autonomy thesis" to argue that the KMT state "was never accountable to political groups or institutions outside the regime."[90] In presenting his thesis (intended as a challenge to earlier interpretations of the Nationalists as the hireling of China's upper classes),[91] Eastman mirrors a larger debate among general theorists about the nature of the state. Whereas a Marxist scholarly tradition had seen the modern state as the "executive committee of the bourgeoisie," a Weberian tradition pictures the state as a "rational" entity operating according to rules of its own making.[92]

Faced with these alternative views, the challenge – as Charles Bright and Susan Harding have summarized it – is to arrive at "a conception of the state that accords it neither too much, nor too little, autonomy from other social forces."[93] But what are the relevant "social forces" with which we should be concerned? In an "advanced capitalist society," perhaps a case can be made that the domestic capitalist class is indeed the critical "social force" with which the regime must interact in the statemaking process. Yet can the same be said for a society like Republican China, where industry was still in its infancy? And what of Communist China, where the bourgeoisie was summarily stripped of its property base?

Like many Third World countries, modern China has been a fragmented society over which no single class could exercise hegemony. If we are to turn to the Marxist tradition for inspiration, the appropriate *locus classicus* would not be *Das Kapital*, where advanced capitalism is analyzed, but *The Eighteenth Brumaire* – where Louis Napoleon's rise to power is interpreted against the background of a divided France in the throes of the transition from an agrarian to an industrial economy. Marx's characterization of Napoleon applies with equal force to a Chiang Kai-shek, Mao Zedong, or Deng Xiaoping: "The contradictory task of the man explains the contradictions of his government, the confused groping about which seeks now to win, now to humiliate first one class and then another."[94]

The classes with which Chinese leaders were forced to deal included not only the old and new elites of landlords and capitalists, but a recently politicized working class (and its leaders) as well. Contrary to the prevalent image of Chinese workers as mere putty in the hands of outside party organizers – to be molded as the latter saw fit, the historical record reveals a remarkable level of labor activism. While KMT-sponsored yellow unions were to some extent able to define labor relations in ways amenable to state officials, workers and their spokesmen were also significant participants in the definitional enterprise. And in part precisely because of the politicization that took place during the years of KMT rule, China's socialist leaders have been compelled to reach their own accommodation with a working class accustomed to militance. If the Nationalists exercised only "dispersed domination" when compared with the "integrated domination" of the Communists, in both cases labor has demonstrated an impressive capacity for resistance. Although the PRC is often characterized as a "totalitarian" regime in which social forces play next to no role in shaping the political agenda, actually the reality or fear of worker protest has exerted a major influence on political events over the past four decades. The waves of repression that have rolled across the Chinese polity each decade since 1949 have all followed on the heels of popular protests in which labor strife was a major concern.[95] Admittedly, the repressive response of the state demonstrates the severe restrictions on popular participation. But it also suggests the extent to which state policies are themselves shaped in reaction to this very participation. Although the outcome is certainly a far cry from the workers' paradise envisioned by Marx and Engels, it nevertheless bears witness to a more influential political role for workers than a recent generation of scholarship on labor history might lead us to expect.

NOTES

1 For a sampling of this important literature, see Ira Katznelson and Aristide R. Zolberg, eds., *Working-Class Formation* (Princeton, N.J., 1986); Richard Jule Oestreicher, *Solidarity and Fragmentation* (Chicago, 1986); Sean Wilentz, *Chants Democratic: New York City and the Rise of the American Working Class* (New York, 1984); Victoria Bonnell, *Roots of Rebellion: Workers' Politics and Organizations in St. Petersburg and Moscow, 1900–1914* (Berkeley, Calif., 1983); Charles F. Sabel, *Work and Politics: The Division of Labor in Industry* (New York, 1982); Ronald Aminzade, *Class, Politics and Early Industrial Capitalism* (New York, 1981); Dick Geary, *European Labour Protest, 1848–1939* (London, 1981); Diane Koenker, *Moscow Workers and the 1917 Revolution* (Princeton, N.J., 1981); William P. Sewell, *Work and Revolution in France* (New York, 1980); Michael P. Hanagan, *The Logic of Solidarity* (Urbana, Ill., 1980); I. Prothero, *Artisans and Politics in Early Nineteenth-Century London* (London, 1979); Barrington Moore, Jr., *The Social Bases of Obedience and Revolt* (Armonk, N.Y., 1978); Herbert G. Gutman, *Work, Culture, and Society* (New York, 1977); Bernard H. Moss, *The Origins of the French Labor Movement* (Berkeley, Calif., 1976); Joan W. Scott, *The Glassworkers of Carmaux: French Craftsmen and Political Activism in a Nineteenth Century City* (Cambridge, Mass., 1974); Stanley Aronowitz, *False Promises* (New York, 1973).
2 Chen Duxiu, "Shanghai shehui" (Shanghai society), *Xin qingnian* (New youth), vol. 8, nos. 1–4 (1980): 67–71 (Emphasis added).
3 "Shanghai jiqi gonghui kai faqihui jilue" (Annals of the inaugural meeting of the Shanghai Mechanics' Union), *Zhongguo gongren yundongshi cankao ziliao* (Reference materials on the history of the Chinese labor movement), vol. 1 (1980), pp. 43–47.
4 *Bao Huiseng huiyilu* (The memoirs of Bao Huiseng) (Beijing, 1983), p. 67. Fortunately for the development of the Communist labor movement, it turned out that a few of their young cadres did have enough patience to work with gangsters. On the efforts of early CCP labor organizers to infiltrate the gangs, see Zhu Xuefan, "Shanghai gongren yundong yu banghui ersanshi" (Two or three things about the Shanghai labor movement and the gangs), in *Jiu Shanghai de banghui* (The gangs of old Shanghai) (Shanghai, 1986), pp. 1–20.
5 Jiang Peinan and Chen Weimin, "Shanghai zhaopai gonghui de xingwang" (The rise and fall of Shanghai's signboard unions), *Jindaishi yanjiu* (Studies in modern history), no. 6 (1986): 46–47.
6 *Zhandou de wushi nian* (Fifty years of battle), (Shanghai, 1960), is the most detailed of these studies.
7 *Shanghai juanyan gongye gaikuang* (Conditions in the Shanghai rolled tobacco industry) (Shanghai, 1950), pp. 35–42.
8 *Shi bao*, 1906/6/13, 1915/2/5, 1916/3/10, 1918/8/5, 1918/8/6, 1918/8/9, 1919/10/8; *Minguo ribao*, 1917/7/21, 1917/7/24, 1917/7/25, 1917/8/2, 1917/8/10, 1918/5/2,

1918/8/4, 1919/11/10, 1919/11/14, 1920/6/23, 1921/3/7, 1921/3/18, 1921/6/25, 1921/6/28, 1921/6/29.

9 Rose Glickman, *Russian Factory Women* (Berkeley, Calif., 1984), p. 162; Louise A. Tilly, "Paths of Proletarianization," in Eleanor Leacock and Helen I. Safa, eds., *Women's Work* (South Hadley, Mass., 1986), p. 37; Patricia A. Cooper, *Once a Cigar Maker: Men, Women and Work Culture in American Cigar Factories, 1900–1919* (Urbana and Chicago, 1987).

10 *Zhandou de wushi nian,* pp. 19–31.

11 Ibid., pp. 32–38.

12 Luo Chuanhua, *Jinri Zhongguo laogong wenti* (Labor issues in today's China) (Shanghai, 1933), pp. 97–102.

13 See Number Two History Archives, Nanjing, #1:2–746, for confidential memos from the director of the KMT Labor Bureau to the minister of finance, allocating generous secret subsidies for the BAT union.

14 *North China Daily News,* 1928/1/18.

15 BAT Pudong archives: August 1933 report of I. G. Riddick.

16 Yao Haigen, 1958/10/28; and Hong Benkuan, 1958/10/24; interview transcripts in the Labor Movement Archives of the Institute of History, Shanghai Academy of Social Sciences (SASS).

17 Archives of the Bureau of Investigation, Taipei, #556.282/810. At the end of 1946, the 25 CCP members at BAT included 12 metalworkers, 5 leaf department workers, 4 rolling department workers, 1 office worker, 1 printer, and 2 schoolteachers. None of these were women.

18 Huang Zhihao, 1958/9/2, interview transcript in the Labor Movement Archives of the Institute of History, SASS.

19 Elizabeth J. Perry, *Shanghai on Strike: The Politics of Chinese Labor* (Stanford, Calif., 1993), chs. 8 and 9.

20 Eric Hobsbawm, *Labouring Men* (New York, 1963), p. 424.

21 Hanagan, *The Logic of Solidarity,* pp. 10–11.

22 Quoted in David M. Mandel, *The Petrograd Workers and the Fall of the Old Regime* (New York, 1983), p. 13.

23 Aminzade, *Class, Politics and Early Industrial Capitalism,* p. 76.

24 On this point, see Hanagan, *Logic,* p. 210. See also Bonnell, *Roots of Rebellion,* p. 444.

25 A Moscow survey of 1908 showed that skilled workers, most notably metalworkers, had a literacy rate of about 90 percent and were considerably more urbanized (measured as the percentage born in the city) than textile workers. Koenker, *Moscow Workers and the 1917 Revolution,* p. 29. Such workers – skilled, well paid, literate, urbanized – led the strike waves of the early twentieth century. Koenker, ibid., pp. 76–78.

26 Natalie Zemon Davis, "A Trade Union in Sixteenth-Century France," *Economic History Review,* no. 19 (1966): 48–69; Natalie Zemon Davis, *Society and Culture in Early Modern France* (Stanford, Calif., 1975) pp. 4–10.

27 Robert J. Bezucha, *The Lyon Uprising of 1834* (Cambridge, Mass., 1974).

28 Eric J. Hobsbawm and Joan W. Scott (1980), "Political Shoemakers," in Eric Hobsbawm, ed., *Workers: Worlds of Labor* (New York, 1984), pp. 103–130.

29 David M. Bachman, *Chen Yun and the Chinese Political System* (Berkeley, Calif., 1985), pp. 72–73.

30 John Cumbler, "Migration, Class Formation, and Class Consciousness: The American Experience," in Michael Hanagan and Charles Stephenson, eds., *Confrontation, Class Consciousness, and the Labor Process* (New York, 1986), p. 42.

31 Aronowitz, *False Promises*, ch. 3.
32 Jonathan Kwitny, *Vicious Circles: The Mafia in the Marketplace* (New York, 1979), p. 143.
33 By the early 1950s, suspicion of Communist sympathies was grounds for expulsion. Kwitny, ibid., p. 144.
34 Jim Clay, *Hoffa!* (Beaverdam, Va., 1965), p. 163.
35 Anton Blok, *The Mafia of a Sicilian Village* (New York, 1974), pp. 6–7, 177.
36 Xue Gengshen, "Jindai Shanghai de liumang" (The gangsters of modern Shanghai), *Wenshi ziliao xuanji,* no. 3 (1980): 162–163; Cheng Xiwen, "Wo dang Huang Jinrong guanjia de jianwen" (What I saw and heard as Huang Jinrong's butler), *Jiu Shanghai de banghui* (1986): 144–148.
37 *Shanghai Municipal Police Files,* microfilm reel #56, D-9319; *Da liumang Du Yuesheng* (Big gangster Du Yuesheng), (Shanghai, 1965), pp. 1–7; Huang Guodong, "Dumen huajiu" (Old tales of the Du residence), *Jiu Shanghai de banghui* (1986): 248.
38 Zhu Jianliang and Xu Weizhi, "Zhang Xiaolin de yisheng" (The life of Zhang Xiaolin), *Jiu Shanghai de banghui* (1986): 343–344.
39 Xiang Bo, "Huang Jinrong shilue" (An account of Huang Jinrong), *Jiu Shanghai de banghui* (1986): 134.
40 "Siyier shibian de qianqian houhou" (Before and after the April 12 incident), *Shanghai gongren yundong lishi ziliao* (Historical materials on the Shanghai labor movement), vol. 4 (1953), pp. 12–35; Wang Jianchu and Sun Maosheng, *Zhongguo gongren yundongshi* (A history of the Chinese labor movement) (Shenyang, 1987), p. 138.
41 On corporatism, see, for example, Phillipe C. Schmitter, *Corporatism and Public Policy in Authoritarian Portugal* (London and Beverly Hills, 1975); and Alfred Stepan, *The State and Society: Peru in Comparative Perspective* (Princeton, N.J., 1978). The characterization of the Nationalists as a corporatist regime has been made in Joseph Fewsmith, *Party, State and Local Elites in Republican China: Merchant Organizations and Politics in Shanghai, 1890–1930* (Honolulu, 1985).
42 Pan Gongzhan, "Shanghai tebieshi shehuiju zhi zuzhi ji gongzuo" (The organization and work of the Shanghai Bureau of Social Affairs), *Qingnian jinbu* (Youth progress), no. 133 (1930): 34–41.
43 Zhu Xuefan, "Shanghai gongren," pp. 6–9.
44 George F. Nellist, ed., *Men of Shanghai and North China* (Shanghai, 1933), p. 110.
45 Ilona Ralf Sues, *Shark's Fins and Millet* (Boston, 1944), p. 78.
46 This was Du's mode of operation during the French Tramway strikes of 1928 and 1930, the Nantao Tramway strike of 1932, the Nanyang Brothers Tobacco Company strike of 1933, the Shanghai Power Company strike of 1933, and the Shanghai Electric Construction Company strike of 1937. See *Shanghai Municipal Police Files,* reels #16–17, D-5310. The British police observed that "the old French opium gang seems to be supplementing its income from smuggling by promoting racketeering in Chinese industrial enterprises." See reel #14, D-4611. Although the financial rewards for Du's services were substantial, the British police offered another, equally important, explanation of the gangster's appetite for labor mediation: "His desire to settle labour disputes aims at winning the confidence of the public and especially the government authorities." See *Shanghai Municipal Police Files,* reel #56, D-9319.
47 Zhu Xuefan, "Shanghai gongren," pp. 6–7.
48 Zhang Jungu, *Du Yuesheng zhuan* (Biography of Du Yuesheng) (Taipei, 1968), vol. 2, p. 155.
49 Sues, 1944, p. 75.

50 Zhu Xuefan, "Shanghai gongren," p. 7.
51 *Shanghai chanye yu Shanghai zhigong* (Shanghai industries and Shanghai workers), (Shanghai, 1939), p. 359; Xue Gengshen, "Wo yu jiu Shanghai fazujie" (The old French Concession of Shanghai and I), *Wenshi ziliao xuanji* (June 1976): 157–158.
52 "Kangri zhanzheng yiqian Shanghai youzheng zhigong de douzheng qingkuang" (Struggle conditions among Shanghai postal workers before the Sino-Japanese war), *Shanghai gongren yundong lishi ziliao* (1954), pp. 1–30; Shen Tiansheng, "Huiyi 1927–1932 nian Shanghai youwu gonghui qingkuang" (Remembering the situation in Shanghai's postal workers' union, 1927–1932), *Shanghai gongyunshi yanjiu ziliao* (1981), p. 29.
53 Joel S. Migdal, *Strong Societies and Weak States* (Princeton, N.J., 1988), p. 141.
54 Number Two History Archives, #720–733, #722:4–233, #722:4–502, #722:4–504.
55 *Da liumang Du Yuesheng* (Big gangster Du Yuesheng) (Shanghai, 1965), pp. 50–51; Zhu Xuefan, "Shanghai gongren," p. 8.
56 Zhu Xuefan, "Shanghai gongren," p. 5.
57 Fan Shaozeng, "Guanyu Du Yuesheng" (Concerning Du Yuesheng), *Jiu Shanghai de banghui* (1986): 221–229.
58 Guo Lanxin, "Du Yuesheng yu Hengshe" (Du Yuesheng and the Constant Club), *Jiu Shanghai de banghui* (1986): 304; Fan Shaozeng, "Guanyu Du Yuesheng," p. 206.
59 Guo Lanxin, "Du Yuesheng," pp. 300–320; Zhu Xuefan, "Shanghai gongren," p. 6; "Hengshe sheyuanlu" (Record of the Constant Club membership), *Jiu Shanghai de banghui* (1986): 369–382; *Hengshe qiuji lianhuan dahui tekan* (Special issue on the spring get-together of the Constant Club), Shanghai, 1934.
60 Huang Guodong, "Dumen huajiu," p. 253.
61 *Shanghai Municipal Police Files*, reel #56, D-9319.
62 Guo Lanxin, "Du Yuesheng," pp. 306–307.
63 Mao Qihua, "Luetan jiefang zhanzheng shiqi Shanghai gongren yundong de yixie qingkuang" (A summary discussion of conditions in the Shanghai labor movement during the war of liberation), *Shanghai gongyunshi yanjiu ziliao*, no. 2 (1982): 1.
64 Fan Shaozeng, "Guanyu Du Yuesheng," pp. 239–242. It may also be that Du was beginning to lean toward the Communists. According to his accountant, Du had developed a number of contacts among future leaders of both the Shanghai and the central PRC government. See Huang Guodong, "Dumen huajiu," pp. 265–267.
65 Gu Shuping, "Wo liyong Gu Zhuxuan de yanhu jinxing geming huodong" (I used the cover of Gu Zhuxuan to carry out revolutionary activities), *Jiu Shanghai de banghui* (1986): 363–366.
66 Lu Xiangxian, *Zhongguo laodong xiehui jianshi* (Brief history of the China Labor Association) (Shanghai, 1987).
67 Of the 69 members of the workers' army on whom we have data, only 8 were from North China and the remaining 61 were from southern locations. "Shanghai gongren-dui duiyuan mingdan" (Name list of members of the Shanghai workers' brigade), 1988, *Shanghai gongyun shiliao* (Historical materials on the Shanghai labor movement), nos. 2–3 (1988): 52–54.
68 "Zongshu Shanghai gongren dixiajun" (Overview of the Shanghai workers' underground army), *Shanghai gongyun shiliao*, nos. 2–3 (1988): 1–7; Zhang Chengzong, "Zuzhi dixiajun, zhunbei wuzhuang qiyi" (Organizing the underground army, preparing for armed rebellion), ibid., pp. 8–12; Zhang Qi, "Huiyi Shanghai gongren dixiajun" (Remembering the Shanghai workers' underground army), ibid., pp. 13–18. *Jiefang ribao*, 1945/8/23, and *Xinhua ribao*, 1945/8/28, reported the news under headlines that read "50,000 Shanghai Workers Rebel."

69 See Shanghai Municipal Archives, #12-1-52, for a listing of these returnees.
70 Including a number of captives from the Eighth Route Army, most of these individuals had been working in Hokkaido for several years before being sent home. Shanghai Municipal Archives, #11-1, 11-9.
71 Mao Qihua, "Luetan jiefang," p. 1.
72 Nicholas R. Lardy and Kenneth Lieberthal, eds., *Chen Yun's Strategy for China's Development* (Armonk, N.Y., 1983); David M. Bachman, *Chen Yun and the Chinese Political System* (Berkeley, Calif., 1985).
73 *Shangwu yinshuguan gonghuishi* (A history of unions at the Commercial Press) (Shanghai, n.d.), pp. 1–2.
74 Andrew G. Walder, *Communist Neo-Traditionalism* (Berkeley, Calif., 1986), pp. 40–42.
75 Martin King Whyte and William L. Parish, *Urban Life in Contemporary China* (Chicago, 1984), p. 33.
76 Walder, *Communist Neo-Traditionalism,* ch. 4.
77 In the early 1950s, the chair of Shanghai's municipal Trade Union Council was also the deputy secretary of the city's Community Party Committee. See Paul F. Harper, "Trade Union Cultivation of Workers for Leadership," in John Wilson Lewis, ed., *The City in Communist China* (Stanford, Calif., 1971), p. 125.
78 François Gipouloux, *Les cent fleurs a l'usine,* (Paris, 1986), pp. 198–205; see also Lynn White III, "Workers' Politics in Shanghai," *Journal of Asian Studies,* vol. 36, no. 1 (1976): 105–107.
79 White, "Workers' Politics," pp. 107–115.
80 Hong Yung Lee, *The Politics of the Chinese Cultural Revolution* (Berkeley, Calif., 1978), p. 137; Lynn T. White, III, "Shanghai's Polity in Cultural Revolution," in Lewis, ed., *The City in Community China,* pp. 325–370; Parris Chang, 1981, "Shanghai and Chinese Politics: Before and After the Cultural Revolution," in Christopher Howe, ed., *Shanghai* (Cambridge, U.K., 1981), pp. 66–90.
81 White, "Workers' Politics," pp. 114–115.
82 On the importance of learned protest repertoires, see Charles Tilly, *The Contentious French* (Cambridge, Mass., 1986). This theme is creatively developed for Shanghai students in Jeffrey Wasserstrom, *Student Protest in Twentieth-Century China: The View from Shanghai* (Stanford, Calif., 1991).
83 Zhang Ben et al., "Shanghai guomian shiqichang gongren douzhengshi" (The history of labor struggles at Shanghai's Number 17 cotton mill), *Shanghai gongren yundong lishi ziliao* (1953), pp. 61–70.
84 Fan Wenxian, "Shanghaishi zonggonghui beiza jishi" (Annals of the assault on the Shanghai Federation of Labor), *Shanghai gongyun shiliao,* no. 5 (1986): 1–6.
85 "Zhengzheng tiegu chuiqing shi" (In appreciation of martyrdom), ibid., pp. 13–22.
86 Lowell Dittmer, *China's Continuous Revolution,* (Berkeley, Calif., 1987), pp. 165–167.
87 Walder, *Communist Neo-Traditionalism,* p. 227.
88 Lardy and Lieberthal, *Chen Yun's Strategy,* p. xiii.
89 Mao Zedong's speech "On the Correct Handling of Contradictions Among the People" in February 1957 called for better education and improved leadership methods as an antidote to strikes that had broken out the previous year. In the spring of 1957, Liu Shaoqi proposed more boldly that union and party officials should themselves participate in strikes to regain the confidence of the workers. See *Joint Publications Research Service,* #41889, p. 58.
90 Lloyd Eastman, "New Insights into the Nature of the Nationalist Regime," *Republi-*

can China, 9, no. 2 (1984): 11. See also Eastman, *The Abortive Revolution* (Cambridge, Mass., 1974).

91 The interpretation of the KMT as representative of the Chinese bourgeoisie or landlord classes can be found in Robert W. Barnett, *Economic Shanghai: Hostage to Politics* (New York, 1941), p. 12; Harold Isaacs, *The Tragedy of the Chinese Revolution* (Stanford, Calif., 1951), p. 182; Barrington Moore, Jr., *The Social Origins of Dictatorship and Democracy* (Boston, 1961), p. 196; and Mao Zedong, *Selected Works* (Beijing, 1967), vol. 1, p. 55.

92 More recently, however, these "alliance" and "autonomy" perspectives have been joined by a third view which allows for the "relative autonomy" of the state. Nicos Poulantzas, 1978, *State, Power, and Socialism,* London, initiated a Neo-Marxist debate about "relative autonomy" by arguing that contradictions within the ruling class meant that the state could not merely reflect elite interests. Subsequently, Theda Skocpol and Kenneth Finegold have elucidated the "specific historical conditions" under which some capitalist states develop "relative autonomy" vis-à-vis industry. See their "State, Party, and Industry," in Charles Bright and Susan Harding, eds., *Statemaking and Social Movements* (Ann Arbor, Mich., 1984), p. 184.

93 Bright and Harding, *Statemaking,* p. 4. For useful efforts to develop typologies of strong, weak, and middling states, see especially Peter J. Katzenstein, "Domestic Structures and Strategies of Foreign Economic Policy," *International Organization* 31 (1977); and Stephen D. Krazner, *Defending the National Interest* (Princeton, 1978).

94 Karl Marx, 1977, "The Eighteenth Brumaire of Louis Bonaparte," in *Selected Works,* p. 178.

95 The Hundred Flowers Movement of 1956–1957 was followed by the brutal Anti-Rightist Campaign; the Cultural Revolution of 1966–1969 was ended by the intervention of the People's Liberation Army; the Democracy Wall Movement of 1978–1979 was quickly snuffed out by public security forces; and the latest round of democracy protests from 1986 to 1989 resulted in the tragic Tiananmen incident.

7

Business conflict, collaboration, and privilege in interwar Egypt

ROBERT VITALIS

Elizabeth Perry begins her chapter in this volume – "Labor Divided: Sources of State Formation in Modern China" – with an insightful summary of recent trends in the historiography of working classes. She argues that in reaction to the "unfulfilled promises of Marxism," recent generations of labor studies "have been obsessed with 'why not' questions: Why did workers not develop a class identity? Why did workers . . . not flock to radical political parties? Why did working-class parties . . . not engineer Marxist revolutions?" Perry is understandably ambivalent about this "search for sources of weakness in the working class." The search has led to a deeper appreciation of the diverse and often conflicting forces that comprise any proletariat. She questions, however, why such "intraclass divisions" are understood and analyzed solely as "obstacles" to political organization and action, a logic that is rooted in the belief in a particular trajectory or class project for labor ("the 'true' mission of the proletariat").[1]

In similar fashion, since World War I analysts have wrestled with the unfulfilled promises of liberalism. Theorists in various colonial and dependent territories asked one "why not" question in particular: Why did the indigenous middle class not engineer bourgeois revolutions? For instance, M. Roy and other delegates to the Third International answered this question by combining imperialism theory and nationalism in a formulation that continues to guide thinking on this subject. Many have since argued that a fundamental division in emerging capitalist classes between pro- and antinationalist (comprador) elements has undermined the capacity of one or another bourgeoisie to play its "historical role" in establishing a modern capitalist order.[2]

The comprador thesis is essentially one variant of the widespread practice of searching for sources of weakness in the capitalist class: Capitalist classes are

I am indebted to all the contributors to this volume, and especially its editors, Atul Kohli, Joel Migdal, and Vivienne Shue, for the close and thoughtful reading of early drafts. In addition, I would like to thank Joel Beinin, Eva Bellin, Nathan Brown, David Gibbs, Ellis Goldberg, Zachary Lockman, Afaf Marsot, Roger Owen, and Robert Tignor for their own generous and critical contributions to this essay.

weak because they are internally divided.[3] Because bourgeois revolutions have proved as elusive as proletarian revolutions in the twentieth century, analysts have had to explain why capitalists appear unable to advance their historical class project.[4] Intraclass divisions, immediately visible in any business community in the form of competing firms and sectors, in outlook, attitude, and so on, play the same explanatory role they play in "new wave" labor historiography. That is, divisions within the business community are also understood primarily as obstacles to collective and socially transforming class action. Once again, the emphasis on, and assumptions about the effects of, intraclass divisions derive from a belief in a particular trajectory or project for the "history-making" bourgeoisie.

Such assumptions underpin the consensus found in much contemporary scholarship on Egypt, which depicts the business community as especially weak and prone to division.[5] According to Bianchi, investors in Egypt constitute "a highly fragmented bourgeoisie, divided not only by such conventional cleavages as sector, region, size, and international competitiveness, but by equally important differences in age, education, ethics, family background, and, of course, political loyalty."[6] Yet any bourgeoisie, of any complexion, weak or strong, would fit this description. The exercise of attributing the relative weakness of Egyptian capitalists to the conflicts and divisions in their ranks is, in reality, deeply flawed. It implies that more powerful classes are somehow less divided by sectoral conflicts of interest and other divisions. In comparison with the advanced industrial economies, the business community in Egypt today remains relatively small and structurally undifferentiated. My point is that the so-called weakness of capitalist classes in Egypt or elsewhere in the Third World cannot be explained simply by pointing to the existence of intraclass divisions because divisions are so far characteristic features of all capitalist classes. Without specifying why such divisions apparently matter more in Egypt, the argument is less an analytical proposition than an act of faith.

This chapter begins to broaden the inquiry into business and politics by examining the competitive conflicts among local Egyptian investors and their relationship to regime change in the interwar Egyptian political economy. It focuses on the five-year period of authoritarian rule during 1930–1935. The course of this regime was charted by Isma'il Sidqi, who took power in June 1930, undermined the constitution, and ruled with an iron fist for three years. The Egyptian king forced Sidqi's resignation (September 1933) while continuing to back the regime. British intervention against the palace, in turn, paved the way for a "transition to democracy" (December 1935–May 1936). The politics of this period, therefore, are often discussed as being a three-way struggle for power among the Wafd, Egypt's only real mass-based party, the king, and the excolonial power, Great Britain.[7]

As I have recently discovered, competitive rivalries and conflicts of interest intersected with virtually every major skirmish fought during this precocious experiment in authoritarianism. In particular, rival coalitions of investors or "business groups" were competing for access to the investment resources of the interwar Egyptian state. Though Sidqi and his successors sought to use these resources to build and sustain business support, economic conditions constrained the regime's ability to accommodate competing interests. The intensifying wars for contracts among business rivals were critical in undermining Sidqi's political coalition, sealing the fate of his government, and shaping the post-Sidqi order.

It has become apparent across different eras, regions, and cultures that the viability of capitalist enterprise depends in large part on access to and appropriation of public resources. Egypt conforms fully to this pattern. Following their occupation of the country in 1882, the British oversaw Egypt's first experiment in capitalist "privatization" and, since the late nineteenth century, virtually every large-scale Egyptian commercial and industrial enterprise has relied on direct and indirect state support, including the transfer of state resources. Through such means, Egyptian investors like the ʿAbbud and Bank Misr groups emerged as powerful units of local private capital accumulation. These rival groups vied for control over markets, industries, and entire sectors by competing for credits, subsidies, licenses, joint venture deals, consultancies, and contracts allocated by state agencies.

In the collaborative arrangements forged between Egyptian investors and state factions, cooperation and conflict existed in uneasy balance. Such relationships exist in all market systems and reflect the "privileged" position of business. Simply stated, business privilege is rooted in the dynamics of a market-driven economy. Markets delegate public authority to private interests. In all market systems, government officials are routinely compelled to acknowledge the social power of capitalists and, to some extent, accommodate to it. The conflicts between business groups and state factions in Egypt reflected the privileged position of local capitalists and took place "because of . . . their sharing major leadership roles in the politico-economic order."[8] In looking at investor coalitions and their strategies for securing shares of state-created markets, this chapter provides a concrete means for disaggregating and analyzing the interactions of state and society in a critical policy domain.

Paradoxically, disaggregation allows us to deepen our appreciation of class-based forms of power. Similar to other forces in society, capitalists face obstacles to broad-based collective action, including the strong cross-pressures of conflict and cooperation generated by markets. Yet markets also confer some unique advantages. Firms, joint ventures, groups, and cartels were all sets of *collective* investors who had regular, direct, and effective access to political authorities in interwar Egypt. Investors were generally not compelled to unite in broader groupings in order to make their voices heard. Nonetheless, Egyptian capitalists were capable of broad forms of collective action in the *limited* arenas where, historically, this even begins to make sense, for example, over issues of redistribution.[9] Once we relax the assumption that Egyptian capitalists or industrialists sought but "failed" to attain what many analysts have imagined to be their "class project," we begin to gain a clearer appreciation of the political and social power of this emerging class, the nature and importance of intraclass cleavages, as well as the channels through which businessmen sought to promote their interests.

EGYPTIAN BUSINESS GROUPS AND THE EXPANSION OF THE SUBSIDIARY IMPORT SUBSTITUTION SECTOR

There is a tendency to think about the course of Egyptian industrialization as if it were a tug-of-war. One force in particular valiantly pulls the economy forward, the others strain to hold it back. This image is clear in the best recent studies of the interwar economy. Rutgers political scientist Eric Davis lionizes the coalition of "native Egyptians" behind the Bank Misr group which intended "to be the *motor force* behind the creation of a modern industrial sector in the Egyptian economy." Princeton historian Robert Tignor breaks with the nationalist consensus to identify the "dynamic and farsighted" cohort of resident non-Egyptian businessmen who he claims were "the real *moving force* for structural economic change." Both authors conclude that "Industrialists" ultimately lost the tug-of-war. Just as the Misr group failed "to establish itself as a viable institution . . . and to create a self sustaining industrial sector," the "Egyptian industrial bourgeoisie never gained an upper hand in the Egyptian political economy." Other social forces, such as "foreign capital" and the country's "landed magnates," managed to defeat them.[10]

One problem with such accounts is that there are few signs of such titanic clashes having taken place in the Egyptian delta towns and villages where interwar Egyptian investors tended estates, traded cotton, and, in addition, ran textile factories. In the south, along the Nile, the country's most notorious captain of interwar industry, 'Abbud Pasha, grew sugar while he tried to raise hydroelectric plants. Even the Misr group, which ostensibly was investing in industry "to lessen Egypt's economic dependence upon the production of long-staple cotton," seemed to have trouble keeping to the path. Within a decade of its founding, as it built its landmark textile manufacturing venture, the Misr group also became the country's single largest, cotton exporter.[11]

Historians generally have found it impossible to pry apart accounts of Egyptian industrial development from the course of post–World War I nationalist politics and especially the countrywide uprising of March 1919 against the British occupation. The founding of the Misr group in 1920, "in the midst of – and in some sense as part of – the struggle for national independence," has left us heroic narratives as well as analytical problems which must be reconciled in making sense of the political economy.[12] For instance, there is a peculiar symmetry to historical accounts. As the leaders of the nationalist movement

failed in their objective of "complete independence," despite the nominal transfer of power by the British in 1922, the national bourgeoisie, too, failed its
alleged objective of "economic independence."[13]

This line of argument provided an intellectual defense for the assault by the
regime of Gamal Abdel Nasser between 1954 and 1961 on the business interests
who controlled the economy.[14] Though it has been easy and, in the context of
post-1952 Egyptian politics, undoubtedly useful to construct the story of the
painful birth of Egyptian industry as a chapter in the epic of the nation, it is an
unreliable guide to the institutions and activities of Egyptian capitalists in the
decades between 1922 and 1952. The identification of an aspiring "Egyptian
industrial bourgeoisie" is itself fraught with problems, given that the creation of
relatively large-scale domestic industries, which began before World War I,
remained essentially a subsidiary investment sector for the local investors that
ran them. In other words, Egypt's most prominent industrialists were simultaneously its most politically powerful landowners, cotton exporters, mortgage
bankers, speculators, and compradors. They successfully integrated these diverse activities and so narrowed the scope of potential conflict over competing
sectoral priorities. The limited expansion of industry in Egypt complemented
rather than undermined the agro-export economy.[15] The most basic and enduring form of conflict within the business community after 1920 was the struggle
of competing capitalists for dominance over these new, albeit limited opportunities for profit and accumulation.

Business group conflict

Once the limited objectives of interwar Egyptian industrial investors are clari-
fied, the problems in the conventional accounts of class are easy to see. In
particular, there is the idea that divisions, for instance, between "native-born"
and "foreign-residential" capitalists, hindered the capacity for collective action
and hence contributed to the weakness and "social and political timidity" of this
class. The argument is entirely circular. The main evidence for its weakness is
the bourgeoisie's "failure" to organize and act to promote their imputed collective interests, presumably, in industrial transformation or in dominance over
other forces.[16]

The Egyptian business community was divided, of course, and the politics of
its members reflected these divisions, but this is simply a recognition of a basic
feature of existing capitalist systems: Investors are divided on most issues.[17] The
regular political activities of interwar Egyptian investors are better understood in
terms of conflict among competitors rather than of concert among a diverse set
of firms, sectors, or class segments. At the same time, the privileged position of
business – in terms of financial resources, access to decision makers, and
information – vis-à-vis other social sectors made it possible for capitalists more
easily to reduce costs to various *forms* of collective action.[18] Rather than

maintain the fiction that "firms" are equivalent to "individuals," or that major investors active in the political economy represent only themselves like any other hypothetical individual, I define business groups, in which coalitions of investors jointly steered sets of companies located in different sectors of the economy, as basic units of interest aggregation and collective action in interwar Egypt. The best-known Egyptian investor coalition was the *Misr group,* a closely linked set of investors led by a business nationalist and publicist, Tal'at Harb. These investors founded Bank Misr, the first completely Egyptian-owned finance institution, in 1920.[19] They gained privileged access to the post-1922 Egyptian state and used political influence to establish the group as a serious force in commercial finance, mortgage banking, cotton export, construction, shipping, building materials, tourism, textile manufacture, chemicals, insurance, and real estate.

Other Egyptian investors also sought shares in these markets, however, which vexed the Misr group and later historians to no end. The most successful competitor was a Glasgow-trained engineer, Ahmad 'Abbud, who launched a career as a contractor for goods and services in 1924. Over the next two decades, 'Abbud and allied investors built a business empire with holdings in every sector of the economy, including construction, shipping, trade, services, and manufacturing. The *'Abbud group* comprised some of Egypt's largest and most well-known enterprises of the era, including the Khedivial Mail Lines, the Egyptian Sugar and Refinery Company (a state-sanctioned monopoly), the Egyptian Omnibus Company, the Egyptian Immobilia Company, and the Fertilizer and Chemical Industries of Egypt.

The owners and top managers of these investor coalitions had regular and predictable access to political decision-makers, unlike most other individuals in Egypt. There is nothing "informal," "traditional" or particularly "Egyptian" about this: It is, in reality, one of the most common forms of capitalist association and interest articulation.[20] The first Egyptian business groups, linking prominent families within Alexandria and Cairo's minority (Greek and Jewish) communities, emerged by the turn of the century as the most important units of interest aggregation within the local business community.[21]

Their influence derived from their control of resources, including markets, which was generally buttressed by the power of the state and the political alliances that investors forged with bureaucrats and politicians. Together with Egyptian landlords, they steered a virtually unregulated commercial, agro-export economy through the last decades of the nineteenth century. Business groups were the local partners in Egypt's first large-scale industrial enterprises. Not surprisingly, then, top British and Egyptian governing officials also cooperated with these business groups during World War I in outlining a strategy for economic diversification, including development of the domestic manufacturing sector subordinate to the dominant export sector. This project received the imprimatur of the state in 1918 when the government issued the *Rapport* of the commission on commerce and industry, a cabinet-appointed panel chaired by Isma'il Sidqi, a bright star in the civil service.[22]

'Abbud, the Misr group, and other new Egyptian investors adopted the multisectoral investment strategies of an earlier generation of capitalists, rapidly advancing to commanding positions within the business community while expanding industry and Egyptianizing existing sectors. Investments in manufacturing enterprise conformed to the limited Import Substitution Industrialization (ISI) project outlined in the Sidqi commission report. The report had recognized the need for cooperation with foreign capital in developing the necessary infrastructure, obtaining machinery and technology, and in securing financing for the most ambitious enterprises.

In the 1880s and 1890s the British-controlled Egyptian state underwrote the creation of a local, predominantly non-Egyptian capitalist class (not to mention the profit margins of London bankers, Manchester spinners, and Brussels finance trusts) through privatization and related transfers of public resources. Engineering marvels of the era, like the construction of the Aswan dam, were celebrated in Egypt not least because they served as a huge source of rents and stimulus to accumulation, in the process changing the contours of city and countryside. In the 1920s and 1930s, the business community, including aspiring Egyptian investors, organized in predictable fashion as a "contested-independent" Egyptian state, proposed ambitious new public works, including urban power plants, electrification of the Egyptian delta, the heightening of the original Aswan dam, and the harnessing of the Nile waters to run new industries.

Because Egyptian businessmen are widely presumed *not* to have played a part in the central political events of the interwar era, the parallel accounts below of (1) the rise and fall of the authoritarian Sidqi regime in Egypt and (2) the 'Abbud group's efforts to develop the domestic power and nitrate sectors are developed in relatively close detail. This narrative strategy is pursued to document my claims about the Egyptian case, as well as to expand the view of where, when, and how conflicts over scarce resources take place in oligopolistically organized market economies.

The following summary will perhaps be helpful to those unfamiliar with the terrain of postcolonial Egyptian politics and society.

Muhammad Ahmad 'Abbud was a maverick Egyptian contractor who launched his career by first investing in the Wafd Party, a coalition of nationalist factions that had pressed for Egyptian independence in 1919. 'Abbud's fortunes skyrocketed, though, after he shifted his investments in favor of an authoritarian alternative to the Wafd. His main objective was to gain the government's backing for a plan to electrify the Aswan dam and use the power to manufacture nitrate fertilizers in Egypt.

Isma'il Sidqi, the quasi-dictatorial prime minister who consolidated power with 'Abbud's help in 1930, ultimately sided with 'Abbud's competitors in a number of key sectoral conflicts. ʿAbbud's failure to obtain backing for the Aswan project led him to transfer his support to alternative factions of the state. Specifically, he joined forces with the palace in its successful effort to weaken and eventually topple the Sidqi government in 1933. However, his interventions to thwart policies at home and, importantly, abroad in the British parliamentary arena helped consolidate a counteralliance of immense value to rival interests.

Hoping to reverse a decline in his economic position, ʿAbbud backed a failed attempt to reconstitute the Sidqi–palace alliance. Instead, the palace acceded to the resurrection of the 1923 constitution, new national elections, and the return of the Wafd Party to power. The regime change permitted ʿAbbud's rivals to consolidate their position in the competition for the Aswan project and other state resources.

ʿAbbud had assembled a formidable coalition to promote the Aswan scheme. It included his local co-investors; allies in strategic ministries and the palace, possibly including the king himself; and a powerful set of foreign manufacturing, finance, and engineering firms. However, the bloc failed to obtain the contract during the 1930–1933 round of negotiations, and gradually saw its position usurped by a rival bloc built around the giant English Electric Company, key members of the Wafd Party, the minister of finance, and local capitalists in the Bank Misr group. Like the ʿAbbud bloc, the strength of this coalition rested in part in its strategic ties to two of the three sides of the political triumvirate that ruled Egypt – in this case, the British Residency and the Wafd.

BUILDING AUTHORITARIANISM: BUSINESS INTERESTS AND THE SIDQI REGIME

Three basic factors account for the appointment in June 1930 of the ambitious and ruthless Ismaʿil Sidqi as Egyptian prime minister. First, the Egyptian king, who was directly responsible for placing Sidqi in office, intended to subvert the 1923 constitution in order to strengthen the power of the palace in the new "liberal" order. Although Egypt was officially a constitutional monarchy, the entire political establishment maintained an ambivalent posture toward the constitution and parliament. King Fuʾad viewed them as threats to what remained of his family's hereditary power and privilege. The main party in the country, the Wafd, championed liberal politics as a weapon with which to defend against the extralegal encroachments of Great Britain and the constant interference of the palace in administrative affairs. When in power, the Wafd and the other, smaller cliques of businessmen, professionals, and landlords interpreted the constitution flexibly. In so doing, they were merely following the lead of Great Britain, which had intervened to bring down Egypt's first popularly elected Wafd government within a year of its taking office in 1924.

This particular imperialist prerogative – intervention – was the second factor in Sidqi's rise to power. Following a failed round of treaty talks with a Wafd government early in 1930, the British also sought an alternative political leadership willing to protect Great Britain's continued interests in Egypt and able to deliver a ratified treaty of alliance with the ex-colonial power. The third factor – and here the British and the palace were no less invested than the country's landlords and the business community – was the deepening economic crisis that racked Egypt. Authoritarianism represented a response to the 1929 Depression.[23]

If the explanation for the advent of the Sidqi regime is straightforward, much about the Sidqi years remains controversial, especially the regime's base of support, the factors that led to the erosion of that support, and the causes behind the collapse of the government in September 1933.[24] For instance, UCLA historian Afaf Marsot asserts that Sidqi "had no popular backing, in fact no backing of any kind save what the king allowed him." This is true, however, only if one discounts the British Residency, strategic parts of the bureaucracy, cultivators seeking relief from falling cotton prices and rising interest rates, bankers, and other embattled sectors.[25]

Segments of the domestic business community and foreign capital had been active in championing an alternative authoritarian coalition centering on the palace since at least the spring of 1928, rallying at first to the side of Muhammad Mahmud, who dismantled parliament, suspended the constitution, and governed by decree for almost sixteen months (June 1928–October 1929). Businessmen not surprisingly celebrated Mahmud's economic plans. As the London *Times* noted with refreshing frankness, Mahmud had chosen "to divert the energies of his country from politics to construction."[26]

Mahmud's ministry made expansion of the country's power resources the centerpiece of a "reform" agenda, a course that Sidqi's 1930 government also pursued. Local investors had been promoting various electrification projects since the early 1920s in conjunction with rival segments of the international power industry. There were three main projects, each associated with a different foreign-local capital alliance. The first, the *Aswan Power Scheme,* centered on electrification of the Aswan dam, in southern (upper) Egypt. Power from the dam would be used to irrigate the nearby provinces and to manufacture chemical fertilizers. An alternative proposal called for electrification of the Egyptian delta, the fan-shaped expanse stretching north from Cairo to the Mediterranean. The main source of power for the *Delta Scheme* would be a steam-driven plant to be constructed near Alexandria. A third plan was based on construction of a new "super" power station in Shubra, a northern quarter of Cairo. The *Shubra Scheme* was designed by the foreign capitalists who dominated Egypt's energy sector to try to prevent other foreign firms from disrupting its monopoly position.

Table 1 summarizes the relationships among local capitalists, international firms, and the projects with which they were primarily associated in the period

Table 1. *Egyptian electrification schemes in 1928*

Project	Local investors	Foreign partners
Delta Scheme	Misr group	English Electric Company Ganz Danubius Siemens
Shubra Scheme	Misr group	Empain group[a]
Aswan Scheme	ʿAbbud	Dudley Docker[b]

[a]The investors known in Cairo as the Empain group were a Brussels-based power finance trust, the Schneider–Jeumont–Charleroi group
[b]Docker, a British financier, fronted an international consortium involving U.S. General Electric, its subsidiary, Associated Electrical Industries (U.K.), and a closely tied engineering arm working out of Brussels and known as Sofina.

before Sidqi took office. The primary goal of international competitors was to capture as large a share as possible of the Egyptian market, and these various projects were instruments toward this end. Thus, English Electric Company and other firms were flexible in their support, ultimately, for one project or another. The local Misr group had strategically positioned itself vis-à-vis these international competitors. The Egyptian investors quietly began contacts in 1928 with the Empain group, the Belgian-based financed trust that dominated Cairo's electricity and transport markets. Two years later, they formed a construction company with Empain and cohorts to build the Shubra station. At the same time, key Misr group figures had also forged ties to rival international firms, including the Hungarian manufacturer Ganz, the German electrical giant Siemens, and the financially strapped U.K. producer the English Electric Company.[27] Bank Misr issued its heralded two-hundred-page study *The Creation of Domestic Industries* in May 1929, in the midst of a battle for the electrification business. Couching a demand for state support for its planned new joint ventures in terms of the national interest, the bank unsurprisingly endorsed the development of hydroelectric power, fertilizer manufacturing, new transport enterprises and railroad electrification, among other projects. As the Mahmud government collapsed, the Bank Misr group deepened its ties to the incoming Wafd administration.[28]

The main local rival of the Misr group in these infrastructure projects was Ahmad ʿAbbud, the contractor whose early career depended on carefully cultivated ties to the Wafd party and to British engineers and equipment manufacturers. ʿAbbud unfortunately lost the Wafd's political backing in 1927 when his chosen candidate lost in a bid to take over the party. He invested heavily from that point on in authoritarianism, dividing his energies between promoting Ismaʿil Sidqi's quest for the premiership and the project to electrify the Aswan dam. I focus on ʿAbbud's interventions in British and Egyptian political arenas as a way to understand more about interests in the interwar economy, strategies of interest articulation, and the political capacities of *competing* Egyptian investors.

Political investments and economic rewards

Political support was crucial during the first days and weeks of Sidqi's frontal assault against the constitution and its defenders. He announced his cabinet on 20 June 1930. On the following day, he announced the suspension of parliament. On 28 June, Ahmad ʿAbbud visited officials at the British Residency (after 1936 the embassy) in Cairo to report his imminent departure for London as an unofficial emissary of the new regime. He wanted to see the British secretary of state on Sidqi's behalf. Once in England, he continued his propaganda mission through the month of July and the bloody antigovernment riots in Alexandria that left twenty-one dead, infantry units occupying the center of the city and British warships headed for the harbor. ʿAbbud traveled to London again in the fall, carrying advance notice of Sidqi's plans for a new constitution "as reactionary in form as in substance."[29]

ʿAbbud realized instant returns from these efforts on Sidqi's behalf, including the appointment of a member of the ʿAbbud group as secretary general of Sidqi's new "party," an organization formed unabashedly to deliver favors. More valuably, Sidqi reshuffled his cabinet in July, appointing an ex-employee and close ally of ʿAbbud, Ibrahim Fahmi Korayyim, as minister of public works. ʿAbbud ensured his reputation as a powerful new force in the economy through this appointment when Korayyim engineered a switch in the contract for heightening the Aswan dam. The original builder was replaced by ʿAbbud and his partners.[30]

ʿAbbud catapulted into prominence during the Sidqi years after nearly a decade of operating as a contractor, a commission agent for overseas manufacturing interests, and local partner to metropolitan financiers. He received the title of Pasha in February 1931 for his "public" service, and although he continued his lucrative canal dredging and commission work, he also expanded into the field of company promotion, investing in construction, shipping, urban transport, and, briefly, oil. Additionally, in partnership with British engineering corporations, manufacturers, and his friend Dudley Docker, one of the world's most powerful financiers, he began to expand his operations into Palestine, Iraq, and Turkey.[31]

There is little doubt that ʿAbbud expected bigger gains. He sought the government's approval for the multimillion-pound electrification joint venture, including the power plant and fertilizer factory at Aswan. The problem with this and ʿAbbud's other enterprises is that he faced stiff competition for the state's limited resources from an array of equally versatile and politically well-placed business rivals. For instance, in contemplating a textile venture, he confronted a domestic market formally cartelized by the Misr and Salvagos groups. His 1933 shipping joint venture faced off against the earlier joint ventures of the Yahya and the Misr groups, both having carved out administrative sinecures of their own. The Yahyas were part of Sidqi's cabinet. Sidqi's minister of communications fought tirelessly for Bank Misr's shipping subsidiary. As ʿAbbud entered Cairo's crowded transport market, the Belgium-based Empain group would attempt to drive him out.[32] And virtually every investor was interested in the electrification business, including Sidqi himself.

The conflict over the power sector

The deep interest in the electrification business is not hard to grasp, given, on the one hand, the drying up of markets for international manufacturers and service firms worldwide, and, on the other hand, the monopoly rents that were involved. The proposed Aswan venture was enormous. ʿAbbud's international partners drew up a grand scheme to cost 30 million pounds sterling, involving an elaborate generation–transmission–distribution network with its center at Aswan. A venture of such magnitude would depend critically on firm political support, and although Docker was reasonably assured of London's backing, the situation in Cairo was less easily managed.

Docker and ʿAbbud approached the Sidqi government with an "interim" plan designed to give the Egyptian government time to investigate the Aswan scheme. They proposed to start by constructing two steam-driven power stations at Alexandria and Cairo and setting up a transmission network in the delta and the region south of Cairo. The ploy was transparent to Sidqi, as he made clear later to the British high commissioner. If ʿAbbud and his allies carried out the Delta Scheme, this would serve as an effective barrier to potential competitors, providing a de facto monopoly.[33] This was precisely the objective of the rival Empain group whom Sidqi, a board member on their tramways enterprise, had been aiding since 1929.

ʿAbbud had access to internal memos that sketched the Belgians' plan to extend their control of Egypt's power sector. These documents also underscored Sidqi's "valuable support." Sidqi's value was confirmed by the furtive but decisive final agreement on the new plant that he orchestrated within weeks of his taking office in June 1930. Noting the secrecy surrounding the affair, the British high commissioner baldly judged it to be a blow for the "British" interests competing in the power sector and recommended somewhat naively that Docker try to take over the Empain group through his own Belgian connections.[34]

The Belgian capitalists dealt a second, more decisive blow to ʿAbbud as he attempted to enter the Cairo transport market, which was the preserve of the Empain group's tramway lines. ʿAbbud and allied Egyptian investors joined with British manufacturers to begin a bus service in Cairo. The Belgians sought to wrest control of the company from the ʿAbbud group or else drive it out of business, and they used their own allies within the cabinet to bring ʿAbbud to the negotiating table. ʿAbbud attempted throughout 1931 to stave off the attempted takeover before capitulating to the Belgians. They took over the second largest block of shares and forced ʿAbbud to pool the company's profits with the tramways, demanding 80 percent of all receipts. Once Empain scored this victory, Sidqi's suddenly conciliatory cabinet approved the company's concession and ushered it through the Senate in the summer of 1932.[35]

ʿAbbud continued to back Sidqi in 1931 while engaged behind the scenes in the war for position in the transport and power markets. The most important documented demonstration of his continued loyalty was the diplomatic mission he undertook in late spring 1931. ʿAbbud returned to London looking to reassure the regime's supporters within the business community following rigged Egyptian elections (May 1931) that had been accompanied by violence and bloodshed.[36]

The archival record nonetheless reveals a great deal about the tensions underlying the alliance between ʿAbbud and different political-bureaucratic factions. Sidqi wanted ʿAbbud's support, obviously, since he valued the influence which ʿAbbud was commonly perceived to wield through his myriad business connections in London. Yet ʿAbbud's support was predicated on obtaining the state's backing for his Aswan venture. For equally obvious reasons, the British Foreign Office valued ʿAbbud's links to U.K. manufacturers and engineering firms, yet officials began to oppose his political initiatives in support of these commercial interests. To put it bluntly, policy makers were enraged by the Egyptian businessman acting outside of the circumscribed space that the Foreign Office traditionally allotted him or any other Egyptian. Following his trip to London in May 1931, the Foreign Office sought to damage ʿAbbud's standing with the Egyptian prime minister.

Ironically, just as the regime's "corrupt" links to ʿAbbud and the businessman's alleged unswervering "service" to the British first become regular themes in the Egyptian opposition press and other venues, ʿAbbud began to find obstacles in the way of his obtaining London's diplomatic support for his business ventures, reflecting a hostility at the Foreign Office that would steadily intensify in the succeeding years.[37] At the same time, Sidqi himself would begin to erect an even more formidable set of barriers to keep ʿAbbud from obtaining the Aswan contract. As competitive pressures intensified, Sidqi's distributive coalition began to unravel and the premier was forced to make costly choices about the distribution of scarce state resources.

ʿAbbud's weakening position vis-à-vis his competitors in the transport and power sectors pushed him in 1932 to reassess his political investment strategy. As will be shown, ʿAbbud abandoned Sidqi and turned to the palace, backing King Fuʾad in his efforts to debilitate and eventually bring down the Sidqi government – a subject of increasing concern both to the British and, of course, to the prime minister. The analysis provides new insights into the factors responsible for the disaffection of elements within the proregime coalition forged by Sidqi.

BUSINESS CONFLICTS AND THE FALL
OF THE SIDQI GOVERNMENT

Relations between Sidqi and ʿAbbud grew increasingly hostile through the summer and fall of 1932. Evidence that Sidqi had begun deliberately to sabotage ʿAbbud's business deals appears in a memorandum from the office of ʿAbbud's partner in the Aswan heightening contract. It records the substance of a meeting with one of the Aswan subcontractors, a close friend of Sidqi who had traveled to London, reportedly at Sidqi's express instructions. The objective was to convince the British engineers to abandon ʿAbbud in any further dealings with the Egyptian state.[38] Sidqi later defended his action by claiming that ʿAbbud was behind a series of highly critical articles that appeared in the London *Daily Telegraph,* in August and September. This alleged newspaper campaign began in August, after London had become the center of private meetings and private intrigues, for instance, between ʿAbbud and the minister of public works, over the Aswan project.[39]

Sidqi's attempt to sabotage ʿAbbud's relations with British capitalists stemmed from the fear that ʿAbbud was attempting to undermine his regime's standing in London. British reports, in fact, date ʿAbbud's increased "influence with palace circles" to the summer of 1932, immediately before what all accounts agree was the beginning of a new, palace-led offensive against the prime minister. The most powerful figure among the king's advisors, Zaki al-Ibrashi, had close ties to ʿAbbud and would help the businessman tremendously in the months ahead. If ʿAbbud was attempting to use his influence in support of the palace and against the premier, it could only have been because Sidqi had failed to support ʿAbbud's investments in the transport and power sectors.

An influential anti-Sidqi voice in London would have been valuable that summer because Sidqi was trying to convince the British anew of his government's popularity and stability. He wanted to begin negotiations with the British for a treaty to resolve outstanding points dating back to Britain's unilateral declaration of Egyptian independence. This goal haunted virtually every Egyptian government from 1922 to 1936.[40] It was a goal which the British Foreign Office shared. The enmity of the Foreign Office toward ʿAbbud and his political activities increased, as we would expect, once ʿAbbud opted to back the palace against Sidqi. It henceforth would become increasingly difficult to separate the commercial rivalries engendered by the Aswan hydropower project from the political power struggle in Egypt that led to Sidqi's resignation in September 1933.

The fall of Sidqi

ʿAbbud played a central role in two attempts to unseat Sidqi, the first in December 1932 and the ultimately successful putsch in September 1933. Sidqi, who suspected ʿAbbud of working with the palace forces, in effect transformed the competition for the Aswan project into a contest over state power, beginning by intervening in the public works ministry scheduled tender call.[41]

According to Percy Loraine, the British high commissioner, by early December there were signs that the cabinet would split over the issue of contracts. Both Sidqi's minister of foreign affairs and Korayyim, ʿAbbud's ally at public works, were reported to be on the verge of resigning. ʿAbbud, who was sometimes described as Egypt's "unofficial" ambassador to Great Britain, had been delivering the same message about the imminent resignations to business circles in London. At the same time, the "official" Egyptian representative in London was blaming the schism on ʿAbbud, who, he claimed, controlled Korayyim and was using him as a weapon against Sidqi.[42]

In January 1933 Sidqi struck by dropping three of his ministers and shifting Korayyim out of public works. ʿAbbud's competitors judged the turbulent political currents to be moving rapidly against him, one predicting that ʿAbbud's fall "would not be long delayed." The Foreign Office seemed anxious to hasten it, judging from records of exchanges with the Residency taking place at the time.[43] ʿAbbud's steadily worsening relations with the Foreign Office, key Egyptian ministries, and the premier weakened his position in an arena crowded with business rivals advancing conflicting agendas for Aswan.

British officials in Cairo sought instructions on whom to support among the many conflicting interests. On the one hand, they were pressed for help by investors from Imperial Chemical Industries; COSACH, which was the U.K.- and U.S.-dominated Chilean export combine; and British shippers with heavy stakes in the lucrative fertilizer trade. All these investors opposed plans to build an import substitution fertilizer factory in Egypt. On the other hand, the British heavy machinery manufacturers that would supply parts of hydroelectric plant and chemical factory desperately wanted the sale. Opposition to the Aswan project also emerged within the Egyptian bureaucracy. The government's financial adviser (a British citizen) marshaled figures purporting to show that the project was a bad commercial proposition and a drain on scarce financial resources. These figures were supplied by the German chemical giant, IG Farbenindustrie, which opposed the scheme as it was already the world's single largest exporter of chemical fertilizers to Egypt.[44]

ʿAbbud joined with the palace in renewing the attack on Sidqi's government in the spring of 1933. His chief co-conspirator was Zaki al-Ibrashi, a close aide of the king's who was becoming one of the country's most powerful personalities (for the British, the most despised) as the palace interfered openly in the administration of the state. The immediate cause of Sidqi's resignation in

September 1933 is usually described as a conflict with the palace over the appointment of a new finance minister. Nonetheless, the British diplomatic staff argued that competing business interests operated behind the crisis, engaged in what Lampson, the new high commissioner, called a "corrupt struggle for the contracts of the Egyptian government." His commercial counselor labeled this the "the heart of the cabinet break-up."[45]

Tellingly, the first assessments of the new ʿAbd al-Fattah Yahya government by the Foreign Office focused on the implications for ʿAbbud's commercial interests. The ʿAbbud–Ibrashi–Korayyim combination warranted special concern, with Cecil Campbell having to assay the difficulties in making a representation against the latter's appointment.[46] The cabinet change would have a vital impact on the future of one contract in particular. As Sidqi's cabinet fell, the U.K. department of overseas trade sought to assess the status of the Aswan hydroelectric scheme. Earlier that month, the Residency staff had submitted a confidential memorandum that noted the hostility of Sidqi's late minister of public works; however, the author presciently added that this "might in no way bind his successor."[47]

THE REIGN OF THE "CONTRACTOR-POLITICIANS"

As the British and others feared, Sidqi's successor proved extremely accommodating to ʿAbbud and his palace patron and probable business partner, Zaki al-Ibrashi. Relations between the British and the new Yahya–palace government quickly deteriorated, leading to the government's fall within a year. Explanations for Britain's decisive return in 1934 to a policy of making and unmaking Egyptian cabinets focus generally on Ibrashi's unwelcomed interference in the state's administration, the "excesses of palace rule," and the "attitudes of intransigent nationalism" on the part of the Yahya government.[48] The question that concerns us here is: "excesses," "interference," and "intransigence" over what?

Competitive conflicts played a decisive role in the post-Sidqi palace offensive. ʿAbbud seized the opportunity following the fall of the Sidqi government to expand his economic interests, in close connection with Ibrashi, the man who fronted in business deals for the king and, once the monarch fell ill, wielded power in Fuʾad's name. The battles for scarce state resources and the resumption of ʿAbbud's political activities in support of the authoritarian order steeled the resolve of the British government to support a change of government in November 1934 and end the reign of the contractor politicians. At the same time, ʿAbbud and his allies confronted a formidable front of Egyptian politicians, business rivals, and British state agents determined to prevent him from participating in the Aswan Scheme. These commercial conflicts were thus intertwined with the eventual restoration of the 1923 constitution and the return of an popularly elected Wafd government to power.

Expansion of the ʿAbbud group

Palace support, a pliant prime minister, and a reliable ally at the ministry of communications encouraged ʿAbbud to undertake specific new ventures. For instance, he and his allies were determined to press ahead on a new and, of course, contested project to widen and modernize the harbor at Alexandria, an arena overseen by Korayyim. For the same reason, ʿAbbud extended his investment activities into a new field by purchasing all the ordinary shares of the Khedivial Mail Line, the Egyptian shipping company controlled by the Inchcape group, owners of the multinational Peninsular and Oriental (P&O) Line. Both these ventures put him on a collision course with an armada of rivals, including the local subsidiary of the oil multinational, Royal Dutch Shell; the Chilean Nitrate Sales Company; various competitors for the harbor works; and the local Misr group, whom the Sidqi government had aided in wresting a lucrative transport concession from the Khedivial Mail Line.[49]

ʿAbbud and co-investors had one faction of the state – the palace – behind them in this quest for the state's business. His entreaties to the British Residency for assistance in his battle to take back the transport concession were rebuffed, however, although he continued to press fruitlessly for British intervention through 1935. British support had, of course, been crucial to the success of his enterprises in the past and remained important for any group endeavoring to obtain the contract for the Aswan project. At the same time, his relations with Korayyim and other Egyptian officials were starting to come under uncomfortably close scrutiny in the press as a by-product of the "Corniche scandal" in which Sidqi was mired. ʿAbbud and his detractors, led by the ex-ministers Sidqi and ʿAfifi, exchanged charges and countercharges, in newspapers, courtrooms, and other venues.[50]

These unsavory revelations contributed to the growing disaffection with the Yahya government on the part of many of the original supporters of the authoritarian regime. The Wafd, of course, had opposed the regime from the first. Party activity, along with a range of antiregime actions launched by student groups and other extraparliamentary groups, continued. In addition, critical parts of the Sidqi coalition were abandoning the regime (or, in the case of Sidqi, had been abandoned by it). The Yahya government steadily lost the confidence of business elites, strategic state agents (no doubt innerved by the constant encroachment of the palace on hallowed bureaucratic turf), and, most important, the British Residency.

The fall of the Yahya government

The spring of 1934 saw a steady stream of visitors to the new British high commissioner, Miles Lampson, including virtually the entire roster of Egypt's business elite. ʿAbbud's name had been purposely omitted.[51] Business interests such as the Misr group and their backers, for instance, Ahmad ʿAbd al-Wahab, the new undersecretary of finance, attacked the corrupt network of palace interests. Henri Naus, the Belgian industrialist who managed the Suares group's sugar-processing monopoly, echoed this view, charging Ibrashi with dominating the administration and dragging the name of his "dear friend and business partner," the king, in the mud. Sidqi meanwhile denounced the ex-mainstays of his rule, ʿAbbud and Fuʾad, every chance he could.[52]

These critics resented the industry of ʿAbbud and his palace allies, for instance, in the Alexandria harbor expansion project where they had packed the relevant government committees with supporters. Likewise, if Sidqi is to be believed, "intrigues" by ʿAbbud forced the resignation of Hafiz ʿAfifi, Egyptian ambassador to London. If so, the act would have likely been a contributing cause of the anti-ʿAbbud sentiment growing within the Foreign Office, where ʿAfifi was well liked and respected. ʿAbbud's rivals, the Misr group, immediately offered the ex-diplomat a prominent position in the group's complex of firms.[53] Needless to say, the Foreign Office resented most of all ʿAbbud's continuing interventions in domestic British political arenas.

Concern for the "stability" of the Yahya–palace government increased markedly with the king's failing health early in 1934, and led ʿAbbud back to London one more time in June. His trip pointed to growing tension between the Yahya government and the British, whose patience – along with the heralded policy of "neutrality" – was clearly on the wane. ʿAbbud sought to diffuse tensions, to reassure influential constituencies about Yahya's intentions, and to gain the palace-dominated regime room for maneuver. Thus he addressed the foreign relations committee of the House of Commons, denouncing the Wafd Party before the legislators and arguing that King Fuʾad represented the only force in Egypt that could guarantee domestic stability and a permanent settlement with Great Britain.[54] He repeated the argument before the powerful British Federation of Industries. The Egyptian businessman remained in London throughout the summer, lobbying for the monarchy with the aid of his paid "consultant," the ex-correspondent for the *Daily Telegraph*.

These activities enraged the Foreign Office, which, among other things, was intercepting ʿAbbud's correspondence with Ibrashi.[55] The Foreign Office was newly determined to "strike and strike without delay at ʿAbbud" and to try and "open a breach" between him and Ibrashi. London ordered the Residency in Cairo to see the king and "discredit" ʿAbbud. The competitive maneuvers in pursuit of the Alexandria harbor contract were denounced as evidence that "the palace corrupts everything it touches" and that "something should be done soon to cut ʿAbbud Pasha." One official likened the situation to the excesses of the Khedive Ismaʿil. Another voiced his objections even more strongly: "[W]e should and at once see the removal of Ibrashi and ʿAbbud."[56]

The widening crisis between the British and the Egyptian government peaked during the course of the long month of October 1934 when a rapid deterioration in the monarch's health exacerbated the sense of crisis. The Foreign Office had given orders for a strict watch to be kept on ʿAbbud, who was attempting to stave off a cabinet change.[57] The British were angered by his return to London, took it as evidence of the palace's intransigence, and intensified their pressure for a new and more cooperative government. One official labeled ʿAbbud, who was "back at his old game," the cause for the British intervention (and, hence, a political crisis) because it meant "a definite disregard by the king of a plain communication to which he could have paid attention much more easily than to the drastic reforms which Mr. Peterson wishes to press on him."[58]

ʿAbbud was apparently counseling the palace that British pressures should be ignored, and that the crisis would abate once Peterson had departed Cairo, as scheduled, late in November. When the dispatch in the *Times* for 23 October 1934 carried ʿAbbud's message, essentially verbatim, officials at the Residency and the Foreign Office moved to correct the deviation from the party line.[59] Prime Minister Yahya did indeed temporize, appointing an ineffectual figure to the newly resurrected post of chief of the royal cabinet late in October, a move clearly designed to placate the British, while permitting Ibrashi (who was officially the director of the royal *waqfs* or charitable endowments) to remain. Five days later, Yahya submitted the resignations of two of his cabinet ministers to the king. On 6 November 1934 he handed in his own.[60]

Business realignment: undermining the ʿAbbud group in the Aswan project

Once again the Foreign Office lauded the likely effects of the cabinet change on ʿAbbud, deciding that he was bound to have less influence with the new government. For one, the new prime minister proved much more accommodating to British wishes than had his predecessor.[61] At the same time, the finance ministry was in the hands of Ahmad ʿAbd al-Wahab, a close ally of the Misr group and a relentless critic of ʿAbbud. Nonetheless, the continuing activities of Ibrashi and ʿAbbud in the months that followed led the British to redouble their efforts to topple them both. The constant British interference in the Egyptian domestic arena, in fact, contributed to undermining the puppetlike Mahir government by the end of 1935.[62] The Foreign Office nonetheless was determined to undermine ʿAbbud's commercial ties to British business.

The clearest example came in February 1935, when British diplomats received reports that, "after a brief interval of semi-eclipse," Ibrashi and ʿAbbud had conspired to block the grant of a concession for new bus lines to a coalition that included ʿAfifi and the Misr group. The British Residency intervened to support ʿAbbud's rival at some cost to the U.K. manufacturers that were partners in ʿAbbud's bus venture. Although the firms ʿAbbud represented in

Cairo had received a total of £E 854.5 thousand in orders in 1934, the Department of Overseas Trade branded him a menace to British commerce and worked covertly to undermine his business connections. The depth of this hostility helps to explain the determination on the part of British commercial and diplomatic officials to strengthen the links between British investors and the Bank Misr group.[63]

It also helps to explain the increasingly partisan support for one particular set of British-identified firms led by the English Electric Company in the competition for the Aswan project. The Foreign Office was intent on stopping ʿAbbud from participating in the scheme. Lampson went so far as to obtain an assurance from the chairman of the board of the EEC that his company had no connection with ʿAbbud. The Foreign Office documents repeatedly stress that the finance minister, who had moved quickly to advance his control over negotiations, was equally committed to locking out ʿAbbud.[64]

The animosity toward ʿAbbud led various Egyptian officials to exaggerate the businessman's influence with the multinational competitors. Thus, when one of the EEC's partners in the proposed project hesitated in its commitment, it was widely believed that ʿAbbud was the cause. This preoccupation with ʿAbbud led the Egyptian government toward negotiations with firms that were ambivalent at best about the project. For instance, Lampson wired back to London that Imperial Chemicals Industries (ICI), another competitor, "had been working very skillfully with the view to creating indecision in the mind of the Egyptian government about the whole scheme."[65]

ʿAbd al-Wahab invited ICI's ostensible German rivals, IG Farben, to submit a scheme as well. This may have been a bargaining ploy; it may also have reflected the influence of the Misr group, which was engaged in cotton-for-fertilizer barter deals with the German nitrate syndicate headed by IG Farben.[66] In any case, IG Farben had no greater interest in building a fertilizer factory in Egypt than ICI. The two giant firms had secretly negotiated the division of Egypt and other export markets. Yet the Egyptian cabinet in June 1935 ordered a round of exclusive negotiations with the EEC–ICI consortium for construction of the Aswan project.[67] The paradoxical result is that ʿAbbud and his foreign partners, the only interests unambiguously committed to constructing the nitrate factory along with the power plant, were locked out of the deal.

For obvious reasons, ʿAbbud sided with the palace in its steadily escalating political offensive against both the British and the British-backed government through March and April of 1935, as the Aswan negotiations were taking place. By mid-April, the British forced the resignation of Ibrashi and his banishment to Brussels. As the repressive order in place in Egypt since 1930 started to collapse late in 1935, ʿAbbud tried investing one last time in authoritarianism.

Mass demonstrations in December 1935 had paved the way for the restoration of the 1923 constitution. Despite the formation of a united front among political parties, factional conflicts ensued over the issues of the composition of a successor regime and the timing of parliamentary elections. The compromise worked out between December 1935 and January 1936 led to the formation of a "neutral" cabinet while deferring elections until later in the year.[68]

Among the remarkable achievements of this period, Isma'il Sidqi staged a political comeback, taking a commanding role in the factional squabbles behind the united front. Sidqi bragged openly of his leadership role to British representatives and of having instigated student riots early in January.[69] He was more circumspect regarding another of his recently concluded alliances. News of a rapprochement with 'Abbud would have likely proved troubling to the diplomats. The politician who had worked so assiduously against 'Abbud's business interests during his last year in office had, by January 1936, accepted a position on the board of the Khedivial Mail Line, 'Abbud's shipping joint venture, and joined forces with the businessman in the Aswan deal.

The alliance made sense for 'Abbud. His economic interests were suffering at the hands of the British state and he had little hope of benefiting by the Wafd's resumption of power. Instead, the businessman was promoting an alternative political solution, namely, a return to the palace–Sidqi dictatorship of 1930, although he vigorously denied any role in the politics of the opposition front.[70]

The competing business interests launched yet another attack on the government's plans to cooperate with the English Electric Company in the Aswan scheme. EEC officials panicked on learning that 'Abbud and Sidqi had apparently obtained the prime minister's cooperation in delaying the presentation of the plan to the cabinet for its approval. The British multinational sought diplomatic support, leading London to manufacture a fictitious rationale for abandoning its policy of neutrality between British competitors and to press the Egyptian government to conclude a final agreement with the EEC and its allies.[71]

Time was running out. Elections were scheduled for early May. The EEC interests and their allies in the British government evinced the growing fear that the project would not be pushed through before the transfer of power to a popularly elected Wafd government. Even before the British high commissioner could intervene, a new political crisis erupted upon the sudden death of King Fu'ad late in April 1936. Despite the last-minute efforts of the British government, state factions remained deadlocked over the Aswan project when Egyptian elections were held during the first week in May.[72]

Lampson received instructions to see the new government immediately and to press for a decision on the Aswan scheme. It was obvious, however, that decision making would not be any more straightforward under the new regime. British officials learned that the Wafd's minister of public works was secretly on the payroll of the English Electric Company.[73]

CONCLUDING REMARKS

Private and public interests formed coalitions, or conflicted, profitably in some cases.[74]

This analysis of business interest conflict in Egypt has introduced a neglected dimension in conventional accounts of interwar-era regime change. Until now, historiographical approaches to Egyptian politics and society in the 1930s have concentrated on ideological change and the vicissitudes of Egyptian nationalism or else have narrated what is familiarly known as the "three-way struggle for power" among the Wafd, the palace, and the British Residency. But these accounts have never sought to explain exactly what was at stake at any point in the contest for control of the post-1922 Egyptian state. One answer to this question emerges over and over again in Ibrashi's "constant interference" over "administrative matters," in Sidqi's maneuvers to fend off the palace, and in the relentless British pressure on the "subservient" government of Nasim throughout 1935.

Commercial rivalries or material conflicts of interest quite clearly intersected with virtually every major political battle fought during Egypt's precocious experiment with authoritarianism. As I have tried to document, businessmen were investing in Egypt's new order. Isma'il Sidqi assiduously courted them because, as Berque correctly notes, the government needed "accomplices."[75] Political scientists might see the Sidqi regime's relations to the business community in terms of the "autonomy" of the state and the "subordination" of societal interests via "patron–clientelism," but Sidqi understood the political economy. Sidqi needed the business community at least as much as investors needed a strongman to steer Egypt through the Great Depression. Sidqi bargained with landlords and capitalists in order to stabilize the economy. Businessmen needed inducements to act. Sidqi made no attempt to appeal to an alternative social base. What is remarkable about the period is the extent to which Sidqi, unlike authoritarians such as Lázaro Cárdenas in Mexico, Getúlio Vargas in Brazil, or Kemal Atatürk in Turkey, avoided expansion of the public sector. The relatively limited resources of the state were one of the only incentives that Sidqi could offer competing investors.

In this struggle among rival business groups and their allies there appears to have been no effective mechanism or agency for coordinating the biggest industrial project of those years, the proposed power and manufacturing development at Aswan, or implementing an alternative or even mediating the many conflicts involved. The British Agency–Residency performed this function in the period 1882–1919, but lost absolute authority over economic decision-making in the postindependence era. In the period under study here, policy was made in an environment marked by increasingly fragmented control over the state's resources, which were being fought over and captured by "particularistic" coalitions of investors and their allies. The 'Abbud group, which linked various foreign and local business partners (e.g., Ahmad Rushdi), "public" officials like Korayyim, and the palace stalwart, Ibrashi, is a case in point. The continued absence of coordination either through voluntary arrangements negotiated by the competing coalitions or through the auspices of the state would prove costly to all parties.

The account presented above contradicts the conventional portrait of Egyptian investors like ʿAbbud merely acting as fronts for foreign business, on the "fringes" of Egyptian interwar politics, and as "clients" of British diplomats and Egyptian cabinet ministers. These familiar and unflattering characterizations reflect and help reproduce a set of problematic assumptions about Egypt's so-called weak bourgeoisie (and its constituent parts) that are derived from a particular narrative about "national capitalism" and how it is supposed to unfold.

By relying on, and conflating, the familiar narratives of national capital and the industrial bourgeoisie, conventional accounts have tended to misspecify the locus of interwar Egyptian business interest conflict, for instance in terms of nonexistent clashes between sectorwide groupings of capitalists (e.g., the Federation of Industries versus the Chamber of Commerce), or in terms of clashes between nonexistent "factions" of capital (e.g., "compradors," "commercial interests"). They have often misjudged the political capacities of Egyptian businessmen. And in essence they have misread the history of the political economy in the 1920s and 1930s.

Thus, the stories that are habitually told about Egyptian businessmen in the 1930s describe why these capitalists "failed" – or at least faltered – in leading Egypt through (what should have been) far-reaching economic and social transformation (the bourgeois or national capitalist project). For instance, in most accounts ʿAbbud stands for a type of investor or a segment of the capitalist class that allegedly served to retard the progressive development of local industry. More generally, class divisions are described and analyzed mainly as a problem for capitalist collective action of the kind – usually left unspecified – that ostensibly would have gained the capitalist class or national capital or the bourgeoisie more power and, axiomatically, would have led to more rapid and more extensive industrialization.

I have tried to tell a different story about Egyptian capitalists and politics here, one that does not rest on the assumption that, over time, capitalists tend to (or should) define and pursue their interests in political arenas through ever more comprehensive organizational forms, and that these more approximate classlike forms of collective action tend to (or should) replace individualistic or particularistic pursuits. Some very simple ideas about politics are usually part of this story – notably, the idea that capitalists organize collectively in interest groups in order to contest for state power (to "capture the state"). Thus, divisions among capitalists serve both as an underlying cause and convenient index of the relative (lack of) power of a particular class.

Even careful analysts can fall prey to the logic of this type of developmental instrumentalism. For instance, in a recent and generally insightful study of capitalists in Indonesia, Richard Robison discusses the importance of monopolies, licenses, and credits to the various Indonesian business factions, but he is careful to underscore that distribution of these resources was "not imposed upon the state by a politically cohesive and powerful bourgeoisie." The point is not meaningful. As I have shown, these are simply not policy arenas around which a "class," cohesive or otherwise, would ever organize. They are instead classic arenas of conflict for competing investors.[76] In interwar Egypt, coalitions of investors like the ʿAbbud group represented a basic institutional form of capitalist collective action, and these competing, multisectoral coalitions regularly and effectively pressed their so-called particularistic concerns, for instance, in the competition for contracts and concessions. The state's resources represented a central arena of conflict for investors, and so-called parasitic relations with the state, which were pioneered by the generation of non-Egyptian (British, French, Belgian, Italian, Greek, etc.) capitalists that preceded ʿAbbud and his "national" cohort, were an essential part of this formative era in Egypt's capitalist economy. The situation is evocative of many contemporary settings, including Indonesia, where a "conglomerate of capitalist factions" has emerged through the steady appropriation of state resources.[77]

Like business interests elsewhere, Egyptian entrepreneurs recognized that their survival in the market depended on the capacity to reduce or eliminate competition. There were at least two, often related processes by which they attempted to secure this goal. The first was through political action, notably the development of ties to strategic actors or sectors of the state apparatus, documented in detail in this chapter. The second was through concentration of resources, a process facilitated by the organization of capitalists into groups. Collective action by these competing investor coalitions continued even as capitalists organized alternative institutional forms. Indeed, the institutionalization of these coalitions probably tended to preempt the use of alternative sectoral forms of political interest articulation (e.g., chambers of industry) for two reasons. First, the highly oligopolistic structure of many markets reduced the need for explicit intrasectoral coordination.[78] Second, these multisector business groups coordinated and centralized decisions for holdings in different markets. The locus of power and decision was the group, not any particular sectoral subsidiary.

I have used the historical materials on Egypt to show that the claims made about "fragmented," "unorganized," and "weak" capitalist classes are either inaccurate or unenlightening, particularly when extracted from a particular kind of long-term, comparative-historical narrative of "development." Within this narrative tradition, of course, virtually *every* case of industrialization since Great Britain has involved the problem of a "weak" bourgeoisie, defined in a very specific sense, as Gramsci conceptualized it, in terms of "hegemony."[79] Most analyses of business and politics in Egypt, however, seem to assume that such "class projects" are real and translatable into specific acts by specific interest groups, organizations, parties, and the like, rather than understanding these ideas in metaphorical terms. And these metaphors evidently can obscure as much as they reveal about the nature of the institutions, strategies, and power of capitalists.

NOTES

1 For the theoretical underpinnings of this critique, see Jean L. Cohen, *Class and Civil Society: The Limits of Marxian Critical Theory* (Amherst: University of Massachusetts Press, 1982), and Ernesto Laclau and Chantal Mouffe, *Hegemony and Socialist Strategy* (London: New Left Books, 1985).

2 This thesis was a mainstay of Chinese Comunist Party theory in the 1920s. See the seminal critique by Alec Gordon, "The Theory of the 'Progressive' National Bourgeoisie," *Journal of Contemporary Asia* (October 1973): 192–203; for an example of its continuing influence in revolutionary thought, see the analysis by the Popular Liberation Forces–Farabundo Martí (FPL–FM) in Tricontinental Society, *El Salvador: The Development of the People's Struggle* (London, 1980), as cited in James Dunkerley, *The Long War: Dictatorship and Revolution in El Salvador* (London: Verso, 1982), pp. 92, 221. The nationalist origins of this doctrine are evident in its widespread dissemination outside revolutionary Marxist circles. For the case of Egypt, see Peter Gran, "Modern Trends in Egyptian Historiography: A Review Article," *International Journal of Middle Eastern Studies*, 9 (1978): 367–371, and Robert Vitalis, "On the Theory and Practice of Compradors: The Role of ʿAbbud Pasha in the Egyptian Political Economy," *International Journal of Middle East Studies*, 22 (1990): 291–315.

3 This same argument about divisions within the capitalist class is used in defense of pluralist approaches to the U.S. case, and against the claims concerning the disproportionate power of the business community here. See, for instance, Robert Hessen, ed., *Does Big Business Rule America?* (Washington, D.C.: Ethics and Public Policy Center, 1987). In interwar Egypt, "national" or "ethnic" divisions in the business community are usually highlighted, for obvious reasons.

4 See Immanuel Wallerstein, "The Bourgeois(ie) as Concept and Reality," *New Left Review*, 167 (January–February 1988): 91–106.

5 For a review and discussion that departs from this consensus, see Alan Richards, "Ten Years of Infitah: Class, Rent, and Policy Stasis in Egypt," *Journal of Development Studies*, 20 (July 1984): 323–338.

6 Robert Bianchi, "Businessmen's Associations in Egypt and Turkey," *Annals*, 482 (1985): 147–154: 153, cited in Robert Springborg, *Mubarak's Egypt: Fragmentation of the Political Order* (Boulder, Colo.: Westview Press, 1989), p. 69.

7 For a recent example of this conventional characterization of interwar Egyptian politics, see Gabriel Warburg, " 'The Three-Legged Stool': Lampson, Faruq and Nahhas 1936–1944," in G. Warburg, *Egypt and the Sudan: Studies in History and Politics* (London: Frank Cass, 1985), pp. 116–157.

8 Charles Lindblom, *Politics and Markets: The World's Political-Economic Systems* (New York: Basic Books, 1977), p. 179.

9 See Theodore Lowi, "American Business, Public Policy, Case Studies and Political Theory," *World Politics*, 16 (July 1964): 677–715.

10 Eric Davis, *Challenging Colonialism: Bank Misr and Egyptian Industrialization, 1920–1941* (Princeton: Princeton University Press, 1983), quotes from pp. 3 and 9;

Robert L. Tignor, *State, Private Enterprise, and Economic Change in Egypt, 1918–1952* (Princeton: Princeton University Press, 1984), pp. 252, 246.

11 Quote from Davis, *Challenging Colonialism*, p. 3. For rankings of cotton exporters, see George Pilavachi, ed., *Egyptian Cotton Year Book for 1931–1932* (Alexandria: Societé de Publications Egyptiennes, 1932), p. 199. For background, see Robert L. Tignor, "Bank Misr and Foreign Capitalism," *International Journal of Middle East Studies*, 8 (1977): 161–181. Conventional historiography of the post-1919 economy treats this apparent contradiction in the investment strategy of the Misr group as a fundamental political problem that requires explanation. I am challenging this assumption and discounting the familiar forms of "theorizing" about it.

12 Joel Beinin and Zachary Lockman, *Workers on the Nile: Nationalism, Communism, Islam, and the Egyptian Working Class, 1882–1954* (Princeton: Princeton University Press, 1987), p. 10.

13 See Marius Deeb, "Bank Misr and the Emergence of the Local Bourgeoisie in Egypt," *Middle Eastern Studies*, 12 (October 1976): 69–86: 82. Tignor, *State, Private Enterprise* titles his account of the economy in the decade following independence "High Hopes Dashed, 1924–1929."

14 I have been influenced in my thinking on this point by the historiographical review of ʿAsim al-Disuqi, *Nahw fahm tarikh misr al-iqtisadi al-ijtimaʿi* (Cairo, Dar al-kitab al-jamiʿi, 1981). For a discussion of the ideological factors that led the left in many countries to embrace "national reformism" and "reconciled them to the apparently unlimited growth of state power," see Nigel Harris, *The End of the Third World: Newly Industrializing Countries and the Decline of an Ideology* (London: Penguin Books, 1987), quote from p. 122.

15 For a parallel case that is developed at great length, see Maurice Zeitlin and Richard Earl Ratcliff, *Landlords and Capitalists: The Dominant Class of Chile* (Princeton: Princeton University Press, 1988).

16 Tignor, *State, Private Enterprise*, pp. 246–247; Deeb, "Bank Misr," pp. 80–82, "The new local bourgeoisie suffered from social and political timidity" and "failed to achieve its goals of economic independence."

17 The numerous divisions among Egyptian capitalists, however, were hardly insurmountable obstacles to broad-based capitalist collective action. The founding of the Association of Industries in 1922, a cross-sectoral association of the country's largest employers, including the sugar industry, the construction industry, the transport and other utility industries, followed an unprecedented level of working-class political action. See Beinin and Lockman, *Workers on the Nile,* pp. 83–158; Deeb, "Bank Misr," p. 74; and Robert Bianchi *Unruly Corporatism: Associational Life in Twentieth Century Egypt* (New York: Oxford University Press, 1989), pp. 68–69.

18 See Mancur Olson, *The Logic of Collective Action* (Cambridge, Mass.: Harvard University Press, 1971); and Thomas Ferguson, "Party Realignment and American Industrial Structure: The Investment Theory of Political Parties in Historical Perspective," in Paul Zarembka, ed., *Research in Political Economy*, vol. 6 (Greenwich, Conn.: JAI Press, 1983), pp. 1–82.

19 The single best account of the Misr group is found in Davis, *Challenging Colonialism.*

20 Other forms include corporations, cartels, trusts, industrywide associations (e.g., a bankers' association), sectorwide associations (chamber of commerce, the National Association of Manufacturers), and cross-sectoral associations (an employers' federation, the Business Roundtable, etc.). For an elaboration, see Claus Offe and Helmut Wiesenthal, "Two Logics of Collective Action: Theoretical Notes on Social Class and Organizational Form," in *Political Power and Social Theory,* vol. 1

(Greenwich, Conn.: JAI Press, 1980), pp. 67–115; and Olson, *The Logic of Collective Action.*

21 This discussion is based on the account in Robert Vitalis, *When Capitalists Collide: Business Conflict and the End of Empire in Egypt* (Berkeley, Calif.: University of California Press, forthcoming).

22 Five businessmen served on the nine-person commission. Three, including Tal'at Harb, were associates of the powerful minority Suares group. A fourth represented the French utilities trust that owned the gas concession in Cairo. The fifth was a leading Egyptian cotton exporter. See Commission du commerce et de l'industrie, *Rapport* (Cairo: Imprimerie Nationale, 1918). For summaries, see Charles Issawi, ed., *The Economic History of the Middle East 1800–1914: A Book of Readings* (Chicago: University of Chicago Press, 1967; Midway rpt. ed., 1975), pp. 453–460; and Tignor, *State, Private Enterprise,* pp. 55–58. Readers familiar with the conventional accounts will recognize at once the revisionist thrust of my summary.

23 Afaf Marsot, *Egypt's Liberal Experiment: 1922–1936* (Berkeley: University of California Press, 1977), pp. 132–137.

24 This discussion draws on Mona Abul-Fadl, "The Sidqi Regime in Egypt (1930–1935): New Perspectives," Ph.D. dissertation, University of London, 1975; Marius Deeb, *Party Politics in Egypt: The Wafd and Its Rivals, 1919–1939* (London: Ithaca Press, 1979); Tignor, *State, Private Enterprise;* Jacques Berque, *Egypt: Imperialism and Revolution* (New York: Praeger, 1972); 'Abd al-'Azim Ramadan, *Tatawwur al-haraka al-wataniya fi Misr min sana 1918 ila sana 1936,* 2nd ed. (Cairo: Maktaba Madbuli, 1983); Marsot, *Egypt's Liberal Experiment;* and Paniyotis Vatikiotis, *A Modern History of Egypt,* 2nd ed. (Baltimore: Johns Hopkins University Press, 1980).

25 Marsot, *Egypt's Liberal Experiment,* p. 138. On Sidqi's support among "financial interests" and "enlightened Egyptians and foreigners," see *New York Times,* 14 September and 2 November 1930, 12 April 1931; and Berque, *Imperialism and Revolution,* p. 441.

26 *Times,* 29 October 1928. For investors' views, see the account of the meeting among Mahmud, the Yahya group, and other Alexandria investors, *Times,* 6 November 1928.

27 Vitalis, "Theory and Practice," pp. 301–302; Clement Levy, *The Stock Exchange Year Book of Egypt,* 1943 ed., p. 695; FO371/12358, J1939/758/16, Memorandum of the Department of Overseas Trade, 13 July 1927; J2449/758/16, Henderson to FO, 26 August 1927; *al-Waq'a'i al-Misriya,* 12 and 19 January 1928; *Pesti Tozsde,* 20 September 1928, translated in FO371/13138, J3032/130/16, Department of Overseas Trade, 22 October 1928; FO371/13877, J1391/1056/16, Lloyd to FO, 5 May 1929; J1476/1056/16, Lloyd to FO, 15 May 1929; FO371/13870/J2382/297/16, enclosing memo by Larkins, 8 August 1929.

28 Tignor, "Bank Misr," p. 170; FO371/13870, J1664/297/16, enclosing dispatch from Turner to Department of Overseas Trade, 22 May 1929; FO371/14636, J1433/130/16, enclosing dispatch from Turner to DOT, 8 April 1930, "Memorandum on the subject of the positions occupied in the Egyptian government service by members of the Muharram family."

29 FO371/14616, J2235/4/16, Cairo Chancery to Egyptian Department, 29 June 1930; J2360/4/16, 'Abbud to Selby, 10 July 1930 and FO Minute (Selby), 15 July 1930; FO371/14620, J3167/4/16, Telegram from Hoare, 22 September 1930. 'Abbud sought assurances that the British would not interfere with Sidqi's "reforms." London officials assured the House of Commons that they would not be part of any "alteration

of the electoral law." *New York Times*, 17 July 1930. If this message was seriously meant to stop Sidqi, perhaps it should have been made stronger. For details of the October 1930 constitution, see Deeb, *Party Politics*, pp. 241–242. The description is from Berque, *Imperialism and Revolution*, p. 442.

30 Deeb, *Party Politics*, pp. 278–281; Robert Keith Middlemas, *The Master Builders* (London: Hutchinson, 1963), pp. 305–306; FO 371/14633, J3291/93/16, Hoare, 4 October 1930; J3459/93/16, Hoare, 11 October 1930; J3558/93/16, FO Minute (Mack) 29 October 1930.

31 *al-Ahram*, 6 February 1970; R. P. T. Davenport-Hines, *Dudley Docker: The Life and Times of a Trade Warrior* (Cambridge: Cambridge University Press, 1984).

32 On the cartel that controlled the textile sector, the state's support and evidence of ʿAbbud's early interest in it, see Robert L. Tignor, *Egyptian Textiles and British Capital, 1930–1956* (Cairo: American University of Cairo Press, 1989), pp. 26, 35; on the shipping business joint ventures, see the series of files in FO371/13878, 1929; and FO371/15417, J699/162/16, Baker (Board of Trade), 6 March 1931; on Duss, see Davis, *Challenging Colonialism*, p. 141; on the transport industry, see Vitalis, "Theory and Practice," pp. 298–300.

33 Davenport-Hines, *Dudley Docker*, p. 211; FO371/15420, J357/357/16, FO Minute, 4 February 1931; and J1606/357/16, Loraine to FO, 7 May 1931.

34 See FO371/14646, letter from ʿAbbud to Turner, 27 May 1930, and enclosing documents titled "Notes from Egypt" and Societé Egyptienne d' Electricité, both dated 25 March 1930; J1978/752/16, Department of Overseas Trade, 17 June 1930; J2595/752/16, P. Loraine, Cairo, 31 July 1930; and J2797/752/16, P. Loraine, Cairo, 6 August 1930. London was suspicious of Docker's connection with the American-born engineer Dannie Heineman, who ran the Brussels-registered utilities corporation Sofina, but they considered the venture "British" finally because of Docker's presumed ownership of the U.K. electrical manufacturer. According to Docker's biographer, "American control of Metrovick was known to a limited circle only." See Davenport-Hines, *Dudley Docker*, p. 180.

35 FO371/16123, J1127/429/16, Turner to Department of Overseas Trade, 19 April 1932, enclosing memorandum by Larkins, "Recapitulation of the History of the Cairo Motor Omnibus Concession"; *Egyptian Gazette*, 7 July 1932; *al-Jarida al-Ra'smiya*, 14 July 1932; Vitalis, "Theory and Practice," pp. 298–300.

36 FO141/766, 801/2/31, Turner to Murray (FO), 21 May 1931. For descriptions of the atmosphere surrounding the elections, see Berque, *Imperialism and Revolution*, p. 443; Vatikiotis, *History of Egypt*, p. 288, and Deeb, *Party Politics*, pp. 243–244.

37 See United States Record Group 59, 1930–1939, 883.6113/60, Jardine to State, 10 February 1932; and *al-Jihad*, 24 February 1932.

38 FO141/759, [The Residency's File on ʿAbbud for 1933], 254/2/33, Memorandum of interview with Commandante Dentamaro, signed E.D.J., 6 September 1932. The rival investor, Emmanuel Dentamaro, was the son of a landowner from Bari, Italy, who owned a construction firm, ran brickworks and quarries, carried out reclamation work, and engaged in speculative land development. See Arnold Wright and H. Cartwright, eds., *Twentieth Century Impressions of Egypt: Its History, People, Commerce, Industries and Resources* (London: Lloyds, 1909), pp. 351–352. Sidqi eventually admitted to the substance of these charges. See, for instance, *La Reforme*, 15 March 1934. Dentamaro was also a principal figure in the Corniche scandal that had embroiled Sidqi.

39 Egyptian diplomats in London claimed that the author of the attacks on Sidqi's regime was in the pay of ʿAbbud. In response to the continuing "hostility" shown

toward Sidqi, a ruthless authoritarian, the Foreign Office planned to limit the correspondent's access to Whitehall. FO141/759 254/1/33, Minutes of First Meeting Held at the Residency, 6:30 p.m., 10 January 1933; FO371/17019, J127/127/16, letter from Peterson to Loraine, 17 January 1933, and FO Minute on Professor Gerothwohl, 16 January 1933; J303/127/16, Loraine to Peterson, 28 January 1933. For the intrigues between ʿAbbud and Korayyim, see *La Bourse Egyptienne,* 25 August 1932; *La Reforme,* 7 and 15 March 1934; *al-Ahram,* 13 March 1934; Proceedings of the Cairo Assize court in libel action brought by ʿAbbud against *al-Siyasa,* 15 December 1934, reported in FO371/18014, J3219/660/16, Peterson to FO, 22 December 1934; J2831/660/16, Peterson to FO, 22 November 1934, enclosing C. D. R. Lumby to L. Smith.

40 See Marsot, *Egypt's Liberal Experiment,* pp. 160–161, on Sidqi's desire for treaty negotiations, as well as for a general summary of the political climate during the summer of 1932. On ʿAbbud and the Palace elites, see FO371/20916, J1989/815/16, Lampson to FO, 16 April 1937, Egyptian Personalities Report, entry on ʿAbbud.

41 *Egyptian Gazette,* 15 and 16 November 1932; FO371/16116, J3398/128/16, enclosing a letter from Larkins (no. 1108), 17 November 1932; Council of Deputies, Committee on Financial Affairs, *Taqrir al-lajna ʿan mashruʿ kahraba khazan Aswan,* Report No. 111 (Cairo: Royal Printing Office, 1948); and ʿAbd al-ʿAziz Ahmad, *Kahraba Misr* (Cairo: Ministry of Public Works, 1955).

42 See FO371/16110, J3362/14/16, Loraine to FO, 10 December 1932, and note by Peterson, dated 22 December 1932.

43 FO371/17019, J424/127/16, letter from Bagg to Loraine, 19 January 1933, Loraine to Bagg, 20 January 1933, and Crowe to Loraine, 16 February 1933; and FO371/17020, J246/246/16, memo by Farrer, DOT, 24 January 1933, for the quote.

44 See the *Times,* 8 August 1932; and Joseph Levy, "Egypt Stirred by Cabinet Dismissals over Demand for Justice, Reforms," *New York Times,* 8 January 1933; FO371/16116, J3398/128/16, Larkins to DOT, 7 December 1932. "State Finance in Egypt"; FO371/17003, J15/15/16, DOT Memorandum, 31 December 1932; J507/15/16, enclosing letter from ʿAbbud to Larkins, 22 January 1933, Farrer to Cairo, 23 February 1933, and letter from Selous to DOT, 11 February 1933; and J2344/15/16, DOT, 27 September 1933, enclosing Larkins's memo, "Hydroelectric Scheme for Generation of Power by Means of the Aswan Dam." The British chemical industries expert attached to the Egyptian department of commerce (ministry of finance), Dr. Fyleman, later admitted to basing all his calculations on the IG Farben report in submitting one of his own to the ministry. Fyleman's report, not surprisingly, concluded that local production of fertilizers would be uneconomical.

45 For the first interpretation, see Deeb, *Party Politics,* p. 249, Marsot, *Egypt's Liberal Experiment,* p. 162, and Ramadan, *Tatawwur,* p. 763, the latter citing – and correcting – Sidqi's memoirs. For Lampson's description, see FO141/498, 218/5/34, draft telegram from Lampson to Simon, 18 March 1934; Selous's characterization is found in the same file, 218/4/34, Minute Sheet, Commercial Secretary for His Excellency [i.e., Lampson], "Abbud and Company versus Dentamaro and Company," Selous, 13 March 1934. I do not mean to dispute the factors emphasized by others, for instance, the recall of Loraine, the failure of Sidqi to initiate negotiations, and so on; but these explanations are not able to explain why the breakup occurred when it did, nor the logic of the cabinet changes. The weight of the ʿAbbud–Sidqi conflict in influencing events would be indirectly confirmed by the vehemence with which ʿAbbud and the palace pursued Sidqi after his resignation through the investigation of what became known as the Corniche Road scandal.

46 FO371/17009, J2329/25/16, Campbell to FO, 25 September 1933.

47 FO371/17003, J2344/15/16, Department of Overseas Trade, 27 September 1933, enclosing letter by Larkins to DOT, 6 September 1933.

48 Marsot, *Egypt's Liberal Experiment*, p. 171; Deeb, *Party Politics*, p. 252, quoting a dispatch from Lampson to Simon, 3 May 1934 (FO407/217, Part CXV, No. 38).

49 For documentation on 'Abbud's takeover of Inchcape's Egyptian interests, see FO371/19094, J9718/1366/16, Lampson to FO, 14 December 1935. For the circumstances behind the sale, see Stephanie Jones, *Trade and Shipping: Lord Inchcape 1852–1932* (Manchester: Manchester University Press, 1989). For business opponents to 'Abbud, see FO371/17020, J246/246/16, DOT Dispatch, 27 January 1933; FO371/18014, 2265/636/16, Peterson to FO, 22 September 1934; FO371/17022, J2863/261/16, Selous to DOT, 21 November 1933; and the series of files in FO371/17999, beginning with J75/75/16.

50 The stories began appearing in March 1934. The political opposition used the ongoing war as an excuse to call for the government's resignation. For a copy of the report issued by the commissions formed to investigate the Corniche scandal, see FO371/17996, J1057/71/16, Lampson to FO, 30 April 1934.

51 See the diaries of Sir Miles Lampson, Lord Killearn, St. Antony's College, Oxford (hereafter, *Killearn Diaries*), 5 March and 4 April 1934.

52 *Killearn Diaries*, 13 April 1934; FO371/17996, J667/71/16, Lampson to FO, 9 March 1934, reporting conversation between Sidqi and the oriental secretary; FO371/17977, J1095/9/16, Lampson to FO, 28 April 1934, reporting a conversation between him and Sidqi. The ex-premier claimed that he was heavily in debt to both Bank Misr and the National Bank of Egypt while the king had closed off "all business avenues" to him.

53 On the harbor scheme see FO371/18014, J1462/636/16, enclosing minutes from the Egyptian Government's financial adviser, Frank Watson, dated 24 April 1934; on Sidqi's charge see FO371/17978, J1228/9/16, enclosing dispatch from Heathcote-Smith (Alexandria) to Cairo, reporting a conversation with Sidqi, 7 May 1934. Lampson affirmed it as well. See his paragraph on 'Afifi in FO371/20916, J1989/815/16, Egyptian Personality Report, 16 April 1937.

54 See the account in FO371/17978, J1670/9/16, J. Loder (MP) to Lord Cranbourn, 12 July 1934.

55 I have made the judgment on the FO's intrigue based on FO371/18019, J1772/1772/16, Green File, labeled Ahmad 'Abbud Pasha. The dispatch in J1772/1772/16, enclosing draft letter from Oliphant to Lampson, 26 July 1934, includes a copy of an intercepted correspondence which Lampson was ordered to destroy. Also see a second letter from Oliphant to Lampson, 3 August 1934. Once again, British diplomats wanted protests lodged with the Egyptian authorities. 'Abbud's lobbying activities continued, nevertheless, much to the consternation of the foreign policy bureaucrats.

56 Surveillance of the businessman continued and the Foreign Office took steps to prevent 'Abbud from meeting with Sir Frederick Leith-Ross, the British government's chief economic advisor. FO371/18019, J1772/1772/16, enclosing draft dispatch to Peterson, 12 September 1934; letter from Kelly to Peterson, 12 September 1934; and the note from Leith-Ross's secretary, 11 September 1934. Quotes are from the minutes appended to J2265/636/16, Peterson to FO, 22 September 1934, Alexandria Harbor Extension Scheme.

57 For one example, see the minute by Thompson appended to FO371/18014, J3219/660/16. 'Abbud, whom he called the "divine crook," had a company director from a

major British engineering firm, J. Stone and Company, visit the Foreign Office and sing his praises on behalf of domestic business interests. The official warned of the danger if the Yahya government fell and ʿAbbud's influence was diminished. However, see Marsot, *Egypt's Liberal Experiment*, p. 172, who suggests that the king was convinced of the need to change the government.

58 FO371/17980, J2521/9/16, minute attached to file. J2521/9/16, enclosing personal and secret telegram from Peterson to Wellesley (my notes do not indicate the date).

59 FO371/17980, J2521/9/16. According to a minute by Somers-Cocks, "Abbud's advice has found its way straight into the *Times*. It is very mischievous. Shows that Mr. Peterson's advice has not been taken and remains to be seen whether the defiance has been prompted by despair or by optimism." The FO planted its own story the next day.

60 This chronology is based on dispatches in the *Times*, 29 October, 2, 5, 6, and 7 November 1934. The delay in Yahya's resignation was due in part to conflicts among the power brokers in agreeing to the next premier. See Ramadan, *Tatawwur*, pp. 767–768.

61 "So pliant and willing a collaborator" was Lampson's assessment of Muhammad Tawfiq Nasim, the new premier. Reference is found in Marsot, *Egypt's Liberal Experiment*, p. 173. Also see the discussion of ʿAbbud in a note appended by Thompson to FO371/17995, J2736/63/16, DOT, 14 November 1934.

62 On the situation confronting the Nasim government, see the very useful discussion in Deeb, *Party Politics*, pp. 253–258; on the early signs of British dissatisfaction with the regime, see FO371/19069, J626/110/16, Lampson to FO, 8 February 1935, and enclosures; on the widespread Egyptian hostility toward the Nasim government and its exhibition of a too blatant subservience to the residency, see the *Times*, 10–12 and 14 December 1935. Writing in the *Times* on 23 October 1935, even the stalwart friend of England, ʿAbbud, found it necessary to condemn the continued denial to Egypt of the "full measure of statehood."

63 The conflict is detailed in Vitalis, "Theory and Practice," pp. 299–300. A breakdown of the figure on exports to Egypt is provided in FO371/19088, J372/372/16, DOT, 28 January 1935. The clearest statement of the FO–DOT position is found in FO141/680, 380/8/35, Oliphant to Lampson, 9 May 1935. On the bank's much-remarked-upon, deepening ties to U.K. industry in the 1930s, see Davis, *Challenging Colonialism*, pp. 141–143, 153; and Tignor, *State, Private Enterprise*, pp. 134–135.

64 See, for example, FO371/19086, J602/348/16,

65 See FO371/19086, J1484/348/16, Lampson to FO, 5 April 1935, reporting interview between Selous [Cairo residency] and Horsfall [EEC executive], 3 April 1935.

66 The Dresdner bank, which held a major interest in Siemens, the manufacturing firm with ties to the Misr group dating back to the late 1920s, was another partner in the barter deal. Details in FO371/19057, J456/J670/J2375/J7334/31/16.

67 See FO371/19086, J2290/348/16, enclosing letter from ʿAbd al-Wahab to EEC, 5 June 1935. Rather than submit the project to open tender, the government decided to rank the proposals and negotiate with the principals one by one, until an agreement was reached. ʿAbbud's proposal was ranked last. Further details of the events leading up to this 5 June 1935 declaration are found in Vitalis "Theory and Practice".

68 The *Times*, 10–12 and 14 December 1935; Marsot, *Egypt's Liberal Experiment*, pp. 171–176; Deeb, *Party Politics*, pp. 257–258; and Ellis Goldberg, "The Wafd 1935 National Congress: Popular Front or Populist Front?," unpublished paper, 1987. The new prime minister was ʿAli Mahir, the ex-Bank Misr board member and director of the royal cabinet.

69 The businessman and authoritarian-at-heart beat his own drum in a remarkable conversation with Heathcote-Smith, the British counsel general in Alexandria. See FO371/20097, J921/2/16, enclosed in Lampson to FO, 21 January 1936.

70 'Abbud made his political preference clear in remarks to a British diplomat. See FO371/20097, J921/2/16, Heathcote-Smith to Lampson, 16 January. On the question of his political activism ("he said he had abandoned politics"), see FO371/20119, J7708/2/16, FO Minute (Mr. Pink), 17 September 1936; for accounts in the Egyptian press on the same question, see FO371/20120, J8211/2/16 Kelly to Houston-Boswall, 13 October 1936; on Sidqi's lobbying on behalf of the Aswan project, see FO371/20139, J445/445/16, enclosing memo by Selous, 8 January 1936.

71 For the company's intelligence on 'Abbud, Sidqi, and the in-fighting within the cabinet, see FO371/20139, J3628/445/16, enclosing letter from Grey [EEC representative in Cairo] to Nelson [EEC, London], 17 April 1936. The deceit on the part of the FO was transparent. For instance, they argued that London's support for EEC was justified because the Egyptian government's (British) financial advisor had finally approved the scheme "in principle since it will prove a savings of the cost of fertilizers." In fact, as Lampson pointed out a month later, the financial advisor was unconvinced that the project would ever prove to be a sound investment. See FO371/20139, J3559/445/16, Lampson to FO, 22 April 1936. Of course, as recorded in Lampson's unpublished diaries, Watson understood who he served, arguing that Egypt's "best interests" *were not* "the right criterion" in the matter. *Killearn Diaries,* 23 April 1936. For the full argument in support of the EEC, see FO371/20139, J2560/445/16, DOT memorandum, 24 March 1936.

72 FO371/20139, J3619/445/16, Lampson to FO, 28 April 1936. For details on divisions within the ministries and Lampson's decision to delay action because of them, see Robert Vitalis, "Building Capitalism in Egypt: The 'Abbud Pasha Group and the Politics of Construction," Ph.D. dissertation, Massachusetts Institute of Technology, 1988, pp. 405–407.

73 FO371/20144, J4104/1553/16, Lampson to FO, 8 May 1936; FO371/20139, J4261/445/16, Farrer to Pink, 12 May 1936, note by Campbell attached to file, and draft telegram to Lampson; and J4845/445/16, enclosing Selous to DOT, 12 May 1936.

74 Berque, *Imperialism and Revolution,* p. 448.

75 Ibid., p. 449.

76 Richard Robison, "Authoritarian States, Capital-Owning Classes, and the Politics of Newly Industrializing Countries: The Case of Indonesia," *World Politics* (1988): 52–74: 65. Although it is possible to imagine situations where sectoral competitors agree to cartelization of the market, for instance, by redistributing shares of the returns from all state contracts.

77 "What then is the political task which confronts the major indigenous capitalist? Primarily it is to secure a guaranteed position in the conglomerate of capitalist factions operating in Indonesia. Given the increasing internationalisation of capital, the prospect of an autonomous and independent indigenous capitalist class, dominating ownership of capital and investment decisions, becomes increasingly irrelevent." Richard Robison, *Indonesia: The Rise of Capital* (North Sydney: Allen & Unwin, 1986), p. 364. Springborg, *Mubarak's Egypt,* provides a good example of the widespread criticism of contemporary Egyptian capitalists as "parasitical." For an extended critique, see Robert Vitalis, "Imagining Capitalists: Ideologies of Class and Client in Egyptian Political Economy," *al-Jadal,* 1 (1991): 54–83.

78 "To an extent, the coordination of business strategies through interest associations or through economic concentration seems to be functionally equivalent." Philippe

Schmitter and Wolfgang Streeck, "Research Design to Study the Associative Action of Business in the Advanced Industrial Societies of Western Europe," unpublished manuscript, n.d., p. 17.

79 Peter Evans and John D. Stephens, "Studying Development Since the Sixties: The Emergence of a New Comparative Political Economy," *Theory and Society,* 17 (1988): 713–745; Antonio Gramsci, *Selections from the Prison Notebooks* (London: Lawrence & Wishart, 1971).

8

A time and a place for the nonstate: social change in the Ottoman Empire during the "long nineteenth century"

REŞAT KASABA

INTRODUCTION

The following quotation is from a book written at the close of the eighteenth century and published in London in 1820.[1] This book chronicles in three volumes the adventures of Anastasius, a Greek sailor, around the Mediterranean provinces of the Ottoman Empire. It is unlikely that it was actually written by the sailor himself, but it is obviously based on firsthand observation. The passage is from a conversation Anastasius is having with his friend Spiridion as they sail off the coast of Rhodes:

"Far as that society has spread its snares, has it so much as left a single small spot on earth, where those yet unborn who should dislike its partial regulations may find room to retire to the enjoyment of their birthright? Or, if there be any such asylum remaining in the wilds of Tartary or the wastes of America, has not society, at any rate, so monopolized all the means of disentangling oneself from its mazes, as to render the gaining these blissful abodes next to impossible? Must we not possess caravans, or vessels, licenses and passports, even to fly to the loneliness of the desert, together with a strength of body and of mind, of which the social institutions take care to deprive us ere we suspect their dangerous power? They cut our claws, they clip our wings, and then they cry out with a smile of derision, "poor pinioned eagle, fly if thou list!" The man who is not wealthy can only escape from society through the gates of death. Nor does he everywhere, I am told, dare to approach even these boldly and honestly. He must, in some countries, smuggle himself out of the world by stealth, and embark for his journey under false colours, lest his body be made accountable for the roving disposition of his soul!"

Anastasius's complaints about forces and regulations that restrict the activities and movements of individuals will strike a familiar chord with anybody who has had to deal with any state bureaucracy in the world. What is interesting, however, is that Anastasius attributes these interventions not to the "state" but to the "society," which suggests an understanding of the relations between Ottoman society and the imperial state that is at considerable variance with many modern analyses.

Most of the commonly held approaches to Ottoman history and the periodizations derived from them take the state as their main focus. In this literature, the trials and tribulations of the imperial bureaucracy are used as the primary raw material for identifying the main turning points of Ottoman history. Here it is always the state that rises and declines, expands and contracts, and, most important, plays a leading role in modernizing its own apparatus as well as the society. Anastasius reverses this perspective and sees the society as the entity that has "spread its snares." Even if we find the slightest evidence that he is correct – that the segments of the Ottoman society did in fact play an important role in regulating their own existence – this will take us quite far in questioning the accuracy of the state-centered paradigms that have held sway in Ottoman–Turkish studies. Such a finding would imply that there were real and effective limits to the extent and effectiveness of the power of the Ottoman state, and that most of these limitations originated from sources beyond the sphere of influence of the central government. This chapter pursues this line of reasoning and inquires whether such a nonstate arena came into being in the Ottoman Empire during the "long nineteenth century."[2] The question is not whether important activities took place outside the purview of the state. Rather, the issue is to what extent this arena limited and defined the content and nature of the state power in the changing Ottoman Empire.

Studying the transformation of the Ottoman Empire from the vantage point of the nonstate domain affords several advantages over alternative approaches. For one thing, focusing on developments that originated from outside the state sector allows us to uncover new elements of dynamism in this historical passage. Under the premises of the old framework, "change" can be discussed only when its source is within the domain of the central state. Movements that originated from or those that fell beyond this stately circle usually have been interpreted as portending a crisis, or, better yet, as disorder that needed to be "dealt with" by the central state. As shaped by this framework, most research topics in Ottoman studies have focused on questions that deal with institutional change, or on analyzing the effectiveness of the state in suppressing or solving certain disturbances and problems.

A corollary to approaching Ottoman (and non-European) history with such preconceived notions has been the importation of two myths about the so-called non-Western societies into this historiography. One such myth is the culturally determined "stasis" of the Ottoman society; the other, the string of absences (in particular, of a middle class and a civil society) that is supposed to explain this social stagnation and underscore the essential difference between this society and the "Western" world.[3] On close examination, however, stasis proves to be more a goal or ideal that the rulers tried to attain than an actual characteristic of the Ottoman Empire. After all, this was a social system ruled by a carefully selected elite who regarded any movement not under their direct supervision as dangerous to the welfare of the imperial domain and who tried to contain it. It is not surprising that when we, as modern analysts, rely on the records of this administrative elite, we also tend to see tranquility and stability as the "normal" and even desirable state of things. In this respect, we become collaborators in an intellectual project that insists on keeping part of its objects silent or, in Eric Wolf's words, "without history"; a project that happens to be also in full agreement with the priorities of the rulers as *they* related to their subjects.[4]

By taking the categories developed by the "state" and accepting the characterizations contained therein as valid, one can believe that the state was indeed the sole source of power in the Ottoman Empire. However, in historical terms, the development of any "state" as an apparatus, and as a hegemonic institution, always takes place simultaneously, in conjunction with and in relation to a nonstate arena. Without the latter, we cannot conceptualize the former or see the primary coercive relationship between the two. In fact, the arguments about the absence of a middle class or a civil society reflect not so much the nonexistence as the actual or desired elimination of such entities or spaces by the forces of the state.

This chapter focuses on three distinct areas that, although beyond the central government's immediate sphere of influence, helped shape the particular measures of reform and, more important, the general contours of state power within the changing Ottoman Empire of the nineteenth century. The first involves the changes in the organization of trade and production that took place within the context of expanding relations with the world economy. These had important ramifications for the social, political, and cultural structures in various parts of the Near East. Here our discussion centers on port cities of the eastern Mediterranean that became the hubs of the growing commercial activity and the loci of a nascent bourgeoisie in the nineteenth century. Although for the most part the expansion of this domain took place independently of the central government, the effects of its presence can be discerned in the measures of reorganization undertaken by the bureaucracy and in the contents of international treaties that the Ottoman government signed during this period. These public acts are generally interpreted as attempts by the Ottoman government to enhance its international legitimacy and to reassert its control over the forces of disintegration, especially in the outlying provinces of the empire. For my purposes, what is equally significant is the degree to which such measures recognized and even tried to accommodate many of these elements that were rooted in the nonstate arena.

The second area of focus comprises the movements of people (seasonal and, in particular, long-distance migration) that seem, at that time and probably earlier, to have been very much an integral part of the organization of the empire's economy. Proper appreciation of a high degree of mobility of peasants and workers will have profound implications for the conception of space and identity, definition of boundaries, and the nature and effectiveness of overrule in the Ottoman Empire. Officially, Ottoman rulers were antagonistic toward such unsupervised circulation of people. As an extension of their concern over security, defense, and taxation, government officials always tried to prevent people from deserting their places of residence. This section discusses the extent to which such interventions were successful in the nineteenth century. It also focuses on the major land legislation of 1858 to see how the continuing presence of a mobile peasant labor force affected the various provisions of this law, and how the law, in turn, tried to deal with this "problem."

The third and the final area relates to the nationalist, religious, and sectarian movements that engulfed the Ottoman Empire during the nineteenth century. Here my concern is not so much with the organization and staging of these movements, or with the political and bureaucratic response to them by the Ottoman government. I will take a somewhat different approach to demonstrate that even though the political discourse of Turkish reform developed in a deliberately cultivated distance from the nonstate arena, the latter still had a formative impact on the former. In bringing together the various strands of their nationalist discourse, the Ottoman–Turkish intellegentsia and bureaucrats were engaged in a continuous dialogue with alternative visions of reorganizing the Ottoman state, be they nationalist, ethnicist, or Islamicist. In engaging in this dialogue, their aim was not so much to win over the Serbians, or the Greeks, but to persuade an imagined third party that theirs was the right, just, and logical way to "save" the empire.

Together, the ensemble of practices, relations, and institutions contained in these three areas constituted a distinct nonstate arena in the dissolving empire. The point of studying this constellation is not merely to acquire new pieces of information, but to develop a new way of thinking about our subject matter. In specific terms, we have to insist on the relevance of the nonstate arena, and of the relationship between this and political structures as a primary locus of dynamism in the Ottoman Empire. In analytical and historical terms, we need to establish that rather than solely submitting to the pressures of the central government, or being molded by them, various processes originating in the nonstate arena constrained and shaped the power of the political authority in the Ottoman Empire.

CITIES, COMMERCE, AND COMMUNITIES

In the Ottoman Empire, historically, port cities such as Salonica, Izmir, Trabzon, Beirut, and Alexandria afforded settings where groups could exist and interact in an environment relatively free from close and constant government supervision. Partly this was because the Ottoman government had left the administrative status of these places vague in order to encourage the continuation of trade in the Mediterranean basin. Most of these cities had long histories of such close connections with other parts of the Mediterranean. Even though some of these connections predated the Ottoman presence in the area, they remained strong throughout the Ottoman rule, earning these cities the reputation of being "free" ports.[5]

After the mid-eighteenth century, the nexus of economic relations linking these port cities to the world economy intensified and changed their nature. Consequently, the territories in and around them became even more detached from the close supervision of the central government. These developments also provided especially the non-Muslim communities with new means of expanding their wealth and influence. In this respect the period after 1840 was particularly important.

Between 1840 and World War I, the Ottoman economy experienced a remarkable expansion. During this period, measured in constant 1880 prices, Ottoman exports increased by nine times, Ottoman imports by ten times.[6] The growth of port cities was even more spectacular. Their population multiplied severalfold, maritime traffic in and out of them registered major increases, and most of them became havens for people not only from their own hinterland but also from other parts of the Mediterranean. As ports, the key axis of the growth of these cities was their involvement in foreign trade. It is important to note that unlike the general trade balance of the Ottoman Empire, which was usually negative, the port cities maintained a positive balance. For example, in the thirty-six years between 1840 and 1876 alone, Izmir's trade generated a cumulative surplus of £16.6 million compared with the total deficit of £69.4 million for the Ottoman Empire as a whole.[7] In earlier periods, these ports had served more as staging points for goods in transit from Asia, but in the nineteenth century, the majority of goods exported from them was produced in their vicinity. It was in these years that Bursa's silk and Izmir's cotton replaced definitively Persian silk and Ankara mohair as the leading exports shipped from the port of Izmir; Lebanese silk became Beirut's key export commodity; and Egyptian cotton dominated the trade of Alexandria. Reflecting these changes, agricultural production registered significant increase in various parts of the Ottoman Empire. In other words, as well as becoming major nodes of exchange in a Mediterranean-wide system of trade, the port cities were emerging as the centers of flourishing economies in their own respective regions.

The expansion of production and trade generated a significant amount of new wealth in these commercially active regions. Contrary to common assumptions, it seems that most of this wealth was actually retained in the places of its creation. For example, in western Anatolia, profit transfers, personal savings, payments for imports, and taxes collected by the central government and its contractors would be the main conduits through which this money could possibly be channeled out of the region. Of these, transfer of profits and personal savings did not absorb a significant part of the new wealth generated in western Anatolia. In the first half of the nineteenth century, except for railroads, there were as yet no major investments by foreign capital, and railroads did not attain a comfortable level of profitability before the 1870s. There was some movement of personal funds across family relations that extended into distant parts of the globe. But such relations served as channels for the flow of wealth in all directions and as such could not have caused a net outflow of funds during this early period. In fact, given the flow of more than 2 million immigrants into the Ottoman Empire in the course of the nineteenth century, it is likely that the movements of people generated a net *inflow* of funds. This was true especially for port cities such as Izmir and Alexandria, which were becoming powerful magnets for people in all of the eastern Mediterranean.[8]

Payments for imports did not constitute a major outflow either. As already noted, port cities enjoyed a consistent surplus in their trade account with the outside world. Furthermore, although more of the import trade was conducted on credit, the exporters insisted on prompt payment in cash. Consequently, payments for imports would frequently be in arrears; thus, at any time, the net gain from export trade would likely be even larger than the one suggested by the foreign trade figures.

As for taxes, port cities and their surroundings had always been among the highest contributors to the treasury of the central government. However, in the nineteenth century, the rate of increase in the revenues generated in these places does not seem to have been commensurate with the rate of expansion of commercial activity in the region.[9] At least on the face of it, there does not seem to have been a major drain on the wealth generated in and around the port cities through the expanding commerce of the Ottoman Empire at that time.

A growing part of the wealth that was thus retained in the regions of its creation fell into private hands because the nineteenth-century trade was organized and conducted almost entirely through private channels. To begin with the sites of production, a certain degree of concentration of land had occurred since earlier periods. But the notables of provincial towns or military and civilian bureaucrats who acquired title to land, rarely, and only in some regions, assumed direct control of production in their holdings. In most cases, the relative sparseness of population as well as the social status and background of this local elite forced it to organize the cultivation of its lands through subcontracting, leasing, and subletting. Therefore, whatever the nature and extent of the titles might have been, almost everywhere the actual units of production were in fact peasant households cultivating small to medium plots under various arrangements of tenancy with their real or titular landlords. An important aspect of this configuration was that by the nineteenth century, willingly or otherwise, the central government had relinquished much of its control over both the owners and the cultivators of land. The tenants, peasants, and landlords therefore acquired a degree of security and freedom to pursue their own interests as they interacted with each other and with merchants and government officials.

The sites of production were linked to regional markets and to port cities through a succession of intermediaries such as tax farmers, caravan traders, merchants-moneylenders, and the agents and brokers of wholesalers, export firms, or government officers. Of these groups, itinerant merchants-moneylenders were in a particularly advantageous position as they were able to move in the hinterland, maintain the necessary contacts, and coordinate the movement of goods from the interior. In tandem with the growing trade, these groups acquired a far-reaching power and influence in commercial networks. In their growth and expansion these constellations remained independent of governmental policies and foreign interventions, and as such became germane to the rise of a nonstate arena in the Ottoman Empire.

The societal changes caused by the growth of the nonstate arena had important implications for the relative position of different ethnic and religious groups in the Ottoman Empire. The most significant among such changes was the rise to prominence of Greeks and Armenians, mostly at the expense of Jews and, to some extent, Muslims.[10] In the course of the late-eighteenth to nineteenth centuries, the Greeks became particularly visible as members of internationally represented families, as sailors, itinerant merchants, agents of European houses, retailers, and bankers in the eastern Mediterranean. They served in all branches of trade and finance in the commercially active regions of the Ottoman Empire and became the perennial intermediaries of the empire's growing integration into the world economy. Thus, more than the Armenians, Jews, Levantines, or the foreigners, the Greeks dominated the growing nonstate arena in such areas as western Anatolia, the Balkans, and North Africa.

The origins and growth of the privileged position of the Greeks occurred in a way that was autonomous not only from the Ottoman government but also from the policies of the European states. The Greeks owed their prominence not so much to the help they received from foreign powers but to the way in which they were spread about the eastern Mediterranean. Their dispersed presence in the area afforded them a network of natural conduits in all directions and the opportunity to take advantage of the openings in the domestic and world markets. In this sense, the support that the Greeks eventually received from outside was more the result and not the cause of their prominence. In fact, when the British were making their initial entry into western Anatolia, they did not see a natural ally in the Greek or any other local community. Far from it. Their initial design was to undermine these local communities with their own representatives, and failing that, to supplant them with members of other (weaker) communities, such as the Jews, who were deemed easier to control.

Many activities that contributed to the growing power and influence of the intermediaries either originated or converged in port cities, which pushed even higher the status of these sites in the nonstate arena. During the second half of the nineteenth century, contemporary observers were describing Izmir as the "queen of the cities of Anatolia, the crown of Ionia, and the gem of Asia."[11] Glimpses of life in non-Muslim quarters of this and other ports reveal all the elements of a civic existence. There were newspapers, schools, professional associations, social clubs, and political organizations that were administered by local councils.[12] Compared with the field of attraction generated by the port cities and the forces that contributed to the growth of coastal areas, the movements of resources and wealth in the opposite direction were thinner and, on the whole, less consequential. Among these were the unceasing acts of brigandage: lootings, robberies, and kidnappings that not only disrupted trade but also, and more important, helped redistribute throughout a wider area in the interior some of the wealth that was concentrating in coastal areas. Thus, within the context of the mid-nineteenth-century boom, the port cities became truly privileged areas that were either the loci or the focuses of activities, relations, and movements that constituted a nonstate arena in the Ottoman Empire.

Most measures implemented by the Ottoman government to reform the administration of the empire were shaped within this general context. We can identify two concerns behind these measures: On the one hand, there was the general goal of keeping the empire together, with the privileged status of the bureaucracy intact. On the other hand, there was the growing realization, on the part of at least some bureaucrats, that circumstances had changed substantially and that to survive, the Ottoman government would have to become a part of these changes instead of attempting to reverse them. Contrary to some perceptions, these two lines of thought did not find their reflections in separate policies, nor did they belong to two distinct "camps" within the bureaucracy. Most of the time they were ingrained in the same policies, which made some of them inherently contradictory or completely ineffective from the outset. Also, the same individual, in opposition or in government, could be seen espousing diametrically opposite views depending on the issue on hand. As a result of such incongruities, the very policies hailed as the formative steps in the emergence of modern Turkey are also identified by other authors as being, for the most part, in line with the classical imperial politics.[13]

The overall drive for saving the empire by reclaiming the original tenets of imperial politics can be attributed to the cultural milieu in which the leading statesmen were trained. Although the main tenets of this "culture" were old and well established, they now existed in an environment that was changing very fast and leading to a considerable loss of power and initiative for the bureaucratic class. Soon officials would find that to carry out their duties and provide for their households they had to become part of the economic networks that had engulfed the empire. One way of achieving this was to seek the help of prominent financiers in the execution of their public and private affairs. Starting with the sultan and continuing from the highest to the lowest rungs of bureaucracy, officials of all ranks hired the services of private bankers. As a result, this predominantly non-Muslim group gained a privileged (but informal) access to the most influential centers of power in the Ottoman administration. At the same time, commercial treaties that the Ottomans signed with European powers opened up other, more formal, ways of integration for the Ottoman state into the regional and global economic networks. When examined from this perspective, it appears that the growing openness that characterized the Ottomans' approach to European states and institutions during the nineteenth century derived from the limitations brought to bear on the power of the central government by the various groups and relations that constituted the nonstate arena. Compared with these constraints, the infusion and spread of Western ideas played more of an auxiliary role in shaping the tone of Ottoman policies during these years.

In addition to the contradictions inherent in pursuing the dual goals of preservation and reform, the particular reform policies were complicated also by the context within which they were formulated. As a result of many and often competing and conflicting influences, in their final form some of these policies turned out to be significantly different from what they would have been like had they reflected solely the will and desire of the bureaucratic elite. For example, between 1840 and 1867 the Ottoman government undertook a series of steps to revise and redesign the system of provincial administration.[14] Examined from one perspective, these steps did involve gradual *re*centralization of the administrative structure by giving more power to the central government and, most important, to its appointees in the provinces. Here, we can point to such measures as redistricting the provinces and rationalizing the provincial boundaries, abolishing tax farming and giving the right to collect taxes to appointed officials, regulating civil bureaucracy, prohibiting government officials from collecting any dues or fees in lieu of their salaries, and passing laws of nationality and passports.

Yet this very process of provincial and administrative reform also included deliberate acts that amounted to recognizing the independent power of various groups in the provinces. For example, some of the local notables were appointed to government posts and with the newly designed provincial councils, members of wealthy families were given a forum for participating in local administration. The councils, or consultative bodies, were to be constituted through a complicated system of elections that would make them somewhat representative and enhance their standing in the eyes of the people.[15] Steps were taken as well to ensure the inclusion and participation of non-Muslims in provincial councils. After a trial phase in the Balkans, such councils were set up in most of the provinces and at each successive level of provincial administration. Yet administrative reform along these lines did not lead to a genuine devolution of power from the center to the provinces and hence to the nonstate arena. For one thing, once established, the councils were incorporated in a new hierarchy where those in the larger administrative units had authority over those in smaller cities and towns.[16] The result was the emergence of a new system of bureaucratic stratification that existed side by side with the old one without necessarily displacing it. In fact, with their claims to "representation" these councils lent a degree of legitimacy to and hence strengthened the imperial administration in Ottoman territories. The selection process for membership in provincial councils was extremely complicated – it was designed to guarantee that there would be a Muslim majority even in regions like western Anatolia where it was difficult to justify such "guarantees" on the basis of demographic composition. As part of these reforms, too, growing cities like Izmir and Beirut were made provincial capitals in the hope that this would pull them closer to the recentralized imperial administration.

The "Treaties of Friendship and Free Trade" signed by the Ottoman government with European powers in the nineteenth century are another group of actions in which the bureaucracy found itself pursuing inherently contradictory goals.[17] Ostensibly the treaties were designed to open the Ottoman markets to foreign goods, to limit or abolish the trade monopolies set up by the central government and its local representatives, and, most important, to make it possible for Britain to help the beleaguered Porte in its battle against rebellious governors including Muhammed Ali of Egypt. Undeniably there was a certain degree of coercion in getting the Ottoman state to agree to sign the treaties, which were primarily designed to help expand the overseas markets for the products of the new British industries. But there was also an element of willing participation and cooperation on the part of the Ottoman bureaucracy to make the agreements a reality. The Ottomans saw them as a means to attract external help in their domestic power struggles and thereby undermine the economic power of some of the influential groups in the provinces. Indeed, treaty-bound liberalization of trade proved to be a significant blow against the position of local officials and governors like Muhammed Ali, who had relied on the income from trade monopolies to finance the organization of their economies and armies, and to assert the autonomy of their administration. But under the circumstances that pertained in the nineteenth century, once free trade was institutionalized, the Ottoman government could not be selective in practicing it. In the end, the foreign trade of the Ottoman Empire increased substantially and Britain became the Porte's leading trade partner; but from these treaties followed some consequences not entirely foreseen or desired by the Ottoman government. For one thing, the increase in the volume of trade directly improved the status of the very groups of intermediaries and merchants who had become the main constituents of the nonstate arena. Most significantly, as part of these agreements some of the non-Muslim subjects of the Ottoman Empire acquired extraterritorial protection by foreign governments. And this privilege enhanced significantly the security of commercial activities and the general status of non-Muslim groups within the empire.

While the Ottoman bureaucracy was pursuing its inherently contradictory policies, the various elements and groups within the nonstate arena were defining and defending their own interests and fields of action, often independently or regardless of what the central government was doing. For example, in 1819 there were riots in Izmir, organized to a large extent by the newly rich Greek merchants against the ecclesiastical authority of the local church and its leaders.[18] Soon, however, the merchant community was divided between those who served only the local markets and those who were involved in foreign trade. The former rallied the members of local guilds to their cause and moved closer to the conservative positions advocated by the church hierarchy; whereas the latter, with the aid of some intellectuals, set up a new school, the Gymnase Philologique. This school, seen as the symbol of the growing power of the more cosmopolitan merchants and businessmen in the Greek community, was to specialize in the instruction of the philosophical modernism developed as an alternative to the conservative teachings of the church. Such an episode demonstrates that the nonstate arena could become the locus of autonomous action, and also the futility of regarding the non-Muslim communities as undifferentiated wholes.

In another example, when the central government sought to convene in Istanbul representatives from all the provinces to solicit their opinions about the provincial councils, local notables, including the leaders of non-Muslim communities, saw this as a ploy to empower the common people. To protect their privileges, these local elites arranged for their own trusted men to participate in the deliberations.[19] When the provincial councils were established, the local notables were quick to take their places in them either directly or through people whom they trusted. Consequently, in most cases, the provincial assemblies became not instruments of reform but sites of struggle among the representatives of the central and local interests, and in most cases they turned into effective barriers against the proposed changes in the status quo.

The causes of the civil war of 1858 in Lebanon can also be traced to changes and divisions in the nonstate arena of the empire. Here, the key to the conflict was that a predominantly Muslim group of tax farmers as well as Christian merchants and peasants resented having to hand over a portion of their newly enhanced earnings to the state authorities or to absentee landlords.[20] Several years of uncertainty, marked by riots in Damascus and the Lebanese civil war, ended when Lebanon was granted a special administrative status. In addition to involving a mechanism for the active participation of various groups in the administration of the province, the new system set up in Lebanon also served as a model for the Provincial Law of 1864 that was soon to be implemented in the Ottoman Empire at large.[21]

We can also find examples of how the different segments within the group of intermediary merchants were active and vocal in advancing their positions against each other and against the Muslim communities in their regions, including the representatives of the central government. It must be noted, however, that in most instances, in their dealings with the central government non-Muslim intermediaries avoided direct confrontation, largely because of the continuing precariousness of their status in relation to Ottoman law and institutions. Under such circumstances, subtle methods such as hoarding money, preemptive purchase of crops, cajoling the peasants into cooperation, circumventing the newly established branch banking, transferring funds within families across short and long distances, proved to be more effective than the more visible forms of resistance in defending the newly constituted space against the encroachments by the central government.

The laws, regulations, statutes, and treaties that were enacted, and the means and methods of central and provincial administration that were created in the Ottoman Empire in the nineteenth century, were not discrete measures. They were part of a long-term process of reorganization and as such their growth was cumulative. Some of these codes survived into the republican period and are upheld even today. That the Ottoman state was forced to accommodate the expanding nonstate arena in formulating these reorganizations meant that no matter how indirectly, the forces and relations located in the nonstate arena have played a formative role in the drafting and implementation of these measures. It is within the context of its recursive relationship with the expanding nonstate arena that the transformation of the imperial bureaucratic apparatus into the Ottoman–Turkish state took place.

To confine this discussion to port cities or to the changes in the status of non-Muslim merchants and their relations with the bureaucracy would present a partial picture of the strengthening of the nonstate arena in the Ottoman Empire. Even though trade was an important part of the imperial system and merchants, especially the larger ones, possessed a significance not necessarily proportional to their numbers, we should not forget that they were at best a sizable "minority" in the Ottoman Empire. As such, representing the nonstate arena exclusively from their perspective would yield a distorted image of the Ottoman society. To appreciate better the developments in this domain, I now broaden my focus to take into account the changes that affected the patterns of circulation of laborers across the various sectors and zones of the Ottoman Empire.

LAND AND LABOR

The rise of the port cities and the growing wealth of the intermediaries could not be sustained without an underlying expansion in agricultural production in the Ottoman Empire. There have been several attempts at calculating the volume of agricultural production in the empire in general and in some of the commercially active regions in particular. These studies indicate a more or less continuous growth during most of the nineteenth century, with particularly high rates around the demanding times of the Crimean War and the American Civil War.[22] It is interesting to examine how this expansion came about. For one thing, there is no evidence of major change in the average size of the units of cultivation, or in the techniques of production employed on these units from early to midnineteenth century.[23] There was a concentration of claims to ownership through tax farming and other methods, but this did not necessarily translate into a change in farming practices. Most of the new "owners" exploited their holdings by utilizing the existing methods of leasing and sharecropping rather than converting them into plantations. In the absence of any significant change in the average size of holdings and the continuing scarcity of modern implements, the only factors that might have been responsible for the absolute increase in the volume of agricultural production are the more intensive use of existing resources or a net growth in population that would make an extensive growth possible. The population of the Ottoman Empire did, in fact, grow during the nineteenth century.[24] Part of this growth was because of the gradual disappearance of plague epidemics, the longer intervals of peace between major wars, and the overall increase in the birthrate, especially in the prosperous regions around the port cities. In addition, coastal areas also benefited from the inflow of Muslim refugees from places that were ceded to other states or became independent in the course of the century.

But the growth of population and immigration from the ceded territories are not sufficient to account for the expansion of agricultural production in the Ottoman Empire. The former was uneven across time and places; the latter did not really begin until after the end of the Crimean War in 1856 and did not become significant before the 1870s. To explain the growth of agricultural production, we need to focus also on the patterns of seasonal and longer-term migration of existing labor within the territories of the empire. More than anything else, it was the mobility of Ottoman peasants that made the intensive use of existing resources possible.

It is not surprising that Ottoman agriculture relied on and made use of migrant labor in the nineteenth century. The agricultural sector always requires access to temporary workers because farm work is usually distributed unevenly across different seasons. What is noteworthy is the increasing numbers of people who participated in these migratory flows, and, more important, the growing distances over which they were willing to travel in order to work in the newly prosperous areas. For example, in 1860 the British consul estimated that out of 991,700 people living in Aydın province, 110,000 were "migratory."[25] It is tempting to attribute the apparent increase in the mobility of labor to the pull exerted by the flourishing economies of port cities and their surroundings. This was undoubtedly an important factor in maintaining the flow of labor, but it does not explain the origins of the increase. After all, if some combination of intensive farming and seasonal migration was essential for any significant rise in agricultural output, it is hard to understand how production could have increased on its own and generated a "pull" for the migrant labor that is supposed to be a prerequisite for this very boom in the first place. Obviously, far from being a mere factor of ex-post adjustment, or a characteristic of only the expansionary periods, circulating labor was very much an integral part of agricultural production in the Ottoman Empire.

Focusing for the moment on the nineteenth century, which included alternating periods of expansion and contraction, we can identify several distinct types of movement of people that could provide a constant source of circulating human power in agriculture. First, there was the regular interchange of labor among small peasant holdings and between these holdings and various activities in urban areas. Since the very beginning, pooling of labor in this manner had been crucial to the vitality and resilience of Ottoman economy – especially its agricultural sector. In the eighteenth century, as new opportunities emerged in rural areas and in coastal towns, such cross-movements intensified and their scope extended to cover larger territories. Ottoman population registers indicate that as early as the 1830s, in the western and southern coastal towns one would be likely to encounter "guest workers" from faraway provinces in the east.[26]

The second type of movement appears to have been better organized than the first one. Starting from the seventeenth century and continuing into the twentieth, local notables in commercially prosperous areas organized the transfer of large numbers of young people from surrounding areas to work on their expanding holdings. Where there was no organized recruitment, people came to these places on their own, in search of employment.[27]

The third group comprised the large numbers of tribally organized people who moved seasonally between higher and lower grounds combining pastoral and farming activities. The important part farming played in their annual cycles distinguishes this group from the better known "nomads" with whom they are sometimes confused. Ottoman administration gave these the special name of *konar göçer* (those who land-leave) and devised separate policies to supervise their movements. In some cases, the distance separating the winter and summer pastures of these tribes was very far, exceeding hundreds of miles. For example, one tribe is reported to have moved between the Adana–Haleb region (an area that falls in southern Turkey and northern Syria today) and as far away as Aydın in western Anatolia.[28] The *konar göçer* tribes moved in a well-organized way as if in a procession, following the same routes their ancestors had taken for generations. Through their mobility and the multitude of activities in which they were involved, these groups constituted one of the crucial links in the organization of the imperial economy.[29]

In addition to these group movements there were also individuals who moved on their own, over long distances, often in pursuit of political protection or economic benefits. The inheritance practices and the distribution of ownership rights in the countryside did not always accommodate growing numbers or respond to fluctuating economic conditions.[30] Therefore, in times of population growth or general social and economic upheaval, young people could escape their obligations temporarily or permanently. Especially in the northern and eastern parts of Anatolia the geographical terrain was such that there always seems to have been an "excess" population ready to move without completely severing their ties to their peasant households.[31] For example, during the nineteenth century most of the porters employed at the Istanbul docks were Kurds and Armenians from eastern provinces. Similarly, almost all the messengers and guards at the foreign consulates in Izmir were of Kurdish extraction.

From the members of peasant households to the refugees of the Russian wars, all of these groups owed their apparent dynamism to forces over which the Ottoman government had little control. For example, if peasants decided to pool their resources or double their activities, it was because they stood to gain by selling the increased product in regional markets. Similarly, merchants mobilized their family connections and conveyed their goods and wealth back and forth across the Ottoman borders when it became profitable to divert goods away from the local markets. Many of the *konar göçer* and nomadic groups moved through their migratory cycles for generations by adapting themselves to changing conditions, including the ebbs and flows of Ottoman rule over them.

For a long time, each type of mobility also afforded the peasants effective means of protecting themselves against the impositions and requistions of the central state. After the eighteenth century, however, the Ottoman administration tried to cast as wide a net as possible to confine and constrain a people spread across a wide territory extending from central Europe to the Hejaz. More often than not the central government had to apply military means to force compliance to its orders of settlement. The government had the most difficulty with the *konar göçer* tribes as it tried different methods of encouraging or forcing them to alter, and indeed abandon, their habits of seasonal migration. One tactic it employed was to arm certain tribes, incorporate them into the Ottoman army, and then use them against rival tribes. Examples of these include the *yürüks* in Rumeli, incorporated into special units called the *Evlad-ı Fatihan* in 1691; the *Fırka-i Islahiye,* used in the pacification of southern Anatolia in the 1860s; and the *Hamidiye Kurds,* who were organized in the 1890s.[32] On a more general level, a series of campaigns was organized to move, relocate, and settle various groups across the shrinking territories of the empire throughout the later decades of Ottoman and the early years of republican history. As with administrative reforms, the central government had to rely on the locally influential people such as the provincial potentate, urban notables, and village chiefs in enforcing many of these measures. Most of these people had a vested interest in having access to a fixed and sedentary (and hence reliable) work force in their localities. But given the relative scarcity of labor, they also wanted to be able to draw on the human power in outlying areas, or, alternatively, to have the opportunity to move themselves. Thanks to their newly attained positions on various levels of provincial administration and councils, the local notables were able to affect the implementation if not the letter of policies pertaining to patterns of migration, ownership, and employment in agriculture. In this way, each of the different patterns of migration became a field of contention between the reforming state and the changing society. Therefore, such movements of people provide a useful angle from which to study the interaction between a state-in-formation and a society-in-constitution.

In the end, in the Ottoman Empire as a whole, many of the reform measures, such as those relating to settling people, were suffused with so many local influences that to this day there is no consensus as to what their real purpose was.[33] For example, the Land Code of 1858 purported to protect small peasant households but failed to introduce a limit on the size of individual holdings; it recognized the idea of private property on land but qualified it with the concept of open fields as well as with various restrictions on what the peasants could and could not do on "their" plots; and, perhaps most important, it did not introduce any principle to regulate the status of peasants on large holdings. Consequently, the peasants' relations with the owners of large estates were left to be determined individually, according to the evolving conditions in different parts of the empire. For example, in Iraq, Syria, Lebanon, and Palestine, the government tried to ban communal ownership (*mush'a*) but did not have the means to enforce such a sweeping measure. Systems of ownership such as *mush'a* had a long history and were rooted in local custom. Some aspects of these systems, such as rotating ownership, were difficult to decipher for an outsider. As such, in addition to regulating farming, *mush'a* was a valuable means of support and security for village communities. Also, different types of communal ownership were more or less open to migration, in the sense both of accommodating outsiders and making it possible for villagers to leave. Furthermore, some communities could switch back and forth between different types, which made it even more difficult for outsiders to intervene.[34] In the end, like other measures of its kind, the 1858 code became all things to all people; it did not change or reverse anything but provided a legal cover for the regionally diverse transformations which were at the heart of the difficulties that the state had set out to address in the first place.

As in the economic and administrative reorganizations, many of the measures that dealt with land grew in a cumulative fashion. With minor changes, the 1858 code remained as the main statute regulating the ownership and cultivation of land in the Ottoman Empire and its main successor, Turkey. This led to the long-term survival of property relations and practices as they evolved in Ottoman lands after the eighteenth century. For those parts of the Ottoman Empire that became Turkey, this has meant both the further entrenchment of small peasant farming and the long-term survival of patterns and arteries of migration.

The local intermediaries who injected large amounts of money in the marketing of agricultural products, the partially dispossessed persons who were willing to move over long distances, and the small peasant households who remained as the key units of production were woven together in an intricate network in the course of the nineteenth century. For our purposes, what is particularly important is that this combination emerged independently of the central government, but developed in relation to the changing Ottoman–Turkish state and, directly or indirectly, left a deep imprint in the policies of reorganization formulated by the Ottoman government during the nineteenth century.

IDEOLOGIES OF STATE AND NONSTATE

The formative impact that the relations and processes rooted in the nonstate arena had on state policies was not confined to trade and production but extended into the ideological and cultural spheres. In some ways, this relationship is the most difficult one to study because often the two domains appeared to represent two separate worlds that were in total isolation from each other. It was very rare, if ever, for any of the key groups of the nonstate sector to be actively involved, individually or through organizations, in shaping empirewide policies or to participate directly in the ongoing transformation of the Ottoman–Turkish state. Most of the time their intervention was indirect and defensive in nature. Herein lies one of the major anomalies of this social transformation in the Ottoman Empire–Turkey. Groups who became so powerful in substantive terms in the nonstate arena continued to be quiescent in political terms and adopted means similar to those recently characterized in a different social context as the "weapons of the weak."[35] This incongruity has led many scholars, old and new, to assume that civil society was absent in the changing circumstances of the Ottoman Empire and the Middle East. Although perhaps tactically convenient, it is not satisfactory to "explain" this anomaly by referring to some essential difference, because this achieves little more than to shift the focus by restating the problem.

There were several historically specific reasons as to why the influential groups identified as having been constitutive of the nonstate arena were not engaged in political action in a prominent way. For one thing, the Ottoman Empire's bureaucratic approach to reform opened a chasm between the rulers and the ruled. Starting from the eighteenth century, the imperial state gradually abandoned many of the classical maxims that had secured its authority and legitimacy in the eyes of the people. It was no longer the protector of the people, guardian of the imperial realm, and an essentially conservative upholder of the Islamic ideals that formed the guiding principles of the policies of the Ottoman state. Its overarching desire now seemed to be to reorganize the empire according to the principles of modernity, Westernism, secularism, and eventually scientific positivism. As the Ottoman bureaucrats became the standard-bearers of reformism, they appeared to be breaking their social pact with the people. Şerif Mardin has described the resultant situation as one of bifurcation between a discourse of reform that was confined to political community and a societal discourse that became increasingly defensive and conservative. Given the substantive difference between the two levels, it became very difficult for any segment of the nonstate arena to breach the gap and affect the political process.[36]

Furthermore, each group in the nonstate arena contained diverse elements that came from a different terrain, socially and even geographically. Simply put, there was little in common within or among the migrant communities, the provincial notables, and non-Muslim merchants to cause them to engage in concerted political action so as to realize the ideal of a collectively imagined Ottoman–Turkish state. In fact, if there was one point on which all of these groups actually agreed, it was their implicit preference for a weak state that did not interfere with their "freedom" to produce, trade, and move. Against this background, Anastasius's complaints at the start of this chapter become more meaningful. More important, it is in this context that some of the arguments concerning the presumed compatibility between Tanzimat reforms and the interests of non-Muslim compradors appear to be misplaced.[37]

Finally, another factor that hampered the long-term growth of concerted political action in the nonstate arena was that some of the intermediary merchants and local notables articulated their interests on a local level, in the direction of various kinds of local autonomy or national independence. Obviously, in most cases, the realization of these latter goals was contingent upon the continuing weakening of the central government. It should be noted here that communal disagreement with the goals of the reform measures was not specific to the non-Muslim part of the Ottoman society. Among Muslims, the Kurds, who were the perennial migrants in Ottoman labor force, staged fierce resistance against the policies that required them to settle for purposes of taxation. In 1845 it took the Ottoman army close to a year to retake the city of Van from a Kurdish contingent that had occupied it in protest of Tanzimat reforms.[38] Similarly, the Shiite groups who had acquired virtual autonomy in Karbala resisted militarily and fought a bloody battle with the Ottoman forces that tried to impose the centralizing precepts of the reform movement.[39]

Even though the lines of communication between the domains of the state and the nonstate were few and far between, it does not follow that the the articulation of the nationalist ideology by the bureaucratic elite occurred in a way that was totally insulated from the nonstate arena.[40] If nothing else, the latter provided a clear and convenient target of opposition that helped the bureaucratic elite to highlight the urgency of their mission. Furthermore, in opposing the various visions that emerged from within the nonstate arena, the bureaucrats had to appropriate some elements and aspects of these rival projects if for no other reason than to argue against, negate, and (hope to) supersede them.

One way to trace the unfolding of this muted dialogue between the two domains is to examine the gradual emergence of militant secularism as one of the key planks of nationalist ideology in the early twentieth century. The religious opposition to bureaucratic reform became manifest in the nineteenth century when not only the Shiites, who were historically discontent with their Sunni rulers, but also the Sunnis had found a venue in the Sufi brotherhoods for rallying their brethren against the centralizing precepts of the government. These communities were organized around alternative local-level interpretations of Islam that had had a long history in the Near East. Their popularity increased and their oppositional character became accentuated in the nineteenth century when many of the reform measures appeared to be too closely in tune with the interests of the Europeans. A key complaint was that the Tanzimat state was neglecting its duty to treat its subjects as a "seamless community." Instead, it seemed to promote a certain hierarchy and a social structure that did not have a clear grounding in Islam.[41]

Initially, the bureaucracy was ambivalent toward religious opposition. During most of the nineteenth century, the leading statesmen and intellectuals thought it was possible to create a new "nation of Ottomans" and obtain the allegiance of all the remaining subjects of the empire, Muslim and non-Muslim alike. Toward the end of the nineteenth century, the growing success of the nationalist and secessionist movements in especially the Balkan provinces forced the bureaucratic elite to rethink these designs. An influential current among them concentrated only on the Muslim subjects of the empire and advocated using religion not only to unite the Muslim Ottomans but also to extend the power and influence of the Ottoman state into Asia. This, too, was quickly abandoned because of the difficulties the Ottoman state faced in the Fertile Crescent, among its own Arab-Muslim subjects, let alone the dreams of unifying the Muslims in different parts of the world. By the turn of the twentieth century, Turkism had emerged as the only remaining alternative in saving the Ottoman–Turkish state. In its initial formulations, this strand of thinking originated from among the Crimean and Caucasian refugees. As such it included the possibility of appealing to the Turkic peoples of central Asia for their support and participation in the creation of a Pan-Turkic Empire, but eventually it settled for the Anatolian peninsula, the core area of the Ottoman Empire.[42]

As the governing ideology moved through these phases, it became not only less open to compromise but also outright hostile to all alternative ideologies and in particular to nonsecular cosmologies. In fact, the way in which the new Turkish nationalism insisted on defining itself as rigidly secular, can be taken as a sign of the perceived threat from, and hence the growing strength of, Islamic and in particular Sufi opposition. Indeed, by the 1920s, with the elimination of competing nationalisms, Sufi brotherhoods had become the main, and perhaps the only, form of organization that was non- or even antistate in Turkey. It is not surprising that the new Turkish republic faced its first and most formidable challenge from these circles immediately after its success in organizing the new state. In the short run, the Turkish state was able to drive most of these movements underground. But the government continued to be apprehensive about their activities. So much so that in 1960, when one of their most prominent Sufi leaders, Bediuzzaman Said Nursi, died and was buried in eastern Turkey, his body was disinterred and transported by military plane to western Turkey, where it was reburied in an unmarked grave to prevent it from becoming a shrine.[43]

CONCLUSION

The way in which the Ottoman–Turkish state and society retreated into two separate worlds suggests that the very process of reform that enhanced the formal strength of the Ottoman–Turkish state also involved the narrowing of the scope and basis of consent this state enjoyed. In this sense, the Ottoman–Turkish state that became better organized, more efficient, and "modern" in the nineteenth and twentieth centuries, had also become "weak" in substantive terms. If social groups, classes, and organizations are able to constitute themselves in an ensemble of arrangements to express and advance their interests, then it is possible for the state surrounded by such practices and ultimately shaped by them, to become strong in substantive terms. I see most of the nineteenth century as one in which such a constellation of practices came into being in the Ottoman Empire; but they fell short of encircling and transforming the state.

At this point, it might be instructive to pose this question in comparative terms and ask why neither the late imperial nor the early republican state attempted to open up real channels of political participation for the various groups who were entrenched in the nonstate arena. Such a scenario would have made the Ottoman state substantively stronger in ways similar to its Chinese counterpart, whose transformation is discussed by Elizabeth Perry in Chapter 6 of this volume. It is beyond the scope of this essay to elaborate all the reasons for the differences in the historical development of the two empires. As already mentioned, some of these had to do with the nature and specificity of the nonstate arena as it developed in the Ottoman Empire. And we should not forget that the Ottoman–Turkish elites deliberately avoided facing the pressures emanating from the nonstate arena. In the late Ottoman and early republican periods the ideologies of state formation were formulated specifically to exclude, not include, many of the groups who had based their power in the nonstate arena – because the continuing quiescence of the nonstate actors and groups made it easier for the military-bureaucratic elite to articulate and develop its own interests as a distinct group, and even as a class.

In the course of the nineteenth century, bureaucrats made substantial progress in reforming the Ottoman Empire. Institutionally, by the end of the century the Ottoman state did appear to be better equipped to administer its territory. Some of the taxes were assessed and collected by centrally appointed, salaried officials; the state institutions had become more diversified and the task of each was better defined; there was a growing body of codified and ever more precise laws; the army was thoroughly professionalized with regular patterns of recruitment and training; and both the civil and military wings of the central government were supported by newly established schools where the future ministers and commanders were educated. In their institutional reforms, the bureaucrats owed their success in no small part to a succession of fortuitous circumstances in the international arena. First, their interest in recentralizing the empire's administration fit perfectly with Britain's Near Eastern policy under Lord Palmerston's leadership during the mid-Victorian era.[44] Then, in the late nineteenth century, Germany's growing interest in the Near East gave the Ottomans a new leverage and a new opportunity to carve a space for themselves in the interstate arena.[45] Finally, the extraordinary circumstances of World War I and the Turco-Greek war that followed it allowed the military-bureaucratic elite of the Ottoman Empire to marginalize and eventually eliminate the two most prominent groups within the nonstate sector: namely, the Greeks and the Armenians. Kurds were the only distinct minority left within Turkey, and they have been in a state of permanent uprising against the Turkish state ever since.

It is the apparent success of the military-bureaucratic elite in strengthening the Ottoman state that made Turkey one of the most popular topics of the modernization literature in the 1950s and the 1960s.[46] But a longer-term perspective such as the one employed in this volume reveals that this success materialized within a context of growing political and economic integration into the capitalist world-system, and that it was almost exclusively confined to the visible aspects of state rule. It is true that the army, the police, and the courts all appeared to be more effective and centralized, but this edifice did not have a substantive basis for its growing power. None of the reform measures involved any attempt at genuine empowerment of a group or an institution that was beyond the field of influence of the central bureaucracy.

The result of these changes was that expanding formal strength coupled with continuing substantive weakness became the perennial characteristic of the state in both the late imperial and the early republican periods of the Ottoman Empire–Turkey. The first major turn toward the substantive strengthening of the Turkish state came only in 1950, when popular classes, especially peasants, were incorporated into the political process in a meaningful way.[47] But that is another story.

NOTES

1 *Anastasius: Memoirs of a Greek* (London: John Murray, Albemarle Street, 1820).
2 The designation of the period between 1789 and 1914 as a historically and intellectually meaningful "long nineteenth century" belongs to Eric Hobsbawm, *The Age of Empire* (London: Pantheon, 1989).
3 Bryan Turner's *Marx and the End of Orientalism* (London: George Allen & Unwin, 1978) remains as one of the best critical reviews of the dominant sociological paradigms as they relate to the study of the Middle Eastern societies.
4 In recent years there have been efforts in the Ottoman historiography to overcome some of these limitations by incorporating new elements from the nonstate arena into fields of analysis. These have revealed many important details on such issues as the organization of work, structure of property, relations within households, and trading groups and their status in Ottoman society. Paralleling these concerns, an effort is under way to develop new methods of approaching the historical material so that the

silences can be deciphered, new voices can be heard, and alternative interpretations can be raised. See the articles in Çağlar Keyder and Faruk Tabak, eds., *Landholding and Commercial Agriculture in the Middle East* (Albany, N.Y.: SUNY Press, 1991). See also H. İslamoğlu İnan, ed., *The Ottoman Empire and the World Economy* (Cambridge: Cambridge University Press, 1987); Donald Quataert, *Social Disintegration and Popular Resistance in the Ottoman Empire, 1881–1908: Reactions to European Economic Penetration* (New York: New York University Press, 1983); Kenneth Cuno, *The Pasha's Peasants: Land, Society, and Economy in Lower Egypt, 1740–1858* (Cambridge: Cambridge University Press, 1992); Amy Singer, "Peasant Migration: Law and Practice in Early Ottoman Palestine," *New Perspectives on Turkey*, No. 8 (Fall 1992): 49–66; and Karen Barkey, "The State and Peasant Unrest in Early 17th-Century France and the Ottoman Empire," *American Sociological Review*, 56, no. 6 (December 1991): 699–715.

5 On İzmir, see Daniel Goffman, *İzmir and the Levantine World, 1550–1650* (Seattle: University of Washington Press, 1990); Elena Frangakis-Syrett, *The Commerce of Izmir in the Eighteenth Century* (Athens: Centre for Asia Minor Studies, 1992). On Salonica, see Nicolas Svoronos, *Histoire du commerce de Salonique au XVIIIe siècle*, Paris, 1953; On Trabzon, see Üner Turgay, "Trade and Merchants in Nineteenth-Century Trabzon: Elements of Ethnic Conflict," in Benjamin Braude and B. Lewis, eds., *Christians and Jews in the Ottoman Empire*, vol. 1 (New York: Holmes & Meier, 1982); on Beirut, Leila Fawaz, *Merchants and Migrants in Nineteenth Century Beirut* (Cambridge, Mass.: Harvard University Press, 1983); on Alexandria, Daniel Panzac, "Alexandrie: Evolution d'une ville cosmopolite au XIXe siècle," *Annales Islamologigues*, 14 (1978): 195–215; Michael Reimer, "Colonial Bridgehead: Social and Spatial Change in Alexandria, 1850–1882," *International Journal of Middle East Studies*, 20 (1988): 531–553; see also *Special Issue on Eastern Mediterranean Port Cities, Review*, 16, no. 4 (Fall 1993).

6 Ş. Pamuk, *The Ottoman Empire and European Capitalism, 1820–1913* (Cambridge: Cambridge University Press, 1987).

7 See R. Kasaba, *The Ottoman Empire and the World Economy, The Nineteenth Century* (Albany, N.Y.: SUNY Press, 1988), and Pamuk, *The Ottoman Empire and European Capitalism*.

8 For population movements, see Kemal Karpat, *Ottoman Population, 1830–1914* (Madison: University of Wisconsin Press, 1985).

9 According to best estimates, in 1872 about 37 million kuruş were collected as tithe in İzmir. In 1879, İzmir's contribution was estimated to be about the same. However, in just the years between 1870 and 1876, the volume of agricultural production in western Anatolia had increased by about 20 percent. Kasaba, *The Ottoman Empire and the World Economy, The Nineteenth Century*, p. 96.

10 See Traian Stoianovich, "The Conquering Balkan Orthodox Merchant," *Journal of Economic History*, 20, no. 2 (1960): 234–313; A. İhsan Bağış, *Osmanlı Ticaretinde Gayri Müslimler* (Ankara: Turhan, 1983); Stelios Papadopulos, *The Greek Merchant Marine* (Athens: Central Bank of Greece, 1972); Braude and Lewis, eds., *Christians and Jews in the Ottoman Empire;* Gerasimos Augustinos, *The Greeks of Asia Minor* (Kent, Ohio: Kent State University Press, 1992).

11 *Illustrated London News*, 17 December 1853.

12 See Tuncer Baykara, *Izmir Şehri ve Tarihi* (İzmir, 1974), p. 110. M. A. Ubicini, *Letters from Turkey*, vol. 1 (London: John Murray, 1856), pp. 249–250.

13 Compare Bernard Lewis, *The Emergence of Modern Turkey* (London and New York, Oxford University Press, 1961), with Halil İnalcık, "Sened-i İttifak ve Gülhane Hattı Hümayunu," *Belleten*, 28 (1964).

14 Roderick Davison, *Reform in the Ottoman Empire* (Princeton: Princeton University Press, 1963), pp. 136–171; İlber Ortaylı, *Tanzimatdan Cumhuriyete Yerel Yönetim Geleneği* (Istanbul: Hil Yayınları, 1985).

15 Ortaylı, *Tanzimatdan Cumhuriyete Yerel Yönetim Geleneği,* pp. 33–45, 67–91. See also Stanford J. Shaw, "The Origins of Representative Government in the Ottoman Empire," in R. B. Winder, ed., *Near Eastern Round Table* (New York: New York University Press, 1969).

16 Davison, *Reform in the Ottoman Empire,* p. 147.

17 R. Kasaba, "Treaties and Friendships: British Imperialism, The Ottoman Empire and China in the Nineteenth Century," *Journal of World History,* 4, no. 2 (1993): 215–241.

18 This account is from P. Iliou, "Luttes Sociales et Movement des Lumières à Smyrne en 1819," in *Structure Sociale Developpement Culturel des villes sud-est Europennes et Adriatiques aux XVIIe–XVIIIe siècles* (Bucharest, 1975), pp. 296–315.

19 İlber Ortaylı, *Tanzimatdan Cumhuriyete Yerel Yönetim Geleneği,* pp. 43–45.

20 Roger Owen, *The Middle East and the World Economy* (London: Methuen, 1981), pp. 160–173.

21 Davison, *Reform in the Ottoman Empire,* p. 143.

22 Donald Quataert, "The Commercialization of Agriculture in Ottoman Turkey," *International Journal of Turkish Studies,* 1 (1980), pp. 38–55; Ş. Pamuk, *The Ottoman Empire and European Capitalism;* Kasaba, *The Ottoman Empire and the World Economy, The Nineteenth Century.*

23 Charles Issawi, *The Economic History of Turkey* (Chicago: University of Chicago Press, 1980), pp. 206–210.

24 Justin McCarthy, *Muslims and Minorities: The Population of Ottoman Anatolia and the End of the Empire* (New York: NYU Press, 1983). Karpat, *Ottoman Population, 1830–1914.* Issawi, *The Economic History of Turkey,* pp. 17–19.

25 Great Britain, Public Record Office, Foreign Office, General Correspondence, FO 78/1533:277–278.

26 Ottoman population registers are in the Prime Ministry's Archives in Istanbul. They are under "Maliye Ceride" (ML-CRD) classification. Examples of guest workers can be found in documents numbered 2, 89, 92. See also Alain Duben, "Turkish Families and Households in Historical Perspective," *Journal of Family History,* 10, no. 1 (Spring 1985): 75–97; Kemal Karpat, *Gecekondu: Rural Migration and Urbanization* (Cambridge: Cambridge University Press, 1976), ch. 2; Çağlar Keyder, "The Cycle of Sharecropping and the Consolidation of Small Peasant Ownership in Turkey," *Journal of Peasant Studies,* 10, nos. 2–3 (January–April 1983): 130–145.

27 Examples of this kind of movement can also be found in the Ottoman Population Registers; for example, ML-CRD 31, ML-CRD 298 (see note 26). See also Gilles Veinstein, "Ayan de la Region d'İzmir et commerce du Levant," *Etudes Balkaniques,* 12, no. 3 (1976): 71–83; Tuncer Baykara, "XIX. Yüzyılda Urla Yarımadasında Nüfus Hareketleri," Osman Okyar and Halil İnalcık eds., *Türkiye'nin Sosyal ve İktisadi Tarihi* (Ankara: Meteksan, 1980), pp. 279–286. Augustinos, *The Greeks of Asia Minor,* pp. 11–32.

28 Cengiz Orhonlu, *Osmanlı İmparatorluğunda Aşiretlerin İskanı* (Istanbul: Eren, 1987), p. 71.

29 See Rhoads Murphey, "Some Features of Nomadism in the Ottoman Empire," *Journal of Turkish Studies,* 8 (1984): 189–197.

30 Alain Duben, "Turkish Families and Households in Historical Perspective," pp. 82, 92.

31 Justin McCarthy, "Age, Family and Migration in Nineteenth Century Black Sea

Provinces of the Ottoman Empire," *International Journal of Middle East Studies,* 10 (1979): 309–323; Karpat, *Gecekondu,* p. 17.

32 Cengiz Orhonlu, *Osmanlı İmparatorluğunda Aşiretlerin İskanı,* p. 4; Cevdet Paşa, *Tezakir,* vol. 1 (Ankara: Türk Tarih Kurumu, 1986), p. 7; Earl Percy, *Highlands of Asiatic Turkey* (London, 1901), p. 131.

33 Compare Ömer Lütfi Barkan, "Türk Toprak Hukuku Tarihinde Tanzimat ve 1274 (1858) Tarihli Arazi Kanunnamesi," in *Tanzimat* (Istanbul: T. C. Marif Vekaleti, 1940), pp. 1–101, with Haim Gerber, *The Social Origins of the Modern Middle East* (Boulder, Colo.: Lynne Rienner, 1987), pp. 67–90.

34 Owen, *The Middle East and the World Economy,* pp. 256–259.

35 James Scott, *Weapons of the Weak: Everyday Forms of Peasant Resistance* (New Haven: Yale University Press, 1985).

36 Şerif Mardin, "The Just and the Unjust," *Daedalus,* 120, no. 3 (Summer 1991): 113–129.

37 See R. Kasaba, "Was There a Compradore Bourgeoisie in Mid-Nineteenth Century Western Anatolia?" *Review,* 11 (1988): 215–228.

38 FO 78/614, 13 June, 10 July, 13 August, 10 October, 1845.

39 Juan R. I. Cole, "Mafia, Mob, and Shi'ism in Iraq: The Rebellion of Ottoman Karbala 1824–1843," *Past and Present,* 112 (1986): 112–143.

40 Two important thinkers who wrote extensively on Turkish nationalism in its formative years are Yusuf Akçura and Ziya Gökalp. See Yusuf Akçura, *Üç Tarz-ı Siyaset* (Ankara: Türk Tarih Kurumu, 1976, rpt. from 1904 ed.); Ziya Gökalp, *The Principles of Turkism* (Leiden: E. J. Brill, 1968, rpt. from 1924 ed.). On Akçura, see François Georgeon, *Türk Milliyetçiliğinin Kökenleri* (Ankara: Yurt Yayınları, 1986). On Gokalp, see Taha Parla, *The Social and Political Thought of Ziya Gökalp* (Leiden: E. J. Brill, 1985). For a general, historical account, see Niyazi Berkes, *The Development of Secularism in Turkey* (Montreal, 1964) and Şerif Mardin, *Religion and Social Change in Modern Turkey* (Albany: SUNY Press, 1989).

41 See Şerif Mardin, "Freedom in an Ottoman Perspective," M. Heper and A. Evin eds., *State, Democracy, and the Military: Turkey in the Eighties* (Berlin, 1988), pp. 23–35.

42 It is interesting to note that from the very beginning, deportations were mentioned as a possible way of dealing with those who did not wish to become part of such a project. See Ahmet Ferit, "Bir Mektup," in Y. Akçura, *Üç Tarz-ı Siyaset,* p. 49.

43 Mardin, *Religion and Social Change in Modern Turkey,* p. 101.

44 The classical account of Britain's foreign policy under Palmerston is Charles Webster, *The Foreign Policy of Palmerston,* 2 vols. (London, 1951). Frank Edgar Bailey, *British Policy and the Turkish Reform Movement* (Cambridge: Cambridge University Press, 1942), was the first thorough analysis of this important relationship. For a recent study of these issues, see C. A. Bayly, *The Imperial Meridian,* London: Longman, 1989.

45 İ. Ortaylı, *Osmanlı İmparatorluğunda Alman Nüfuzu,* Istanbul: Kaynak, 1983; U. Trumpener, *Germany and the Ottoman Empire, 1914–1918* (Princeton: Princeton University Press, 1968).

46 For example, Daniel Lerner, *The Passing of Traditional Society* (New York: Free Press, 1958); C. E. Black, *The Dynamics of Modernization* (New York: Harper & Row, 1966).

47 See Ç. Keyder, *State and Class in Turkey* (London: Verso, 1987); R. Kasaba, "Populism and Democracy in Turkey, 1946–1961," E. Goldberg, R. Kasaba, J. Migdal, eds., *Rules and Rights in the Middle East* (Seattle: University of Washington Press, 1993), pp. 43–68.

9

Peasant–state relations in postcolonial Africa: patterns of engagement and disengagement

MICHAEL BRATTON

INTRODUCTION

At the heart of the contemporary crisis in sub-Saharan Africa lies a deep estrangement between state and society. State elites and peasant producers – arguably the two most politically relevant categories of social actor in Africa – have yet to engage each other fully in a mutually advantageous project of national development. To date, these groups have not arrived at a working consensus to reconcile the quest by state elites for political survival with the aspirations of ordinary Africans for economic well-being.

The essence of the postcolonial history of sub-Saharan Africa is therefore an unresolved political struggle: On one hand, political elites wish to extend the authority of the state over scattered populations, most of whom live in rural areas; on the other hand, peasants remain determined to preserve a realm of authority within which to make decisions about their own lives. The struggle between these groups centers on the classic issue of early modern economic development: Who will produce and who will dispose of economic surpluses from agriculture, and on what terms?

The argument presented here is that a state–peasant struggle persists in African countries because neither party has the power resources to resolve it. Both state and peasant organizations are more effective at asserting political autonomy than they are at building political capacity. Neither has succeeded in capturing the other. Thus the upshot of their interactions more commonly has been reciprocal political disengagement rather than joint engagement in a con- certed effort to reach shared goals.

But we should not draw an overly combative or pessimistic image of state– society relations in postcolonial Africa, thereby overlooking factors that help to forge struggle into accommodation. Although elites and peasants both seek to maximize their own political autonomy, each reluctantly discovers that it is mutually dependent. State elites are driven by a revenue imperative, whether to finance the burgeoning apparatus of the developmental state or to satisfy the patronage requirements of more predatory forms of governance. Public officials would prefer to extract revenues from diverse sources, but commonly find that they must fall back upon slim and unpredictable pickings from the peasant sector. The government thus faces the challenge of whether to strike a compromise that addresses the interests of the most productive elements within the peasantry. Peasants, for their part, try to improve household welfare by generating flows of cash income from market production and off-farm employment. In so doing, they invariably encounter agencies of the state that monopolize or regulate markets. Producers must thus assess whether the benefits of using essential government services outweigh the costs of submitting to public regulation.

The relationship between state and social actors is therefore ambivalent and contradictory, a love–hate relationship. State actors seek to transform society by imposing a planned vision of the future on it, but they cannot be effective at this task for long without seeking legitimacy from among society's members. For their part, societal actors resent public regulation but are sometimes willing to accept it as part of the price of access to the substantial resources which the state controls. This dialectic of mutual attraction and repulsion is the source of movement and dynamism in state–society relations.

The love–hate relationship between state and peasantry in Africa is played out within rural organizations. This chapter examines the agricultural production and marketing organizations that govern the rural political economy in Africa. Since before independence in Africa, state policy makers have attempted to prescribe peasant production practices, for example, by establishing commodity production schemes on which peasant producers grow cash crops for export. Even where peasant production has not been fully encapsulated, policy makers have promulgated laws and regulations making it mandatory for independent smallholders to sell agricultural produce only through official marketing boards and cooperatives.

Alternatively, and often in reaction to governmental initiatives, peasants have attempted to construct their own rural organizations. For example, they have created informal trading networks to cater to local demand or to bypass inefficient official channels to national and international markets. And where independent small farmers have become deeply involved in agricultural marketing, they have sometimes formed political associations to defend and advance their group interests.

Whether rural organizations are sponsored by the state or by social actors, state officials and peasant producers vie to own and shape them. Because rural organizations are subject to contestation, they do not always perform as intended by the actors who establish them. State-sponsored production schemes targeted at poor farmers may be captured and milked by elite social groups at the local level. Peasant associations that begin as autonomous social movements may ultimately be co-opted by the rural extension agencies of the state. The actual outcomes depend on balance between the power resources brought to bear by peasants and the state respectively.

The first part of this chapter suggests a framework to help analyze these state–society relations. The framework takes the form of a power analysis in which the main explanatory factors are the political initiatives (to engage or disengage) and power resources (of political autonomy and political capacity) of organized social actors. Specifically, I ask: Do state officials and other social groups seek out or avoid one another? What power resources do they bring to bear in the process? Do simultaneous political initiatives from state and society reinforce or counteract?

The second part of the chapter offers an interpretation of the evolution of postcolonial African politics as a sequence of shifting state–society relations. This four-stage sequence is a conceptual construct derived from the initiatives of state and social actors to engage with, or disengage from, one another. It summarizes the central tendencies from a variety of national experiences and thus may deviate from the precise chronology of events in any particular country. Its outlines are as follows: Initially, in the afterglow of national independence, policy elites and peasants expressed a common political agenda by mutually engaging in state-sponsored commodity production schemes. As economic planners endeavored to expand the reach of the state across the countryside through marketing cooperatives, peasant producers became disillusioned with the political controls and economic costs associated with these institutions, and withdrew their support from the state. Still later, while peasants independently reorganized themselves into informal trading networks, the state encountered a severe fiscal crisis, resulting in disengagement by both state and society. Finally, although political relations in many African countries remain stalled at this stage, autonomous farmer associations in select places attempted to initiate a mutually empowering policy dialogue with the state.

ORGANIZATIONAL POWER ANALYSIS

The state in society

Political inquiry consists of the study of power as it is pursued and used by social actors. Power – the ability to secure compliance to one's will – is difficult for individuals to obtain when acting alone. To mount a credible bid to exercise power, individuals must combine with others; thus power is accumulated and exercised in the context of political organization. And because power is a scarce resource, it tends to crystallize within a limited number of such organizations.

The structure of political organizations may be more or less formal and – especially in sub-Saharan Africa – the informal sector of politics has broad scope. Some organizations may be so informal – for example, ethnic or class movements or clienteles of personal patrons – as to be better conceptualized as social forces. In other instances, purposive actors may construct specialized organizations with a legal identity and an administrative structure with leaders, staff, and members. Through these formal organizations, they undertake a program of action geared to an explicit set of political goals.

Of all political organizations, the state is the largest, most formal, and most powerful. Yet the state is only one form of organization among many: It is an organization *within* society that coexists and interacts with other formal and informal political organizations. The uniqueness of the modern state is that the elites who control its power seek hegemony by claiming to institute universal and binding rules to govern social behavior.[1] A contextual definition, which identifies state agencies as species of a wider genus of political organization, has important advantages over a state-centric approach. A state-in-society perspective enables the analyst to recognize that political power resides at numerous locations, not just at the political apex occupied by state executives. If diverse social actors decide to organize themselves, power can be aggregated beyond the reach of the state and be used as a counterbalance to excessive political centralization. In short, state elites do not automatically enjoy a monopoly of political power, but must bid for it in competition with an array of formal and informal political organizations.

If the distribution of power is the result of political competition, then state–society relations are necessarily indeterminate. In most instances, the decisions of state elites will prevail, but occasionally the collective preferences of other social actors will do so. The state may dominate in the teeth of forceful social resistance or with willing acquiescence from members of society. Similarly, nonstate actors may get their own way by staking out non-negotiable demands and sticking to them, or by accommodating their preferences to those of state elites. Thus, while state–society interactions often lead to conflict, they can also involve reciprocity, organizational adaptation, and mutual gain. The analytic task, therefore, is to identify the conditions under which state and social actors assert, and sometimes share, political power.

Political initiatives: engagement and disengagement

When political actors seek to influence the behavior of others, we can speak of political engagement. When they make no such claim, or actively try to evade the claims of others, we may describe their initiative as political disengagement. This lexicon derives from an emerging literature in comparative politics that questions the universal applicability of the state-centered "engagement paradigm."[2] Donald Rothchild and Naomi Chazan, by way of trying to conceptualize informal political and economic activity in Africa, pose "disengagement as an alternative to incorporation."[3]

This chapter extends these ideas toward a systematic and comparative framework. Political initiatives appear in four basic forms, depending initially on the intent of political actors and their location in society:

- *State-sponsored engagement* refers to efforts by state elites authoritatively to regulate social behavior. This type of political initiative includes, inter alia, pacification of national territory, promulgation of legal codes, and efforts to plan centrally economic production, distribution, and exchange.
- *State-sponsored disengagement* refers to retrenchment by state elites who encounter limits to the reach of public authority. It is manifest, for example, in concessions of liberated areas to rebels, in devolution of legal jurisdictions to traditional or religious authorities, and in reforms to liberalize and privatize economic activities.
- *Society-sponsored disengagement* refers to actions by ordinary citizens to withdraw from the realm of state authority or otherwise to evade compliance with official directives. Examples include refugee flight, popular disregard for civil and criminal laws, and black-marketeering.
- *Society-sponsored engagement* refers to collective action by citizens to influence the allocation of public resources or gain control of state power. Examples include voting, lobbying, patronage claims, political protests, and armed resistance.

The resources of power: autonomy and capacity

The political initiatives taken by state and social actors are not entirely voluntaristic. The choice to engage or disengage in political action, and the likely success of such initiatives, are conditioned by the actors' access to power resources. We must thus untangle the components of power itself. Debates on the contemporary state would suggest that the power has two basic dimensions: political autonomy and political capacity.

Autonomy means the latitude of social actors to take political initiatives unconstrained by the claims of others. With reference to the state, Theda Skocpol has defined autonomy as the ability of political elites "to formulate and pursue goals that are *not* simply reflective of the demands or interests of social groups, classes or society."[4] Beyond the state, the notion of autonomy applies wherever the members of *any* social organization attempt to define a protected realm within which to make independent decisions. An organization is autonomous to the extent that the interests of its members, in contrast to some external force, drive a distinctive program of political action.

Capacity is the ability to implement political decisions. Again with reference only to the state, Skocpol defines capacity as the means "to implement official goals, especially over the actual or potential opposition of powerful social groups or in the face of recalcitrant socioeconomic circumstances."[5] It is clear that the concept of political capacity can also refer to *any* organization, regardless of the arena in which it operates. Capacity exists when an organization possesses the full range of resources – human, financial, material, coercive, and symbolic – required for implementers to get things done. As far as political organizations are concerned, the symbolic resource of political support is particularly important. Although in the short run, leaders may implement a political agenda using only coercion – and in the medium term using only material rewards – they must legitimize their leadership in the long run by promoting shared values.

The current literature on the state tends to blur the distinction between political autonomy and political capacity. Eric Nordlinger confuses the two concepts by measuring one in terms of the other, arguing that "a state is autonomous to the extent that it translates its own preferences into authoritative actions."[6] Joel Migdal suggests that "the question of 'who makes the rules' . . . leads us to examine the central elements of the state's capabilities" without exactly specifying whether and how autonomy enables capacity.[7] Skocpol is clearest about the supposed relationship between these concepts: "The explanation of state capacities is closely connected to the explanation of autonomous goal formation by states, because state officials are most likely to try to do things that seem feasible with the means at hand."[8] In short, analysts seem to concur that capacity describes the limits to autonomy.

Yet political autonomy and political capacity are analytically distinctive properties of social organization and should be treated as such. Whereas autonomy answers the question "who initiates?," capacity tells us "how implementation is achieved." Autonomy refers to the process in which actors set goals for organizations, whereas capacity signifies the means of goal realization. These attributes are discrete: Whereas they often appear together and reinforce one another, they do not necessarily do so. An organization may enclose enough inviolable political space to enable leaders to make independent decisions; but, at the same time, it may be unable to mobilize the necessary resources to implement these decisions. Conversely, an organization may have plentiful resources but be constrained in using them because it is restricted – say, through co-optation – from setting independent goals.

As far as the accumulation of political power is concerned, autonomy takes precedence over capacity. The most basic issues of political struggle concern ends rather than means. The leaders of an organization that enjoys autonomy can, under the most favorable circumstances, set the agenda in political disputes. Even if they cannot unilaterally ensure the outcome of a contested issue, the leaders of an autonomous organization at least have the negative power of withholding support from any claim to issue an authoritative command. By contrast, the leaders of an organization that has considerable capacity but lacks autonomy may find themselves party to a political action not of their own making. Thus, whereas capacity cannot substitute for autonomy, the reverse may be true. Indeed, autonomy is the quintessential "weapon of the weak" enabling any social organization, at minimum, to disengage from the political fray.

While political autonomy is the secret weapon of smaller social organizations, political capacity is the backbone of the state. Stated differently, political capacity is distributed asymmetrically across organizations in favor of state agencies. After all, Weber's famous definition of the state posits a claim to an exclusive monopoly of the basic political resource of coercion. And with regard to the capacity to extract and accumulate other critical human, financial, and material resources, the state must be regarded as preeminent. Interestingly, however, state elites have great difficulty in cornering the market on the crucial symbolic resources that endow institutions with permanent popular value. Indeed, a monopoly of coercive and productive resources, if not legitimized through regular elections and economic performance, can prove to be an albatross around the neck of the state. Under circumstances where monopolistic state agencies are performing poorly, political legitimacy readily flows to alternative organizations in society, which are then well placed to use popular support in a bid for influence or power.

Thus, political autonomy is the cornerstone of power; it lies at the heart of struggles between state and society. It provides the starting point for the analysis in the following paragraphs. Although most writers on the state dwell on the autonomy of the state, Alfred Stepan's more sophisticated analyses suggest that the autonomy of institutions in civil society is a factor affecting the success of state elites at regime installation.[9] An organization in society, for example, exists to differentiate the interests of its membership from those of other civic groups and also from those of the state elite. Empirically, neither state nor social actors are ever able to maximize the property of autonomy to a point where they are able to make decisions entirely without reference to external considerations. At best, each enjoys relative or partial autonomy, although the boundary between the state and social arenas may be constantly contested and shifting. As Allen Isaacman has said, "jockeying and negotiating to reshape [this] partial autonomy represent[s] the principal terrain of struggle" between state and society.[10]

Autonomy without capacity: organizations in Africa

Just how much autonomy and capacity do political organizations display in African contexts? Let us discuss this question with reference to peasant and state organizations in turn.

Because peasants stand with one foot in the domestic household economy and another in wider systems of production, exchange, and authority, they have ambiguous relationships to state and market. As agriculturalists who control the land they work and who use household labor to meet most of their production needs, peasants are potentially politically autonomous. On the other hand, peasants also produce small amounts of commodities for sale, and thus are vulnerable to domination by outsiders who seek to appropriate economic surpluses, either directly or by use of state power.

Africa is a continent of peasant societies, with an average of about 70 percent of the population engaged in agricultural occupations.[11] Agriculture constitutes the basic means of subsistence because opportunities are meager for earning off-farm income in rural Africa. Rural households are only partially incorporated into capitalist production-and-exchange relations, and African peasantries remain relatively undifferentiated along class lines. With a few exceptions – notably in the high-rainfall uplands – African rural societies have yet to be torn apart into classes of land-owning capitalist farmers and landless tenants and proletarians. For the most part, the process of class formation is incomplete, with rural populations being only "semicapitalist" or "semiproletarian." The principal distinction within the peasantry lies between those who produce only for household consumption and those who earn income from marketing agricultural surpluses. This distinction is important for present purposes, for it is the second group, the market-oriented producers, who interact most regularly with the agricultural agencies of the state.

Access to land and control over family labor is the source of peasant political autonomy, enabling African peasants to "shield critical resources and to implement individual remedies to combat . . . oppression."[12] Within various externally imposed constraints, peasants in Africa have been able to decide "to produce when and what they wanted."[13] The most entrepreneurial producers have exercised what Terrence Ranger calls a "peasant option," that is, to obtain income from agricultural commodity production while maintaining access to land and labor, and insisting on the right to make independent farm management decisions.[14] In other words, the top stratum of the peasantry has sought to enter the market on its own terms while at the same time avoiding state efforts to regulate and reorganize agricultural production.

Although peasant producers enjoy autonomy, they have rarely been able to construct organizations with a strong capacity to represent political interests. During decolonization in Africa, peasants were late in adding their weight to the nationalist coalition and their role was largely limited to providing a pool of followers for urban-based, middle-class political leaders. Peasants played a leadership or catalytic role in anticolonial resistance only through protests against agricultural regulation or where land hunger was prevalent. In postcolonial times, peasants have become politically demobilized, disassembling into the household, community, migrant, and urban realms. The scattered pattern of peasant settlement, the low levels of education among rural dwellers, and their widespread distrust of non-kin "strangers," have all militated against collective political action. Organizations that do emerge among peasants – such as agricultural work groups or savings clubs – tend to address economic rather than political issues, and to be local in scope and parochial in vision.

Turning now to the state in Africa, it, too, enjoys political autonomy, especially from the agrarian elements in society. The state in Africa is a set of alien political institutions, originally imported from abroad. During the colonial period, public officials employed an uninhibited scope of decision making to impose European codes of law and regulation on African societies. Usually without consideration of popular preferences, the colonial authorities decided to draw national boundaries, to raise revenues through taxation of the peasantry, and to compel cash crop production. Although the colonial state clearly lacked the political capacity to implement policy in local arenas without collaboration from indigenous auxiliaries, it exercised almost absolute power in newly created national arenas.

The autonomy of the state and the fault line between state and society was temporarily breached at the time of decolonization. In the first years of *uhuru,* the new African political leaders felt beholden to satisfy the demands of the populace that they had mobilized through promises of the good life. In time, however, because they lacked resources to bring about broad-based rural development and because they came to savor the fruits of power, the new political elites reasserted the primacy and autonomy of the state. They reclaimed a role as rule givers for society by undermining electoral and legislative institutions and introducing one-party and military regimes. In some countries, the arbitrary fiats of personal dictators elevated autonomous decision-making to an obscene art.

At the same time, the political capacity of the state declined. From the outset, the state apparatus was hamstrung by gross shortages of trained and experienced personnel, in large part because the colonial authorities had failed to prepare Africans. Rapid Africanization of the public service after independence was usually accompanied by a loss of technical and managerial expertise. Moreover, African political leaders embarked on state intervention in precisely the area where skills were shortest: namely, the comprehensive planning and management of economic production. As state enterprises foundered – in agriculture among other sectors – their losses undermined the fiscal foundation of the state.

In postcolonial sub-Saharan Africa, therefore, two general institutional conditions inform state–society relations. All organizations – whether based in the state or elsewhere in society – are characterized, first, by relative political autonomy, and, second, by limited political capacity. Although all organizations are incompletely formed and short of resources, their autonomy nonetheless endows them with adeptness at evading political claims from beyond their own boundaries. As shown in the next section, both state officials and peasant producers in Africa have undertaken initiatives to engage one another on joint activities in the agricultural sector. Yet most such initiatives have failed to flourish, either economically in terms of increased export revenues and household incomes, or politically in the form of mutual empowerment of state and peasant organizations. These disappointing results can be traced not only to the limited capacity of any sort of organization in Africa to effect planned change, but also to the fact that political actors, in both state and society, are sufficiently independent to retreat beyond each other's reach.

PATTERNS OF PEASANT—STATE RELATIONS IN AFRICA

State elites and other social actors launch simultaneous political initiatives to obtain preferred political outcomes. The actual outcome – Who, if anyone, prevails? Is there compromise? – is shaped by the balance of power in such encounters.

Analysis of political outcomes will be most fruitful with reference to concrete cases, preferably of specific state agencies and peasant organizations in individual countries. As a preliminary step, the remainder of this chapter offers a general sketch of the evolution of state–society relations in sub-Saharan Africa in the postcolonial era. Depending on whether the political initiatives of state elites and peasants have reinforced or conflicted, different patterns of state–society relations have prevailed. The postcolonial era began with mutual efforts at political engagement, but this happy coincidence soon gave way to less productive patterns of interaction as first the peasantry, and later the state, began to withdraw and disengage. Only recently have we seen occasional signs of organized efforts by market-oriented peasants to reengage in the market and state arenas.

State and society engage: production schemes

Immediately after independence, the political capacity of the state to reach out, control production, and deliver services in the countryside was at a peak owing to flows of foreign technical and financial assistance. Peasants, flushed by the experience of nationalist mobilization, were willing to grant widespread legitimacy to their new rulers, and expected to take advantage of the first fruits of development. Therefore, the interests of both state planners and market-oriented farmers coincided in favor of planned agricultural production schemes. Such schemes illustrate a form of rural organization that resulted from the mutual engagement of social actors inside and outside of the state.

Even though production schemes were initiated by a ministry of agriculture, a land settlement board, or a parastatal corporation, they employed a peasant form of production. Unlike state farms, where peasants became wage laborers, production schemes were organized around smallholder plots in which peasants continued to enjoy access to their own land. The prototypical form was the settlement scheme, defined by Robert Chambers as "an organized attempt to introduce change" within "a visible land unit" that involved "a movement of population, and an element of planning and control."[15] In Africa, settlement schemes ranged in size from Sudan's giant Gezira Scheme, supporting over a million settlers on 1.8 million acres, to microprojects involving less than a hundred acres and a handful of smallholders. The purposes of such schemes included one or several of the following: land reform, refugee rehabilitation, cash crop production, soil conservation, irrigation, or farm mechanization.

First introduced during the colonial period, production schemes became a favored instrument of national development planners in Africa in the 1960s. From the perspective of the state, they provided a controlled environment in which to introduce technical innovation and boost output of foreign-exchange-earning cash crops. By concentrating scarce investments in high potential areas, planners hoped to demonstrate that peasant agriculture could be restructured and modernized. From a societal perspective, settlement schemes were attractive to peasants because they promised access to productive resources – whether land, tillage, extension, or credit services, usually at subsidized rates – that were not generally available in the rural hinterland. To the extent that the schemes enabled profitable agricultural production and offered improved standards of living, peasants had a strong incentive to join. Indeed, agricultural production schemes in tropical Africa were typically oversubscribed, with waiting lists of applicants far larger than the number of available plots.

Yet the price of economic opportunity for peasants on production schemes was a loss of political autonomy. The schemes were governed by a managerial staff appointed by the relevant state agency, who were distinguished from settlers by sharp differences in income, education, and status. Chambers suggests that "clear territorial boundaries, physical isolation and a community of 'subjects' [gave] a manager a position in which he might easily come to regard himself as a sort of chief with sovereignty over his settlers."[16] The important decisions regarding the constitution and operation of the scheme rested with agricultural bureaucrats: for example, the criteria for tenant selection, the arrangements for land tenure, the choice of crop and production method, the means of payment for produce, and the rules for tenant representation. State managers sought to regulate tenant behavior in accordance with the technical requirements of the production process, such as the timely distribution of water on irrigation schemes and the efficient deployment of tractors on mechanization schemes. Their commands were backed by a capacity to enforce sanctions: verbal and written warnings, legal prosecutions, even eviction from the scheme itself.

Conflicts commonly arose when official objectives diverged from the interests of farmers. For example, tenants wished to move freely back and forth to the communities whence they came; yet management wanted to limit absenteeism. Scheme managers also sought compliance with instructions on land use, livestock holdings, and crop husbandry; but tenants found ways to avoid implementation, often in order to invest time in private economic activities. Management preferred a sense of physical orderliness, with settlement patterns designed for administrative convenience; tenants had a looser, organic vision, with amenities laid out to facilitate social intercourse.

In the struggle between state and social actors on production schemes, peasants suffered a critical disadvantage: They were less well organized than the state agency, not only having sacrificed political autonomy but also lacking political capacity. The very fact that production schemes involved population movement or the selection of "better" farmers meant that social relations – the glue of small-scale organization – was disrupted. Scheme farmers became isolated from their home communities and from one another. While homogeneous in social class terms, tenant communities were often culturally heterogeneous, mixing persons of diverse ethnic backgrounds who found difficulty in combining for collective action. The position of women was weakened, not least by severed attachments to networks of mutual support. Again in Chambers's words: "A social nakedness has to be endured by settlers at least in the early stages of settlement."[17]

The mismatch in power resources meant that mutual engagement led to the dominance of the state and the subordination of those peasants who participated in production schemes. The social organizations induced by the settlement bureaucracy – for example, tenants' advisory committees – served principally as a sounding board for management and a channel to communicate management's version of the rules for scheme operation. In some cases, tenants' advisory committees were charged to enact or approve disciplinary actions, including evictions from the scheme, thereby providing protection and legitimacy for management. The object of induced social organization on the scheme was to free public officials to concentrate on matters of technical and economic efficiency. Thus, while permitting a greater degree of democratic representation than the paternalistic colonial structures, production schemes in postcolonial Africa still promoted a technocratic and bureaucratic organizational culture. By subordinating peasant participation in decision making within centrally determined rules, successful production schemes constitute the best example in rural Africa of state-structured social relations.

Every form of rural organization suffers its own internal contradictions. From the perspective of the state, settlement schemes were expensive: as special projects they addressed ambitious goals and had a highly visible profile; at the same time, however, they absorbed scarce resources, stretched the capacity of the state at service delivery, and were not always productive. Grand schemes – such as the Volta River Settlements in Ghana and the Pilot Village Settlements in Tanzania – were therefore prime targets for spectacular failure.

From a peasant perspective, the attractiveness of a scheme depended on whether the selection of tenants and the organization of production were perceived as voluntary. Settler families were easily reminded of colonial regimes of compulsory cultivation and sometimes came to regard themselves as temporary employees of government. Production scheme managers often found that "penalties [were] generally easier to apply widely than rewards which [were] often from their very nature limited to relatively few individuals."[18] For peasants who entered the schemes, political autonomy and opportunities for political association were reduced. For this reason, schemes were vulnerable to defection. The longevity of a particular production scheme thus depended critically on whether peasants perceived that privileged access to economic services or agricultural incomes outweighed the costs of the loss of political autonomy.

State engages/society disengages: marketing cooperatives

Because African state elites never gained sufficient political capacity to blanket the countryside with production schemes, they were led to adopt alternative forms of rural organization by which to attempt to engage the peasantry. The marketing cooperative represented a looser form of state–society relations: Producers continued to work on independent smallholdings rather than on residential schemes, and agricultural officials, rather than aiming to directly supervise production, instead sought to manage the disposition of agricultural surpluses. Marketing cooperatives, administered by a specialized government department within the ministry of agriculture or office of the president, were the most common form of organized political initiative taken by the state in the African countryside.

Administrators promoted an official network of agricultural cooperatives on the grounds that they would enable peasant political participation and self-management. Cooperatives were supposed to be governed by principles of open and voluntary membership, internal democratic accountability, and profit sharing. The goals of cooperatives were distinguished from those of business corporations in that the maximization of profit was to be balanced against the welfare needs of members. In practice in African countries, the power of members to make decisions was restricted, not only by the need to remain economically competitive in the marketplace, but by management requirements imposed by the state. Few African cooperatives became production collectives. Most concentrated on service functions such as agricultural input distribution or the sale of agricultural produce, occasionally providing other services, such as commodity processing, banking, and insurance.

First initiated by colonial regimes, agricultural marketing cooperatives expanded rapidly in the period immediately after independence. In Kenya, for example, membership of agricultural marketing cooperatives grew from under 200,000 to almost 1 million farmers between 1961 and 1977.[19] In Zambia in 1965, President Kaunda launched a popular program of cash grants to peasants willing to form and register agricultural cooperatives.[20] State and peasantry seemed to have a shared interest in cooperative organization: "Small farmers are drawn to cooperation as the preferred means of improving their lot . . . political leadership is drawn to cooperation as a half-way house between direct state implementation of economic activities and . . . the regulation of private enterprise."[21]

In retrospect, the cooperative movement in postcolonial Africa expanded too rapidly for its own good. Although large numbers of cooperative societies were registered on paper, their presence was not widely supported or deeply institutionalized. Elected management committees were captured by local political elites, who were more interested in personal financial gain than in broadly increasing the agricultural incomes and social welfare of members. Many of the new cooperatives were inactive or nonviable, and even the profitable ones suffered from deficits of leadership and professional skills. All too often they were plagued with mismanagement, malfeasance, and internal conflict.

In the face of poor performance, government policies toward the cooperative movement shifted from promotion to consolidation. By the end of the first decade of independence, central government began to exercise powers of direct intervention. While justifying the reorganization of cooperatives in terms of rooting out corruption, state intervention invariably violated the principle of democratic membership control. Ministers dissolved elected committees and appointed new officeholders, seized financial records and assets, and forced societies to amalgamate to form unions. In some cases, these measures were taken without due cause in an effort to prevent local leaders from accumulating an independent power base. Ghana represents an extreme case: Nkrumah repressed his political opponents in the Ashanti cocoa cooperatives in the 1960s; and his successors only tolerated, then formally liquidated, cooperatives by 1977.

State intervention typically focused at the apex of cooperative organization because national political leaders did not have the means to undertake detailed direction of local societies. State control of the peasantry through marketing cooperatives was also limited to periodic crisis situations.

Because the state lacked capacity to supervise peasants directly on their own land, political leaders came to rely heavily on indirect policy measures such as the administrative regulation of agricultural markets.[22] Agricultural marketing cooperatives constituted an important link in the regulatory chain. As agents of the national commodity marketing boards, they implemented at the grass roots the key policy measures that underpinned the extraction of agricultural surpluses from the countryside. As legal representatives of the board, cooperatives performed to exercise monopsony power over "regulated" commodities; administer fixed prices and quality grading standards; and deduct loan repayments and other charges from payments made to producers.

Under these circumstances, the marketing cooperative became an extension of the state apparatus. Whether peasants were willing to offer allegiance to this form of organization depended critically on the terms under which agricultural commodities were traded. If peasants obtained a fair price in relation to the costs of production, they were likely to engage as participants in the cooperative enterprise. The cooperative movement was most popular in countries like Kenya and Côte d'Ivoire where farmers were paid for their products according to world market prices and without deduction of undue administrative charges. In these places, where the return to export crops was higher than to marketable food crops, peasants willingly reallocated land and other agricultural resources toward production for export.

The key issue for peasant members of agricultural marketing cooperatives was therefore whether they could obtain an attractive income in the face of deductions made by the state and by the cooperative itself. Even under relatively favorable conditions, peasant support was less than wholehearted. In a study of agricultural marketing cooperatives in Kisii, Kenya, Torben Bager found that only 18 percent of members attended general meetings, 24 percent did not know who owned the cooperative society, and 41 percent stated that they would like their society to be independent of the cooperative union as deductions were too high.[23] Other common peasant concerns included delays in crop payments, the lack of clarity about the purposes for deductions, and the misuse of funds by committee members or staff. Until these issues were resolved, members were unlikely to perceive marketing cooperatives as their own property, but – perhaps correctly – as parastatals.

Wherever agricultural marketing cooperatives in Africa served as a device for generating revenue for the public treasury, peasants usually chose to withdraw support. This began with "everyday" forms of resistance. Farmers used credit from the cooperative to buy nonagricultural goods and services; they applied fertilizer supplies on food rather than cash crops; or they avoided loan repayment. They knew that the marketing board or agricultural finance corporation often lacked the will or capacity to enforce sanctions for rebellious behavior. In the extreme, peasants left the official marketplace entirely and sought new forms of livelihood: either by abandoning cash crop production, retreating into subsistence, or, as demonstrated in the next section, by establishing informal trading networks to bypass the cooperative. A loss of peasant confidence was most likely where state or local elites plundered the organization's resources for personal gain. When this happened, peasants " 'voted with their feet', leaving the cooperative an empty shell."[24] In short, they disengaged.

State and society disengage: trading networks

When peasants disassociated themselves from cooperatives and from administered markets, they looked for alternative ways to obtain commodities to maintain household production and consumption. They sought to reestablish ties to agricultural and other markets, only now outside the purview of state control. While continuing to exercise the option of exit from the state arena, producers organized their own independent trading networks. They attempted to "beat the system" by constructing a substitute set of exchange relations. They helped to create, or participate directly in, "that part of the economy variously referred to as the second, parallel, informal, underground, black or irregular economy."[25]

In scope and formality, trading networks range from ad hoc village markets to organized smuggling rings that span international frontiers. Because they are designed to circumvent the state, trading networks are an explicitly autonomous form of social organization; but because they are based on face-to-face relations, they often lack organizational capacity. Furthermore, because informal trade robs the public coffers of tax revenue, it also leads to a diminution of state capacity. In time, African governments have little choice but to reduce their regulatory presence in the countryside and to allow social initiatives and structures to replace planned interventions. In sum, trading networks promote, and flourish under, conditions of mutual disengagement between state and society.

The explosive growth of the second economy has been one of the most striking social phenomena of the postcolonial period in Africa. It consists of all those economic activities that occur without being officially recorded and that may deprive the state of revenue. Some of these activities may be illegal, such as smuggling across customs frontiers or bribing state officials, but others may be simply antisocial, such as hoarding scarce goods for profit. As early as 1970, the value of the illicit export trade in coffee and peanuts in Zaire and Senegal respectively exceeded the annual net turnover of the central marketing boards. By 1980, in Ghana and Uganda, the size of the second economy was estimated to approach, if not exceed, the size of the official gross domestic product.

The participation of peasants in the second economy is based on access to assets for the production of tradeable commodities such as food, fish, game, and export crops. In a situation where producers no longer have confidence in the operation of official markets, agriculture can become partially decommercialized. During the 1970s and 1980s, peasant producers in many African countries cut back or abandoned the production of export crops in response to falling world or local prices and the nonavailability of consumer goods. Producers retreated, if not into subsistence, then into the cultivation of food crops alone. One result was that food became more readily available in rural than in urban markets. Under these circumstances, farmers began to send supplies to family members in town to exchange for items that were difficult or expensive to obtain in the countryside such as fertilizer, kerosene, or cooking oil. Whether such exchanges worked to the benefit of small producers depended a great deal on who occupied the key intermediary positions in rural–urban trade. Most often, merchants quickly positioned themselves to reap profitable margins from unofficial markets.

Janet MacGaffey describes an interesting case in which kinship connections formed the basis of a major long-distance trading organization among the Nande of North Kivu, Zaire.[26] The network began when young Nande men first collaborated to grow coffee and to smuggle it – by headload, bicycle, and truck – across the border into Uganda, where producer prices were higher and consumer goods were more readily available than in Zaire. They made handsome returns, particularly after the windfall rise in world coffee prices in 1976. In Uganda, coffee was bartered directly for motor vehicles, spare parts, and manufactured goods that were shipped back to Zaire for sale. These local currency profits were then reinvested in legal enterprises, most notably coffee plantations, urban real estate, and wholesaling. The Nande now constitute a trading diaspora that dominates the distribution of dried beans and fresh vegetables from rural Kivu, through the regional entrepôt of Kisangani, to the capital city of Kinshasa. According to MacGaffey, they are part of a nascent commercial bourgeoisie that owes its class position not to offices within the state, but to an independent productive base within society.

The fact that African citizens autonomously undertake a wide gamut of organized economic activity has profound political implications for the state. The state is particularly vulnerable at the border regions of its territory. Because international frontiers in Africa artificially divide social groups who regard themselves as nations, border regions have always been porous and difficult to police. Trade among kin has often been cross-border trade. To make matters worse, African political elites have always suffered from a limited administrative capacity to extract income taxes, and instead have tended to rely for public revenues on fees, tariffs, and margins from the import–export trade. When trade is conducted primarily through illegal or informal networks, such taxes become difficult to collect; public revenues diminish, especially in valuable foreign exchange. The emergence of society-based trading networks therefore exacerbates the fiscal crisis of the state.

Under these circumstances, the state apparatus begins to disintegrate at the edges. Reduced public budgets lead to cutbacks in public services and regulatory activities, especially in the rural periphery. Public administrators discover that stagnant government salaries do not keep pace with mounting inflation. Absenteeism takes a heavy toll on administrative efficiency as state employees spend time away from their desks in search of food and other basic necessities. Many civil servants, concluding that their family's prospects are brighter in the second economy, begin to "moonlight" at second jobs or in petty trade. Almost all urban dwellers establish household gardens and some move back to the land in search of subsistence. With fewer human resources and financial resources, the will of state elites and the capacity of state agencies inevitably dissipate. Because "the official legal-normative framework is . . . discredited,"[27] state elites have little choice but to concede ever greater amounts of rule-making authority to social actors. The state itself begins to disengage from society.

It may be argued, following Nelson Kasfir, that state and *magendo* (second economy) are interpenetrated.[28] Although it is indeed often impossible to get things done in the second economy without collusion from state officials, this does not attest to a strong residual capacity on the part of the state. When public officials accept bribes to turn a blind eye to an illegal activity, they are not extending the state's authority but reducing it. And when officials engage in private accumulation and trade – even if only through relatives, intermediaries, and employees – they are acknowledging that their behavior is not governed by legal commands. The participation of state officials in the second economy amounts to a deconstruction of the formal architecture of the state in the face of a more compelling set of social imperatives.

The disengagement of the state has been formalized in those African countries where the government has applied a package of structural adjustment reforms to the economy. These reforms include some or all of the following measures: removal of administrative controls in favor of market prices, dissolution of loss-making public enterprises, reductions in public sector employment, and opportunities for private traders to enter agricultural markets. MacGaffey notes with irony that the second economy operates according an approximation of free market principles; therefore, "some of the steps advocated by the World Bank for resolving the crisis in food production [in Africa] are already in effect!"[29] The combined impact of both informal peasant trading initiatives and pressure from international financial institutions is therefore consistent; in both cases it leads the state to retrench, withdraw, and disengage from society.

State disengages/society engages: farmer associations

The retreat of the state leaves an organizational vacuum between state and society. In some African countries, this void is filled with uncertainty, even violence; in others, it is occupied by new, more popular forms of rural organization.

Farmer associations represent a form of rural organization through which actors based in society once again take the initiative to engage the state. The hallmark of the farmer association is that it is autonomous, being a voluntary union contracted among a membership of farmers themselves. It is typically a formal mode of organization, with specialized functions distributed within a differentiated structure, and with an implementation capacity based on the mobilization of resources by the members themselves.

Formal voluntary associations do not arise automatically or frequently in a social context of scattered communities of small agricultural producers. Several preconditions seem to be necessary: an ideology of reciprocity and a tradition of collective action in the agricultural sector; a strong set of shared economic interests, often embracing farmers engaged in the production of a particular commodity; the availability of models of economic interest association, for example, the large-scale commercial farmer unions in former settler colonies; and a favorable economic environment in which agricultural surpluses can be disposed of at a profit beyond the household. In practice, this means there should be open, legal markets and efficient agricultural institutions, conditions that are gradually being met in those African countries undertaking economic adjustment reforms.

Farmer associations arise because of the difficulty faced by individual households in pursuing the "peasant option" alone. For small farmers seeking income from agricultural sales, economies of scale in commodity circuits are most accessible through combination. Enterprising farmers form community-based groups to tackle shared problems such as the high price of improved technology or the unreliability of transport linkages between farm and market. Solutions take the form of bulk purchasing at agricultural inputs or group contracting of agricultural services. In addition, small producers often find it expensive to operate in the second economy. They are unable to take full advantage of the market opportunities because of the high cost of illicit transactions: markups, bribes, and the danger of legal prosecution. The second economy offers small producers little choice but to buy at a premium and sell at a discount. They therefore sometimes decide to reenter official markets and to make efforts to adjust the prices in those markets in their favor.

In several African countries, enterprising farmer-leaders have taken the initiative to combine community-based organizations into regional or national associations. These organizations often adopt a federated structure with members electing representatives to higher levels. In Senegal and Burkina Faso, there are numerous regional peasant associations that express members' views to local government councils and that are linked together in an international network known as L'Association Six-S. In Zimbabwe, there is a national smallholder unions, the Zimbabwe Farmers' Union (ZFU), which represents small- to medium-scale cultivators. In Kenya, peasant farmers have amalgamated with large-scale commercial operators in a national lobby known as the Kenya National Farmers' Union (KNFU). Alongside the KNFU is a diverse set of commodity-specific membership associations for grain, dairy products, and, most importantly, coffee.

These organizations function to improve the delivery of agricultural services to members. This involves direct commercial undertakings: Members pay fees and hire staff to run credit, insurance, information, input, transport, and processing services. In Kenya, farmer organizations handle commodities worth an estimated 40 percent of gross domestic product. Because these organizations have a presence at national level where public policy is made, they may also act politically by giving voice to the policy concerns of peasant farmers.[30] The most powerful policy tool for government control of the agricultural sector is commodity pricing. In Kenya, Zambia, and Zimbabwe, farmer organizations engage in policy advocacy on agricultural prices more often than on any other issue. Whereas the leaders of some organizations (e.g., KNFU) favor decontrol of all agricultural prices, others (e.g., ZFU) prefer to maintain public subsidies on inputs and transport. Other issues around which farmers organize are land distribution, credit availability, and late payments by agricultural marketing boards.

African farmer organizations use various strategies to engage in policy advocacy. Whereas L'Amicale du Wallo and other regional associations in Senegal employ informal, face-to-face contacts with policy-makers through local patronage networks and coalitions, the ZFU supplements this approach by preparing policy position papers for formal submission to the cabinet, for example, on land reform. Whereas the Zambia Cooperative Federation (ZCF) takes an accommodating position toward the government, for example, by acceding to government requests to take over select agricultural marketing services from the state, the Kenya Cooperative Planters' Union (KPCU) has confronted the government directly by calling out its members in boycotts of coffee deliveries, most recently when the government sought to reestablish administrative control of coffee payments.

What has been the result of these peasant efforts at political reengagement? It is difficult to attribute directly agricultural price policy changes to the activities of a small farm lobby in former settler colonies that inherited price regimes that favored producers. But when agricultural commodities are in short supply, for example, owing to disturbed weather conditions, maize farmers in Zimbabwe and coffee farmers in Kenya have been able to win price or payment concessions from the government. Other farmer policy victories can also be noted: For example, in 1979, the Gezira Tenants' Union in Sudan won adjustments to, and delayed implementation of, a plan to charge farmers for land and water used for growing household food crops; in 1984, the ZFU's predecessor won eligibility for its members for selection to settlement schemes under the government of Zimbabwe's land reform program; and in 1989, the KNFU persuaded the Kenyan government to provide seasonal loan insurance and write off the bad debts of smallholders.

There appears to be no immediate relationship between a farmer association's success at policy reform and its strategy of policy advocacy. In the successful cases just cited, the organizations used both informal and formal methods, sometimes confrontation and sometimes accommodation. Rather, to understand the political potential of farmer associations, we must return to the earlier discussion of the power resources of state and social organizations. The autonomy of farmer associations is not at issue because they usually begin as self-appointed entities. But even if they win legitimacy through broad membership and democratic accountability, farmer associations still face problems of organizational capacity. They cannot afford to confront the state unless their members control a strategic resource on which the state relies as the primary source of foreign exchange: as with coffee in Kenya, cotton in Sudan. Similarly, a farmer association cannot use formal methods of policy advocacy unless it builds a capacity at policy analysis that can rival or complement that of the government.

Thus, the initiatives of African farmer associations at political engagement have resulted in public policy reform only under exceptional circumstances. More often, a weakly articulated peasant political voice remains unheard by defensive governments who shelter behind official regulations and bureaucratic institutions. Only rarely does agricultural policy-making through structures of consultation allow peasants to have a seat in public negotiations. As one national farmer leader declared in frustration: "The government doesn't take private advice. Our influence is superficial. The law should provide a bargaining procedure." As he saw it, the challenge for farmer associations was to secure responsiveness and accommodation from the agencies of a disengaged state.

CONCLUSION

This chapter has proposed a framework for studying state–society relations based on the political initiatives of social actors (to engage or disengage) and deriving from the power resources (autonomy and capacity) of social organizations. This framework has been applied to the complex love–hate relationship between state elites and peasant producers in postcolonial Africa. These groups of social actors are attracted to one another because neither can realize their economic goals alone; yet they are mutually repelled because of a political desire to preserve decision-making autonomy.

Certain patterns of peasant–state relations emerge from the analysis and are expressed through familiar types of rural organization. State elites in Africa have succeeded in directing peasant production only within bounded and privileged pockets in the countryside (the production scheme). Official efforts to influence the behavior of the mass of landholding cultivators through price controls and marketing organizations have foundered (the marketing cooperative). Instead, peasants have learned to fend for themselves in the marketplace by adopting coping mechanisms that avoid or bypass the structures of the state (the trading network). In a few cases, peasants have constructed formal organizations to acquire agricultural services or to pressure the state on agricultural policy (the farmer association).

Broadly speaking, each pattern can be argued to have emerged sequentially as a result of unresolved tensions in preceding patterns. For example, because state planners were unable to encapsulate the entire countryside in centrally managed production schemes, they had no choice but to adopt looser forms of rural organization by encouraging independent smallholders to join marketing cooperatives. In turn, marketing cooperatives required peasants to shoulder such heavy institutional costs that peasants ultimately shrugged them off in favor of private trading networks. Still later, the disadvantages of operating outside the law drove many peasants to reengage in political arenas, this time determined to adjust the rules in regulated markets in their own favor.

This is not to make an absurdly sweeping claim that a single line of historical evolution in peasant–state relations applies to all parts of postcolonial Africa. In some countries, production schemes and marketing cooperatives continue to thrive, especially for specialized export commodities. International smuggling of agricultural commodities is more prevalent in some regions of Africa than in others, depending on relative differentials in cross-border prices. Farmer associations are still an exceptional form of rural organization, and even in the countries where they do exist, they often relate more closely to local, rather than central, governments. Because all empirical cases are to some degree distinctive, future detailed analysis of state–peasant relations must therefore be disaggregated, not only by country and historical era, but also by agricultural-ecological zone and by stratum of the peasantry.

In general terms, however, much can be learned from studying the unfolding processes of state–society relations. Who seeks to transform whom? Does anyone prevail? What policy and organizational accommodations are struck? The general outcome for postcolonial Africa is that, although in some countries new strata of peasant agricultural producers have entered capitalist markets, there has been relatively little political transformation. The postcolonial state remains an exotic institutional transplant without deep roots in indigenous soil; peasants, isolated on their rural smallholdings, remain unincorporated into the mainstream of national policy making. In general, a lack of reciprocal influence has arisen because organizations within the state and peasantry both possess political autonomy, yet both lack political capacity. This combination of power resources has meant that organizations on each side have been better equipped to undertake evasive strategies of political withdrawal than to engage in ambitious efforts at structural transformation. The prevailing image of African politics, therefore, is one of mutual disengagement. And the current lack of reciprocity in state–society relations is both a manifestation and a cause of stalled socioeconomic development on the continent.

Yet all is not lost. Because every pattern of state–society relations is fraught with internal tensions, there is always room for social actors to exercise a degree of political initiative. The retreat of the African state creates both obstacles and opportunities. While it removes policy makers even farther from citizen claims for accountability, state-sponsored disengagement also opens up new arenas in which autonomous popular organization can grow and consolidate. Over time, peasants may be able to accumulate enough power within nonstate social arenas to endow their own organizations with a newfound political capacity. Through these organizations, peasants may eventually be able to take compelling initiatives to shape state policies that respond to popular demands. Through this type of political engagement, social actors will lend legitimacy to incumbent governments and thereby enable a constructive process of mutual empowerment that will strengthen not only society, but the state too.

NOTES

1 Joel Migdal, *Strong Societies and Weak States: State–Society Relations and State Capabilities in the Third World* (Princeton: Princeton University Press, 1988), p. 396. Victor Azarya, "Reordering State–Society Relations: Incorporation and Disengagement," in Donald Rothchild and Naomi Chazan, eds., *The Precarious Balance: State and Society in Africa* (Boulder, Colo.: Westview Press, 1988), pp. 3–21.

2 Victor Azarya and Naomi Chazan, "Disengagement from the State in Africa: Reflections on the Experience of Ghana and Guinea," *Comparative Studies in Society and History*, 29 (1987): 106–131. See also Albert Hirschman, *Exit, Voice and Loyalty: Responses to Decline in Firms, Organizations, and States* (Cambridge, Mass.: Harvard University Press, 1970); Goran Hyden, *No Shortcuts to Progress: African Development Management in Perspective* (London: Heinemann, 1983); Migdal, *Strong Societies and Weak States;* Michael Bratton, "Beyond the State: Civil Society and Associational Life in Africa," *World Politics*, 41, no. 3 (1989): 407–430.
3 Rothchild and Chazan, eds., *The Precarious Balance*, pp. 124–148.
4 Theda Skocpol, "Bringing the State Back In: Strategies of Analysis in Current Research," in Peter Evans, Dietrich Reuschmeyer, and Theda Skocpol, eds., *Bringing the State Back In* (New York: Cambridge University Press, 1985), p. 9 (emphasis added).
5 Ibid.
6 Eric Nordlinger, "Taking the State Seriously," in Myron Weiner and Samuel Huntington, eds., *Understanding Political Development* (Boston: Little, Brown, 1987), p. 361.
7 Migdal, *Strong Societies and Weak States*, p. 397.
8 Skocpol, "Bringing the State Back In," p. 16.
9 Alfred Stepan, *State and Society: Peru in Comparative Perspective* (Princeton: Princeton University Press, 1981), p. 84.
10 Allen F. Isaacman, "Peasants and Rural Social Protest in Africa," University of Minnesota, Institute of International Studies, Working Paper No. 1, Series 1 (1989): 3.
11 World Bank, *Sub-Saharan Africa: From Crisis to Sustainable Growth: A Long-Term Perspective Study* (Washington, D.C.: World Bank, 1989), p. 277.
12 Isaacman, "Peasants and Rural Social Protest," p. 3; Hyden, *No Shortcuts to Progress*.
13 Ibid.
14 Terrence Ranger, *Peasant Consciousness and Guerilla War in Zimbabwe: A Comparative Study* (Harare: Zimbabwe Publishing House, 1985), p. 25.
15 Robert Chambers, *Settlement Schemes in Tropical Africa: A Study of Organizations and Development* (London: Routledge & Kegan Paul, 1969), pp. 11, 39.
16 Ibid., p. 157.
17 Ibid., p. 175.
18 Ibid., p. 182.
19 Torben Bager, *Marketing Cooperatives and Peasants in Kenya* (Uppsala: Scandanavian Institute of African Studies, 1980), p. 25.
20 Stephen Quick, "The Paradox of Popularity: 'Ideological' Program Implementation in Zambia," in Merilee Grindle, ed., *Politics and Policy Implementation in the Third World* (Princeton: Princeton University Press, 1980), pp. 45–52.
21 Crawford Young, Neal Sherman, and Tim Rose, *Cooperatives and Development: Agricultural Politics in Ghana and Uganda* (Madison: University of Wisconsin Press, 1981), pp. 215–216.
22 Robert Bates, *Markets and States in Tropical Africa: The Political Basics of Agricultural Policies* (Berkeley: University of California Press, 1981), pp. 11–61.
23 Bager, *Marketing Cooperatives*, pp. 81–85.
24 Young et al., *Cooperatives and Development*, p. 222.
25 Janet MacGaffey, *Entrepreneurs and Parasites: The Struggle for Indigenous Capitalism in Zaire* (New York: Cambridge University Press, 1987), p. 22.

26 Ibid., pp. 143–164.
27 Azarya and Chazan, "Disengagement from the State in Africa," p. 130.
28 Nelson Kasfir, *State and Class in Africa* (London: Frank Cass, 1984), pp. 84–103.
29 MacGaffey, *Entrepreneurs and Parasites,* p. 140.
30 Michael Bratton, "Non-Governmental Organizations in Africa: Can They Influence Public Policy?" *Development and Change,* 21, no. 1 (1990): 87–118.

10

Engaging the state: associational life in sub-Saharan Africa

NAOMI CHAZAN

CIVIL SOCIETY AND STATE–SOCIETY RELATIONS

The fourth decade of African independence has coincided with a renewed interest in the nature of associational life on the continent. Observers, noting the number and variety of nongovernmental organizations, have viewed their current salience as a significant milestone in the restructuring of African political life.[1] A major gap exists, however, between the grand theorizing on social organizations and the available empirical evidence.[2] It is hardly surprising, therefore, that the conceptual tools employed to examine these phenomena have yet to transcend the intellectual confinement of the state–society dichotomy.

The notion of civil society, occupying the middle ground between communal groups and state structures, has been introduced to fill this void. First and foremost a linkage concept, civil society is "becoming an all-encompassing term to refer to social phenomena putatatively beyond formal state structures, but not necessarily free of all contact with the state."[3] When the term is not used loosely as a synonym for society, it has been conceptualized in the African context, alternately, as a necessary precondition for state consolidation, as the key brake on state power (and consequently in constant confrontation with the state), as a benign broker between state interests and local concerns, or as a medley of social institutions that interact with each other and with formal structures in ways that may either facilitate or impede governance and economic development.[4]

The divergent opinions regarding the relationship between society, civil society, and the state not only reflect a lack of clarity on the definition and extent of

The research for this article was supported by the Harry S Truman Research Institute for the Advancement of Peace at the Hebrew University of Jerusalem. Galia Zabar-Friedman and Nurit Hashimshoni provided invaluable research assistance. Thanks are also due to the participants of the two workshops on "State Power and Social Forces: Domination and Transformation in the Third World," for their critical comments and suggestions.

civil society in Africa, but also demonstrate the limitations inherent in viewing the structure and organization of civil society merely as the palpable product of differing modes of state–society interaction. The conceptual vision that either pits society against the state or allows for cooperation or collusion with the state inevitably yields a mechanistic view of the political domain, which neglects both the weblike structure of the human landscape and the fluid nature of social exchanges.

State formation and the emergence of civil society are related but not identical processes. A state-in-society framework requires that at least as much attention be devoted to the study of the crystallization of civil society as to the consolidation of the state as an organization within society that claims to make binding rules for all its members.[5] Indeed, "much of the contemporary resurgence of the state in political theory obviously is constructed around the connections between the organization of state authority and the organization of society, most especially the organization of collective action."[6] This is especially true in the African context, where contemporary states and civil societies have been molded simultaneously (albeit separately) within the rich social tapestry of the continent in the course of the twentieth century.

But if increasingly sophisticated attention has been devoted to the state in recent years, the dynamics of civil society have hardly been explored with equal vigor. The purpose of this chapter is to outline an approach to the analysis of the processes of the formation and fluctuation of civil society in Africa and to explore its implications for an understanding of the structure of states, societies, and the contours of politics on the continent.

The starting point for such an examination is the presumption that both the state and society are neither monolithic nor organic entities and must be disaggregated so that their dynamics can be traced and understood.[7] The state encompasses a complex set of institutions that operate at different levels of human agency. Similarly, the social forces that make up society embrace a wide variety of movements, networks, cells, and formal organizations that differ substantially in size, scope, purpose, composition, and resources. Not all social associations are part of civil society; some organizations contribute to its growth and others do not. Civil society is separate from the state but relates to the state: parochial associations that do not evince an interest beyond their immediate concerns, groups that do not have a concept of the state independent of their own aims, and those totally controlled by state agencies are excluded from its domain. State organs and social groups continually engage each other in multiple settings that are arenas of struggles for domination and accommodation. The constantly changing interactions that occur in these spaces mold and redefine the nature of state structures and social forces, generating an ongoing, mutually transforming, dynamic.[8]

Civil associations provide critical organizational settings for such exchanges. These middle-level groups are viewed as conceptually distinct both from ascriptive or local-level social forces and from political society that develops around the state. They occupy crucial positions at the interstices of economic, social, cultural, and political fields. Within these frameworks various human, symbolic, material, and political issues are contested and negotiated, and power is either aggregated, redistributed, or dispersed.[9] They are thus vital focuses of analysis for those concerned with unraveling the ways "in which people at different levels of social agency have mobilized and organized resources, allies and ideas in a continuous effort to cope with changing circumstances."[10] Situationally, these groups constitute the locus of interaction of different levels of social organization and "force attention to the institutions and arenas in which decisions are articulated."[11] These associations and institutions together form the structural building blocks of civil society, which horizontally joins diverse interests and groups at various levels in normatively bounded organizational settings (in contrast to the state, which establishes a vertical focus for such activities).

The concentration on intermediate social organizations affords the opportunity to place transactions at the center of political analysis and not as their outcome. If the state–society relationship is indeed recursive,[12] then the precise features of specific states, societies, and political dynamics are as much the consequence as the cause of interactions in these settings. In this view, economic life, social structures, and state organizations are conditioned by distinctive kinds of exchanges occurring at intermediate levels of social organization.[13] This "social intertexture . . . forms the stuff of political life."[14] It offers an indispensible lens through which to trace changing political relations and their external manifestations in varying regime forms (which reflect shifts in the nature and extent of organizational interlocking).[15]

Political activities occur at different levels and reflect diverse contents of interchange.[16] The outcome of these transactions may result in total transformation, state incorporation of society, societal control of large portions of the state, or various forms of state–society disengagement.[17] In this perspective, then, politics is viewed in broad terms as the process of negotiation, struggle, accommodation, and redistribution of resources and hence power in society.[18]

The basic analytic task facing those concerned with understanding civil society in Africa involves studying how civil power coalesces and how it is translated into political terms. This challenge may usefully be tackled initially by examining the dynamics of the emergence of voluntary associations as well as the extent of their coalescence into a civil society that relates to, but is separate from, the state. Adopting a "historical sociology of action" approach deeply rooted in the constantly changing circumstances of modern Africa,[19] in the following pages a preliminary (and admittedly highly schematic) attempt will be made to address these questions through an examination of intermediate social organizations in Africa and their interactions during four historical phases: the colonial phase, the postcolonial phase, the crisis of the 1980s, and the current stage of economic and political reordering.

The main contention of this broad overview is that the development of civil society in Africa has paralleled processes of state formation on the continent: Its scope and degree of consolidation are a key measure of the extent of stateness; its various forms are a crucial indicator of the nature and variety of state types in different parts of the continent.[20] The combination of apparent strength and substantial powerlessness that characterized many African states during the first three decades of independence attests to the fragility of civil society during this period.[21] The symbiotic relationship between state and civil society is a recognition of the fluidity of power and of its aggregation in integrative or dispersion in diffuse social spaces.[22] The power, autonomy, and capacity of states is therefore a function of the relative autonomy of civil society.

This is particularly true in the African context. The two key stages of state construction in recent African history (during decolonization and since the crisis of the 1980s) have also been periods of vibrant associational activity, indicating that social organizations not only react to government measures but also adapt to circumstances and therefore play a major role in the construction and allocation of power in particular settings. Thus in the 1980s the emergence of new forms of associational activity relieved some African states of their obligation to divert resources for daily consumption, while simultaneously making them more accountable to newly empowered social groups.

Today, therefore, the capacity to uphold democratic forms of government "is likely to depend more on the development of associational life and the further empowerment of civil society rather than on the action of the state and its agencies."[23] The reordering of power arrangements is consequently as much an outcome of the dynamic interplay of a variety of actors in different arenas as of shifts in policy or of the capacity of state agencies. The specific features of political life in Africa have been a result of these constantly changing transactions. The transformative potential of these exchanges depends on the expansion and organization of civil society.[24]

THE DYNAMICS OF CIVIL SOCIETY IN AFRICA

The colonial phase

African social organization has relied, perhaps more heavily than in any other part of the globe, on group affiliation and group action. Precolonial African politics revolved around ascriptive and functional groups that varied widely in scope and organizational complexity. Economic and political standing was a corollary of social identification. With no great tradition of politics, arrangements for the regulation of public affairs depended on complex rules arrived at by negotiation between social groups. Indeed, "the most distinctive contribution of Africa to human history has been precisely in the civilized art of living reasonably peacefully without a state."[25]

Colonialism, however, altered this picture dramatically. The redrawing of political boundaries and the imposition of foreign rule nurtured the emergence of dual societies: The colonial administration relied on the development of patronage systems based on elaborate hierarchies of personal power while simultaneously enabling the gradual emergence of a new, albeit contained, civil society around the colonial apparatus.

The midcolonial period in Africa coincided with the rapid expansion of organizational life in all parts of the sub-Sahara.[26] People joined associations not only because they were born into them, but also to promote their interests, to enhance their standing in the community, and to cope with new and unfamiliar environments.[27]

The new types of organizations (encompassing literally hundreds of different forms of groups) fell into four broad categories. The first consisted of voluntary associations, ranging from ethnic organizations, through kinship groups, credit unions, burial societies, sports clubs, literary societies, women's organizations, old-boys' and -girls' networks, youth movements, and mutual aid societies, to cultural organizations and recreational groups.[28] The second encompassed occupational organizations including producer cooperatives, trader associations, craft guilds, professional associations, organizations of chiefs, workers movements, and, in most areas, also (usually heavily restricted) trade unions.[29] The third category comprised religious organizations, which referred not only to a diversity of churches (of both a missionary and independent sort) and Islamic brotherhoods, but also to a medley of groups established by religious institutions to cater to the needs of their adherents.[30] And in many rural areas, an array of traditional and new community-based associations thrived.[31]

Most of the newly formed groups were based in the urban areas and initially launched by incipient elites who, while offering services to migrants to the city and opening opportunities for upward mobility, were themselves heavily dependent on the colonial apparatus. Although some were inspired by European organizations and others derived from traditional African institutions, their emergence paralleled the introduction of colonial state structures and they shared a similar location in proximity to the colonial apparatus. In many respects, therefore, they constituted the kernel – however limited in composition and small in scale – of a new civil society in each African territory.

These groups attempted to achieve three main purposes. First, they sought to fulfill the needs of their members, many of whom were migrants in search of employment, housing, and support in the transition from rural to urban life. Their activities consequently centered heavily on obtaining, controlling, and distributing resources.[32] Some organizations (most notably churches) had external sources of funding that afforded them a large measure of operational maneuverability (this was true for Pentecostal and millenarian groups such as the Seventh Day Adventists as well as for African branches of established denominations). Other groups (especially professional organizations, such as legal and medical associations) taxed their members, but depended on developing avenues of access to colonially generated resources. And still other organizations (farmers' cooperatives, trade unions) themselves controlled either land or labor and could, under certain circumstances, expand their spheres of material autonomy as well.

Second, the new associations were concerned with establishing and maintaining their position in the emerging social context by expanding their membership, establishing norms of conduct, and devising mechanisms for participation, decision making, and leadership rotation. Intermediate organizations consequently devoted a good deal of their energies to group consolidation and to the assertion of their authority over their members. Thus, associations as diverse as the Ibo State Union in Nigeria, the Harrist religious movement in West Africa, or the East Africa Association in Kenya established a specific organizational structure (often copied from Western models), usually consisting of fairly elaborate internal organs including committees, decision-making forums, and detailed provisions for the selection of officeholders.[33] Incentives were given to members to adhere to the rules established by the group, and sanctions were imposed on those unwilling to conform to its dictates. Emphasis was also placed on the recruitment of new members (who almost by definition came mainly from a small stratum of upwardly mobile, Western-educated individuals drawn to the colonial metropolises) and on their induction into the norms of behavior established by the founders.[34]

Success in these inner-directed activities varied substantially from group to group. The degree of institutionalization of particular associations had an important bearing on their cohesion, autonomy, and capabilities. Thus ethnic unions, professional organizations, and most religious groups succeeded in constructing branches at various levels and achieved a modicum of continuity, whereas many service, welfare, and some imported youth groups remained fairly amorphous. Clearly those associations able to give their members a sense of belonging, mold them into a network of effective groups, provide them with a common purpose, coordinate their activities, and carve out a position in the colonial structure, were also able to achieve a modicum of organizational, symbolic, and mobilizational autonomy.[35]

Third, these social associations sought to interact with each other and with broader economic, social, administrative, political and even international entities.[36] The nature of social group transactions in colonial Africa depended not only on the extent of group resources but also on the skills and the goods held by other social forces or by the colonial state. Patterns of investing surplus generated by productive activities furnished an important indicator of the directions and substance of transactions at this juncture.[37] In many parts of Africa urban-based associations sought to direct resources to the procurement of goods at the local level and to long-term investments in education as a means of assuring entry into the orbit of the colonial state.

These transactions in most parts of colonial Africa took place primarily along a vertical axis ranging from the local level to the colonial state (and at times beyond). Some intermediate social groups – and especially religious and ethnic associations – established strong links with local constituencies while vying with each other and with other types of groups for access to avenues of communication with colonial authorities. Thus, while the forms of exchange were inherently unequal, civil associations occupied a clearly defined, albeit quite minuscule, middle space in social exchanges. The methods of interchange inevitably involved a degree of subordination and incorporation. Associational life flourished by arrangement, toleration, exclusion, evasion, default, muted resistance, or by some combination of these ingredients.[38] The sphere of civil society was hence both discrete and contained. Overlapping membership in a series of organizations and some multifunctionality (as in youth movements) enabled a measure of communication between groups, but these generally lacked coherence and breadth.

The small scale and limited cohesion of civil society at this time helped shape the image of the colonial state, which was simultaneously precarious and aloof. In Bratton's terms,[39] the state agencies established by the British and the French enjoyed a great deal of autonomy but had limited capacities. They could utilize either material incentives or coercion to ensure compliance, but they did not have the ability to gain symbolic or social ascendancy. The remoteness of the colonial state from African societies was exacerbated by the reluctance of colonial powers to nurture an African economic bourgeoisie that could act as a channel of communication and interaction. The incipient managerial elites who congregated in the new social associations could hardly fulfill such a role.

The structure of the formal order in these frameworks was fragmented and dispersed. In most situations, European rulers bypassed civil associations, establishing control directly over stringently demarcated local communities through the sophisticated employment of local collaborators. They adopted a top-down, central-local, pattern of extraction and distribution that limited the flow of entitlements between increasingly distinct and purportedly mutually exclusive local collectivities.[40] The British, and in many instances the French, ruled through local patrons and were as dependent on their durability as these strongmen were dependent on the colonial state.[41]

By inventing tradition and formalizing it, colonial rulers not only contributed to undermining their own penetrative capabilities, but also intensified the disarticulation between the patronage-propelled colonial administration and the rudimentary civil society that was crystallizing at the same time.[42] At the local level, rival strongmen competed with each other over access to the colonial center and control over the dispersion of its resources. The paradoxes inherent in the structure of these colonial exchanges generated a growing conflict between the middle-level social groups that made up civil society and the externally controlled administrative apparatus.

Involvement in associational activities afforded opportunities for social mobility, communication of new ideas, leadership training, participation in the state arena, and, progressively, opposition to the colonial order. In many respects, these organizations constituted prepolitical networks that used the colonial state as their frame of reference. Virtually every nationalist leader received his political education in these settings and drew on the political support they proffered. Civil associations were the foundation upon which anticolonial movements were constructed in the immediate postwar period. From this perspective, decolonization may be viewed as the process of the empowerment of that civil society which developed in tandem with the colonial state.

In most parts of Africa the confrontation between colonial rulers and mass political movements was brief and relatively devoid of violence. In these instances, although the proliferation of civil associations was the precondition for the rise of anticolonial organizations, once the colonial powers had agreed in principle to transfer power, nationalist leaders emanating from these groups, in search of local support, attempted to control them and moderate their demands.[43] No alternative bases of legitimacy could be established under such circumstances. Only in areas where the anticolonial struggle was protracted and intense (such as Angola, Mozambique, and Zimbabwe) did the reinforcing relationship between intermediate social groups and the nationalist movements involve some institution building and consequently endure into the early years of independence.

If Africa had entered the colonial era with strong civil societies and frequently without states, by the end of the period of foreign rule key elements of civil society underwent a process of *étatisation,* taking over control of the state apparatus. In this transformation, not coincidently, middle-level social organizations were enfeebled. Thus, "decolonization opened new struggles between and within loosely integrated, heterogeneous, and often multiple coalitions for control over the state apparatus itself. The dynamics of this process shaped the subsequent course of change, including the trajectory of ruling-class formation."[44]

The manner in which civil society was merged with the colonial administration had a critical impact on the specific nature of individual states. In some countries, where internal competition for state power on the eve of independence was intense (Ghana, Cameroon, Uganda), opposition groups sustained the activities of their associational networks. In these cases, however, severe rifts appeared in elite circles. In other countries (Côte d'Ivoire, Kenya, Tanganyika, Zambia) opposition groups were weak and the new leadership was fairly cohesive. In these instances efforts were made to depoliticize social organizations and to control their activities. Civil society was effectively wedded to the administration and underwent a process of contraction. In another set of states (Nigeria, Zaire) ethnoregional leaders assumed power at the state level, forcing opponents to entrench themselves in regional strongholds. Regardless of the precise conditions, therefore, not only did the visibility of social organizations decline, but their interests were redefined.

The first phase of the process of the emergence of civil society in Africa coincided with the creation of an array of social organizations clustered around the new urban areas. Because of the separation of power between state and civil society in the colonial setting as well as the creation of a parallel administrative-social network, these organizations gradually accumulated sufficient political resources to take over the colonial state apparatus. This transformation left a partial vacuum at the intermediate level on the eve of independence, presaging a period of uncertainty and fluctuation in societal transactions.

The postcolonial phase

The first twenty years of African independence were characterized by a process of consolidation of an urban-based administrative society through the refinement of clientelistic networks and the implementation of corporatist policies that nurtured the emergence of authoritarian regimes. The politicization of colonially rooted patronage systems during decolonization contributed to the reorganization of state institutions and substantially altered the terms of societal exchanges.[45] Although many social groupings at the middle level survived the transfer of power and new ones were created, their relative salience declined with the proliferation of grassroots associations locally and government-controlled organizations at the national level. Under these circumstances the balance of forces operating on the associational scene shifted, and civil organizations were relegated to subsidiary roles. Their weakness contributed both to the exposure of state institutions to direct pressures from certain social interests and to the concentration of many other social endeavors in small independent enclaves unrelated to the state, thereby contributing to the diminution of state autonomy on the one hand, and, on the other hand, to the substantial reduction in state power throughout the continent.

Continuity in the intermediate range of associations was visible in a variety of areas, and particularly among occupational groups. In every African country existing professional organizations proliferated and new ones were established (for example: lawyers, doctors, teachers, nurses, accountants, university lecturers, engineers, bankers, contractors). Skilled workers and traders, previously severely circumscribed, were organized, frequently changing names (although not composition) if restrictions were placed on their operations. Religious activity also expanded and subsidiary welfare and youth groups became a crucial part of the associational landscape at this time. Established and independent churches attracted growing numbers of adherents, and new churches were formed in many parts of the continent.[46] Muslim associations also came to the fore. Islamic welfare and advocacy groups were set up throughout West Africa, and the 1970s witnessed a resurgence in the activities of major brotherhoods and radical sects.[47] Many of the service, leisure, mutual help, and rotating credit associations persisted into the independence era as well. These were joined by health groups and by local branches of international nongovernmental organizations (NGOs) such as the Red Cross, Save the Children Fund, UNICEF support groups, St. John's Ambulance Associations, or various refugee relief committees.[48] Recreational groups diversified as tennis, polo, and golf were introduced into capital cities. And football, by far the most popular sport, took on renewed momentum when league and inter-African competition commenced and existing clubs were institutionalized.

Not all intermediate social organizations were a carryover from the colonial period. Student groups were undoubtedly the most important to emerge in the early years of independence. The establishment of full-fledged universities was accompanied by the creation of vibrant (and often highly politicized) student unions on each campus (the National Union of Ghanaian Students and the National Association of Nigerian Students were particularly visible), as well as a variety of specific student organizations (such as debating societies, glee clubs, and preprofessional groups).[49] Women's organizations also developed substantially during this period, with a good deal of their energies devoted to social welfare and income-generating activities.[50] In many urban areas such as Kampala, Accra, and Lusaka, in fact, gender displaced age as the primary socioeconomic determinant of status.[51]

Middle-level social institutions in the postcolonial period continued to be based in the major cities. But their expansion and growth depended on their ability to recruit newcomers and branch out into smaller urban areas. Unlike in the past, new migrants were rarely attracted to the ranks of established groups (which often possessed an elitist aura), and residents of the rural areas were not easily drawn into their nets.[52] Thus, although civil associations grew in number and variety at this juncture, they did not necessarily expand in size or increase in relative importance.

In contrast, in the migrant quarters of the cities and at the local level small-scale grassroots organizations recorded substantial gains during the course of the 1960s and 1970s. These included a vast array of local improvement societies, craft shops, security associations, small-scale women's cooperatives, support groups, spiritualist churches and particularistic sects, Koranic reading groups, prayer societies, hometown associations, community youth organizations, work brigades, and traditional recreational groups.[53] These specific and limited networks, although rarely attempting to expand beyond the local level, played an important role in the regulation of daily life.[54] The desire for community not only increased their attractiveness, but generally also served the purposes of precarious rulers concerned with preventing the aggregation of interests beyond the local level.

Indeed, at the state level leaders launched another, countrywide, set of social institutions in an attempt to control social groups and constrict major social forces (trade unions, students, women) seen as potential sources of political unrest.[55] In some instances, the new governments created monolithic structures (farmers, workers, student and women's organizations) meant to displace existing groups and carry out their specific functional tasks.[56] This trend was most pronounced in socialist-oriented regimes (Guinea, Mali, Tanzania, Ghana under Nkrumah), but in the case of trade unions was commonplace throughout the continent.[57] In other countries an alternative strategy was pursued: the creation of umbrella organizations to bring together the multiplicity of groups working in similar spheres (such as associations of professional bodies, national councils of churches, women's bureaus, national youth councils, national sports associations). In either event, the result of these actions was to try to impose corporatist arrangements on an extremely heterogeneous organizational scene.

Thus, although the associational terrain became more heterogeneous than in the past, independent social groups were enveloped and their range of maneuverability severely confined. "The suppression of autonomous unions and experiments in communal farming should come as no surprise. States in Africa are insecure – politically, economically, and socially – and their leaders are likely to perceive any organization they cannot control as a direct threat."[58]

The variegation of types and levels of social groupings in the postcolonial phase meant that the picture of associational life became differentiated not only functionally, but also spatially and organizationally. Vast discrepancies in size, location, membership, objectives, capabilities, and durability highlighted the inequality that developed in the social sphere at this juncture. Associational groups were spread out along a vertical range, significantly affecting the substance and manner of social interactions.

Civil associations and local groups employed two contrasting strategies (of exploitation and evasion) in their transactions with other organizations and official agencies. The first, and most carefully documented, were patron–client ties. The disruption of competitive party politics in most African states within a few years of independence and the restrictions placed on intermediate social groups meant that few institutional mechanisms were available for the interlocking of local communities and state organizations. Personalistic networks came to fill this void and, in different countries, new groups of intermediaries, brokers, and emissaries oversaw the exchange of goods for compliance.[59] Clientelistic modes of interchange were particularly open to distortion, diversion, subversion, and corruption.[60] They frequently nurtured intense competition among vying factions, while significantly increasing the cost of political maintenance.[61]

The second method was far less instrumental or extractive. Intermediate social associations and some local communities tried to adopt a strategy of retrenchment, closing themselves off to unnecessary influences from above and nurturing their own dynamic arrangements backed by specific group values.[62] Localism, by highlighting autonomy and limiting contacts among communities, not only impeded horizontal communication so necessary for the crystallization of civil society, but also had the effect of circumscribing opportunities for penetration by outside agencies, compelling official organs to nurture personalistic links and thereby reinforcing patronage ties. Civil society in the postcolonial period, to the extent it existed at all, tended to congregate within the limited niches outside these clientelistic and particularistic social spaces.[63]

Competition between various groups revolved, first, around a struggle for members, frequently conducted through very different attempts to meet the human, material, symbolic, and emotional needs of potential recruits. Smaller grassroots organizations and religious bodies were more successful in this regard than state-sponsored groups (whose instrumental appeal was not inconsiderable)[64] because in these settings reciprocity and trust became the foundation for social exchanges.[65] Issues of access to resources also invited confrontation. Local groups and peasants did enjoy a modicum of autonomous control over certain resources, but depended heavily for capital and amenities on links with other organizations or with powerful patrons. Concern with access was particularly prominent among middle-level groups, which controlled few resources of their own. They came to rely either on external flows or, more notably, on the umbrella organizations that had become a funnel for the distribution of funds and expertise. Thus, they were forced into some contact, and frequently accommodation, with corporatist groups.

Inevitably, these conflicts also assumed overt political forms. Many groups at the intermediate level (but much less so at the local or countrywide rungs) sought either to influence policy, affect the composition of decision makers, or in extreme cases to bring about a fundamental change in the structure of power relations.[66] Indeed, the quest for an independent political role by many intermediate groups, however enfeebled, became a hallmark of the first two decades of African independence.

The multiple confrontations between various levels of social organization clearly influenced the quality of their exchanges. The relationship between intermediate and umbrella organizations (such as market women collectives and government-sponsored women's federations or student movements and state-controlled student associations) was, in most countries, highly conflictual. The greater the number of intermediate organizations coexisting with state-sponsored groups, the more intense and protracted were these struggles. This pattern first became apparent in the case of trade unions and national labor federations, which were in constant contestation.[67] A similar dynamic developed in student quarters, especially in Uganda, Kenya, Côte d'Ivoire, Nigeria, and Ghana.[68] It was visible, too, among farmer and producer associations, and, in the 1970s, also among different types of religious groups. These confrontations were indicative not only of the limits of corporatist policies but also of the incomplete nature of hegemonic pretensions and the unsettled character of social exchanges in many postcolonial settings.

Grassroots organizations, on the other hand, interacted with intermediate and broader social institutions in a more variegated manner. To be sure, often relations with either local officials or with parent organizations replicated struggles in other settings. But in many cases grassroots groups opted to avoid unnecessary contacts with each other or with official agencies.[69] Alternatively, especially in the case of local improvement groups, certain associations preferred to enter into collaborative arrangements with national agencies, since some politicians were viewed as amenable to the demands of the community and more susceptible to direct pressures from below. This was particularly true in single-party regimes where elections were held periodically (Tanzania, Kenya, Senegal, Zambia, Côte d'Ivoire, and Cameroon).[70] Contacts between grassroots and intermediate groups tended to be more sporadic: Trade networks and family relations supplied some meeting points,[71] but comprehensive coalitions developed only at times of severe political stress, as in Ghana and Uganda in the latter part of the 1970s.[72]

Interactions in specific countries consequently took place almost exclusively along vertical lines. Horizontal links at the local and intermediate levels were virtually nonexistent. More significantly, the growing connections between local groups and officially sponsored countrywide organizations severely limited the operational parameters of intermediate social groupings, which all too often found themselves paralyzed by these alliances.[73]

These trends help explain the structure of the aggregation and distribution of power in postcolonial Africa. In broad strokes, it appears that at the national level two divergent processes occurred simultaneously. First, states became more porous to selected societal demands transmitted through clientelistic systems. The consolidation of personalistic networks to tie officials with local communities, primarily in the rural areas, left officials at various rungs of the administrative apparatus particularly vulnerable to demands from various patrons on whom they relied for cooperation and backing. The relative autonomy of administrative institutions was consequently undermined and their capacities significantly eroded.[74] Regimes, on the other hand, relying on diverse patterns of exclusion and inclusion, became more autonomous from many social pressures. The narrower the social base of specific regimes, the less accountable they became;[75] those leaders with few social roots (most notably Idi Amin in Uganda; Macias Nguema in Equatorial Guinea; Jean-Bedel Bokassa in the Central African Republic; Samuel Doe in Liberia) also veered heavily toward the repressive. Thus, many states could not develop spheres of decision making independent of patronage pressures, while authoritarian governments found it increasingly difficult to penetrate the protective armor of social groups.[76]

The structure of society in the postcolonial order was also ambiguous. Large social organizations lacked autonomy but experienced an increase in capacity, effectively becoming extensions of the state apparatus. Some intermediate and local groups were similarly engaged, while others maintained independence but did not possess the capacity to pursue their aims beyond their narrow organizational confines.[77] Because these pockets of independence were obscured by highly visible corporatist processes, the significance of these niches and their role in the maintenance of (an admittedly much enfeebled) civil society has been frequently overlooked.[78]

The picture of state–society relations that emerged in the postcolonial period was therefore one not necessarily of strong social aggregations confronting weak states capable only of fragmented control, but, rather, of diverse and unequal social organizations that, in different circumstances, either preyed on the state, dissociated themselves from its agents, substituted for its lacunae, or, alternately, succumbed to its dictates. Those regimes which were most shielded from direct social pressures could protect technocratic elites from political demands and develop some administrative capabilities. The degree of insulation from what Thomas Callaghy has described as the pervasive "postcolonial syndrome" became a mark of durability.[79] But even in these instances, the position of the state itself remained tenuous, confirming the close connection between weak and fragmented civil societies (the size and strength of individual social groups notwithstanding) and ineffective states.

The political dynamics of the first two decades of African independence revolved around conflicts between shifting coalitions based on differing organizational interests. Although almost all countries were subjected to authoritarian rule and consequently to a blurring of the distinctions between public and private,[80] this took on a multiplicity of forms. In some countries (Côte d'Ivoire, Malawi, Kenya) elite cohesion sustained bureaucratic forms of government, but undermined the coalescence of civil society. In others (Nigeria, Ghana, Uganda) elite factions fomented deep-seated cleavages and the rotation of state power – usually via military coups – between competing groups. The 1970s were punctuated by the emergence of highly coercive forms of authoritarian regimes in Uganda, the Central African Republic, and Equatorial Guinea, as well as (less forcefully, perhaps) in Zaire, Guinea, and Togo.[81] In these countries the repression of associational life and the activation of sophisticated techniques of local evasion yielded extremely erratic and personalistic forms of governments marked by capricious behavior. And in many places ethnic and professional alliances sustained neotraditional regimes (Niger, to mention but one).

By the late 1970s, however, it became apparent that these neopatrimonial arrangements could not be sustained indefinitely. Patronage politics not only induced regime instability and undermined state autonomy, but in due course also reduced state capacities.[82] If a combination of centralization and powerlessness characterized public institutions, civil society, in contrast, was marked by an admixture of fragmentation and dissensus. Competition over access and control neither encouraged societal coherence nor promoted development goals. African states and civil societies consequently tended to undergo a visible contraction. The diminution of civil society was accompanied by a parallel process of state immobilization.

The crisis phase

At the end of the second decade of independence economic conditions in most African countries had deteriorated drastically, political relations were marked by growing uncertainty, and the prospects for the amelioration of the exigencies of daily existence were dim. Although the extent of the unraveling of the fabric of economic, social, and political life varied from country to country,[83] people had to devise new means of fending for themselves in a situation where choices were limited and opportunities drastically constricted.

In these conditions both state agencies and social networks experienced a process of implosion: the scale of activities contracted, the range of contacts diminished, the size of overarching coalitions was reduced, and linkage arrangements were undermined. State leaders consciously divested themselves of responsibility for the material well-being of large portions of their populations. As the process of official de-linkage gathered momentum,[84] social groups sought to develop more effective mechanisms for self-sufficiency. Economic and political crisis coincided with the localization, and in severe cases, the atomization, of civil society, dramatically magnifying problems of governance.

Associational life underwent significant structural reordering at this juncture. The most noticeable changes took place at the local level, where the multiplication of communal associations was everywhere in evidence. Entrepreneurial, credit, banking, and barter groups were established alongside new welfare associations, mutual aid societies, educational initiatives, and self-defense groups. For example, in the community of Idere in Oyo State, Nigeria, more than fifty credit and loan (*Egbe*) associations were documented in the mid-1980s.[85] In other parts of Nigeria, Sara Berry and Joel Barkan and his collaborators reported growing investments in extended social networks rooted in communal affiliation.[86] In Ghana, a substantial number of local groups emerged in the rural areas and in the poorer neighborhoods of the major cities. In Tanzania, local initiatives were set in motion to compensate for failing government services. "The crisis thus opened up new economic and political spaces that allowed for the emergence and strengthening of viable voluntary organizations, especially at the communal level."[87] And in Kenya, interest group formation in and around the ever-expanding informal sector increased markedly.[88]

The rise of these separate local initiatives, reflecting a not inconsiderable measure of suspicion, apprehension, and cynicism toward official organs,[89] can be attributed primarily, unlike previous undertakings of this sort,[90] to concrete attempts to fulfill basic needs in the face of enormous poverty. The emphasis on locale and the variety of organizations at the community level were directly related to scarcity, to the absence of basic commodities, to impeded access, and to the perceived futility of the quest for influence on official institutions.[91] Thus, although community-oriented activities proliferated, efforts to use local associations as the foundation for spanning communities were sparse.

The key victims of this organizational reorientation were state-sponsored umbrella organizations and monolithic corporatist structures, which almost disappeared from the associational stage. Those that continued to exist (such as some trade unions, student associations, and women's groups) became noticeably more autonomous in their outlook and activities. These groups spearheaded the opposition to authoritarian regimes in Kenya, Zaire, and Nigeria, and in Burkina Faso, Liberia, and Ghana were instrumental in organizing their violent overthrow in populist-oriented coups.[92]

Even at the intermediate level voluntary ethnic, occupational, recreational, and leisure societies contracted, whereas economic and religious networks expanded. The religious resurgence that emerged at this time was evident in both Muslim and Christian quarters. As spiritual, Pentecostal, and charismatic movements blossomed in many countries,[93] Islamic fundamentalist sects garnered strength, primarily in northern Nigeria (the Maitatsine movement), Senegal, and the Sahel belt. Significantly, established churches and the veteran Muslim brotherhoods displayed a plurality of repertoires that proved inherently mutable and eminently adaptable to changing contexts.[94] A similar pattern was discernable among trading networks, which developed methods of bypassing official restrictions and frequently succeeded in establishing new commercial channels independent of state control.[95] Entrepreneurial, credit, banking, and barter groups were established alongside a second generation of transport collectives, producer cooperatives, and distribution systems.[96] New regional markets developed, and ingenious mechanisms were elaborated to cope with the increasing shortages in basic commodities. Thus, during the early years of the African crisis of the 1980s the growth of the voluntary sector was accompanied by its localization.

Activities of societal organizations (mostly of the communal variety) focused heavily at this juncture on the implementation of a repertoire of survival strategies.[97] These included, first and foremost, massive involvement in the informal economy. The elaborate second economy became the central funnel for the distribution of goods and a vital setting for petty manufacturing and small-scale agricultural production.[98] Second, migration of large numbers of people (within Africa and to target countries abroad), increased. Third, many people designed spiritual and social techniques to make do with less, adapting attitudes ranging from fatalism to indifference. Finally, in a few places self-encapsulation mechanisms were activated as the exit option was explored by local communities.[99]

The successful implementation of these coping techniques relied heavily on lateral interactions with similarly placed groups, primarily through interlocking commercial networks. Thus, to establish an effective distribution system it became necessary for specific groups to maintain a relationship with producers, food contractors, transporters, loan associations, and market-based traders.[100] These links had to be based on some measure of accommodation and the creation of mechanisms of arbitration to avoid undue friction (in Uganda, for example, trading groups hired armed guards to protect produce from well-organized highway robbers);[101] they did not necessarily lead to joint action on a countrywide basis.

In these conditions vertical contacts diminished in importance. Since avoidance of official dictates and minimalization of contact were at the root of the new avenues of interaction, old, state-based, patronage networks were undermined. Hierarchical engagement was frequently replaced by miniaturized horizontal links cemented through new forms of patronage revolving around locally based traders and entrepreneurs.[102] Local associational activity underlined the activation of self-reliant techniques, often reminiscent of the quiet rebellious tactics employed during the colonial era.[103] These measures served to limit further the already meager penetrative capacities of official organs, which in any event had themselves reduced allocations to local projects and curtailed their involvement in educational and welfare activities.

In these circumstances the autonomy and capacity of state structures were further eroded as the shrinkage of the official arena became evident throughout the continent. Collaborative interactions between state and society were minimized, communication between different levels of social interaction almost ceased, and pockets of mutual detachment became more commonplace. Power was dispersed to parochial networks that lacked autonomy and possessed only limited capabilities. It is crucial in this context to note that although crisis bred a local associational revival in Africa, the emphasis placed on survival techniques, as well as the parochial nature and limited size of many of the new organizations, did not endow civil society with essential organizational and material resources to expand its scale or to assert control over the newly molded social and economic spaces that emerged at this juncture. In effect, state structures and social institutions became embedded in small, narrowly delimited, niches. The symbolic and human foundations for the redefinition and consolidation of civil society were laid down but scarcely realized in the early part of the 1980s.[104]

The reordering phase

The African economic and political crisis peaked in the mid-1980s as the calamitous conditions engulfing the continent were compounded by the onset of drought and famine.[105] Local survival strategies were inadequate in the face of the spread of absolute scarcities. And most African states were literally bankrupt and incapable of dealing with the severity of the human immiseration they had helped engender.[106]

Both social organizations and state entities lacked a sufficient resource base to grapple with the crisis, rendering them increasingly dependent on external flows. In the mid-1980s, most African governments acceded to the conditionalities of the International Monetary Fund (IMF) and the World Bank, agreeing to undertake sweeping economic liberalization measures and adopt structural adjustment programs (SAPs) in return for heavy capital injections from abroad.[107] The thrust of these programs favored privatization, the reduction of official price controls, incentives to local producers, fiscal austerity, the imposition of user fees for government services, and, most significantly, an emphasis on investment in the agricultural sector and a concomitant streamlining of the bureaucratic apparatus. At the same time, the institutional capacity of social organizations was promoted not only through official programs, but also by way of substantial direct transfers of funds and commodities from international NGOs.[108] Thus, the resources of voluntary groups were augmented just as African states, however reluctantly, adopted neoclassical economic policies.

The period of economic readjustment and structural reordering set the stage for the further expansion of associational life (especially at the intermediate level), permitting the reemergence of the outlines of civil society in forms not dissimilar to those that prevailed in Africa on the eve of decolonization. The impetus for additional associational growth not only yielded further institutionalization, but also fostered additional group diversification with important implications for regime reorientation in the 1990s.

The most important development during the latter part of the 1980s was at the middle rung: civil associations – such as professional, student, and women's groups – experienced a resurgence, and additional intermediate organizations were appended to the associational roster. In countries as diverse politically as Nigeria, Tanzania, Kenya, Gabon, and Zaire, civil liberties unions, human rights associations, political debating forums, countrywide welfare and service organizations, and consumer protection groups were formed. These institutions not only contributed to what was described as a veritable explosion of associational life in Africa;[109] they also injected an explicitly political dimension into the associational arena, pressing for guarantees for basic human rights and advocating sweeping democratic reforms.[110]

At the local level, existing grassroots associations continued to operate and were buttressed by a new spate of voluntary development organizations (VDOs) and hometown improvement societies, creating a constituency for welfare and self-help projects on a countrywide scale.[111] In response, many governments tried to resurrect corporatist arrangements in an attempt to reassert a modicum of control. Thus, in Nigeria a Directorate for Social Mobilization (DSM) was created in 1987 to coordinate a regime-initiated campaign for social action.[112] In Ghana the government made an effort to reestablish control over the Trade Union Congress. In Kenya and Côte d'Ivoire, as well as Nigeria, student activities were restricted. In Zaire and Cameroon, supervision of established churches was tightened,[113] and throughout most of Africa corporatist modes of student, worker, farmer, and women's action were reinstated.

The outcome of these multiple initiatives has been to increase the number and heterogeneity of social organizations in contemporary Africa. The pluralization of institutional life is, first and foremost, proof of the existence of available political space (either by design or by default) and of the diversification of social structures. Not all organizational developments have, however, necessarily contributed to the consolidation of civil society. The expansion of voluntary activities requires a more differentiated approach to the analysis of their contribution to the establishment of a civil order.

Social organizations in Africa have operated in recent years on a variety of levels and possessed a wealth of contents and goals. Those groups that are holistic in aim, seek to deal with all the needs of their members, and consequently demand total allegiance, are virtually by design antithetical to the concept of civil society. Thus some fundamentalist religious groups, ethnic associations, parochial networks, or ideological movements either ignore the state or seek to replace it, leaving little leeway for ideas or interests beyond their own particular purviews. It would appear that the concentration on partial and clearly delimited interests (frequently reinforced by the density of institutional forms) fosters an outward orientation conducive to the construction of civil society.

The internal structure of different organizations and their capacity to mobilize human and material resources also affect their role in civil society. Many indigenous membership groups have been able to attract new members, but do not always possess the means to achieve their aims. NGOs with transnational links frequently control resources, but do not have the constituency to pursue their goals.[114] Even if, on balance, associational autonomy is more central to the vitality of civil societies than the availability of resources,[115] some combination of the two appears to be essential. Moreover, the norms nurtured within various groups, a still gravely under-researched area, are critical for maintaining a rhythm of civic involvement over time.

The diversity of associational orientations and structures has been reflected in the growing repertoire of strategies they employ. Many local organizations, especially those geographically remote from the capital cities, have continued to resort to techniques of self-enclosure, local retrenchment, or evasion. Grassroots associations in both rural and urban areas have also employed more subtle methods to express their positions, including impassivity, indifference, mimicry, and ridicule. Many have engaged in illicit activities, and some have used overt tactics, such as vigils, demonstrations, and petitions. Depending on their specific purposes, group strategies have been designed to support, collaborate with, exploit, evade, defy, confront, or take over official institutions.

The interplay of voluntary groups with government institutions at this juncture has taken place at all levels of interchange, and has consisted not only of struggles for domination but, equally as significantly, of negotiations and bargains over various forms of accommodation.[116] Many of these interactions in the latter part of the 1980s also focused heavily on the burgeoning informal sector. Economic activities in this sphere included the development of microindustries and small manufacturing cooperatives, the revival of local markets, shifts in patterns of agricultural production, and the creation of new distribution networks.[117] By the end of the decade most productive economic activity was concentrated in the informal sector. Concurrently, certain social programs were taken over by welfare and service organizations, including sanitation, housing, local policing, and major aspects of health and education.[118]

A new breed of elites began to emerge in this context. These entrepreneurs were not, like many of their predecessors, either necessarily associated with the state or dependent on its resources.[119] Alternative avenues of accumulation and social stratification had developed in the course of the 1980s (expedited by cutbacks in the public sector), leading to the emergence of an economic middle class that began to carve out a place for itself independently of salaried workers.[120] Despite the marked social inequalities that developed in this process (not insignificantly linked to the implementation of austerity measures),[121] the elites that coalesced at the middle rungs of social organization shared many interests and possessed some of the means for their realization.

But if a high degree of interlocking was achieved at the middle level, mostly around the informal economy, at the local level identity, religious and service group autonomy was frequently granted official sanction, yielding considerable social fragmentation. And at the state core, collaboration and conflict remained highly visible.

The diversity of associational activities since the adoption of structural adjustment programs also affected the shape of social exchanges. While specific groups carved out their own spheres of autonomous action and amassed material, social, and symbolic resources independently, they also at times encouraged the elaboration of wider communication networks along horizontal lines. Thus, some purely local organizations, such as improvement societies, farmer cooperatives, and credit unions, either established regional and even national networks or regularized their connections with neighboring groups dealing with related issues. Some aggregation of social interests took place in the process. Simultaneously, several officially controlled social institutions detached themselves from state control, usually in response to member demands. With straddling between the parallel and the official markets widespread, vertical and lateral transactions intersected at the middle level of social organization in a new symbiotic relationship that implied neither state domination nor local subordination.[122] This trend was reinforced by the mitigation of the urban bias in the new economic plans and the reversal of the terms of trade between urban and rural areas in many parts of the continent.

The gradual population of the middle level by local groups and national associations (however hesitant and piecemeal) did in some instances permit the translation of economic and cultural concerns into a more effective policy voice.[123] A profile of those organizations able to exert an influence has gradually been constructed. These associations have a discrete constituency (regardless of size), they are endowed with well-developed participatory structures, some resources and technical expertise, and a younger, relatively well-educated leadership core. All these associations appear to be linked to the money economy, their members have undergone some process of commercialization, and they maintain communications that span the urban–rural divide.

The outcome of these processes has been to enable some aggregation of associational life and to nurture the emergence of a civil society rooted in local institutions and resources.[124] The fortification of social organizations, coupled with the growth of autonomous accumulation channels (through the assertion of a marked preference for informal sector activities over survival strategies), enhanced social communication. The flourishing of the press in wide sections of East, West, and Central Africa, as well as increased attempts by government to muzzle the media, were an indication of the spread of autonomous information networks. As a result, separate economic, social, and political niches bound by explicit rules and culturally prescribed values were molded.

The weblike expansion of the associational realm was not, however, necessarily accompanied by a retreat of state agencies.[125] In very important respects, the strengthening of civil society has also had the effect of enhancing both the autonomy and the capacity of the state. Structurally, developments at both societal and state levels were mutually reinforcing.

Relations between social groups and state agencies have assumed two major forms in recent years. On the one hand, many countries achieved some tacit understanding regarding a division of labor. Civic, local, and economic associations were given a wider berth than in the past, while state bodies continued to operate in their own separate spheres. On the other hand, new forms of conflict surfaced. The quest for official control over social activities did continue in the reordering phase, at times breeding serious confrontations between social groups and political leaders. In countries such as Nigeria and Sudan, government manipulation of nationality and religious particularism was pitted against emerging popular notions of citizenship.[126] Moreover, urban groups, most adversely affected by SAPs clashed with government forces in Zambia, Zaire, Congo-Brazzaville, Côte d'Ivoire, Nigeria, and Liberia in 1989 and 1990, highlighting the extent to which vibrant associational life was frequently accompanied by political unrest fomented by social inequalities. The employment of modified exit options was thus accompanied by the enhancement of voice.[127] Because both social groups and state structures coalesced separately on a countrywide basis, the freedom from the state in Africa reaffirmed the freedom to determine its character.[128]

The crisis of the 1980s may have paved the way both for the expansion of associational activity and for the strengthening of state agencies; it did not, however, necessarily provide guidelines for the regulation of their interaction. Clearly, institutional trends have significantly affected the location and distribution of power in many African countries. These developments have implied that the hegemonic arrangements that could be imposed when associational networks were dispersed and national patronage networks were institutionalized (as in the early years of independence), could no longer be sustained.

Since the nature of emergent power designs has been more spatial than vertical, the redistribution of power locations has called attention to the need for a new kind of political architecture that respects autonomous spaces and finds innovative ways of weaving them together. Most recent grassroots- and intermediate-level demands have focused squarely on finding ways to reduce government intervention, on fending off rather than tapping the state.[129] With interest in gaining access to state resources diminishing and pressures for the removal of restrictions multiplying, political dynamics may be moving away from the extractive principles that propped up three decades of authoritarian rule in Africa. In these conditions, populist, parochial, and democratic options exist.

Most discussions on political reform have, however, centered on prospects for liberalization and possible democratization.[130] It seems that 1990, much like 1960, marked a crossroads in African political history. In the course of that year more than half the countries in sub-Saharan Africa underwent some political changes, most notably involving the introduction of multiparty competition.[131] The issue of whether this threshold also constitutes a turning point leading to the transformation of the political order in Africa is likely to be scrutinized and debated for some years to come; what is not disputed is that civil associations have played a vital role in this process. "The emergence of social forces outside the tributary grasp of the state in turn empowers civil society, strengthening pressures for accountability. Meaningful accountability, in turn, is the key to democracy."[132]

The current quest for regime reorientation has focused on four major aspects of political reordering. The first has involved some normative and conceptual reevaluation. Previous African experiments with formal democratic rule have generally failed.[133] In various parts of Africa debates are taking place on the formulation of specifically African notions of democratic government, in an attempt, as one observer commented, to reinvent democracy to suit the particular contextual conditions of contemporary Africa.[134] This process has been most advanced not only in Nigeria, Ghana, and Benin, where democratization efforts have resulted in officially organized discussions on political futures, but also in other countries, such as Kenya, where liberalization has been forestalled, resulting in a variety of alternative suggestions emanating from intermediate groups for viable democratic government.

Regime redefinition has, second, reopened a search for suitable institutional arrangements, most notably stressing the revival of multiparty competition. In

1989 and 1990, many one-party states succumbed to popular pressure applied by coalitions of social groups and lifted prohibitions on multiparty competition (including Côte d'Ivoire, Benin, Mozambique, Togo, Congo, Zaire, and Zambia). In these and other countries several suggestions have also been made to establish monitoring devices to ensure greater accountability, to guarantee judicial autonomy, to protect social pluralism, and to nurture subsidiarity.[135] However, these moves to multipartyism, a sign of liberalization, have frequently been used to thwart more profound demands for democratization.

A third element of regime reorientation has taken on structural dimensions. In the context of economic liberalization and the divestment of state corporations, some countries have begun to set in motion processes of decentralization and to explore the viability of federal and confederal arrangements.[136] In Ghana, for example, district-level elections were held in 1988 and early 1989, ostensibly as a prelude to renegotiating the rules of the political game at the national level.[137] Similar experiments are being planned in other countries as well, with the proposed constitution for a third Nigerian republic containing important clauses on the devolution of powers to the local level.

The fourth aspect of regime restructuring has been initiated by external sources and has stressed a concern with issues of governance. By the end of the 1980s international financial agencies and major donor countries began to link continued economic assistance to changes in political arrangements. The imposition of political conditionalities by foreign agencies has not only evoked important discussions on the connection between economic reform and regime reconstruction,[138] but has also reopened the question of the connection between political arrangements and administrative efficacy.

The focus on regime reformulation, championed by many civil associations, is an integral part of the economic rehabilitation and social reconstruction of African countries in recent years. Political dynamics have focused on regime changes because they are the key to the operational and conceptual articulation of the new shape of state–society relations. If the main feature of state–society exchanges has been the protest against injustice and elite hegemony, the contemporary African discourse on political change, much like that currently taking place in other parts of the globe, has concentrated on different notions of democratization. These debates have been tailored to the economic exigencies of the continent today: "Democratic forms of rule in Africa are not luxuries to be casually entertained or dispensed with on the road to development. On the contrary, they are necessary for development."[139]

Voluntary associations have thus constituted one of several factors contributing to regime reformulation at the outset of the 1990s. Yet, although social groups have helped to undermine statism and to provide frameworks for the formulation of local interests and concerns, not all associations contribute to the construction of civil society, which is a precondition for the coalescence of democratic and just political orders.

Civil society, much like the state, was enfeebled at the beginning of the 1980s. The pervasive crisis of the 1980s had the effect of rupturing postcolonial modes of social transaction and establishing the conditions for an associational resurgence in many countries. Where these trends have involved the reemergence of intermediate social groups, they have come together with the definition and reassertion of state capacities, highlighting the close connection between civil society and stateness in contemporary Africa. Whether these processes will have a transforming effect on political dynamics still remains to be seen. From a political perspective, Africa in the 1990s, both more marginalized internationally and more dependent on external resources,[140] is in its second phase of decolonization, immersed in an ongoing struggle for independence.

CIVIL SOCIETY AND STATE CONSOLIDATION: SOME IMPLICATIONS

In the preceding pages an attempt has been made to look at state–society relations through an examination of intermediate social organizations and their relationship to associational life and state agencies on the continent. In the course of the analysis, it has been possible to clarify some key points related to the definition, emergence, and transformation of civil society in Africa. First, it is abundantly clear from this discussion that civil society encompasses only one portion of what has become a complex and diverse associational scene. What distinguishes those groups incorporated in civil society from other associations is their partial nature: They are separate from but address the state. These networks do not attempt to offer total solutions to existential problems (as do some sectarian organizations), nor do they seek to capture the state (as do some populist groups). They therefore occupy a conceptual – although not always a locational – middle, nurturing both horizontal and vertical ties.

Second, it is possible to pinpoint with greater precision the conditions for the rise of civil society. Associational vitality appears to be related to conditions of flux, generated by the opening of new opportunities, conscious changes in official structures, the onset of economic or political crisis, or the breakdown of other linkage mechanisms. Many groups in Africa arose as a channel for detachment from the state or as a means of protest against state repression. Indeed, those groups that contribute to the elaboration of civil society have thrived at two important conjunctures: in the oppositional context that developed when state control was challenged (in both the colonial and the postcolonial periods), and when efforts to maintain state exclusiveness, for whatever reasons, have declined. There seems, however, to be a correlation between the emergence of civil society and the simultaneous relaxation of monopolistic tendencies on the one hand, and the closure of exit options on the other hand. Both statism (which invites populism) and state decay (which evokes localism) stymie the growth of civil society.

Third, therefore, the very particular circumstances required to nurture civil life highlight a specific combination of factors related to external conditions as well as to domestic trends. Although civil society can develop only when opportunities for escape are foreclosed and when the coercive capacities of official agencies can no longer ensure compliance, its emergence depends heavily on the expansion of channels of communication and the accumulation of shared experiences. Commercialization surely plays a role in this process, but so, perhaps more significantly, does the concomitant fortification of autonomous social classes that evolve from the aggregation of a variety of associational interests. These groups need each other and the state in order to maintain their independence. In turn, the African experience amply demonstrates that when no such strata have developed or when they have taken over the official apparatus, states cannot function properly over a protracted period of time.

Fourth, some of the reasons for the interdependence of states and civil society have been illuminated. The state as an organization in society can assert its centrality if it succeeds in obtaining the acquiescence of other social groups. In order to do so, short of physical elimination, it must grant them some margin for maneuverability. Civil associations, precisely because of their partial nature, prop up the state without mounting a challenge to its existence. From this perspective, states and civil societies (which may take on a variety of forms) reinforce and empower one another.

Finally, there appears to be a close tie between different types of states and regime forms. The absence of civil associations buttresses authoritarian regimes, just as particularistic and holistic associations constitute a severe threat to democratic governments. The recent political history of sub-Saharan African states underlines the importance of not confusing all associational activity with democratic propensities, just as it accentuates the potential contribution of truly civic associations (whose partial structural properties require normative moderation) to the strengthening of a variety of democratic modalities.

The shape of the social order and the nature of state constructs have been treated in this exploration as the visible results of ongoing societal transactions. Such an approach redirects analyses away from the prevailing focus on structures and reemphasizes the need to trace the processes of the interplay of institutions and agency over time. In all probability the contours of contemporary states cannot be adequately determined unless the various parameters of civil society are identified with precision and their institutional, material, and symbolic properties are more carefully explored.

These processes have important ramifications for the study of political trends. The neglect of sociology and social dynamics in recent years – as political economy concerns, institutional preoccupations, and symbolic reconstructions of reality have predominated – has made it increasingly difficult to grasp political patterns and to account for rapid shifts in the contours of political life. The theoretical challenge is consequently doubly pressing: Without mediating concepts to bridge ideological, structural, economic, and behavioral phenomena, it may be virtually impossible to create explanatory frameworks capable of capturing the complex interactive reality of contemporary developments.

Africa, like many parts of the world today, is undergoing a comprehensive reevaluation of the prevailing rules of the political game. Its recent experiences, while hardly as dramatic as those taking place in Europe and portions of Asia and Latin America, are nevertheless no less significant or instructive. In all probability the lessons gleaned from the close analysis of recent African developments can yield important insights into similar processes occurring elsewhere. But for these dynamics to be fully comprehended, it might be necessary to revise conceptual approaches and theoretical orientations drastically. This chapter has attempted to suggest some possible interactive guidelines for such a much more thoroughgoing reconsideration.

NOTES

1 See Michael Bratton, "Beyond the State: Civil Society and Associational Life in Africa," *World Politics,* 41, no. 3 (1989): 407–430; Samir Amin, "La Question Democratique dans le Tiers Monde Contemporain," *Africa Development,* 14, no. 2 (1989): 17; and Goran Hyden, "Governance and Liberalization: Tanzania in Comparative Perspective," paper presented at the American Political Science Association, Atlanta, August 1989.

2 A discrete body of general analyses, mostly in article form, has appeared in recent years. See, for example, besides Hyden, "Governance and Liberalization," also Goran Hyden, "African Social Structure," in Robert Berg and Jennifer Whitaker, eds., *Strategies for African Development* (Berkeley: University of California Press, 1986), pp. 52–80; Robert Fatton, "State and Civil Society in Africa," paper presented at the Thirty-second Annual Meeting of the African Studies Association, Atlanta, November 1989; and Michael Bratton, "The Politics of Government–NGO Relations in Africa," *World Development,* 17, no. 4 (1989): 569–587. At the same time, there is a plethora of microstudies on individual organizations. Research on social organizations, especially at the intermediate level, has been neglected, creating an empirical vacuum with adverse theoretical and conceptual implications.

3 Dwayne Woods, "Civil Society in Europe and Africa: Limiting State Power Through a Public Sphere," paper presented at the Thirty-third Annual Meeting of the African Studies Association, Baltimore, November 1990, p. 1.

4 See, for example, the differing conceptualizations of civil society contained in Jean-François Bayart, "Civil Society in Africa," in Patrick Chabal, ed., *Political Domination in Africa: Reflections on the Limits of Power* (London: Cambridge University Press, 1986), p. 11; Robert Fatton, "Bringing the Ruling Class Back In: Class, State and Hegemony in Africa," *Comparative Politics,* 20, no. 3 (1989): 253; Goran Hyden, *No Shortcuts to Progress: African Development Management in Perspective* (Berkeley: University of California Press, 1983), passim; and Larry Diamond, "Introduction: Roots of Failure, Seeds of Hope," in *Democracy in Developing Countries: Africa* (Boulder, Colo.: Lynne Rienner, 1988), esp. pp. 20–23. For a different classification, see John W. Harbeson, "State, Society and Civil Society in Africa: Where Do We Go from Here?," paper presented at the American Political Science Association, San Francisco, September 1990.

5 The notion of the state as a social organization is developed in Joel S. Migdal's "Strong States, Weak States: Power and Accommodation," in Myron Weiner and Samuel P. Huntington, eds., *Understanding Political Development* (Boston: Little, Brown, 1987), p. 396.

6 Bert A. Rockman, "Minding the State – Or a State of Mind?: Issues in the Comparative Conceptualization of the State," *Comparative Political Studies,* 23, no. 1 (1990): 28.

7 These ideas are spelled out in detail in Joel S. Migdal's chapter, as well as in the other chapters in this collection.

8 This argument is succinctly summarized in Joel S. Migdal, "The State in Society: Struggles and Accommodations in Multiple Arenas," *States and Social Structures Newsletter,* 13 (Spring 1990): esp. 2–3.

9 Sara Berry, "Coping with Africa's Food Crisis," manuscript, Boston University, 1987, p. 1.

10 Sara Berry, *Fathers Work for Their Sons: Accumulation, Mobility and Class Formation in an Extended Yoruba Community* (Berkeley: University of California Press, 1985), p. 6.

11 Jane Guyer, "Perestroika Without Glasnost," in Carter Center, *Beyond Autocracy in Africa* (Atlanta: Emory University, 1989), p. 148.

12 Shaheen Mozaffar, "The Policy Dimension of State–Society Relations in Africa," paper presented at the Thirty-second Annual Meeting of the African Studies Association, Atlanta, November 1989, p. 6. Also see Shaheen Mozaffar, "Putting the State in Its Place: Theoretical Implications of State–Society Relations in Africa," paper presented at the American Political Science Association, San Francisco, September 1990.

13 Naomi Chazan, "State and Society in Africa: Images and Challenges," in Donald Rothchild and Naomi Chazan, *The Precarious Balance* (Boulder, Colo.: Westview Press, 1988), p. 338. Also see Otwin Marenin, "The Managerial State in Africa: A Conflict Coalition Perspective," in Zaki Ergas, ed., *The African State in Transition* (London: Macmillan, 1987), pp. 61–85.

14 Vivienne Shue, *The Reach of the State: Sketches of the Chinese Body Politic* (Stanford, Calif.: Stanford University Press, 1988), p. 27.

15 See Frances Hagopian's chapter in this collection.

16 Naomi Chazan and Donald Rothchild, "Corporatism and Political Transactions: Some Ruminations on the Ghanaian Experience," in Julius E. Nyang'oro and Timothy M. Shaw, eds., *Corporatism in Africa: Comparative Analysis and Practice* (Boulder, Colo.: Westview Press, 1989), esp. pp. 180–181. Also see Larissa Adler Lomnitz, "Informal Exchange Networks in Formal Systems: A Theoretical Model," manuscript, Mexico City, Universidad Nacional Autónoma de México, 1988, and Larissa Adler Lomnitz and Claudio Lomnitz Adler, "La Representación Simbólica del Poder: Política, Ritual y Símbolo en la Compaña Presidencial del Partido Revolucionario Institucional de México," manuscript, Mexico City, 1989.

17 See Joel Migdal's chapter in this collection.

18 Another advantage of this approach is that it allows for multiple ways of examining politics in fragmented societies or in conditions where states are weak or incapacitated. For an excellent example, see Elizabeth Perry's chapter in this collection.

19 Jean-François Bayart, *L'Etat en Afrique: La Politique du Ventre* (Paris: Fayard, 1989), pp. 19–31.

20 Thanks are due to Michael Bratton for his insights on this point.

21 This point is made for India in Atul Kohli's chapter in this collection.

22 I prefer this formulation to that of a "love–hate relationship" suggested by Michael

Bratton in his chapter in this collection, because it better conveys the ambivalent relationship between state and society he seeks to capture.

23 Adigun Agbaje, "Mobilizing for a New Political Culture," paper presented at the Conference on "Democratic Transition and Structural Adjustment in Nigeria," Stanford, Hoover Institution, August 1990, p. 45.

24 This point is made for preindustrial societies by Marc Howard Ross, "Political Organization and Participation: Exit, Voice and Loyalty in Preindustrial Societies," *Comparative Politics,* 21, no. 1 (1988): 73–74.

25 Bayart, *L'Etat en Afrique,* p. 58.

26 This analysis is based on abundant evidence from many countries. In the interest of space, few references will be made to specific case studies here. For a general overview, however, see Immanuel Wallerstein, "Voluntary Associations," in James Coleman and Carl Rosberg, eds., *Political Parties and National Integration in Tropical Africa* (Berkeley: University of California Press, 1966), pp. 318–339.

27 Naomi Chazan, Robert Mortimer, John Ravenhill, and Donald Rothchild, *Politics and Society in Contemporary Africa* (Boulder, Colo.: Lynne Rienner, 1988), pp. 72–74.

28 See P. C. Lloyd, *Africa in Social Change* (Harmondsworth: Penguin, 1969); Kenneth Little, *West African Urbanization: A Study of Voluntary Associations in Social Change* (London: Cambridge University Press, 1965); Thomas Hodgkin, *Nationalism in Colonial Africa* (New York: New York University Press, 1957); and Chris Allen and Gavin Williams, eds., *Sociology of 'Developing' Societies: Sub-Saharan Africa* (New York: Monthly Review Press, 1982).

29 Elliot J. Berg and Jeffrey Butler, "Trade Unions," in Coleman and Rosberg, *Political Parties and National Integration in Tropical Africa,* pp. 343–381.

30 Margaret Peil, *Consensus and Conflict in African Societies: An Introduction to Sociology* (London: Longman, 1977), pp. 235–239.

31 In many rural areas small populist movements developed. These organizations did not attempt to expand their activities beyond the local level and developed few contacts with other similarly constituted groups. For one analysis, see Martin Kilson, "Anatomy of African Class Consciousness: Agrarian Populism in Ghana from 1915 to the 1940s and Beyond," in I. L. Markovitz, ed., *Studies in Power and Class in Africa* (London: Oxford University, 1987), pp. 50–66.

32 M. K. Schutz, "Some Observations on the Functions of Voluntary Associations with Special Reference to West African Cities," *Human Relations,* 9 (1977): 803–816.

33 For a classification based partly on organizational complexity, see James S. Coleman, "Nationalism in Tropical Africa," *American Political Science Review,* 48, no. 2 (1954): 404–426. Also, for a detailed case study, see James S. Coleman, *Nigeria: Background to Nationalism* (Berkeley: University of California Press, 1958).

34 For a general discussion of these issues in voluntary associations, see Milton Esman and Norman Uphoff, *Local Organizations: Intermediaries in Rural Development* (Ithaca, N.Y.: Cornell University Press, 1984), pp. 81–100.

35 Peil, *Consensus and Conflict in African Societies,* p. 32.

36 Richard Hodder-Williams, *An Introduction to the Politics of Tropical Africa* (London: George Allen & Unwin, 1984), p. 164.

37 Berry, *Fathers Work for Their Sons,* p. 5.

38 Victor T. Le Vine, "Parapolitics: Notes for a Theory," paper presented at the Thirty-second Annual Meeting of the African Studies Association, Atlanta, November 1989, pp. 17–20.

39 See the chapter by Bratton in this collection.

40 I am indebted to Sara Berry for these insights. Her current comparative work on the

relationship between state processes and agricultural production promises further elaboration of these points.

41 Joel S. Migdal, *Strong Societies and Weak States: State–Society Relations and State Capabilities in the Third World* (Princeton: Princeton University Press, 1988), p. 141.

42 The distinction between civil society and the primordial public is inspired by the differentiation between the civil and primordial publics in the seminal article by Peter Ekeh, "Colonialism and the Two Publics in Africa: A Theoretical Statement," *Comparative Studies in Society and History,* 17, no. 1 (1975): 91–112.

43 For a detailed comparison of the role of voluntary associations in the nationalist struggle, see Immanuel Wallerstein, *The Road to Independence: Ghana and the Ivory Coast* (Paris: Mouton, 1964). For an analysis of the process of moderation, see pp. 107–121.

44 Catherine Boone, in her chapter in this collection.

45 For an excellent discussion of the significance of the political (as opposed to structural) properties of African states at this juncture, see Catherine Boone, "State Power and Economic Crisis in Senegal," *Comparative Politics,* 22, no. 3 (1990): 341–357.

46 For one of many accounts, see Burgess Carr, "The Church in Africa," *Africa,* 40 (1974): 58–59.

47 Christian Coulon, "Le Reseau Islamique," *Politique Africaine,* 9 (1983): 68–83, and Guy Nicolas, "Islam et 'Constructions Nationales' au Sud du Sahara," *Revue Française d'Etudes Politiques Africaines,* 165–166 (1979): 86–107.

48 For details on the picture in West Africa, see Willard R. Johnson and Vivian R. Johnson, *West African Governments and Volunteer Development Organizations* (Lanham, Md.: University Press of America, 1990). Also see the excellent paper by Aili Nari Tripp, "Local Institutions and Grassroots Party Dynamics in Urban Tanzania," paper presented at the American Political Science Association, Atlanta, September 1989, p. 5 and elsewhere.

49 William John Hanna, "Students," in Coleman and Rosberg, *Political Parties and National Integration in Tropical Africa,* pp. 413–445.

50 Kenneth Little, *African Women in Towns* (London: Cambridge University Press, 1973). For one of many excellent case studies, see Rayah Feldman, "Women's Groups and Women's Subordination: An Analysis of Policies Towards Rural Women in Kenya," *Review of African Political Economy,* 27–28 (1983): 67–85.

51 For one of these case studies, consult Claire Robertson, *Sharing the Same Bowl: A Socioeconomic History of Women and Class in Accra, Ghana* (Bloomington: Indiana University Press, 1984).

52 Sandra Barnes, "Voluntary Associations in a Metropolis: The Case of Lagos, Nigeria," *African Studies Review,* 18, no. 2 (1975): 75–88, and Sandra Barnes and Margaret Peil, "Voluntary Association Membership in Five West African Cities," *Urban Anthropology,* 6, no. 1 (1977): 80.

53 For details, see Richard Sandbrook, *The Politics of Basic Needs: Urban Aspects of Assaulting Poverty in Africa* (London: Heineman, 1982); Hyden, *No Shortcuts to Progress;* and, for one specific case study, C. K. Brown, "The Ghanaian Rural Youth: Resource for Social Development," *Ghana Social Science Journal,* 5, no. 1 (1978): 26–46.

54 Barbara Thomas, *Politics, Participation and Poverty: Development Through Self-Help in Kenya* (Boulder, Colo.: Westview Press, 1985), p. 5.

55 Boone, in her chapter in this volume, suggests that this is a form of "colonization" and "domestication."

56 For a discussion of corporatism in the African context, see Nyang'oro and Shaw,

Corporatism in Africa; for a definition, consult Thomas Callaghy, *The State Society Struggle: Zaire in Comparative Perspective* (New York: Columbia University Press, 1984), p. 16.

57 Yves Person, "Les Syndicats en Afrique Noire," *Le Mois en Afrique,* 172–173 (1980): 22–46. Also see Richard Sandbrook and Robin Cohen, eds., *The Development of an African Working Class* (London: Longman, 1975).

58 Michael Schatzberg, *The Dialectics of Oppression in Zaire* (Bloomington: Indiana University Press, 1988), p. 15.

59 Chazan et al., *Politics and Society in Contemporary Africa,* pp. 172–177.

60 Richard Joseph, *Democracy and Prebendal Politics in Nigeria: The Rise and Fall of the Second Republic* (London: Cambridge University Press, 1987), has described this process as the prebendalization of African politics. Although frequently used in the recent literature as a synonym for corruption, prebendalism, in the more classical Weberian sense, is also an indication of the looseness of central control and the paucity of state resources.

61 Rene Lemarchand, "The Dynamics of Factionalism in Contemporary Africa," in Ergas, *The African State in Transition,* pp. 149–165.

62 For three excellent case studies of this dynamic, see Goran Hyden, *Beyond Ujamaa in Tanzania: Underdevelopment and an Uncaptured Peasantry* (Berkeley: University of California Press, 1980); John Dunn and A. F. Robertson, *Dependence and Opportunity: Political Change in Ahafo* (London: Cambridge University Press, 1973); and Sandra Barnes, *Patrons and Power: Creating a Political Community in Metropolitan Lagos* (Bloomington: Indiana University Press, 1986).

63 For a case study, see Margaret Peil, *Nigerian Politics: The View from Below* (London: Cassell, 1975), who argues forcefully that social spaces emerged particularly in intermediate social groups.

64 This tension is discussed superbly in Bjorn Beckman, *Organizing the Farmers: Cocoa Politics and National Development in Ghana* (Uppsala: Scandinavian Institute of African Studies, 1976) and Richard Jeffries, *Class, Power and Ideology in Ghana: The Railwaymen of Sekondi* (London: Cambridge University Press, 1978).

65 Goran Hyden, "Governance: A New Approach to Comparative Politics," paper presented at the Thirty-first Annual Meeting of the African Studies Association, Chicago, October 1988.

66 Naomi Chazan, "The New Politics of Participation in Tropical Africa," *Comparative Politics,* 14, no. 2 (1982): 169–189.

67 For general analyses, see Berg and Butler, "Trade Unions" (pp. 367–370), and Robin Cohen, "Resistance and Hidden Forms of Consciousness Among African Workers" (pp. 18–22), *Review of African Political Economy,* 19 (1980). For an excellent case study, see Jeff Crisp, *The Story of an African Working Class Ghanaian Miner's Struggles* (London: Zed Books, 1984).

68 See Joel Barkan, *An African Dilemma: University Students in Ghana, Tanzania and Uganda* (London: Oxford University Press, 1975). Also see Naomi Chazan, "The Manipulation of Youth Politics in Ghana and the Ivory Coast," *Genève-Afrique,* 15, no. 2 (1976): 38–63.

69 See Jean-François Bayart, "Le Politique par le Bas en Afrique Noire," *Politique Africaine,* 1, no. 1 (1980): 53–82.

70 Hodder-Williams, *An Introduction to the Politics of Tropical Africa,* p. 166. For a series of excellent case studies that highlight the patronage links of one-party states, see Fred Hayward, ed., *Elections in Independent Africa* (Boulder, Colo.: Westview Press, 1986).

71 See Berry, *Fathers Work for Their Sons,* p. 57.

72 For a discussion of the Ghanaian coalition of intermediate groups and popular organizations, see Naomi Chazan and Victor T. Le Vine, "Politics in a 'Non-Political' System: The March 30, 1978 Referendum in Ghana," *African Studies Review,* 22, no. 1 (1979): 177–208.

73 Strategies of organizational autonomy and governmental control and their impact on the operational space of civil associations are analyzed in depth in Bratton, "The Politics of Government–NGO Relations in Post-Colonial Africa."

74 This is the same argument posed by Catherine Boone in her chapter for this collection. For a contrary view, see Robert Fatton, "The State of African Studies and Studies of the African State: The Theoretical Softness of the 'Soft State,' " *Journal of Asian and African Studies,* 24, nos. 3–4 (1989): 170–187.

75 John Lonsdale, "Political Accountability in African History," in Patrick Chabal, ed., *Political Domination in Africa: Reflections on the Limits of Power* (London: Cambridge University Press, 1986), pp. 126–157.

76 This dilemma is discussed in Joshua B. Forrest, "The Quest for State 'Hardness' in Africa," *Comparative Politics,* 20, no. 4 (1988): 423–442. The debate between those who view the African state as overly autonomous and those who insist on its embedded character had become particularly acrimonious in recent years. Compare Fatton, "The State of African Studies and Studies of the African State," and Robert Price, "Neo-Colonialism and Ghana's Economic Decline: A Critical Assessment," *Canadian Journal of African Studies,* 18, no. 1 (1984): 163–193. My position is that these debates confuse regime autonomy with the state, which, with few exceptions, has not proven to be endowed with autonomous characteristics. For a fuller analysis, see Naomi Chazan, *An Anatomy of Ghanaian Politics: Managing Political Recession, 1969–1982* (Boulder, Colo.: Westview Press, 1983).

77 Frank Holmquist, "Defending Peasant Political Space in Independent Africa," *Canadian Journal of African Studies,* 14, no. 1 (1980): 157–167.

78 Bratton, "Beyond the State: Civil Society and Associational Life in Africa."

79 Thomas M. Callaghy, "Lost Between State and Market: The Politics of Economic Adjustment in Ghana, Zambia and Nigeria," in Joan M. Nelson, ed., *Economic Crisis and Policy Choice: The Politics of Adjustment in the Third World* (Princeton: Princeton University Press, 1990), pp. 257–319.

80 Rockman, "Minding the State," p. 48.

81 Samuel Decalo, *Psychoses of Power: African Personal Dictatorships* (Boulder, Colo.: Westview Press, 1989).

82 On regime instability, see Chris Allen, "Staying Put: Handy Hints for Heads of State," paper presented at the Symposium on Authority and Legitimacy in Africa, University of Stirling, May 1986. On the erosion of state capacities, see, for example, Larry Diamond, "Class Formation in the Swollen African State," *Journal of Modern African Studies,* 25, no. 4 (1987): 567–596.

83 The centrality of the "trough factor" is discussed extensively in the recent works of Thomas Callaghy. See Thomas M. Callaghy, "Toward State Capability and Embedded Liberalism in the Third World: Lessons for Adjustment," in Joan M. Nelson, ed., *Fragile Coalitions: The Politics of Economic Adjustment* (New York: Overseas Development Council, 1989), pp. 115–138.

84 Pierre Jacquemont, "La Destatisation en Afrique Subsahariennes: Enjeux et Perspectives," *Revue Tiers Monds,* 29, no. 114 (1988): 291–299.

85 See Jane Guyer, "Experience of Government and Issues of Governance in a Rural Area: An Interpretation Based on Ibarapa, Oyo State," paper presented at the Conference on "Democratic Transitions and Structural Adjustment in Nigeria," Stanford, Hoover Institution, August 1990, p. 29. Guyer goes on to suggest that, "The possibil-

ity cannot be ruled out that as the nature of the incumbents of chieftancy shifts, that 'traditional' institution might provide the political space and protection in which new community and regional organizations can develop in the rural areas" (p. 30).

86 Sara Berry, "Coping with Confusion: African Farmers' Responses to Economic Instability in the 1970s and 1980s," in *Working Papers in African Studies*, 141 (Boston University: African Studies Center, 1989), p. 5; Joel D. Barkan, Michael L. McNulty, and M. A. O. Ayeni, "Hometown Voluntary Associations, Local Development and the Emergence of Civil Society in Western Nigeria," paper presented at the Thirty-third Annual Meeting of the African Studies Association, Baltimore, November 1990.

87 Tripp, "Local Institutions and Grassroots Party Dynamics," p. 42.

88 Jennifer Widner, "Interest Group Structure and Organization in Kenya's Informal Sector: Cultural Despair or a Politics of Multiple Allegiances?," *Comparative Political Studies*, 24, no. 1 (April 1991): 31–55, and Alan Fowler, "The Role of NGOs in Changing State–Society Relations," paper presented at the Thirty-third Annual Meeting of the African Studies Association, Baltimore, November 1990, p. 4.

89 Several case studies of popular political cultures have recently underlined the degree of mass alienation from officialdom in many parts of the continent. For an overview, see Naomi Chazan, "African Political Cultures and Democracy: An Exploration," paper presented at the Conference on "Political Culture and Democracy," Stanford, Hoover Institution, September 1988. Also see Thomas Callaghy, "Culture and Politics in Zaire" (Washington, D.C.: Department of State, Bureau of Intelligence Research, 1987), and Ernest Wilson, "Politics and Culture in Nigeria" (Washington, D.C.: Department of State, Bureau of Intelligence Research, 1988).

90 This is suggested by Jeffrey Herbst, "Migration, the Politics of Protest, and State Consolidation in Africa," *African Affairs*, 89, no. 355 (1990): 183–203.

91 This point is emphasized in my analysis of Ghana during this period. See Naomi Chazan, "Liberalization, Governance and Political Space in Ghana," paper presented at the Thirty-first Annual Meeting of the African Studies Association, Chicago, October 1988.

92 For more details on Ghana, see Donald I. Ray, *Ghana: Politics, Economics and Society* (London: Frances Pinter, 1986). For Burkina Faso, see Rene Otayek, "Burkina Faso: Between Feeble State and Total State, The Swing Continues," in Donald B. Cruise O'Brien, John Dunn, and Richard Rathbone, eds., *Contemporary West African States* (London: Cambridge University Press, 1990), pp. 13–30.

93 For the evidence from Ghana, see Kwesi Jonah, "Crisis and Response in Ghana" (Kingston, Jamaica: University of the West Indies, Institute of Social and Economic Research, April 1989), p. 34.

94 See Jean-François Bayart, "Les Eglises Chrétiennes et la Politique du Ventre: La Partage du Gâteau Ecclesial," paper presented at the Thirty-second Annual Meeting of the African Studies Association, Atlanta, November 1989.

95 For details, see the contribution included in Gracia Clark, ed., *Traders Versus the State: Anthropological Approaches to Unofficial Economies* (Boulder, Colo.: Westview Press, 1988). Also see Chaire Robertson, "The Death of Makola and Other Tragedies," *Canadian Journal of African Studies*, 17, no. 3 (1983): 469–495.

96 Willard Johnson, "Notes on 'Community Governance,' 'High Politics' and Informal Governance by Aid Agencies," in Carter Center, *Beyond Autocracy in Africa*, pp. 14–19.

97 For an overview of these techniques, see James C. Scott, "Everyday Forms of Resistance," in Forrest D. Colburn, ed., *Everyday Forms of Peasant Resistance* (London: M. E. Sharpe, 1989), pp. 3–31.

98 The best case study of this phenomenon is Janet MacGaffey, *Entrepreneurs and Parasites: The Struggle for Indigenous Capitalism in Zaire* (London: Cambridge University Press, 1987).

99 I have not elaborated on these activities in these pages, as I have written on them extensively in other publications. See Naomi Chazan, "Patterns of State–Society Incorporation and Disengagement in Africa," in Donald Rothchild and Naomi Chazan, eds., *The Precarious Balance*, pp. 121–148. Also see Victor Azarya and Naomi Chazan, "Disengagement from the State in Africa: Reflections on the Experience of Ghana and Guinea," *Comparative Studies in Society and History,* 19, no. 1 (1987): 106–131.

100 The way this system worked in one country is described in Gracia Clark, "Price Control of Local Foodstuffs in Kumasi, Ghana," in Clark, *Traders Versus the State,* pp. 57–80.

101 Some of the more violent aspects of the informal economy are discussed in Nelson Kasfir, "State, *Magendo,* and Class Formation in Uganda," *Journal of Commonwealth and Comparative Politics,* 21, no. 3 (1983): 90–110.

102 René Lemarchand, "The State, the Parallel Economy, and the Changing Structure of Patronage Systems," in Rothchild and Chazan, *The Precarious Balance,* pp. 149–170.

103 For a good description of these tactics, see A. Adu Boahen, *African Perspectives on Colonialism* (Baltimore: Johns Hopkins University Press, 1987), pp. 63–81.

104 Bratton, "The Politics of Government–NGO Relations in Africa," using quite different terminology, has pointed out similar issues in the analysis of associational life in Africa in the 1980s.

105 By far the best analysis of the problems of impoverishment in Africa is the recent study by John Iliffe, *The African Poor: A History* (London: Cambridge University Press, 1987).

106 Richard Sandbrook, *The Politics of Africa's Economic Stagnation* (London: Cambridge University Press, 1985).

107 For an assessment of the first phase of the structural adjustment regimen, see The World Bank, *Sub-Saharan Africa: From Crisis to Sustainable Growth* (Washington, D.C.: World Bank, 1989).

108 Ann Drabek, ed., "Development Alternatives: The Challenge for NGOs," Special Supplement, *World Development,* 15 (1987): 2.

109 Tripp, "Local Institutions and Grassroots Party Dynamics in Urban Tanzania," documents this process in East Africa. For Nigeria, see Adebayo O. Olukoshi, "Associational Life During the Nigerian Transition to Civilian Rule," paper presented at the Conference on "Democratic Transition and Structural Adjustment in Nigeria," Stanford, Hoover Institution, August 1990, esp. p. 1 ("no period has been as vibrant associationally in Nigeria as the period since 1986").

110 Larry Diamond and Oyeleye Oyediran, "Military Authoritarianism and Democratic Transition in Nigeria," paper presented at the American Political Science Association, San Francisco, September 1990, p. 31.

111 Johnson and Johnson, *West African Governments and Volunteer Development Organizations,* esp. pp. 5–24.

112 Agbaje, "Mobilizing for a New Political Culture," pp. 5–6.

113 Bayart, "Les Eglises Chrétiennes et la Politique du Ventre."

114 Pearl T. Robinson, "Transnational NGOs: A New Direction for U.S. Policy," *Issues,* 18, no. 1 (Winter 1989): 41.

115 See Bratton's chapter in this collection.

116 See Donald Rothchild and Michael Foley, "African States and the Politics of

Inclusive Coalitions," in Rothchild and Chazan, *The Precarious Balance,* pp. 233–264.

117 Lillian Trager, "A Re-Examination of the Urban Informal Sector in West Africa," *Canadian Journal of African Studies,* 21, no. 2 (1987): 238–255. Also, for one case study, see Cyril Kofie Daddieh, "Economic Development and the Informal Sector in Ghana Reconsidered: Notes Towards a Reconceptualization," manuscript, Cambridge, Mass.: Harvard University, Center for International Affairs, African Studies Program, 1987.

118 Pieter Van Dijk, "Collaboration between Government and Non-Governmental Organizations," *Development,* 4 (1987): 117–121.

119 The suggestion that this group has channeled resources from the state arena to undertakings in the parallel economy is raised by Fatton, "The State of African Studies and Studies of the African State," and Irving Leonard Markovitz, "African Capitalism in Comparative Perspective: African Entrepreneurship in Senegal," paper presented at the American Political Science Association, San Francisco, August 1990, p. 1. Other studies, such as that conducted by Tripp, "Local Institutions and Grassroots Party Dynamics in Urban Tanzania," p. 19, claim that profits gained in the informal sector appear to be reinvested in enterprises in this sphere as well.

120 Again, see MacGaffey, *Entrepreneurs and Parasites: The Struggle for Indigenous Capitalism in Zaire,* for details.

121 The social consequences of SAP are now being examined in some detail. For two case studies that highlight the extent of social disparities resulting from these programs, see Tade Akin Aina, "The Social Consequences of SAP," paper presented at the conference on "Democratic Transition and Structural Adjustment in Nigeria," Stanford, Hoover Institution, August 1990, and Jonah, "Crisis and Response in Ghana."

122 Fatton, "Bringing the Ruling Class Back In," p. 257.

123 For a superb and sophisticated case study, see Jennifer Widner, "The Discovery of 'Politics': Smallholder Reactions to the Cocoa Crisis of 1988–1989 in Côte d'Ivoire," paper presented at the Thirty-third Annual Meeting of the African Studies Association, Baltimore, November 1990.

124 Frantz Telmo Rudi, "The Role of NGOs in the Strengthening of Civil Society," *World Development,* 15 (1987): 121–127.

125 Shue, *The Reach of the State,* pp. 125–152, makes this point forcefully for China in the pre-Maoist era.

126 For an explication of this thesis in Nigeria, see Daniel Bach, "Managing a Plural Society: The Boomerang Effects of Nigerian Federalism," *Journal of Commonwealth and Comparative Politics,* 27, no. 2 (1989): 218–245.

127 See Albert O. Hirschman, *Exit, Voice and Loyalty: Responses to Decline in Firms, Organizations and States* (Cambridge: Harvard University Press, 1970).

128 Cf. Hyden, "Governance and Liberalization: Tanzania in Comparative Perspective," p. 7.

129 Guyer, "Experience of Government and Issues of Governance in Rural Africa," p. 21. The point is also made emphatically by Tripp, "Local Institutions and Grassroots Party Dynamics in Urban Tanzania," p. 18.

130 An entire body of literature on democratization in Africa has appeared in recent years. The discussion was sparked by the pioneering work of Richard Sklar, "Democracy in Africa," *African Studies Review,* 26, nos. 3–4 (1983): 11–24, and by his subsequent article "Developmental Democracy," *Comparative Studies in Society and History,* 19, no. 4 (1987): 686–714. Larry Diamond has been instrumental in

promoting the discussion. See Diamond et al., *Democracy in Developing Countries: Africa.*

131 These events are described and analyzed masterfully by Michael Bratton and Nicholas van den Walle, "Popular Protest and Political Reform in Africa," in Goran Hyden and Michael Bratton, eds., *Governance and Politics in Africa* (Boulder, Colo.: Lynne Rienner, 1991).

132 Babacar Kante and Crawford Young, "Democracy in Africa and the Senegalese Elections," paper presented at the Thirty-second Annual Meeting of the African Studies Association, Atlanta, November 1989.

133 For a view that suggests that democracy in Africa has been stronger than heretofore suggested, see John A. Wiseman, *Democracy in Black Africa: Survival and Revival* (New York: Paragon House, 1990).

134 Bayart, "Civil Society in Africa," pp. 124–125. For an intriguing set of insights into this rethinking, see the articles in Peter Anyang' Ny'ongo, ed., *Popular Struggles for Democracy in Africa* (London: Zed Books, 1987).

135 Larry Diamond and Harvey Glickman have written extensively on these aspects of democratization. See the various contributions in Carter Center, *Beyond Autocracy in Africa.* Also see John Dunn, "The Politics of Representation and Good Government in Post-Colonial Africa" in Chabal, *Political Domination in Africa,* pp. 158–174.

136 David Booth, "Alternatives in the Restructuring of State–Society Relations: Research Issues for Tropical Africa," *IDS Bulletin,* 18, no. 4 (1987): 23–30.

137 Republic of Ghana, *District Political Authority and Modalities of District Level Elections* (Accra: Ghana Publishing Corporation, July 1987).

138 For a summary of the problematics inherent in some of these discussions, and for an analysis of the issue of the sequencing of economic and political reforms, see Thomas M. Callaghy, "Political Passions and Economic Interests: Comparative Reflections on Political and Economic Logics in Africa," paper presented at the American Political Science Association, San Francisco, August 1990.

139 Michael Ford and Frank Holmquist, "Crisis and Reform," in Naomi Chazan and Timothy Shaw, eds., *Coping with Africa's Food Crisis* (Boulder, Colo.: Lynne Rienner, 1988), p. 234.

140 Thomas M. Callaghy, "Africa and the World Economy: Caught between a Rock and a Hard Place," in John Harbeson and Donald Rothchild, eds., *Africa in World Politics* (Boulder, Colo.: Westview Press, 1991).

PART IV

CONCLUSION

11

State power and social forces: on political contention and accommodation in the Third World

ATUL KOHLI AND VIVIENNE SHUE

A STATE-IN-SOCIETY APPROACH

The recent renewal of intellectual interest in the state has made a number of salutary collateral contributions to the field of comparative politics. One of these has been to provoke a certain rejuvenation of the comparative study of politics and society in the low-income countries of Asia, Africa, and Latin America. Moving beyond the lamentable dialogue of the deaf to which the debates between both modernization and dependency analysts had descended in the 1970s, numerous stimulating monographs published during the 1980s have been successful in "bringing the state back in" to Third World studies.[1] It often happens in the social sciences, however, that new gains made on one analytical front may only give rise to yet newer and yet more challenging problems of analysis on other fronts. Against this generic malady, the recent state-oriented studies have shown no immunity.

Furthermore, a common tendency to mistake analytical claims for empirical ones has shown itself to be especially problematic for this line of inquiry and research. The general analytical claim concerning the primacy of state can easily lead, for example, to the fallacious view that states in low-income settings are always and inevitably the most significant social actors on the scene. And the research agenda that, in turn, can flow from a view of the state-as-domineering-Leviathan is almost bound to be deficient for the study of most countries in Asia, Africa, and Latin America, where really-existing states have so rarely achieved such colossal proportions, and where those that might be classified as genuine goliaths have so often proved to be but crippled giants. The present volume, therefore, moves away from a strict statist orientation; it argues instead for a frame of reference that puts the mutual interactions of the state and society at its focal center.[2]

This volume's introductory chapter, by Joel Migdal, lays out such a framework. While accepting the analytical distinction between authority and association, or between the state and society, the framework stresses instead the interconnectedness of state and society. To serve as a starting point here, three general considerations featured in Migdal's framework are worth reiterating. First, it is important to *disaggregate the state*. State power at the pinnacle is seldom monolithic; careful dissection of the center is essential. This piece of the truth is, perhaps, already widely recognized. We want to stress in addition, however, that a research focus on lower levels of the state – away from the capital city – and a focus on the links between those lower levels and the capital city, may have much to teach us both about power distribution within a state and about that state's capacity to define and implement a specific policy agenda.

Second, it is important to remember that *the boundaries between state and society are generally blurred*. Necessary (and neater) analytical distinctions notwithstanding, it is essential that we now pay careful attention in our work to just how numerous are the points at which, and to just how many-layered are the modalities (both structural and ideational) by which, state and society are in fact linked or intertwined. The specificities in each prevailing complex of state–society linkage, overlay, and embrace take on great significance in actually understanding the conduct of politics at mid- and grassroots levels, and this is especially so in settings where organizational and emotive distinctions between the public and private realm are not well established. A deliberate analytical sensitivity to both the ubiquitousness and the variety of state–society linkage is thus required now if we are to advance our understanding of states' simultaneous embeddedness in and relative autonomy from other operational social forces.

Finally, and related to these first two considerations, the framework proposed here argues for a greater degree of self-consciousness, in both our descriptive and our analytical work, of *the "recursive," that is, the mutually transforming, nature of state–society interactions*. A steady focus on the state's developmental capacities may, perhaps, be appropriate for a handful of the newly industrializing countries, or the NICs, but, for most low income countries, influence flows between state and society tend to be mutual. This mutuality of influence suggests that a research focus on state capacities needs to be complemented with considerations of a given state's social setting. And this claim, in turn, leads to two analytical implications.

First, it tends to redirect our attention back to some of the more conventional political sociological concerns and questions, for example: What are the social determinants of state power? Such a focus, admittedly, may carry with it certain of its own analytical liabilities. It can make it more difficult, for example, to take account of and give due weight to international factors and variables that may, in reality, impinge heavily on the state–society relationship under study.[3] However, it is worth noting explicitly that such a political-sociological approach need not represent a return either to structural-functional or to the more closed Marxist models of political power. As discussed in greater detail in the sections that follow, the initial assumptions of our framework are quite different: in the Weberian spirit, we avoid conceptualizing social change as unidirectional, moving toward a known end point; and we begin also by asserting the analytical separation of state and society, even as we urge special attention to the linkages between them and to their often "recursive" interrelationships.[4] Second, our emphasis on understanding the state's social setting tends to open up new research questions concerning politically significant social changes, such as the evolving nature and extent of civil associational life and the processes by which civil society may emerge, even in low-income settings.

The merits of such an analytical recasting are always to be found in the echoes they either do or do not elicit in actual empirical research. The empirical essays in this volume are thus both informed by and help elucidate the utility of the general framework. They speak for themselves and require no elaborate summaries here. The purpose of this conclusion is, instead, just twofold. First, we lay out some general issues, in an attempt to situate the present volume and the work of its ten contributors in a larger intellectual tradition. And second, we review and discuss the materials of this volume at an intermediate level of generality – that is, between the general framework and the specific empirical studies – so as to focus on some of the more important analytical and thematic contributions made by this collection as a whole.

THE INTELLECTUAL BACKGROUND

Our current approaches to the study of political and social change in developing countries have been profoundly influenced by antecedent intellectual debates concerning the process of modernization in Europe.[5] The great transformation of the countries of Western Europe from agrarian to industrial political economies engendered a number of bold, yet conflicting, scholarly interpretations. Karl Marx, Emile Durkheim, and Max Weber, for example, all sought to conceptualize the nature of Europe's transformation, to explain its dynamics, predict its future, and identify the heroes and the villains of historical change. The intellectual influence of these three early thinkers has both enriched and, on occasion, misled the latter-day study of contemporary developing countries.

Marx's materialist interpretation of history led him to view capitalism as the motor force that propelled Western Europe's great transformation.[6] Indeed, capitalism, as a system of economic production, was responsible both for great increases in economic productivity and for the relative immiseration of the working class. Marx expected this process of relative immiseration to precipitate proletarian socialist revolutions. When such revolutions did not materialize, some of his followers – beginning with Lenin himself, in the early years of this century, and extending all the way down to the dependency theorists still working today – shifted the analytical emphasis decidedly away from the political strivings of the proletariat and, instead, toward the relentless searches for overseas markets and products engineered by capitalists, and by capitalist countries, in their drives to counter declining rates of profit.

What Marx saw as the revolutionary high drama of capitalist accumulation and human exploitation appeared to Durkheim as but the long and typically lonely journey of mankind toward its future in industrial society.[7] Never forgetting the violent history of revolutionary France, Durkheim was concerned about the implications of this protracted and disorienting transformation for the stability, the "social solidarity," of industrial Europe. Industrialization, Durkheim noted, entailed the specialization of tasks in production and distribution and thus led to increasingly finer divisions of labor in society. Differentiation of social roles, in turn, undermined the cultural unity of preindustrial society – what Durkheim referred to as "mechanical solidarity" – because this kind of unity was based on persons performing essentially similar roles and possessing similar world views. Specialization engendered individualism; it led to different life experiences and different values and attitudes toward society. Diversity and the lack of integration in a society's value system could, therefore, in turn threaten social solidarity.

Durkheim's analysis of the great transformation of Western European societies focused attention on the process of industrialization, its accompanying refinements in the division of labor, and the resulting changes in a society's value system. The image of this transformation put forward in Durkheim's writings was one of a process with a clear beginning, and an end. The mechanical solidarity of preindustrial society was slowly supplanted by and moving toward the "organic solidarity" of industrial society; the in-between, transitional periods were characterized by anomie and possible social breakdown. In the writings of later theorists, this image of Durkheim's was to inspire, first, the formulation of the well-known dichotomy of "tradition" and "modernity," and second, the idea of "modernization" – the troubled transition from one to the other.

The diverse concerns of Marx and Durkheim can be compared and contrasted on many dimensions. These thinkers shared, however, two characteristic approaches to the analysis of European transformation that are especially relevant to the subject of this volume. First, both considered their respective analyses of capitalism and industrialization to be of quite general significance; as other societies underwent such transformations – and in due course they would – the social dynamics within them would be similar to those observed in that first handful of Western European countries. Second, both theorists tended to focus analytical attention primarily on matters of socioeconomic structure.

For Durkheim as for Marx, the great dramas of the great transformation were located not in the state, but in the society. The state and politics were, for both, peripheral to the major processes of change under way. Although both paid some attention to the state, they each considered a state's actions and a society's politics to be primarily a reflection of more fundamental dynamics of socioeconomic shift and variation. Whatever may have been the merits of such perspectives for the study of industrializing Western Europe, their general significance for the study of Third World development has turned out to be limited. The roles and actions of states in the late-industrializing countries have been of considerably greater significance than in the cases observed by Marx and Durkheim; this historical fact alone necessitates a more balanced state–society perspective.

By contrast to Marx and Durkheim, Max Weber was both less general in his theoretical ambitions and more sensitive to the mutual interaction of politics and society.[8] One of Weber's central concerns was to explain why capitalism and industrialization took root in Western Europe rather than elsewhere. He explored a number of world religions in the belief that religious teachings had a profound influence on "this-worldly," or secular behavior. His argument tracing the "elective affinity" between the Protestant ethic and capitalism left a number of important methodological legacies for future comparativists: premodern culture and social structure have a significant influence on whether a society will "naturally" evolve into a developed capitalist one (against both tradition–modernity and Marxist frameworks); because there is often a gap between the motivations of the social actors and the unanticipated consequences of their actions, social change may proceed in a manner not understood by the participants (against "rational choice"); and the best way to theorize about significant social transformations is to ask historically and spatially limited questions (against grand theorizing).

Weber's political-sociological concerns spanned the issues of the rise of the modern state, the patterns of authority and legitimacy, the role of leadership, and the nature of bureaucracy as the quintessential "rational" organization. Taking the unification of Germany as salient historical background, Weber was concerned about its "catching up" with politically and economically more advanced England. Dealing with such "modern" issues, Weber was naturally led to focus on the problems of carving out cohesive and centralized states, and on the creative roles of political leaders. The enduring relevance of Weber's work for contemporary comparative studies is in part the result of the continuing pervasiveness of similar political problems, even into the second half of the twentieth century.

The recent attempts by comparativists to "bring the state back in" have often been building on precisely this half of Weber's contribution. But Weber, it should be remembered, was as sensitive to the sociological determinants of politics as he was to the roles and structures of the state. The dominant impact of modern capitalism for Weber, after all, was not the growth of the state but the spread of rationality. And the rise of the modern, bureaucratized state was to be understood as an integral aspect of this *larger* trend toward the reconceptualization and reorganization of society. Weber, furthermore, tended explicitly to treat the market as an arena of power conflicts. In this arena, he saw the "market situation" as helping to determine the unequal "class situation" of individuals and groups. Thus, Weber understood the power of social groups and of states to be continually influenced by the shifting nature of power distributions in the market. Finally, we cannot overlook the fact that Weber devoted considerable attention in his writings to issues of status and to subjective identifications that he regarded as helping to transform individuals with shared beliefs into power groups, thus often decisively influencing and shaping the actual distribution of power in a society. It is on this, more full and more balanced, state–society interpretation of Weber that this volume builds.

Marx, Durkheim, and Weber dominated the nineteenth-century study of social structural transformations in Western Europe;[9] problems of modernization and development were not widely examined during the first half of the twentieth century.[10] During that period, Western scholars were concerned primarily with the two world wars and with issues of capitalism versus socialism. When, after World War II, most former European colonies became sovereign states and the United States emerged as the leading world power, the coincidence of these two global changes spawned considerable scholarly interest again in the problems of development. This more recent political-sociological scholarship on development has proceeded in three waves or "generations" of concerns: the concern with tradition, modernity, and modernization; the focus on the continuing legacy of colonialism in relations of dependency; and the concern with "bringing the state back in." Each approach has made valuable and lasting contributions to the comparative study of developing countries. Each, however, has also been analytically skewed – the modernization and dependency approaches toward apprehending the social determinants of politics, and the statist approach toward discerning the political-structural sources of social change and continuity.

Modernization approach.   In the 1950s and 1960s, a rich and diverse body of literature on modernization and development appeared in the United States, only to be followed by numerous critical (and some sympathetic) reviews.[11] Much too much, it can be argued, has already been written about this framework, so only a few comments are necessary here. It was Talcott Parsons' ambitious attempt to develop a general theory of society around the concept of a "functioning social system" that provided the theoretical inspiration for much of this intellectual effort.[12] Parsons conceived of all societies as systems of interacting parts. The constituent parts of a social system were actors, endowed with roles and status positions, and sharing a common cultural orientation. As culture tended to define group membership ("insiders" and "outsiders"), a social system, because it was characterized by shared culture, tended to be relatively self-sufficient. Moreover, because social systems tended to persist, certain system-maintaining functions common to all of them helped reproduce shared cultural orientations from one generation to the next. Parsons, basing his efforts on such reasoning as this, then attempted to identify the common "pattern-maintaining" functions of social systems; he hoped that others would use them, finally, as a basis for structural-functional analyses of different societies.

Like Durkheim, Parsons sought to devise a classification scheme for social systems. The resulting conceptualization was dichotomous, as Durkheim's had been: All societies were either traditional or modern. Because social systems consisted of interdependent parts, traditional and modern social systems could be defined by "bundles" of coexisting and covarying attributes. Modern society, for example, was likely to be characterized by achievement orientation, functionally specific political and economic structures, and differentiated roles. Traditional society, by contrast, would be characterized by ascriptive orientations, little division of labor, and fused roles. Parsons believed that a scheme of this type would be helpful in classifying all social systems and would thus provide the basis for a more dynamic theory of modernization.

Parsons' abstract formulations had an undeniably profound impact on the subfield of comparative development. And when the study of politics in developing countries finally emerged from its drenching in this very deductive sociological exercise, the role of the state, in the hands of leading political scientists, had been reduced and subordinated to something understood as the "primary need" of a society's "pattern maintenance." The effects of such a reductionist mode of conceptualizing politics were clear, for example, in the influential work of Gabriel Almond. In spite of his more recent protestations to the contrary,[13] Almond then considered the "political system" to be that subsystem of the social system which performed the tasks of "social integration" and "adaptation."[14] Politics was what it does; and what it did was to help a society integrate and to adapt. Even though Almond referred favorably to Weber's writings, his basic conceptualization of politics betrayed a tendency against which Weber had warned stringently: a tendency to define the state in terms of the ends of political action. It is, therefore, not at all surprising that this mode of conceptualizing politics made it logically difficult even to generate a balanced formulation, one capable of recognizing the processes of mutually conditioning interaction that take place between state and society.

Much more might be said on these and related themes.[15] The main points, however, are these: Much of the modernization literature was moved by a normative concern for the preservation of "social solidarity," and much of it also tended to view political conditions as derivative of socioeconomic change. The preoccupation with the destabilizing consequences of socioeconomic development was inspired by nineteenth-century intellectual concerns. Durkheim, remember, descried a France in which private entrepreneurial energies were fast propelling the public upheavals of industrialization. The destabilizing consequences of such fundamental socioeconomic change must have appeared, to nineteenth-century Europeans, to be important enough to be placed at the center of intellectual inquiry.

The extrapolation of this mode of inquiry to more contemporary concerns, however, carried with it the assumption that twentieth-century developing countries would experience processes and perils fundamentally similar to those confronted in "developing" nineteenth-century Western Europe. This assumption has not been borne out. The main agent of socioeconomic change within most Third World countries has not, in fact, been the entrepreneur; it has been the state. The relative absence of entrepreneurial initiative is actually very often a crucial part of the explanation for the continued underdevelopment that plagues these societies. State actors, not surprisingly in these circumstances, have often seen their role as necessarily one of stepping into the breach, precisely in order to promote socioeconomic development. These state actors have deliberately pushed the processes of social change, looking for haste more than harmony. Yet, at the same time, many postwar, postcolonial states have turned out to be hemmed in by domestic and international forces on the one hand, and chronically unstable and ineffectual on the other hand. How can we best conceptualize the simultaneous tendencies of many Third World states to be dominant (in the sense of controlling resources and decisions) and yet not very effective? This is one of the main subjects up for discussion in this volume. Not all aspects of the matter may be settled here, but one thing, surely, is clear: A theoretical framework that treats politics and the state mainly as a dependent variable, influenced and determined by still "more fundamental" socioeconomic changes, cannot focus attention on some of the most salient political-economic relationships of interest.

The dependency perspective.   Strains of Third World nationalism and neo-Marxism combined during the 1960s and 1970s to give rise to a trenchant line of criticism aimed against the modernization perspective. Radical critics found the modernization approach wanting, not only in its substantial interpretations of the problems of developing countries, but also on methodological and ideological grounds. On issues of substance, dependency-oriented critics disagreed with the modernization school's assumption that the Third World countries were in "the early stages of development." For these critics, underdevelopment was to be understood as a product of the encounter between the capitalist West and the colonized people of Asia, Africa, and Latin America. Colonialism itself fostered underdevelopment. Then, even after the granting of formal sovereignty, continuing ties of economic dependency served to maintain neocolonialism. And these contemporary relationships of dependency, like the old ones, worked to the political-economic advantage of the developed West, and to the disadvantage of the underdeveloped Third World.

Beyond dissenting from the modernization perspective on issues of substance, dependency advocates professed different methodological and ideological allegiances. They found modernization approaches to be methodologically ahistorical and overly formal. They argued for historically oriented scholarship that was nevertheless rooted in theoretical assumptions about the primacy of the economic whole, especially the primacy of capitalism as a system of cross-national relations of dominance and dependency. Ideologically, they chastised modernization scholars for providing the intellectual cloaks to cover continued Western designs for dominating and exploiting the Third World. By contrast, they perceived themselves as championing the liberation of the Third World from both capitalism and imperialism.[16]

Like the modernization approach, the dependency approach has made some valuable and lasting contributions to the political-economic study of development. The most significant of these are: (1) It recognizes that contemporary developing countries differ in important respects from the industrializing Western countries of the past; (2) it draws attention to world economic conditions as constraints on contemporary developing countries; and (3) it focuses on the interaction of political, social, and economic variables in the systematic study of development.

Subsequent waves of criticism arose, as we would expect, to point out problematic aspects in the dependency approach as well. The early dependency theory asserting that the Third World's integration into the world capitalist economy actually produced negative development – underdevelopment – has, as a result, now nearly vanished. A revised dependency position, which suggests that dependent development is possible within the constraints of a world economy, has fairly demolished the flawed but logical framework of early dependency thinking. A dependency-oriented approach remains a significant one in the literature. Yet it has been becoming increasingly clear, through the findings of these and other studies, that specific Third World governments and their chosen policies also bear much of the actual responsibility for both "success" and "failure" at development.[17] The differential dynamics of development are being molded by the Third World states – some effective and some not so effective – and not by international economic factors alone.

This recognition of the significant role of state authorities and politics in development bids fair to dilute some of the theoretical thrust of the dependency framework itself, however. This dilemma, in fact, highlights a problem of much of the Marxist-inspired scholarship of Third World politics, namely, that the logic of political explanation must remain, in the end, reductionist. Even though the significant role of the state in development has been widely recognized in neo-Marxist scholarship, varying explanations of this role share one blind spot: they insist that this phenomenon must reflect the interests and goals not of the political elite, but of specifiable economic actors. If the state exhibits "relative autonomy," that must be the consequence of a "Bonapartist" condition whereby the social situation does not permit the establishment of a clear class hegemony, and political authorities emerge as significant mediators. If the state adopts policies further enmeshing domestic economies with the world economy, that must be a reflection of the altering class balance in favor of those representing the interests of world capitalism. And changes in political organization, especially toward authoritarianism, must result from shifting economic needs to sustain and reproduce capitalism.

We do not here dispute the accuracy of any of these specific propositions. Our point is a more general one. Important and profound insights concerning politics in developing countries have been generated by scholars working in both the modernization and the neo-Marxist traditions. And as argued in the sections that follow, we here unabashedly incorporate quite a few of these into our own eclectic framework. Yet we believe that there are limits to how far one can strain the logic of social determinism in political analysis. Many issues of state–society relations in development are simply better analyzed by abandoning the nineteenth-century analytical commitment to an evolutionary and social logic of politics.

Bringing the state back in.   Dissatisfaction with both the modernization and the dependency approaches has called forth numerous responses, many of which are theoretically anarchic. Some coherent analytical concerns, however, have been voiced by scholars troubled by the tendency in both the modernization and the dependency approaches to reduce politics to socioeconomic variables. These scholars have, in various ways, attempted to restore the significance of the autonomy of the political to their respective analyses of development issues.[18]

There are two main ways of interpreting the analytical assertion concerning the autonomy of the political. First, political variables may be understood to have independent significance because those who control state power are in a position to take decisions of far-reaching socioeconomic consequence. Although these political decisions may on occasion reflect the interests and pressures of other powerful actors – at home or abroad – they usually manifest the interests and ideologies of the state authorities. State actions are thus political choices. Although choices are always made within constraints, they are, nevertheless, choices. Patterns of state intervention in society can thus be empirically analyzed for understanding both why specific development strategies or options were adopted and, more important, the consequences of the political choices for political and economic change.

The other sense in which political variables are of autonomous significance has to do with the continuity that political traditions often exhibit. Political cultures and structures are not altered readily in response to socioeconomic change. Authoritarian values and structures, for example, are not easily transformed simply by the spread of education or the rise of a middle class. Patterns of regime action and inaction, as well as the mode in which political demands are made, and their intensity, are thus likely to be as much a product of the political past as of present socioeconomic conditions.

These analytical assertions clearly do not add up to a new theoretical perspective. They have, however, propelled a body of literature that has come to be recognized as "statist." The current volume can be viewed as both a continuation of and a dialogue with this statist approach. One of our main analytical assertions is that some of the statist literature has gone too far in its emphasis on the autonomy of the political. This general contention is supported by nearly all the essays in this volume and is discussed further later in this chapter. If modernization and dependency approaches erred on the side of socioeconomic determinism, the statist literature errs on the side of political determinism. Tracing our roots back to Weber, we argue instead for a more balanced state–society perspective.

GENERAL THEMES

When viewed collectively, this volume's essays can be read as addressing three interrelated state–society themes or issue-areas: the capacities of states in low income societies to legitimate their domination and to pursue their socioeconomic agendas; the roles of various social forces (such as social classes and class fractions, formal and informal civil associations) in the politics of these low-income settings; and the circumstances that may facilitate or prevent mutual empowerment of state and society. The contribution these essays make toward furthering the analysis of each issue must be explored in some detail. Before that, however, three general comments or caveats are in order.

The objects of analysis in these three issue-areas, though related, are also distinct. The first issue of state power helps focus on the state as both an independent variable (the impact made by varying state capacities) and a dependent variable (the determinants of varying state capacities). The issue of old and new social forces, by contrast, shifts analytical attention away from the state and toward changes in society at large. The third central issue-area, understanding the prospects for the simultaneous strengthening of state and society, stands squarely at the intersection of the other two. It is the contention of this volume that our ability to grapple with each of these issues is enhanced when we approach them from the state-in-society perspective.

The relative "newness" of the three central themes invoked in this volume varies. The issue of state capacity, for example, has certainly received a fair amount of scholarly attention over the last decade. This discussion has ranged from characterizing the malaise and evaluating the apparent "weakness" of the African state, to explaining the contrasting apparent "efficacy" of state power in some of the more spectacularly successful newly industrializing countries. Several authors in this volume contend, however, that situating the study of state capacity in its broader social setting modifies and sharpens our understanding of why only some states succeed at their politicoeconomic tasks, whereas many others do not. The scholarly concern with the second of our themes, namely, the role of social forces in low-income settings, is growing. The historical essays in this volume on the role of social classes detach the study of class from a philosophy of history and thus offer fresh insights into how to study the political impact of both business groups and workers. As for the dynamics of associational life and the rise of civil society, the present volume underlines the significance of this currently emerging research focus by both reflecting and contributing to it. The third issue – of mutual empowerment of state and society – is one that has not yet received much scholarly attention. And what is said here is not by any means intended to be taken as the last word on the matter. It is, rather, just the beginning of what we hope may be one of the contributions of the kind of work we propose and illustrate. By moving away from a state-versus-society orientation, which creates a misleading sense of power conflicts as zero-sum games between state and social actors, several authors in this volume are provoked to raise questions instead about the conditions under which the capacity of both state elites and social forces to pursue their goals may be enhanced.

As a final general comment, we should note the progressive or chronological dimension that has tied the three interrelated themes of the volume together in a specific order. Many low-income countries, especially those in Asia and Africa, emerged from colonial rule with a nationalist elite at the helm, ready to initiate far-reaching plans to "develop" their societies. Some of these efforts were to bear fruit; others did not. It is hardly surprising, therefore, that the question of how best to understand different states' capacities to establish domination and to initiate change would be one important analytical concern of a volume such as this. For many of these countries, it was only *after* this first postwar phase – only after those early efforts at state-led development in both the more "successful" and the less "successful" cases – that a host of other social forces were to react, sometimes adopting a more aggressive-competitive, sometimes a more passive-obstructionist role in the public sphere. Although the specific patterns of resistance and collaboration among state and other social actors have varied sharply in different low-income settings, one general trend, a clear second wave, a "new politics" demanding scholarly attention, emerged with the appearance of more pronounced associational or non-state-led political action. Then, lastly, as both state elites and social groups settled into controlling certain power resources, and as both actively pursued their respective aims, an important, even newer set of questions began to materialize on the research agenda: Are there any conditions (in environments of persistent poverty) under which *both* state *and* other social groups or forces may be empowered? Are there conditions under which they may be mutually empowering? What are these conditions? And would sustained economic development and democracy open up such prospects where they have not yet come into view?

States: autonomy, capacity, legitimacy

Four chapters in this volume, those by Frances Hagopian, Vivienne Shue, Catherine Boone, and Atul Kohli, directly speak to the issue of state power in low-income settings. While each essay addresses some themes other than that of state power, and some other chapters are also concerned with the issue of state power, central to these four is an analysis of a state's capacity to achieve its goals. Although focused on the state, they are reacting to one or more of the following misleading "state-centric" assumptions made in the current literature: that the state is an all important actor in the drama of contemporary social change; that the nature of state institutions is the key for understanding the impact of the state on social change; that certain states are somehow "autonomous" from their social settings, and that this "autonomy" may alternatively be the basis of "state strength" (as, for example, in some newly industrializing countries), or of "state weakness" (as, for example, in some African countries).

Hagopian and Shue provide "revisionist" accounts in the best sense of that word, both suggesting that states conventionally understood to be "strong" and "efficacious" turn out, on closer examination, to have important limitations. In Chapter 2, Hagopian argues that Brazil's military regime (1964–1984) was not as "rational" and "efficacious" as often depicted in the "bureaucratic-authoritarian" or the "dependent development" models that have been applied to the Brazilian case. On the contrary, it is clear in retrospect that the Brazilian military failed in its political project to rid the Brazilian polity of traits it deemed undesirable, namely, traditional clientelism and polarizing populism. In order to explain this failure, Hagopian takes us away from the seemingly modern-rational top of the political pyramid, and down into the innards of the polity, that is, to the level of regional and local politics.

The Brazilian military was involved in a "class project," aimed at generating high growth, while simultaneously repressing the left and the working class. As has also been true for other rulers in other countries, coercion and torture did not provide infinite ruling resources to the Brazilian military; sooner or later, they needed a modicum of legitimacy to rule. Given their strong preference for authoritarian politics and given also the conspicuous class nature of their politicoeconomic project, however, this was not an easy order for the regime to fill. Yet eventually, the necessity to restore some legitimacy led Brazil's military rulers to allow a round of relatively free popular elections of candidates for seats in the national Chamber of Deputies and the Senate. Because a significant proportion of the Brazilian population remained politically undermobilized and deeply entrenched in patron–client power networks embedded in the state itself, the military must have calculated that freer elections alone could not serve as a vehicle to generate class-type social polarization and political action. This calculation turned out to be essentially correct, but the results of the 1974 elections were nonetheless to bring home to the military regime another major problem with their governing formula. The government-supported party did rather poorly at the polls, thus spotlighting the growing unpopularity of the military regime.

Hagopian shows that the military government's next strategy to cope with what had to be regarded as a still threatening legitimacy gap was to try strengthening the hand of traditional elites in the regions. It was hoped that these elites would mobilize the support of their dependents to shore up the government's sagging popularity. The paradoxical result, however, was that the power of the "traditional politicos" increased at the expense of the "rational bureaucracy." When the eventual transition to a civilian regime occurred in the 1980s, therefore, these traditional politicians in the regions were well positioned to emerge once more as crucial power brokers in the new "democratic" polity.

If Hagopian successfully demonstrates the limited capacity of the military rulers to implement political change, other revisionist accounts of Brazilian authoritarianism have similarly been tracing the economic failures of that experiment to the regime's legitimacy needs.[19] This new image, of political and economic failure rooted in limited state power, one may note, contrasts sharply with the earlier analyses of the Brazilian military regime, wherein not only was the presumed efficacy of these rulers regarded as the main reason for their initial emergence, but the very combination of authoritarianism and technocracy was also seen as responsible for the turn toward a new type of development – dependent development.[20]

In Chapter 3, Shue, in her reinterpretation of the crucial case of China, argues that the effective reach of the Maoist party-state was shortened, not extended, over time. She attributes the state's declining capacity to govern mainly to a growing disjuncture between the state and society. The party-state that arose in China following the Communist revolution successfully undertook a number of far-reaching social changes. This capacity to initiate deep changes was in part a function of the fact that the Communist Party had mobilized numerous social groups into the political arena. The party had thus, in the early years, created new power resources within Chinese society. As the victorious revolutionary party came to control the structure of state, these firm linkages between state and society, via the party, enabled the regime to implement such profound tasks of social engineering as land reform, collectivization, and nationalization of business and commerce.

Over time, however, the postrevolutionary society and economy, according to Shue, went through a process of "cellularization." Imposition of the Chinese version of collectivized agriculture, and of limits on personal mobility and on commercial transactions across enterprises and regions, engendered numerous small and discrete, cell-like socioeconomic units. As millions of these miniaturized units of life and labor adjusted as best they could to economic planning and to political and procedural demands of the domineering state, the possibilities for linking the state with genuine and vibrant social forces were gradually eroded. Cadres and people living and working in these effectively isolated units often resorted to deception to deal with the barrage of edicts emanating from the state. Local politics, in consequence, came gradually to be restructured along neotraditional lines of localistic protection and personalistic patronage networks and factions. A glaring gap emerged between the state's relentlessly progressive public discourse, which was based on impersonal categories of class, on the one hand, and the far less noble realities of local politics, which, on the other hand, were based on localist deception and patronage. The highly centralized and dictatorial Chinese state in this way found it increasingly difficult to mobilize genuine social support for its own political and economic programs, even though it retained a certain capacity to whip up mass campaigns of shocking social energy and destructiveness. The ironical outcome in China, therefore, was that what began as a sweeping social-revolutionary movement linked to a well-organized and highly efficacious party-state gradually deteriorated into a regime of ideological obsession lacking almost any genuine social base beyond that of the party-state apparatus itself, a regime that therefore was to find it increasingly difficult to govern either legitimately or effectively.

In contrast to Hagopian and Shue, Boone and Kohli do not attempt to revise the prevailing image of the nature of the state in their respective areas of study. Instead, they provide new accounts of the malfunctioning of the state in Africa and India. In Chapter 5, Boone, for example, argues against the view that traces the "malaise" of the African state to the "superimposed" nature of state power in that part of the world. She suggests instead that the crisis of governability in many African countries is rooted in the overexploitation of peasant agricultural societies by state elites.

Boone traces the roots of this pattern of state exploitation of society back to the colonial period. She argues that the colonial state in Africa was designed to facilitate surplus extraction from an economy based on peasant agriculture. The absence of a landed aristocracy in many African countries created favorable conditions for indirect rule by local "strongmen," who themselves became key links in a chain of exploitation that connected the parasitic colonial state to its small peasant producers.

The postcolonial state, according to Boone, basically continued this pattern. A new political class emerged as the de facto rulers in many of the new African countries. In enhancing their own control over the operations of state, they tended to further the exploitation of the peasantry. As before, given the continued absence of market-based, capitalist agriculture, surplus extraction on behalf of the new political class required the use of fairly naked political power. Rule by strongmen, both in national capitals and in local areas, reflected this larger pressure to maintain an authority-based system of surplus acquisition. In the modern environment, however, where the ideal of sustained growth had become a norm in national economies as well as in the international discourse of "development," the African system came to be seen as marred by a deep contradiction: Continuing to squeeze the peasantry only diminished the prospects for genuine economic growth, and only further undermined the resource base on which the power of indigenous African rulers would have to rest. Low growth and political vulnerability came to feed upon each other.

If Boone discovers a social logic to the malady of the African state, and that social logic has to do with a system of surplus appropriation, Kohli, in Chapter

4, also sees a social logic behind the growing crisis of governability in India, but with a difference. A crucial variable for him is the breakdown of established patterns of authority in India's villages. The emergence of new patterns of economic activity and the spread of democratic politics have undermined the authority of members of high castes, or of other "big men," over the masses. This shift has made it nearly impossible to reproduce the old pattern of rule in India wherein the national leaders, belonging to the Congress Party, had forged patronage-based alliances with "big men" at the intermediate and the local levels of the polity. Instead, the emergence of new free-floating political resources – numerous political groups making demands – has created conditions that attract populist and personalistic rule.

Personalistic and populist rulers, in turn, tend not only to further deinstitutionalize the polity, but are also not very efficacious in solving pressing problems. Such leaders do not readily perceive the need to build political institutions; rules and procedures of institutions like parties put limits on the discretionary power of personalistic leaders. Without parties, in turn, the links between leaders and their supporters, or between the state and society, remain weak. Elections are won on general, nonprogrammatic promises, and it becomes very difficult to translate these general mandates into specific policies. Major policy decisions repeatedly evoke considerable opposition, even from former supporters, and, just as repeatedly, governmental initiatives eventually falter. Policy failure in turn paves the way for other populist challengers, thus perpetuating the cycle of centralization and powerlessness.

To summarize, the four essays with the state as their main focus of analysis provide two important modifications to prevailing state-centric analytic tendencies. First, the chapters by Hagopian and Shue highlight how states conventionally thought to be "strong" and "efficacious" were actually laboring under important limitations. The Brazilian state under the military and the Chinese state under Mao may still have been a good deal more "efficacious" than, say, the Indian state or some of the colonial and postcolonial states of Africa. Nevertheless, the general implications of Hagopian's and Shue's work are important. If "modern" states generally presumed to have been all-pervasive and domineering turn out, on closer inspection, only to have exercised a putative reach that exceeded their actual grasp on their respective societies, chances are that numerous nonstate variables were, and are, influencing the processes of social change in these, and in most other, low-income countries. Although "bringing the state back in" may thus have made an important contribution to comparative political sociology, it is just as crucial to remember that a fair amount of the real drama of social change continues to be located in social realms reacting with, but in important ways residing also "beyond," the state.

Second, the analyses of factors limiting state capacities offered in the four essays also leave us with a similar general message. None of these essays subscribes to the view that "strength" or "weakness" of the state is primarily a function of such state attributes as degree of centralization, technocratic competence, or insulation-disconnectedness ("autonomy") from society. On the contrary, these essays call attention to the fact that a focus on state attributes alone generates numerous unresolved analytical paradoxes: Centralization seems to go hand in hand with powerlessness; technocratic competence does little to resolve a state's legitimacy problems; and a given state's "autonomy" from social groups may be as much a source of "weakness" as of "strength."

Paradoxes such as these vanish, however, when accounts are historically specific and when the objects of analysis are not primarily state attributes but state–society relations. The simultaneous tendency toward centralization and powerlessness, for example, say, in India but also in other cases, can be understood as a function of the growing fragmentation of political society. Technocratic competence, as in Brazil under the military, may have enhanced the state's capacity to pursue technically correct economic policies but did little to strengthen the government's legitimacy; sooner or later, the state had to incorporate power brokers at the lower levels of the polity, thus internalizing some very traditional forms of power management within the framework of what had been a seemingly modern-rational, even authoritarian, state. Finally, the much vaunted concept of a state's "autonomy" from society emerges from these essays either as something of an illusion or as a recipe for very little. In the case of Africa, Boone argues that the state's seeming disconnectedness from society was the ironic product of a governing design primarily aimed at suppressing social organization in favor of appropriating the social surplus. In the case of China, the party-state's capacity to lead and to manage declined as the society it sought to govern was "cellularized" by its own aggressive social engineering policies and plans, and as the initially legitimate and resilient authority links between the state and society were, in the process, themselves also parcelized and attenuated.

Social forces: class fractions, coalitions, and groups

To adopt a state-in-society perspective means, among other things, to strive toward a more balanced consideration of *both* the capacities of states *and* the roles of a variety of social forces in shaping the politics of low-income countries. And striving for a more balanced treatment, in turn, presses us to reconsider the categories in which we have been accustomed to conceptualize both social structure and social action in our various Third World case studies. Three of the chapters in this volume, those by Resat Kasaba, Elizabeth Perry, and Robert Vitalis, make particularly pointed and helpful contributions in this effort to reconceptualize relevant social forces. All three are historical and draw attention to the political roles of social classes. But the "class analysis" deployed in these essays departs significantly from some of the standard assumptions of a Marxist philosophy of history.

Explicitly rejecting the Marxian tendency to ascribe predetermined historical roles to particular classes, the three authors also reject the "Why not?" questions that have dominated so many recent studies of class politics in the first and third worlds. Why didn't the working class, in this society or in that one, successfully organize itself to challenge bourgeois domination and to overthrow capitalism? Why didn't the emerging capitalist class, in this society or in that one, manage successfully to establish and consolidate a modern capitalist political-economic order? What were the special "weaknesses" of these classes that prevented them from assuming their proper historical roles? Questions such as these, our authors argue, all too clearly and unfortunately reflect the misguided determinism that underlies them by assuming a unidirectionality of social development that brushes aside most of the interesting (and important) contingencies of history. Questions such as these require us to analyze classes in low-income countries in terms of "what they are not" instead of "what they are." And this, by the same twist of logic, leads us to comprehend them not in terms of how they actually did behave in specific historical circumstances but, perversely, in terms of how they did not behave. Kasaba, Perry, and Vitalis frame their studies to proceed very differently.

With data drawn from several decades of working-class politics in Shanghai, in Chapter 6 Perry provides a keen comparison of the roles of various urban social forces under the Guomindang and the Communist Party in prerevolutionary China. She begins by accepting that Chinese society has been deeply fragmented during most of this century, and by pointing out that the Chinese working class in particular was broken down into a number of divergent subgroups or fractions. She rejects the assumption that such intraclass divisions are inevitably a recipe for "weakness," however. That a society or a social class is internally divided need not mean that it is "politically impotent," she argues. Different segments of a fragmented society, even different class fractions for that matter, may well be capable of effecting important and influential linkages with state actors or organizations. These linkages need not be supposed always to amount to a simple "capture" of the state by a given class fraction. In fact, far more often when segments of society and political movements (or states-in-the-making) make common cause for a time, neither partner gets exactly what it wants from the arrangement. But each side may nonetheless find its resources and its options quite decisively affected, even transformed, through the partnership. Thus, by taking seriously the political potential of small but crucial class fractions, and by examining carefully how that potential was or was not realized through actual linkages with elements of state in specific historical circumstances, we should be able to learn more both about the prevailing patterns of state–society interaction and about the "recursive," or mutually transformative, aspects of those patterns of interaction.

Perry explains why and how the Guomindang and the Communist Party each came to draw its labor constituency from separate segments of the Shanghai working class. Even in the early days, workers could clearly have discerned that the parties were separated by significant differences in political ideology and political strategy – one stressing the tactics of militant class struggle, the other the tactics of collaborative class harmony. But factors such as individual skill level, native-place ties, and workplace experience were probably more salient than ideology per se in giving some workers an affinity for one party over the other. The Communists tended to attract support from skilled artisans who had originally migrated to Shanghai from the south, people who belonged to guilds and native-place associations and who, through these organizations, had acquired some experience of collective action against employers in pursuit of higher wages and job control. The Guomindang, in contrast, tended to attract its support from semiskilled workers, new recruits to the industrial work force, people who were more often from the north. These recent arrivals not only lacked training and job security, they lacked the guild mentality and communal experiences of the skilled craftsmen. They were much more prone to become dependent on underworld gangs in the competition for jobs, and more dependent on good relations with employers to keep their jobs in confused times.

These differing social groups carried different social organizational imperatives and proclivities with them as they were incorporated into their parties' labor movement plans, and as their needs and aims were assimilated into the two parties' political programs. The Guomindang labor organization evolved into an elaborate constellation of patron–client and protection networks connecting laborers and foremen with street gangsters, drug kingpins, and "respectable" high-placed businessmen and politicians. The Communist labor organization, resting on a strong ethos of workshop and small-unit solidarity, was constructed of numerous tiny cells that were linked, in the guild tradition, into a set of large and radical unions promoting worker welfare. While both types of labor organization were effective politically up to a point, both also set limits on the direction and pace of change their parties, once in power, could pursue. The Guomindang's gang base and its patron–client system of payoffs and political rewards made it difficult for the government to reach out to and attract support from other segments of the Shanghai working class. The Communists' association with the Chinese labor aristocracy and its values of small-unit solidarity led the government to enshrine the *danwei* (small unit) ideal as the foundation not only of worker welfare but of all urban social life after 1949. The vested interests of myriad *danwei*, especially those in the state-run industrial sector, would later stand clearly in the way of the state's responding equitably and innovatively when confronted with the challenge of employing and motivating succeeding waves of industrial work force entrants. Both the Guomindang state and the Communist state were constrained – in organizational capacity and in policy responsiveness – by the nature of their early bargains and linkages with specific working-class fractions. This leads Perry to conclude that "trying to impose rule on highly fragmented societies, new states necessarily enter into pacts with receptive social elements. Yet such accommodations may imprison the state in preferential relationships that serve ultimately to inhibit a broader base of support."

In Chapter 7, Vitalis's close study of business conflict and politics in Egypt during the early 1930s generates an analysis of the capitalist class very similar in its working assumptions and in its conclusions to the analysis of Chinese working-class politics provided by Perry. Vitalis begins by recognizing the importance of intraclass divisions among Third World capitalists, but rejects the assumption that the fundamental division must inevitably be between nationalist and comprador elements. He rejects also the expectation that intraclass division must lead to class "weakness" and political ineffectuality. Likewise, Vitalis discards as too simplistic the informing question of many recent studies of markets and politics in the Third World, "How does business go about capturing the state?" Divided states and divided business interests should be assumed instead, he argues, to interact in highly complex ways through fluctuating market conditions and through changes of political regime. The result may not be the outright "capture" of one side by the other, yet business groups often do succeed in tilting the political process in their favor.

In the Egyptian case, both the state and the capitalist class were divided into sets of competitive coalitions. Key state players at that time included the Wafd Party and an assortment of its leading politicians, the Egyptian king and his palace politicos, along with a number of overt and covert representatives of residual postcolonial British interests and influentials. The key capitalist players, on the other side, were organized into quite far-flung and diversified rival investor groups, encompassing complex networks of agricultural, entrepreneurial, and industrial interests and holdings. In competition for credits, subsidies, licenses, joint venture deals, consultancies, and contracts – most of these privileged opportunities dispensed by Egyptian state agencies – such rival business groups fought "for control over markets, industries and entire sectors" of the developing Egyptian economy. Although state agencies were in a position to dispense opportunities or to withhold them from rival investor groups, those agencies could hardly be said to have enjoyed much autonomy from the organized business interests in society. If the state was to succeed in its project of economic development, it patently needed both the organizational skills and the capital that only those diversified business groups could provide. And the business groups, for their part, were dependent on the state for resources and preferential terms only it could deliver. Divided as they were, and with both "sides" engaged in the rational pursuit of self-interest, the stage was set for considerable political intrigue around major business deals.

Coalitions of capitalists sought to use their influence in political circles to reduce or eliminate competition from rival coalitions in the marketplace; coalitions of state actors sought to use their support in business circles to manipulate political outcomes and to eliminate competition from rival factions bidding for power. To illustrate the scope and style of business politics during that period, Vitalis examines several historical examples in great detail, but he also paints an overall picture in which businessmen in fact turn out to be efficacious political actors: Intrigues around hotly contested investment ventures were critical to the fall of at least one Egyptian government, and influential also in shaping the repertoire of viable political options – indeed, in shaping the fundamental political terrain, of the times.

Vitalis stresses the near inevitability of division within emerging capitalist classes. The intrinsically competitive nature of the relations among different business interests in the marketplace finds its natural reflection in competitive strategies of interaction with the state and in clashing political goals. But Vitalis posits no inevitability about the political forms such intraclass divisions will assume. The salient forms of intraclass political division are likely to be heavily influenced, he suggests, by the peculiarities of the structure of the markets in which they compete and in which their social relations are embedded. In the oligopolistically structured markets of 1930s Egypt, leading business interests tended to coalesce into large investor groups and networks. The very bold sorts of collective (and competitive) actions such diversified coalitions were prone to (and fit to) engage in left their mark both on the day-to-day political landscape within the divided state apparatus itself and on the overall process of state building in interwar Egypt. Had the marketplace been structured differently, capitalist intraclass conflict would likewise have been structured differently and capitalists would have pursued different kinds of strategies with different implications for the processes of state building and political change.

On the brightly colored frieze of Egyptian capitalism and politics painted for us by Vitalis, the mutual embraces of "state" and "society" are passionate and close – often painfully so. In the ornate Ottoman tapestry woven for us in Chapter 8 by Kasaba, however, "state" and "society" do not ever quite embrace; always disengaged, they nonetheless gaze raptly at each other, and each is profoundly influenced by what it sees. In their efforts to rethink the dynamics of social forces in relation to the state, Perry and Vitalis move in close, as if with microscopes, dissecting the sinews of social organization to reveal their constitutive class fractions, coalitions, and groups. Kasaba, by contrast, steps back from his subject in order to discern some of the longer and larger processes of social formation and evolution at work in the making of Turkish political history.

To study state–society interactions under the changing Ottoman Empire of the nineteenth century, Kasaba selects three spheres of social evolution for discussion: first, changes in the organization of production and trade associated with increasing commercialization of the Ottoman economy; second, changes in agriculture and employment yielding greater and greater geographical mobility among peasants and workers; and third, the sharp rise of nationalist, religious, and sectarian ideologies and movements across the empire as the century wore on. "Together," Kasaba argues, "the ensemble of practices, relations, and institutions that are contained in these three areas constituted a distinct nonstate arena in the dissolving empire." Kasaba wishes precisely to "insist on the relevance of the nonstate arena" because in the very relationships between this sphere of social life and the structures of state, he believes, can be found "a primary locus of dynamism" in the late history of the Ottoman Empire.

It is mistaken to suppose that social forces were simply subordinated to the vision and will of the modernizing imperial state. Rather, Kasaba maintains, "various processes that originated in the nonstate arena constrained and shaped the very nature of the power wielded by the political authority." The transformation of the imperial bureaucratic system into the modernizing Ottoman-Turkish state took place, as he illustrates, in the context of this recursive relationship with the expanding nonstate arena.

The very ideology of Turkish nationalism, for example, was enriched and "shaped by the presence" of alternative religious, ethnic, and antistate ideologies in society. The nationalist Turkish intelligentsia, whether consciously or unconsciously, according to Kasaba, were continually engaged in a "dialogue" with other nationalisms. And out of their effort to distinguish their own vision of the future from the alternatives surrounding them grew the particular brand of secular nationalism that was to sustain the modernizing Turkish state. In fact, the very way in which the ultimately prevailing version of Turkish nationalism "insisted on defining itself as rigidly secular" should be understood as testimony to the perceived threat – that is, to the potential political power – of those alternative ideologies. Defeated social forces commonly leave indelible imprints on their victorious adversaries, of course, much as the winners may wish either to claim such stigmata as their very own creations or, more often, simply to obscure them from public view.

While the nonstate arena came to contain many influential institutions and groups, Kasaba notes that these social forces rarely took part in direct political action – either with or against the state. Although extremely powerful in substantive terms, these forces remained essentially quiescent politically, adopting evasive and defensive, rather than participatory or interventionist, strategies of interaction with political authority. Kasaba explains this missed opportunity in two ways. First, these sui generis social forces had little in common with one another that would have tended to unite them in collaborative political action. Second, the changing Ottoman state itself, reacting to the presence of these new forces in the polity, adopted a number of policies and reforms designed to deal with and defuse their potential political authority. State reform measures, however, were never intended genuinely to empower any of these possibly challenging groups and institutions in the nonstate arena. They aimed, instead, either to play these groups off against each other or to co-opt them into collaboration within the state power system itself. This mode of coping with social forces in the nonstate arena, Kasaba concludes, allowed the apparatus of state to proliferate and undeniably magnified the appearance of state capacity and control. But disengaged as the state actually was from popular movements, ideologies, and organizations, its robust appearance was at best misleading. The formal strength of the Ottoman state belied its substantive weaknesses.

Social forces: civil associations

Problems of engagement and disengagement between state and society are at the core of two other essays included here, those by Michael Bratton and Naomi Chazan. Both authors deal, in boldly cross-temporal and cross-national comparisons, with the very broad sweeps of social and political change that have been taking place in the states of Africa, especially since decolonization. Both reach specifically for an understanding of the conditions and the patterns of interaction that have emerged between state authorities, on the one hand, and civil associations, on the other. They focus on questions about the organization and intensity of associational life, in the way that Kasaba generates preliminary maps of the nonstate arena. They then go on to explore what they each regard as a rolling sequence of experimental-constructive state–society engagements and of defensive-disenchanted disengagements, an alternately hopeful and frustrating sequence that has characterized the struggle in many African states for both economic and political solvency.

Bratton confines his study in Chapter 9 to rural social organizations and to peasant–state relations. He outlines a four-phase sequence in these relations, beginning with a period of mutual engagement, through the agency of state-sponsored cash crop production and marketing schemes, promoted by many new governments in the immediate aftermath of national independence. During phase two, peasant farmers tended to become disillusioned with these cooperative schemes as economic payoffs failed to materialize and as the organizations themselves were used more as means to extend the state's authority into the hinterland than as vehicles for improving peasant livelihood. Peasants, choosing to "disengage" themselves from involvement in the state's agencies, plans, and visions, withdrew their support from these organizations. In phase three, as peasants were independently reorganizing themselves into informal or private production and trade networks, the states in question tended to fall increasingly on economic hard times. Facing serious fiscal crises, and unable or unwilling to carry the costs of so many failing rural organizations, states, too, chose "disengagement" from their ties to rural producers, allowing peasants to fend for themselves in production and the marketplace. Finally, while state–society relations remained stalled in this condition of mutual disengagement in many parts of Africa, in some few cases, according to Bratton, we have seen a move into a fourth phase of tentative reengagement, an opening of a dialogue between state agents and social groups that builds more or less consciously upon the lessons of past failure. Each stage in this general sequential model, Bratton argues, emerged not capriciously or accidentally, but logically, and out of the "unresolved tensions" present in the previous stage.

For Bratton, state–society relations are generally conceived as contentious, even highly conflictual. This, no doubt, is related to the fact that the social group he studies is peasants, and peasants everywhere, after all, tend to exhibit deeply problematic relations with agents of state power. Associational life, in Bratton's essay, takes the form of rural organizations (of production, trade, and so on), which are fought over by representatives of state, on the one hand, and by groups in society, on the other. Control over them is contested because such social organizations can "constitute *instruments* employed by social actors to realize political objectives." The goal of both sides to the conflict is to "own and operate" a politically autonomous entity because they "cannot make an effective political initiative of any kind if they do not" possess such an organization. With control over an autonomous organization, "they are well placed to mount a successful disengagement initiative." If their organization also possesses political capacity, they can mount an "engagement initiative" aimed at influencing the behavior of others. Bratton explains the stronger tendency toward disengagement in the African environment by pointing out that most rural African social organizations score high on "autonomy" but low on "capacity." Thus, those both state-operated and societally operated have habitually been better equipped to assay evasive strategies and political withdrawal maneuvers than to attempt drives for political outreach, extension of influence, or transformation of the preferences or behaviors of others. In this way Bratton explains, in terms of both structure and learning, the apparently chronic disarticulation of rural associational life and state power in postcolonial Africa, which otherwise might be understood only as a series of tragically missed opportunities or failures of will.

Chazan in Chapter 10 also develops a four-phase sequence of state–society interaction, which, although it does not entirely parallel Bratton's sequence, nonetheless bears a number of important similarities to the periodization and processes he describes. However, she does not confine herself to the peasantry or to any other single social group. She seeks, instead, generalizations that may be applied to the whole of civil society in Africa, which she conceptualizes as "the middle ground between communal groups and state structures." And although Chazan recognizes the tendency toward disengagement between state and civil society as a powerful one in Africa, "the main contention" of her essay runs in a somewhat different direction: She aims to demonstrate instead that "the development of civil society in Africa has paralleled processes of state formation on the continent." She sees state and civil society as sharing a "symbiotic relationship" and goes so far as to assert that the "combination of apparent strength and substantial powerlessness which characterized many African states during the first three decades of independence attests to the fragility of civil society during this period" because the "power, autonomy, and capacity of states is . . . a function of the relative autonomy of civil society." When the institutions of civil society are robust, Chazan argues, the capacities of the state may also expand, and she then demonstrates this reinforcing relationship by establishing that the periods of most autonomous action by civil society coincided with those of the most vigorous state-building on the African continent.

Chazan contends that civil associational life grew in diversity and importance in Africa at the very same time that colonial states were in the ascendant and consolidating their systems of rule. These rising civil associations would eventually come to serve as the trellises upon which anticolonial movements were to grow. "From this perspective," Chazan comments, "decolonization may be viewed as the process of the empowerment of that civil society which developed in tandem with the colonial state." But as civil society went through this process of *étatisation,* moving to take control of the state apparatus, many intermediate-level social organizations were, in consequence, deprived of both substance and a cause, and were thus enfeebled. Most of the new postcolonial states moved to fill the social gap with institutions of their own making. These institutions, many of them corporatist or socialist-type mass organizations, were deployed by state rulers more to contain social forces deemed potential sources of political unrest than to engage them in constructive social action. Then, in the aftermath of these organizational initiatives, according to Chazan, certain adaptive patterns set in that were deeply corrosive of effective state–society interaction and that were, incidentally, strikingly similar to some of the patterns described by both Shue (for China) and Kohli (for India).

The postcolonial elaboration of patron–client networks and clientelistic modes of exchange, with its accompanying phenomena of political factionalism, subversion, and corruption, made African states more porous to selected social demands and interests, it is true; but at the same time, it made those states far less capable of dealing efficiently and equitably with genuine public needs. Meanwhile, as social forces withdrew from involvement with the sundry dubious agents and agencies of the state, an age-old self-protective organizational tendency toward localism was intensified, "limiting contacts among communities" and thus miniaturizing the valid, and the active, units of civil society. Institutions of both state and society, therefore, were not only disarticulated, they were diminished. In some states, the "narrower the social base of specific regimes, the less accountable they became." These states' headlong evolution in the direction of "centralization and powerlessness" frequently gave rise to the capriciousness and repression of venal, self-annihilating personal dictatorship; state "autonomy" thus became a formula for very little – leading more to predatory behavior than to developmental efficacy. At the same time, as units of civil society were further fragmented or cellularized, their social power, too, was progressively shaved and constricted. During the long crisis of the 1970s and 1980s, therefore, African states and civil societies were not only mutually disengaged, they were mutually disempowered as well.

Chazan goes on to show that during the most recent period – thanks largely to "the conditionalities of the IMF and the World Bank," which demanded sweeping economic liberalization and structural reform measures before they would issue loans to African states to cope with their chronic fiscal crises – we have witnessed a marked resurgence of African civil society, "rooted in local institutions and resources." With this resurgence, once again, has come a new set of opportunities and possibilities for states to grapple with and learn to employ. Initial indications, Chazan reports, are that the symbiosis of past periods may again be coming into play. During the late 1980s, she finds, "the strengthening of civil society also had the effect of enhancing both the autonomy and the capacity of the state. Structurally, developments at both societal and state levels were mutually reinforcing."

In this last important respect, Chazan's assessment of the fundamentally reinforcing nature of state–society relations in Africa deviates somewhat from the more conflictual model offered by Bratton. But whatever the differences in emphasis, these two chapters, along with those discussed in the preceding section, do move in tandem toward a distinctive contribution to the larger theoretical goal of reconceptualizing the relevant units of "society" in its re-cursive relations with "the state."

The five society-centered essays in this volume tend to adopt a view that the political behavior and the power capacities of social groups are, at least in part, contingent; that is, the political action and influence of a social group are not wholly predictable just by examining the relative position of that group within the social structure. Social classes, for example, are not simply more or less powerful depending on their relative control over property. While property is clearly a potent political resource, and the propertied often do get their way in politics, a wide range of political power balances involving the propertied and the propertyless are possible, even workable. Similarly, levels of associational activity do not covary in any simply or direct fashion with levels of economic development. These five chapters, when read together, underscore further that, of all the contingencies or contextual variables molding the political behavior of social groups, the nature and the role of the state itself often turn out to be among the most important.

Perry and Vitalis, for example, proceed by disaggregating social classes into their various key "fractions" for analysis. Perry thus examines the behavior of Chinese working-class fractions and discovers that the underlying variations in their political behavior reflected both the "premodern" origins of the fractions and the prevailing larger context in which unified state power had nearly disinte-grated. Vitalis similarly shows that Egyptian business groups were efficacious or inefficacious depending largely on their particular relationships with state authorities. Kasaba proceeds differently, drawing attention not to class fractions but to the role of larger historical processes that gradually cumulate to create distinctive "nonstate arenas" of social action – both structural and ideological – developing in juxtaposition to state authority. Finally, Bratton and Chazan undertake to analyze the universe of "civil associations," as well as the specific structures, opportunities, and processes of learning that condition the emergence and interaction of civil society in relation to the state.

A general theoretical approach emphasizing the mutually transforming relationship of state and society is, then, clearly flexible enough to be employed with a variety of societal analytics. How we should imagine and address the social field of action is in no way restricted by such an approach. The important thing to bear in mind is, rather, that the political behavior of social groups tends to be context-specific. While prevailing state forms and relative access to property, as well as the underlying patterns of production, surely provide some broad boundaries on the probable and possible political action of groups, these turn out to be no more than *broad* boundaries. We should thus be encouraged to think in new ways about the actual or potential power of social groups and about the dynamics of the societies we study. In addition, thinking in new ways about the forces at work in our particular case studies should help us when we use those cases in the search for answers to still larger questions. What factors, for example, go into determining how certain class fractions become highly influential whereas others remain politically insignificant? What are the conditions under which a "nonstate arena" can develop in low-income countries? What are the conditions encouraging and discouraging the emergence of "civil society"? When new social groups do engage state power, what are the determinants of their actions and of the outcomes of their actions for the polity as a whole? What are the factors determining whether the emergence of new social forces ultimately leads toward democratization of the polity? toward political instability? or toward reinforcing and strengthening state authority?

Mutual empowerment of state and society

The proposition that state power and social forces in low-income settings may, under certain circumstances, enter into relationships that are mutually reinforcing (or mutually empowering) is given its most forthright consideration in Naomi Chazan's ambitious and optimistic essay on the relatively unstructured and fluid states and societies of Africa. But the possibility of mutual empowerment is raised by several other authors here as well, authors analyzing an assortment of more and less tightly structured political settings.

Reşat Kasaba, for example, talks about the decline of the Ottoman imperial order and the rise of the twentieth century's modernizing authoritarian Turkish state. "If social groups, classes, and organizations are able to constitute themselves in an ensemble of arrangements to express and advance their interests, then it is possible for the state surrounded by such practices and ultimately shaped by them, to become strong in substantive terms." Kasaba interprets the Turkish case precisely as a missed opportunity for mutual empowerment.

Atul Kohli, working in India's popular democratic setting, also raises the possibility of mutual empowerment. But, he argues, because Indian society has been increasingly fragmented even as the system of political authority has been subjected to a series of deinstitutionalizing periods of personal rulership, special attention must be paid to the mechanisms of mutual empowerment. The phenomenon of mutual empowerment – for example, the condition of state authority and social demand supporting and reinforcing one another – depends on the viability of institutions that can link state power with social forces. And in a competitive democracy like that of India, this must mean political parties – well-organized, disciplined parties that can generate and offer to the electorate alternative social goals embodied in coherent policy programs. Such parties have emerged, with mutually empowering effects, in the local politics of some Indian states. But at the national level, Kohli shows, the drift has been in the other direction – toward state powerlessness and social frustration.

Even Vivienne Shue, working in the very highly structured setting of Chinese Communism, employs the notion of mutual empowerment to help conceptualize both some of the dilemmas and some of the opportunities present in the mammoth project of reforming state socialism. Although the circumstances and the nature of the two polities were obviously very different, Shue nevertheless chronicles a process of deepening societal fragmentation along with intensifying state powerlessness under Mao that, in several interesting respects, resonates with Kohli's account of the Indian political trajectory. With both social forces and political authority in China in a state of relative enfeeblement, any process of mutual reempowerment would, as in India, depend primarily on the development of viable mechanisms linking social demand to state power. But whereas the competitive electoral Indian setting required the building of broad-based and resilient political parties to fill this need, the unitary party–state system and the distinctive revolutionary socialist ideology that shaped the Chinese political setting required the invention of some very different kinds of linking mechanisms or institutions. And in the 1990s, as Shue argues, we may be seeing the beginnings of just this sort of institution building embodied in the host of new, corporatist-style civil associations now emerging to play key roles at different points in the Chinese polity.

Thus, mutually empowering relations between state and society arise both as a helpful conceptual device and as a genuine (though often a missed) political opportunity in several of the essays here – including ones on modernizing authoritarian regimes, personalist dictatorships, state–socialist and populist democratic systems. Thus, although many questions may still remain concerning the conditions for and limits on mutual empowerment, a general conclusion of some importance nonetheless seems warranted.

When conceptualizing power in low-income settings, it is helpful to think of it as having both distributive and collective dimensions. Power in some senses is like wealth; it can accumulate, and it can be divided. While a few in society may always possess more power than others, a related issue concerns just how much power there is to go around. Some societies simply have more power with which to define and achieve collective goals than others. It would take us too far afield to attempt to develop this point further here. Suffice it to say that the power resources of a society tend to vary with such conditions as the state's capacity to "penetrate and centrally coordinate the activities" of that society,[21] the levels of consciousness and organization of social groups, and most important, whether the goals of state elites and of organized social groups tend to converge or diverge. These issues can become considerably more complex in highly stratified class societies, wherein state actors often ally with dominant economic classes. In such settings, power as a distributive resource – who has it more than others – is likely to dominate the political discourse. Nevertheless, just below the surface we are apt to find lurking the issue of how much collective power the society possesses to achieve its national goals. And it is our concern with this dimension of power that, in part, spurs our interest in studying the conditions under which both state and society are mutually empowered. Our contributions to this end are preliminary, but we put them forward speculatively, as a promising line for future research and theoretical refinement.

SHARED UNDERSTANDINGS

A collection of essays that are as scattered over space, time, and regime type as those gathered here is bound to contain a certain diversity, even an apparent looseness. At the risk of repetition, therefore, it seems worthwhile to conclude by reiterating a few of the more fundamental commonalities in orientation that all these authors do share as well as some of the common themes their chapters develop. These are orientations and understandings that it is hoped may be found useful to others.

The research reported here is neither "state-centered" nor "society-centered." It approaches the formations and transformations of states and societies as reciprocal, rather than autonomous, processes. It accepts that states in part constitute their societies; and societies in part constitute their states. It dwells deliberately at the intersections of state and society, and focuses on the mutually conditioning interactions that occur between segments of state and of society.

We present this state–society approach, fully aware that it is not "new"; similar ideas have been around for a long time, at least since Weber. We acknowledge also that this approach tends to privilege the kind of painstaking, historically specific research that can be slow to cumulate findings of more general significance. We therefore make no claims either to sensational original-ity, or to newfound theoretical shortcuts for understanding complex Third World realities. What we offer instead is a balanced frame of reference that we believe will be helpful in orienting future empirical research, whether country-specific or broadly comparative. We would point out, moreover, that numerous ap-proaches of the past, claiming theoretical breakthroughs, have often led only to dead ends. The postwar intellectual history of the development subfield is studded with such failed attempts to make a "paradigm shift": political develop-ment, dependency, statism, and soon, perhaps, the rational choice approach. Exaggerated intellectual product differentiation may bring short-term profes-sional rewards, but it inevitably defeats our better purposes. It generates fads and false starts that more often than not most heavily afflict our graduate students, at great intellectual costs to us all.

Aside from the general orientation, several more specific and thematic conclu-sions emerge from this volume. Three are worth repeating at the end. First, the issue of why some Third World states are more effective at establishing author-ity and at facilitating socioeconomic change than others is of considerable interest to development scholars. Over the last decade several of them have traced state effectiveness back to a state characteristic they call "autonomy." While the concept of "autonomy" is allowed to remain murky in some of this work, the general suggestion seems to be that a state's disconnectedness or insulation from society can be helpful in enabling state elites to accomplish their political goals, both locally and at the national level. Yet our collective insights move in nearly the opposite direction. Growing disjuncture between the state and society, in several of our cases, appears not to release but, rather, to reduce a state's ability to reach into and across society to effect change. Clearly, more research is needed. It is likely that state effectiveness will turn out to be a trait that varies not only across countries, but within countries, both over time and across policy areas. It is also likely that "effectiveness" will be found to result from a subtle but complex mix of how states simultaneously incorporate some, and insulate themselves against other, social demands. Whatever the eventual findings, our firm conclusions at this stage are more methodological than sub-stantial: The study of a state's relative effectiveness is best pursued not by a primary focus on that state's organizational characteristics, but by tracing the manner in which the state and society are linked, including the links between state elites and dominant social classes.

The importance of studying the actual political roles of social classes in the Third World is another prominent theme in this volume. Although substantial insights can be gleaned in this chapter's summary (and, of course, traced in greater detail in individual chapters), our general conclusions with respect to this issue can, again, be best summarized as a methodological statement. The study of social classes in the past has been distorted by the association of class-oriented questions with a particular philosophy of history. The "why not" questions – that is, why classes, whether capitalists or workers, do not act out their historical missions – have thus tended to dominate the research agenda. We maintain instead that it is important now to study (describe and explain) the real, on-the-ground, political proclivities and actions of those who share similar positions in the division of labor. It ought not to be necessary to reiterate (although we are afraid it is) that the position of social actors in the division of labor is not the only important basis for political association. Class alone does not determine political behavior. Nevertheless, social relations around production are significant enough that no analysis of state–society relations in a Third World setting can be satisfactory or complete without a clear-eyed understanding of underlying class relations and of the past and present political roles of contending social classes.

Finally, as one ponders future trends in the Third World, it seems nearly certain, on the one hand, that political elites in low-income settings will continue to resort to state intervention as means to mold patterns of social change, while on the other hand, various social groups will continue to demand a greater say in influencing how the state operates. Patterns of state–society interaction will thus continue to demand our analytical attention. In the recent literature on the state, state–society interactions have often – perhaps most often – been conceived of as antagonistic, as struggles, even as zero-sum conflicts. Our authors accept that for some social groups or segments, this is indeed an accurate rendering of the nature of their interactions with the state. But it is not always so. Some interactions (or linkages) between state segments and social segments can and do have the effect of creating *more* power for *both* sides. Some, of course, favor one side over the other. Some vitiate the powers of each side. And in still other cases, state actors ally with select social groups against other groups.

The studies reported here suggest, therefore, that analysts of social change in low-income countries would be well advised to stay away from an exclusive state-versus-society framework; the other important possibilities specifically to bear in mind should include: mutual empowerments of state and society; tactical disengagements between elements of state and society; and alliances of domination, that is, alliances between state actors and certain social groups at the deliberate (or the negligent) expense of others. The repertoire of state–society interactions is at least this rich.

NOTES

1 The reference is to Peter Evans et al., eds., *Bringing the State Back In* (Cambridge: Cambridge University Press, 1985). An incomplete list of other recent state-oriented works would include the following: Alfred Stepan, *The State and Society: Peru in Comparative Perspective* (Princeton: Princeton University Press, 1978); Ellen Kay Trimberger, *Revolution from Above: Military Bureaucrats and Development in Ja-*

pan, Turkey, Egypt, and Peru (New Brunswick, N.J.: Transactions Books, 1978);
Robert H. Bates, *Markets and States in Tropical Africa* (Berkeley: University of
California Press, 1982); John Waterbury, *The Egypt of Nasser and Sadat: The
Political Economy of Two Regimes* (Princeton: Princeton University Press, 1983);
Richard Sandbrook (with Judith Barker), *The Politics of Africa's Economic Stagna-
tion* (Cambridge: Cambridge University Press, 1985); Atul Kohli, *The State and
Poverty in India: The Politics of Reform* (Cambridge: Cambridge University Press,
1987); Peter Evans, "Predatory, Developmental and Other Apparatuses: A Compara-
tive Political Economy Perspective on the Third World State," *Sociological Forum*
(Fall 1989): 561–587; Stephan Haggard, *Pathways from the Periphery: The Politics
of Growth in the Newly Industrializing Countries* (Ithaca, N.Y.: Cornell University
Press, 1990); and Robert Wade, *Governing the Market: Economic Theory and the
Role of Government in East Asian Industrialization* (Princeton: Princeton University
Press, 1990).

2 The editors of this volume have, in their own recent and respective works, been
moving toward such a position. For example, see Vivienne Shue, *The Reach of the
State: Sketches of the Chinese Body Politic* (Stanford, Calif.: Stanford University
Press, 1988); Joel Migdal, *Strong Societies and Weak States* (Princeton: Princeton
University Press, 1989); and Atul Kohli, *Democracy and Discontent: India's Grow-
ing Crisis of Governability* (Cambridge: Cambridge University Press, 1990).

3 This, as most of the authors represented here would readily acknowledge, does show
up as something of a blind spot in work taking a state–society, or a state-in-society,
focus. An earlier generation of modernization scholars, thinking and writing about
Third World politics during the Cold War, a prolonged period of hardened international stalemate, may be excused, perhaps, if they tended to neglect certain international variables. Most of us, however, have grown up with "dependency theory."
And regardless of our individual evaluations of that body of thought, we tend to take
it for granted that the external environments of nation-states are of critical significance in understanding Third World politics. In the second half of the 1980s, if one
needed a reminder, we have all been forcefully shown once again that sudden sea
changes on the international scene (and long-term, more subtle changes, as well) can
have profound effects on domestic affairs, including state–society interactions, in the
Third World. Obviously, the analytical problem of striking the right balance between
external and internal variables can, to a certain extent, be ameliorated by framing
more of our case studies cross-temporally. But ultimately, Third World "societies"
and their "states" will need to be conceived and understood as porous entities –
porous not only vis-à-vis one another, but also vis-à-vis transnational forces of all
kinds. We leave such a postdependency modification of a state–society framework
for a subsequent endeavor.

4 For a good discussion of how this Weberian standpoint is distinct, and why it is
preferable, over other major theoretical traditions in political sociology, namely,
structural-functional and Marxist, see Reinhard Bendix, *Nation-Building and Citizenship* (Berkeley: University of California Press, 1977), Conclusion. Also note that,
although focusing mainly on state–society relations, Bendix is quite sensitive to the
international influences on processes of social change.

5 The argument is distinct, but this section does draw on some materials presented
earlier in Atul Kohli's "Introduction" to Atul Kohli, ed., *The State and Development
in the Third World* (Princeton: Princeton University Press, 1986). Specialists in
comparative politics may wish to skip this section because it reviews familiar materials. Its main contribution is to trace our intellectual lineage back to a more balanced
understanding of Weber and other classical thinkers.

6 For a summary review of Marx's political-sociological writings, see Anthony Giddens, *Capitalism and Modern Social Theory* (Cambridge: Cambridge University Press, 1971), Part 1, and Raymond Aron, *Main Currents in Sociological Thought,* 2 vols. (New York: Anchor Books, Doubleday, 1965), 1: 145–236. A good book-length study of Marx's writings is Shlomo Avineri, *Social and Political Thought of Karl Marx* (New York: Cambridge University Press, 1971). For a sampling of Marx's own writings relevant to the present discussion, see the following selections in Robert C. Tucker, ed., *The Marx–Engels Reader* (New York: Norton, 1972): "German Ideology, Part I," 110–166; "Wage Labor and Capital," 167–190; and "The Eighteenth Brumaire of Louis Bonaparte," 436–525.

7 A review of Durkheim's political-sociological concerns is available in Giddens (fn. 6), Part 2, and Aron (fn. 6), 2: 11–118. A good book-length study of Durkheim is Robert Nisbet, *Sociology of Emile Durkheim* (New York: Oxford University Press, 1973). For a sampling of Durkheim's own writings relevant to the present discussion, see Emile Durkheim, *The Division of Labor in Society* (New York: Free Press, 1969), esp. Book 1, chs. 1–3, sec. 7.4, and the Conclusion.

8 A summary review of Weber's concerns is in Giddens (fn. 6), Part 3, and Aron (fn. 6), 2: 219–318. For useful book-length studies of Weber's political and sociological writings, see David Beetham, *Max Weber and the Theory of Modern Politics* (London: George Allen & Unwin, 1974), and Reinhard Bendix, *Max Weber: An Intellectual Portrait* (New York: Anchor Books, Doubleday, 1962). For a sampling of Weber's political-sociological writings, see H. H. Gerth and C. Wright Mills, eds., *From Max Weber: Essays in Sociology* (New York: Oxford University Press, 1958), esp. chs. 3, 4, 7, and 8.

9 Because some of Weber's major writings were published after the turn of the century, the term "nineteenth-century" as used here includes work published before World War I.

10 Some of the works of Joseph Schumpeter, Thorstein Veblen, and Bronislaw Malinowski would, of course, count as exceptions to this generalization.

11 For a sampling of these reviews, see Reinhard Bendix, "Tradition and Modernity Reconsidered," *Comparative Studies in Society and History,* 9 (April 1967): 292–346; Samuel Huntington, "The Change to Change," *Comparative Politics,* 3 (April 1971): 283–322; Mark Kesselman, "Order or Movement? The Literature of Political Development as Ideology," *World Politics,* 26 (October 1973): 139–154; Andre Gunder Frank, *The Sociology of Development and the Underdevelopment of Sociology* (London: Pluto Press, 1971); Tony Smith, "Requiem or New Agenda for Third World States," *World Politics,* 37 (July 1985): 532–561; and Gabriel Almond, *A Discipline Divided: Schools and Sects in Political Science* (Newbury Park, Calif.: Sage, 1990), esp. ch. 9.

12 The following discussion is based on Parsons, *The Social System* (New York: Macmillan, 1951), esp. chs. 1, 2, and 7.

13 See Almond, *A Discipline Divided,* passim.

14 See Almond's "Introduction," in Gabriel Almond and James Coleman, eds., *The Politics of the Developing Areas* (Princeton: Princeton University Press, 1960), esp. p. 7.

15 In addition to the references in footnote 12, for a fuller discussion see and follow the footnotes in Atul Kohli, "Introduction," in *State and Development,* esp. pp. 9–14.

16 The strengths and the weaknesses of the dependency approach to development have also been widely discussed in the literature. See, for example, Gabriel Palma, "Dependency: A Formal Theory of Underdevelopment or a Methodology for the Analysis of Concrete Situations of Underdevelopment?," *World Development,* 6

(1978); and Tony Smith, "The Underdevelopment of Development Literature," *World Politics,* 31 (January 1979): 247–289. This, however, is not the place to review those issues. Here we can only reiterate some of the themes important for this volume.

17 For a review of the literature on "success," see Robert Wade, "East Asia's Economic Success: Conflicting Perspectives, Partial Insights, Shaky Evidence," *World Politics,* 44 (January 1992): 270–320. For a parallel discussion of "failure," see Sandbrook, *The Politics of Africa's Economic Stagnation.*

18 See the references above in note 1.

19 See Albert Fishlow, "A Tale of Two Presidents: The Political Economy of Crisis Management," in Alfred Stepan, ed., *Democratizing Brazil: Problems of Transition and Consolidation* (Oxford: Oxford University Press, 1989), pp. 83–119.

20 See, for example, Fernando Enrique Cardoso, "Associated-Dependent Development: Theoretical and Practical Implications," in Alfred Stepan, ed., *Authoritarian Brazil: Origins, Policies and Future.* (New Haven: Yale University Press, 1973), pp. 142–178.

21 Michael Mann describes this as a state's "infrastructural power." See Mann, "The Autonomous Power of the State: Its Origins, Mechanisms and Results," in John A. Hall, ed., *States in History* (London: Basil Blackwell, 1986), esp. pp. 113–119.

Index

ʿAbbud, Muhammad Ahmad, 177, 180–181, 183, 184, 185–186, 188, 189, 190–194, 196
ʿAbbud group, 176, 179, 180, 186, 190, 195–196, 197
ʿAbd al-Wahab, Ahmad, 191, 192, 193
ʿAfifi, Hafiz, 191
Africa, 3, 25–26, 108–134, 231–233, 237–252
  colonial rule in, 110, 111–119, 238–239, 307
  colonial society in, 258–263
  decolonization of, 119, 120, 121, 239, 262
  democratization in, 276–277, 288n, 289n
  dependency and modernization theories of, 108–109
  drought and famine in, 271–272
  economic control in, 124–125, 130–131, 132–133
  land reform in, 128–129
  marketing cooperatives in, 122–123, 129, 130, 243–245, 251, 315
  nationalist movements in, 120–121
  patron–client networks in, 110, 126, 127, 129–130, 131–132, 139n, 263, 267
  peasant associations in, 232–233, 238, 248–251, 252, 266
  peasant farming defined, 135n
  peasant–state relations in, 122–124, 130, 231–232, 237–238, 240–252, 307, 309, 315–316
  peasant trading networks in, 132, 238, 245–248, 270
  political control in, 123, 124, 125–128
  political organizations in, 233–234, 239
  postcolonial syndrome in, 268
  regime consolidation in, 109–110, 122, 131, 132, 133–134
  ruling class formation in, 121–122, 134, 136n, 274, 307

  second economy in, 246–248, 274
  social organizations in, 257–280, 316–318
  trade in, 124–125, 138n
  See also specific country
Agriculture
  associations, 79–80, 232–233, 238, 248–251, 252, 259, 260, 266
  collectivization of, 68–69
  in colonial state, 112–113, 115–116, 307
  growth of production, 218–219
  marketing cooperatives, 122–123, 129, 130, 243–245, 251, 315
  peasant–state relations, 122–124, 130, 231–232, 237–238, 240–252, 307, 309, 315–316
  trading networks, 132, 238, 245–248, 270
Alexandria, in Ottoman Empire, 210, 211, 212
Alienation, 286n
Almond, Gabriel, 299
Alves, Márcio Moreira, 52, 60n
Ames, Barry, 51
L'Amicale du Wallo, 249
Amin, Idi, 267
Anastasius, 207, 208, 224
Angola, 262
Anthropology of the state, 15–16
Anxi Chamber of Commerce, 80–81
Anxi County Tea Study Association, 81–82
Apprenticeship system, 151
Aquino, Corazon, 90
ARENA. *See* National Renovating Alliance
Argentina, 37, 48, 49, 60n
Aronowitz, Stanley, 152
Artisan trades, and labor movement, 150–152, 161–163
L'Association Six-S., 249
Aswan Dam project, 180, 181, 182, 183–184, 185, 186, 187, 188, 189, 193, 194
Atatürk, Kemal, 195
Autonomy, 235, 236, 237, 322